Rethinking
the
Western
Tradition

*The volumes in this series
seek to address the present debate
over the western tradition
by reprinting key works of
that tradition along with essays
that evaluate each text from
different perspectives.*

The
Idea
of a
University

J O H N   H E N R Y   N E W M A N

Frank M. Turner, *Editor*

Contributors

Martha McMackin Garland

Sara Castro-Klarén

George P. Landow

George M. Marsden

Frank M. Turner

Yale University Press

New Haven & London

Published with assistance from the foundation established in the
memory of Amasa Stone Mather of the Class of 1907, Yale College.

Set in Times Roman type by
Keystone Typesetting, Inc.
Printed in the United States of America by
Vail-Ballou Press, Binghamton, New York.

Library of Congress Cataloging-in-Publication Data
Newman, John Henry, 1801–1890.
The idea of a university / John Henry Newman ; Frank M. Turner, editor ;
contributors, Martha McMack in Garland . . . [et al.].
p. cm. — (Rethinking the Western tradition)
Originally published: London ; New York : Longman, Green, 1899.
Includes bibliographical references and index.
ISBN 0-300-06404-7 (cloth : alk. paper). — ISBN 0-300-06405-5 (pbk. : alk. paper)
1. Education, Higher — Philosophy.   2. Universities and colleges — Philosophy.
3. Newman, John Henry, 1801–1890 Idea of a university.   I. Turner, Frank M.
(Frank Miller), 1944– .   II. Title.   III. Series.
LB2321.N54   1996
378′.01 — dc20   95-38832
CIP
A catalogue record for this book is available from the
British Library.

The paper in this book meets the guidelines for
permanence and durability of the Committee on
Production Guidelines for Book Longevity of the
Council on Library Resources.

10 9 8 7 6 5 4 3 2 1

Editor's Dedication

For

James D. Kenney, M. D.

and

W. Bruce Lundberg, M. D.

with

Admiration and Affection

Contents

been chosen because of their close relationship to and expansion upon the ideas Newman originally enunciated in 1852 and because of their particular relevance to issues of literature, science, and religion under debate in late-twentieth-century universities.

The text for this edition is the posthumous "New Impression" published in 1891 by Longmans, Green. It includes all changes Newman made after 1873.

Three elements of the editorial apparatus of this volume require comment. The first is the section entitled "Reading *The Idea of a University.*" From his own experience teaching *The Idea of a University,* the editor has become keenly aware of the difficulties that many readers, especially undergraduates, encounter when first presented with the work. Suddenly they find themselves members of an audience of Irish Catholic laymen sitting in Dublin in 1852, listening to lectures by a recent convert whom their bishop has appointed as rector of a new Catholic university that many of them did not want founded. Readers discover that Newman commences *in media res,* with few introductory remarks. Consequently, the editor has sketched the broad arguments that Newman develops in his discourses and later essays. This sketch is to help readers understand where Newman's arguments commence and why he is making them.

Next follows an extensive analytic table of contents, a topical outline of the subjects Newman addresses in each discourse or essay. The information in this section is intended to aid readers in following the direction and content of Newman's presentation. This section should also help readers discover those parts of *The Idea of a University* that invite comparison and contrast and also to discern where Newman picks up a subject or argument he has treated earlier. The analytic table of contents is thus intended to be a road map through what is at first unfamiliar terrain.

For those who may be reading this volume in a classroom setting or who may wish to use it in a discussion group, the editor has also provided a set of questions that may spur thought or discussion. These may also allow readers to think about Newman's views as they relate to contemporary universities.

Second, Newman printed a few footnotes that gave minimal information about his sources. He cited many quotations and did not footnote them. He also often omitted material from his quotations without so indicating. The Notes on the Text reprint Newman's substantive footnotes, cite sources for all his quotations or translations, provide translations of all the French, Latin, or Greek texts quoted, and interject a few brief explanations of topics that may be unfamiliar to readers.

Editor's Preface

In the almost century and a half since its publication, John Henry Newman's *The Idea of a University* has exerted extraordinary influence over the discussion and conceptualization of higher education. In an era when universities and colleges, their curricula, their missions, and their financing have become the center of both concern and controversy, it is fitting that Yale University Press bring out a new edition of this classic work in its series Rethinking the Western Tradition. Newman's volume drew deeply upon that tradition and in turn has contributed much to the manner in which it has been understood and taught to succeeding generations of students. Thus, thinking and rethinking through Newman's arguments, values, and presuppositions is to probe the intellectual and religious heritage of the West and its transmission in institutions of higher education.

It is the purpose of this edition to place the greater part of the text of *The Idea of a University* before contemporary readers alongside a series of interpretive essays. All of the commentators, like Newman himself, have been involved in the idea and the reality of American universities. Each of the essayists has not only taught and published in the mainstream of Western literature and history but has also served as an administrator at the departmental or university level, fostered technological change in university teaching, or commented extensively on university life.

Newman composed *The Idea of a University* in two parts. The first is the series of discourses he delivered in Dublin in 1852 and published that year. The second is a series of ten lectures and essays on University Subjects which Newman prepared between 1854 and 1858 for particular occasions in the Catholic University while he was its rector. These were first published as *Lectures and Essays on University Subjects* in 1859 and then as the second section of *The Idea of a University* from 1873 onward. Publication of the entire text of the *Lectures and Essays on University Subjects* would have been economically prohibitive. Consequently, the present edition consists of the nine discourses that Newman made the core of his 1873 edition and four selections from the University Subjects. The latter have

Third, the editor has prepared a Glossary of Names, the second section of which lists saints. Newman was enormously widely read and made frequent reference to persons in both sacred and secular history whom most readers today do not know and who may have been unfamiliar to many members of his audience. The identifications in the glossary are extremely brief; readers may then use standard works of reference for further information. Rather than attempt to guess which names might be familiar and which unfamiliar, the editor has identified all names, including many that are commonplace. The brevity of the identifications in no manner reflects the intrinsic historical or religious importance of the person identified or the significance Newman attributed to the person.

For a fully annotated edition of *The Idea of a University,* readers are directed to Ian Ker's critical edition published by Clarendon Press in 1976. This work has been invaluable to the present editor, as have the editorial materials of Martin J. Svaglic in the University of Notre Dame Press edition of *The Idea of a University* (1982) and Dwight Culler's *The Imperial Intellect: A Study of Newman's Educational Ideal* (1955).

A list of suggested reading is included for those who may wish to explore particular topics raised by Newman or the authors of the interpretive essays.

The editor would like to express his appreciation for the encouragement of Jonathan Brent of Yale Press, who originated the concept of the series Rethinking the Western Tradition, and his thanks to John Ryden, the Director of Yale University Press, for his support and friendship.

Frank M. Turner
John Hay Whitney Professor of History
Yale University

Note on the Life of
John Henry Newman

John Henry Newman was born on February 21, 1801. He grew up in a moderately evangelical Anglican family. In June 1817 he entered Trinity College, Oxford, and he took his undergraduate degree in 1820. Two years later he became a fellow at Oriel College, Oxford, at a time when its fellowship was the most distinguished in the university. Newman was ordained into the ministry of the Church of England in 1824. Four years later he became vicar of St. Mary's, the Oxford University church, and held that position until 1843. He published ten volumes of sermons from those years.

Commencing in 1833, Newman along with other Oxford-connected clergymen began to publish *Tracts for the Times*. These publications sought to establish the independence of the Church of England from what the authors believed to be the state's improper intrusions following the passage of the Reform Bill of 1832. As the Tractarian Movement, or the Oxford Movement, as it is also called, developed during the 1830s certain of its members, Newman among them, became increasingly attracted to the Roman Catholic Church. Newman in Tract 90 (published in 1841) contended that it was possible for Church of England clergy to believe many elements of religious faith normally associated with Roman Catholicism and still conscientiously continue to serve the Church of England. University authorities quickly condemned Tract 90, and so did the bishops of the Church of England during the next several years. In 1843 he resigned his pulpit at St. Mary's. In October 1845 he was received into the Roman Catholic Church. The year of his conversion he published *An Essay on the Development of Christian Doctrine*.

After studying in Rome and being ordained as a Roman Catholic priest, Newman returned to England. In 1848 he founded the Oratory of St. Philip Neri, which established itself in Birmingham the next year. In 1851 Archbishop Cullen asked Newman to come to Ireland to preside over the establishment of a Roman Catholic university in Dublin. Newman accepted the invitation. One result of his academic work in Ireland was his writing the essays that today compose *The Idea of a University*.

In 1852 Newman delivered five lectures in Dublin on the character of a university. He later wrote five additional lectures that he published but did not deliver. Each of these lectures and essays appeared as an individual pamphlet. In 1852 Newman published these essays with other materials as *Discourses on the Scope and Nature of University Education. Addressed to the Catholics of Dublin.* During his active rectorship (the university came into being only in 1854), Newman also delivered a number of lectures for special occasions. He published ten of these in 1858 as *Lectures and Essays on University Subjects.* The next year he printed a revision of the 1852 volume as *The Scope and Nature of University Education.* In 1873 Newman gathered both works, again considerably revised, into a single volume entitled *The Idea of a University Defined and Illustrated I. In Nine Discourses delivered to the Catholics of Dublin II. In Occasional Lectures and Essays addressed to the Members of the Catholic University.* Thereafter this work became known popularly as *The Idea of a University.* Newman would continue to refine and re-edit the prose right up to the ninth edition published in 1889, the year before his death.

Newman's experience as a university administrator was a mixed one. He felt he never received adequate support from Cullen. Further, the Irish Catholic lay community was suspicious of the Catholic University. Many still preferred to send their sons to Trinity College, Dublin, which though Anglican had high social standing and a long historical tradition. Newman left Dublin and the Catholic University in 1858 and returned to Birmingham. The Catholic University itself eventually became part of the new Royal University of Ireland in 1882.

Newman's own life continued to be quite eventful. He was an extremely active and prolific writer within the English Roman Catholic community. In 1864 the Anglican clergyman Charles Kingsley wrote an article that Newman understood to accuse him and other Roman Catholic priests of dishonesty. Newman responded in his most famous work, *Apologia pro Vita Sua,* in which he traced his life from evangelicalism through the Oxford Movement to Roman Catholicism. That volume returned Newman to the center of English intellectual life. In 1870 he published *The Grammar of Assent,* in which he defended the grounds of religious belief. In 1878 he returned to Oxford for the first time since 1845. The next year, Pope Leo XIII named Newman to be a Cardinal in the Roman Catholic Church. On August 11, 1890, Newman died in Birmingham, having lived almost exactly half his life in the Church of England and half in the Roman Catholic Church.

Reading *The Idea of a University*

I

NEWMAN'S ARGUMENTS

One's first encounter with *The Idea of a University* can be very challenging. The reader is immediately thrust into certain local problems that Newman encountered as the recently appointed rector of the Catholic University in Dublin. Both Newman and the reader must work their way through those issues before reaching questions that are more readily accessible and recognizable as part of more recent concerns in higher education. Newman must first address the issue of why a Catholic university is necessary. That this issue comes first in the book often surprises readers, but it was *the* issue on the mind of Newman's Dublin audience. There were alternative university choices available to Irish Catholic youth. Newman needed to demonstrate the necessity for and unique qualities of the new institution being founded. Second, as Newman's task unfolded itself, he had to persuade his audience that their sons should receive not only an education in a Catholic university, but also a liberal rather than a professional education. Finally, throughout his discussion Newman needed to walk a fine line in explaining the relationship of such secular subjects as literature, history, and science to religious teachings and religious authority in the Catholic University. Although each of these was a separate issue and each moved in and out of Newman's range of immediate concern, they were always in the back of his mind.

In the Nine Discourses that constitute the first section of *The Idea of a University,* these issues led Newman to explore three broadly interwoven themes. First, he argues that there exists a particular need, as understood by the pope and the Irish bishops, for a distinctively Roman Catholic university. Such a university, unlike other contemporary Protestant, religiously mixed, or secular universities, will teach the Roman Catholic doctrine of God. Newman argues that by definition those alternative institutions that do not teach theology as a science are not fully universities because through this fundamental omission, they do not teach universal knowledge.

Indeed, Newman defines a university as a place for teaching universal knowledge in order to mandate the presence of theology as a science of sciences. This is a key argument for Newman because the Irish Catholic laymen in his audience were generally satisfied with religiously mixed institutions whose faculties and students could function peacefully by not addressing religious knowledge. At the same time while criticizing the theological failings of non-Catholic universities, whether secular or Protestant, Newman contends that they may nevertheless provide important models for other aspects of education. This latter contention permits Newman to draw upon his experience at Oxford University for many of the values and goals of instruction he will champion.

Assuming that he has persuaded his listeners of the necessity of including theology and thus of a distinctly Roman Catholic university, Newman must still convince them that such a university should provide liberal learning rather than vocational or professional instruction. Attempting to achieve his audience's assent to this proposition constitutes Newman's second theme and for many readers the most memorable argument in the volume. Newman argues that university education is virtually by definition distinct from instruction for a vocation or a profession. The purpose of a university education is the achievement of a particular expansion of outlook, turn of mind, habit of thought, and capacity for social and civic interaction. This argument fills the central portion of the original discourses and leads Newman to refer specifically to the debates over Oxford education that had taken place earlier in the century in pamphlets and periodical literature.

As a third theme, Newman distinguishes between what a university may purport to do as a university and what the Roman Catholic faith may do as true religion. Newman sees the university as a human institution that may and should produce a person of broad knowledge, critical intelligence, moral decency, and social sensitivity, but not as an institution that can fundamentally transform fallen, sinful human beings. The university can produce through liberal learning the person Newman describes as the Gentleman. To become a Gentleman, however, despite its polish and other benefits, is not to rise above the natural man. The liberally educated Gentleman is not to be confused with the Christian, just as education in philosophy, literature, and science, which prepares the student for life in fallen human society, is not to be confused with attainment of genuine moral virtue. The person of real moral virtue, as opposed to a person possessing some kind of expedient earthly virtue, can only be produced through the teachings, faith, and practice of the Roman Catholic Church.

Throughout the Nine Discourses, there exists a tension, which has sometimes confused readers, in Newman's understanding of the natural human
being and the Christian. For Newman the world of knowledge as found in
the liberal arts pertains to the natural man and participation in human society, and the university must teach such knowledge. But the Catholic
University understands such liberal learning as pertaining only to life on
earth and not to the ultimate good of a human soul in eternity. Newman
repeatedly oscillates between addressing issues that refer to the natural
human being and those that refer to the good of an individual's soul. In this
regard, Newman urges a maximally expansive view of the knowledge that
should be present in a university while warning that such knowledge must
not displace in the human imagination the necessity for receiving religious
truth through the Church. To produce persons capable of active contributions to society, the university must educate them in history and literature,
from which they will be exposed to the record of the moral evil of fallen
human beings. They should also become familiar with the physical sciences, which if pursued too exclusively will lead to indifference to religion.
The distinctive feature of a Catholic university, which includes the teaching
of Roman Catholic dogma, is that by its very nature it will prevent students
from confusing the excellent ends of liberal education and the still higher
ends of true religious faith.

Newman continues to pursue these same themes in his discussions of
University Subjects, but there he turns his attention to particular areas of
study. In his lecture "Christianity and Letters" he again distinguishes human literature from religious revelation. Literature is the manifestation of
the human spirit in its achievement of what he terms *Civilization*. It is
important to see how Newman tends to limit Civilization to the lands surrounding the Mediterranean and western Europe. Newman emphasizes his
case for teaching ancient Greek and Roman literature, instead of more
recent European literatures, because the latter derive from the former. Here
Newman provides a classic argument for the maintenance of a recognizable
literary canon within a liberal education. He also urges the priority of
literature over science in education.

In his lecture "Catholic Literature in the English Tongue" Newman
expands his commentary about the character of literature. He commences
by raising the issue of what might be an English Catholic Literature, but he
quickly explains that his real concern is what it will *not* be. Thereafter, he
probes the question of what constitutes a National Literature. As in the
previous essay, he presents it as an achievement of natural human beings.
Languages and literatures emerge as historical and national facts that exist

as the secular, cultural situation into which one is born. Within national literatures there already exist classic works that in effect forged the language and that continue to influence writing, including that of the present day. Newman outlines the writers who he believes created the English language. He portrays such literatures as a national inheritance, which individuals whatever their religious faith must inevitably use and by which they will find much of their intellectual and cultural existence shaped. Newman suggests that because of the character of the contemporary periodical press, the generation of English classics may have come to an end.

Newman, however, did not think that the advances of science were nearly ending. During his lifetime most English readers assumed that there was a conflict between religion and science. There had been quarrels over the impact of science on what most of his contemporaries called *natural theology,* but which Newman called *physical theology.* Other disputes centered on the difference between scientific theory and the content of biblical narrative. Newman's attitude toward the physical sciences in "Christianity and Physical Science" and "Christianity and Scientific Investigation" offers remarkable support for the scientific enterprise. Unlike many Christians of his day, whether of Roman Catholic or Protestant persuasion, Newman believes that there is little real conflict between science and religion properly understood. God is the author of both modes of knowledge, so there can be no fundamental disagreement. He believes that scientists and theologians should tend their own distinct spheres of knowledge and not intrude upon the other's intellectual territory. He also contends that many scientists have been hostile to religion because theologians have often overstepped their mark.

At the core of the problems between science and religion, Newman argues, is the deductive character of the theology and the inductive character of physical science. Theologians are developing deductively the implications of a divine revelation once given to the Apostles. Physical scientists are inductively investigating nature to acquire and accumulate new knowledge. The two processes are fundamentally different. It is when a person switches the methods from one arena to the other that the difficulty, confusion, and conflict commence. In particular he criticizes the Protestant effort to seek inductive knowledge of nature from reading the Bible, which as one part of apostolic truth should be explored deductively for theological truth rather than for scientific information.

Newman's dissent from many of his contemporaries on another important issue allows him to be much more tolerant of the advancing science than were numerous other religious thinkers of his day. The latter often believed

that the truths of revealed religion were confirmed by the scientific investigation of nature, which they thought could demonstrate the existence and
the benevolence of God. Newman considers this a mistaken attempt to turn
theology into an inductive science. But no less important, as Newman
makes clear in these lectures, the arguments for the existence of God drawn
from what he terms *physical theology* do not persuade him. Like the Scottish philosopher David Hume before him, Newman thinks that the observation of nature does not inherently lead either layman or scientist to a belief
in God. Consequently if a person pays intellectual attention only to science,
such a person will likely become indifferent to religious truth, which does
not necessarily intrude upon scientific observations. Moreover, the kind of
religious truth that others attempt to draw from physical theology is to
Newman's mind inadequate and unworthy of true theological knowledge.
The God set forth in physical theology is simply not the God set forth in
Catholic theology. For those reasons Newman thinks it essential that a
university teach the truths of religion alongside the truths of science.

In "Christianity and Scientific Investigation" Newman discusses what
he regarded as the limitations placed on science in that context. Here he is
addressing the extent of freedom of thought and expression in a university
that adheres to a clear religious mission. He portrays such a university as a
place of considerable mutual tolerance on the part of scholars and students
examining a vast array of ideas. He calls for much "elbow room" in the
world of secular thought. He suggests the university may set some boundaries on the publication and dispersion of scientific discoveries and theories
that might be religiously unsettling. Nevertheless, Newman tends to believe
that errors introduced by allowing considerable freedom in scientific investigation and other secular subjects will be temporary and in time corrected.
Although these views are more conservative than thinking about publication of scientific or other research in today's university, Newman's opinions
on these subjects were in his own day sufficiently open to criticism from
religious authorities in Dublin that he chose only to print this essay and did
not deliver it as the public lecture he had planned.

II

ANALYTIC TABLE OF CONTENTS

By means of this analytic table of contents, the reader can follow the
general direction of Newman's arguments and the subjects he addresses.
The reader may also more easily find those portions of Newman's discus-

sions that bear directly on each other, though they are in different discourses or addresses.

Preface

A University defined – Relationship of a University to the Church – Why the Pope wishes to establish a University – Distinction between Academies and Universities and between discovery and teaching – Church wants education of Catholic youth to be on par with that of Protestants but in a Catholic form – Irish Catholics have been historically denied education – The real cultivation of the mind defined – Benefits of the training and formation of the intellect – Critique of "viewiness" and of periodical literature – Previous authority of Universities now lodged in the literary world – Catholic prelates seek to resist these tendencies

Discourse I – Introductory

Accusations of lack of utility and religious exclusiveness brought against Oxford and Cambridge earlier in the century – Newman's view on education as a product of his whole life's experience – Both Catholics and Protestants may hold similar views of a University – Philosophy of education based on natural order rather than on revelation – Newman as a Catholic may and will thus appeal to Protestant experience in education – Universities to be considered from standpoint of human reason and wisdom – Education a matter of practice and expedience, not immutable truth – Ecclesiastical authority has declared for a pure University system for Catholic youth – Some Catholic parents will regard the goal as impractical, but the Pope has chosen this path – Power and authority of the Papacy through history – What the Papacy has achieved in Ireland and England

Discourse II – Theology a Branch of Knowledge

Can the idea of a University exclude theology? – Can the useful arts and sciences be given priority over the liberal arts and sciences? – Universities now being created without Theological Chairs – How can theology be excluded if Universities are to teach universal knowledge? – Universities should teach universal knowledge – Logical inconsistency of excluding Theology unless it is asserted that Theology is not a science – Central purpose of human association may not be compromised without undermining the character of the association – Those who advocate universal knowledge may not sacrifice a form of knowledge itself – If there is a God, a University must profess the science attendant to God – Existence of God is a truth of the natural as well as of the supernatural order – Evangelical Protestantism has taught religion to be based on feeling rather than on reason – This attitude leads to exclusion of Religion from Universities – Attack on Lord Brougham's views of religion as sentiment – Natural religion suggests a basis of truth for religious doctrine – Catholic doctrine of the belief in God – Contemporary non-Catholic writers do not mean by the term *God* what Catholics mean – Non-Catholics reduce God to a constitutional monarch – The God of physical theology merely a manifestation of subjective feeling – Hume's views discussed – Religious doctrine is a form of knowledge and thus belongs in a University

Discourse III – Bearing of Theology on Other Branches of Knowledge

Critique of setting religion apart from public secular knowledge – Knowledge constitutes a single whole – Sciences represent partial views of the mind – Man is viewed differently according to the science employed – Sciences supplement each other – No single science can be dogmatic – Universe cannot be contemplated without thought about God – There must exist a science of the sciences – Exclusion of theology means less than complete knowledge, and it prejudices the truths associated with other sciences – Imagine a University that omitted all study of the human mind – Ignoring divine agency the equivalent of denying God – Natural Theology different from Physical Theology – Theology is the Science of God – Doctrine of God – Place of Theology in intellectual world from time immemorial assures its prescriptive right in the University – Religious Truth a condition of general knowledge

Discourse IV – Bearing of Other Branches of Knowledge on Theology

Facts supplied by Revealed Religion supplement knowledge of other sciences – Omission of Divine Knowledge leads to ignorance – Exclusive pursuit of secular sciences a danger to Religion – Human nature naturally insists on views that coordinate thought and experience – Man of one idea carries single point of view to excess – Absence of Theology leads to perversion of other sciences attempting to fill the vacuum – Painting, music, architecture may attempt to subjugate religion – Exclusive study of a single subject leads to opposition to religion – Claims of Political Economy to be a Moral Science – Political Economy sets accumulation of wealth as basis of virtue and religion – Truth of men of science not the whole truth – History given more authority than it warrants – Theology can defend itself only if present in the University – Summary of argument for inclusion of Theology in the University

Discourse V – Knowledge Its Own End

All university subject matter the acts and words of the Creator – University portrayed as gathering of teachers of individual sciences who learn from each other – Philosophical habit of mind flows from liberal education – Knowledge capable of being its own end – Cicero's distinction of differing pursuits of knowledge – The Liberal Arts defined and distinguished from the servile, the commercial, and the professional – Bacon's association of science with the Useful Arts – Praise for Aristotle – Liberal Knowledge as a Gentleman's knowledge – Knowledge becomes a Science or Philosophy when informed by Reason – Knowledge a good before a power – Knowledge as habit, possession, inward development – Education distinguished from instruction – Useful Knowledge directed toward secular objects – Christian Knowledge directed toward eternal objects – Incapacity of philosophy to teach virtue – Aims of Useful Knowledge low but attainable – Francis Bacon discussed – Differing ends of Liberal and Religious Knowledge – Distinction between virtue and knowledge – Liberal Knowledge does not make men morally better – Liberal Knowledge makes the Gentleman – Liberal Knowledge as the cultivation of intellect not of virtue

Discourse VI – Knowledge Viewed in Relation to Learning

English language lacks term to express intellectual proficiency – Function of the University is intellectual culture – Acquisition of mere knowledge distinguished from Liberal Education – Knowledge of mutual relations of things rather than of things only – Men of information have not achieved the Liberal Education – True enlargement of mind is capacity to view things in relationship to each other and to the whole – Mind disciplined to perfection of its powers described – Mistakes besetting University education: overemphasis on memory, smattering of shallow learning, mechanical learning – University as a particular kind of community more important than instruction alone – The educative powers of the community of youthful scholars – Self-education preferable to many other systems – Praise for the capacity of independent self-learning

Discourse VII – Knowledge Viewed in Relation to Professional Skill

Cultivation of intellect lies in apprehension of truth – Role of habit and discipline – Mind disciplined for its own sake constitutes Liberal Education – *Edinburgh Review* attack on Oxford recalled – Oriel College, Oxford, remembered – Dr. Copleston and others defending Oxford education – John Locke's arguments favoring useful education – Quotations from *Edinburgh Review* critique of Oxford – Liberal Education useful when properly understood – Utility of Liberal Education compared to utility of health – Liberal Education prepares one for numerous vocations – Position of Professional Education within a University – Extracts from Mr. Davison's essay – Role of University in cultivating public mind, purifying public taste, and preparing students for public life

Discourse VIII – Knowledge Viewed in Relation to Religion

Summary of Discourses V, VI, and VII – Right Reason leads mind to the Catholic Faith – Modes of Religion – Religion of Civilization distinguished from Catholicism – Catholicism as system of pastoral instruction and moral duty – Temporary nature of personal religious experiences and resolutions – Knowledge can draw mind from what may harm it – Knowledge provides a discipline aiding the mind to avoid evil – A "fastidiousness" that helps to avoid evil – Radical difference between mental refinement and genuine religion – Civilized age transforms sin into offense against human nature rather than God – Philosophical or Gentleman's religion defined – Critique of eighteenth-century versions of Religion of Philosophy exemplified in Lord Shaftesbury's morality – Refinement of intellect ends in excusing sensuality – The Gentleman the creation of Civilization not of Christianity – Philosophical morality embellishes the exterior and transforms pride into self-respect – The Gentleman described – Qualities of the Gentleman and morality of Civilization may be realized both inside and outside the Church

Discourse IX – Duties of the Church Towards Knowledge

Summary of previous argument – Church must have jurisdiction of University lest the latter become the rival of the former – Liberal knowledge apprehends truth as beautiful – Useful knowledge apprehends truth as power – Danger that the Beautiful will become a substitute for faith, that Theological Truth will be ignored, and that spirit of Catholicism will be adulterated – No real collision between Physical Science and Catholicism, but a long history of hostility nonetheless – Satisfaction in laws of nature indisposes one to thoughts of a Moral Governor – Physical Science moves by induction, Theology by deduction – Only one revelation – Protestantism moves by induction – Natural knowledge pertains to earthly matters before the introduction of evil – Catholic Church entrusted to remedy the consequences of introduction of evil – Physical science is part of advanced civilized age – Church must protect Revealed Truth inside and outside the University – Literature the voice of natural and thus fallen, sinful man – Literature naturally leads to understanding of moral evil – Christian Literature a contradiction in terms – Literature included in the University to prepare men for the world – Church must not exclude Literature but must demand inclusion of its own teachings as well – Praise of St. Philip Neri

University Subjects

I. Christianity and Letters. A Lecture in the School of Philosophy and Letters (1854)
Universities have historically been formally centered in the Faculty of Arts – Survey of the course of Civilization – Comments on non-Western Civilizations – Civilization defined as those countries surrounding the Mediterranean – This civilization equated with Human Society and the Human Mind – This same Civilization has been the chief setting for Christian society – Analogies between Christianity and Civilization – Homer, the first Apostle of Civilization – Rise of the Liberal Arts as part of the history of European Civilization – Function of literature of Greece and Rome in forming mind of European Civilization – Professional Studies were never intended to displace the Liberal Arts – Study of the Classics preferable to that of the Sciences – Jerusalem the fountainhead of religious knowledge, Athens of secular knowledge – Rome has benefited from and dispenses knowledge of both traditions – Hope that the founding of the School of Philosophy and Letters will be just the beginning of greater things

II. Catholic Literature in the English Tongue (1854–1858)
Difficulties in discussing the concept of Catholic Literature in English – Essay will concentrate on what it is not – Catholic Literature in English is literature by Catholics, not about Catholic subjects – Catholic Literature not

synonymous with Theology – A Catholic Literature has no particular concern for the physical sciences – In the abstract a non-Catholic might fill the
chairs of the physical sciences in a Catholic University – The scientific
treatises of both non-Catholics and anti-Catholics are of use to a Catholic
University – Literature defined as thoughts conveyed under the forms of
a particular language – A Classical English Literature has already been
created – Literature as a historical and national fact – Catholic Literature
cannot displace Classical English Literature – Development of language
and literature over time as facts of nature – Masters of composition as the
creators of the language – A National Literature as a great work of man that
Catholics cannot overcome – All secular literatures are bad when weighed
against truth and morality – National Literatures the offspring of natural
man – English Literature is Protestant, but not atheistic or immoral – Comments on Shakespeare and on English philosophers – Classics of a National
Literature defined – A particular language and literature improve over
time – Classics both perfect literature and discourage further advance –
Impediments to the rise of new classics – The present age marks the end of
English classics – Catholics must use the language and literature they have
inherited to write about Catholic subjects

*III. Christianity and Physical Science. A Lecture in the School of
Medicine (1855)*
Popular assumption of antagonism between Physics and Science –
Distinction between natural and supernatural world and knowledge of
each – Properly understood, Theology and Science will not contradict each
other – Physicist acting as physicist will not contemplate final causes – The
Theologian addresses final causes – Quotations from Macaulay on Protestantism and Roman Catholicism, respecting natural theology – Holy Scripture does make some comments on the natural order, but they need not
occasion conflict – Physics and Theology do not quarrel, but Physicists and
Theologians have quarreled – Neither group has been content to stay on its
own ground – Theology is deductive, Physics inductive – Theology develops a revelation given only once; Physics seeks new knowledge –
Critique of popular interpretations of Scripture that contradict physical
sciences – Experimentalists have intruded on ground of Theology well
beyond the defense they need to make against introducing final causes into
science – For last three centuries, wrong efforts have tried to make Theology an experimental science – Theology and Baconian method are mismatched – The error has come from seeking Baconian knowledge of Scripture rather than having recourse to the authoritative teaching of the Catholic

Church – Character of Natural or Physical Theology and its misuse, being put too prominently forward – Scripture and Antiquity do not contain all religious truth – Physical Theology cannot by its very nature teach Christian truth – God of Physical Theology can become an idol or lead to belief in pantheism – Profession of Atheism perhaps preferable to profession of self-deceptive faith in Physical Theology

IV. Christianity and Scientific Investigation. A Lecture Written for the School of Science (1855)

Anxiety raised by science among religious men is needless – Expansive character of subjects taught in a University – Manner in which a University incorporates a broad range of studies and blends them into a single social establishment – University is the equivalent of an empire to philosophy and research – University representing the philosophy of an imperial intellect – Truths cannot be contradictory despite appearances – Members of a University community ought to behave in a neighborly way when there seem to be discrepancies between Reason and Revelation – Catholic faith allows scholars to face truths without nervousness – Discussion of opposition of Catholic Church to Copernican System – Necessity for freedom in the investigation and discussion of the physical sciences, if one assumes no assault on dogma, intrusion on the proper realm of theological teaching, or shocking of the popular mind – Summary of previous argument – Elbow room desirable in domain of scientific thought, not in theology – Minds not intent on unbelief must be allowed to pursue their ideas and to encounter criticism – Error is not permanent – Science as pursued in good Catholic faith

III

QUESTIONS FOR REFLECTION

Preface

a. To what extent does Newman indicate what his ideal of "universal knowledge" includes? Either in 1852 or today, would all subjects of human thought and activity be included in "universal knowledge"? Then or now, how would selections be made? How has the content of the ideal of "universal knowledge" changed between 1852 and the present? What intellectual and social forces have contributed to those changes?

b. Why does Newman draw a distinction between teaching and discovery? Are they always separate activities? How do they contribute to each other? How do both contribute to the educational experience of students?

c. What does Newman mean by the phrase "real cultivation of the mind"? How does he relate it to Irish Catholics achieving social advancement and overcoming the prejudices they have confronted? How might this idea affect the experience of minority groups today? To what extent has education as a path to social and economic mobility, rather than as a path to knowledge, accounted for the broad public support for university education in the past half-century?

d. In the Preface and elsewhere in *The Idea of a University,* Newman criticizes the periodical press and popular publications. What is the criticism that he brings to bear against them? Are there any parallels to be drawn to modern culture – the influence of popular media, television, and electronic games?

Discourse I

a. What does Newman mean when he declares that "the philosophy of Education is founded on truths in the natural order" (16)? How does this point of view allow him to draw upon the experience of Protestant universities? What lessons does he draw from them?

b. What are the factors that Newman outlines as working against the effort to establish "a University, of which Catholicity is the fundamental principle" (20)? Why does Newman believe that some of these factors appeal to Irish Catholics in 1852? What arguments might support or criticize the idea of a college or university being organized today according to either religious principles or some set of social and political ideals?

c. What is the purpose of Newman's praise for the role of the papacy in the history of England and Ireland? Why does he outline the history of its achievements in those lands?

Discourse II

a. Why does Newman regard as "an intellectual absurdity" the establishment of universities without provision for teaching Theology (25)? How does this argument relate to his contention that universities are places for teaching universal knowledge? Could the arguments he uses for Theology also be used to defend the teaching of other subjects or the teaching of particular political points of view in a University? Does Newman's argument permit any limits to what fields of study might be offered in a University?

b. What are Newman's criticisms of Protestant Evangelical theology, which roots religious faith in feeling? Why does he think that this Protestant concept of religion works against the inclusion of Theology in a University?

c. Compare and contrast Newman's presentation of the idea of God as understood in natural theology and in Roman Catholic theology. Why does he regard the former as reducing God to the level of a "constitutional monarchy" (37)?

d. What is the implication of Newman's conviction that "religious doctrine is knowledge" for the inclusion of Theology in the University (39)? What arguments might be brought forth today for including Theology in a University's program of study? Are modern arguments the same as Newman's? Would the academic aims of departments of religious studies or divinity schools, which are parts of present-day universities, satisfy Newman's concerns?

Discourse III

a. What is the argument that Newman sets forth as coming from persons opposed or indifferent to the presence of Theology in the University?

b. How does Newman portray the various sciences as correcting each other? How does this presentation lead him to contend that Theology must be included among the sciences taught in the University? Why is Theology "a science of sciences"?

c. What is the distinction Newman draws between real Theology and other sets of ideas that he sees merely posing as Theology? How does the view of God as taught by Theology differ from that taught by physical theology?

d. What does Newman mean when he urges, "Religious Truth is not only a portion, but a condition of general knowledge" (57)?

Discourse IV

a. What relationship does Newman establish between Revealed Religion as a form of knowledge and secular subjects as a mode of knowledge? Why does Newman claim that to overlook the knowledge of revelation will leave large areas of ignorance? What is the basis of Newman's argument, toward the close of the discourse, that if Theology is not taught, the other sciences will usurp its role?

b. What is Newman's "man of one idea" (61)? How does this figure relate to those intellects whom Newman portrays later in the discourse as pursuing only their own fields of study, little concerned about other forms of knowledge? Does one encounter such single-minded people today?

c. What is the relationship that Newman draws between Religion and the Fine Arts? What occurs in the Fine Arts if they are separated from Religion? What moral powers does Newman associate with the Fine Arts?

d. What does Newman see as the social and intellectual goals of Political Economy? Why does he contend that Political Economy can only lead to an inferior form of virtue?

Discourse V

a. What are the characteristics of the university community of scholars that Newman portrays in the opening section of this discourse? Is this a fair description of a university or college community today?

b. Why does Newman believe that knowledge may be pursued as an end in itself? Why does he emphasize liberal learning as establishing a habit of mind?

c. How does liberal learning differ from commercial or professional education? Is it possible for professional or business education to include elements of liberal knowledge and liberal learning?

d. What is the basis for Newman's assertion that Lord Bacon, in relating the sciences to useful knowledge, had transferred them from the realm of liberal learning? Is Newman correct, or is he simply attempting to protect some areas of thought and instruction from having to compete with the sciences? Are the physical sciences as taught today part of liberal knowledge?

e. What is Newman's distinction between philosophical knowledge and mechanical knowledge? Why does Newman repeatedly insist that the Philosophy of Utility and useful knowledge aim only toward a low form of knowledge, learning, and instruction? Is this conviction valid? Is it still shared by people who teach and study in universities? According to what values today do university students and faculties establish a hierarchy of studies.

f. What does Newman mean when he declares, "Knowledge is one thing, virtue is another" (89)? What is the distinction between intellectual excellence and moral excellence? In an age when meritocratic judgments and evaluations often determine the schools one may enter and the professions one may pursue, does Newman's distinction have any present-day validity? How important is character? Does Newman believe that universities as universities can or should determine moral excellence? Can or should universities today attempt to form character and cultivate moral excellence or foster awareness of differing moral values?

Discourse VI

a. Why is the accumulation of mere knowledge – for example, through training the memory or producing "men of information" – *not* what Newman means by a Liberal Education (98)? How does Newman's argument on this matter relate to the present-day view that students may achieve a Liberal Education simply by having a wide array of different subjects from which to choose for their programs of study?

b. What does Newman mean by his assertion that "the power of viewing many things at once as one whole" represents the only true enlargement of the mind (99)? How might such a power be achieved? Are there experiences in college and university education today by which one can acquire such an intellectual vantage point? Is this a realistic goal for education, or simply an impractical ideal?

c. Newman declares, "A University is . . . an Alma Mater, knowing her children one by one, not a foundry, or a mint, or a treadmill" (109). To what extent is this an accurate description of the modern university? What elements of university life contribute to the recognition of individuality among students? Is the classroom the best site for such recognition, or are other activities – such as athletics, drama, music, fraternities, and religious groups – more likely to produce such an atmosphere in the university?

d. Although Newman emphasizes learning throughout his volume, in this discourse he also stresses the importance of the student community and the manner in which students educate each other. What is the "sort of self-education" that he admires in the English Protestant universities (111)? Does he see the life of the student community as equally or even more important than the instruction they receive? Would Newman's comments have validity in university settings where many students commute or where many students are not of the traditional college age?

Discourse VII

a. Why does Newman regard the disciplining of the mind for its own sake as a higher goal than the disciplining of the mind for a particular profession or vocation? Here and elsewhere, what does Newman actually mean by achieving mental discipline?

b. What were the accusations that Newman reports being brought against Oxford University by the writers in the *Edinburgh Review?* Why does he relate their criticisms to John Locke's educational ideas? Are there any writers today whose criticisms of contemporary universities resemble those leveled against Oxford?

c. How does Newman present the Liberal Education as "useful"? Is Newman's argument that the Liberal Education allows one to "take up any one of the sciences or callings" valid in the present world of specialized learning (118)? What aspects of present-day liberal education work to open the way for later vocational choices and later intellectual attainment? What are "a power and a grace" that Newman contends the Liberal Education brings to a variety of occupations (119)? Are Newman's arguments in favor of the Liberal Education the same as those of Copleston and Davison, the defenders of Oxford against the *Edinburgh Review,* whom he quotes?

d. How do you reconcile Newman's defense of a Liberal Education, which has no professional end, with his contention that the practical end of a University is "that of training good members of society" (125)? Should that goal be the University's most important practical purpose? What aspects of present-day University education and experience prepare students to be good members of society? Is there agreement in the contemporary University world as to what kinds of people constitute good members of society?

Discourse VIII

a. What are the varieties of religion that Newman outlines in the early portion of this discourse? Among these, what does he mean by "the Religion of Civilization" (129)?

b. Why does Newman contend that Knowledge, rather than religious experience, may be a better discipline for moral activity? How does Knowledge supplement religion as a source of moral discipline?

c. What is "a gentleman's religion" (136)? Why is Newman so concerned with conscience being replaced by a moral sense? What are the dangers he portrays arising from the "Religion of Reason" and "a godless intellectualism" (137)? How do the passages from Lord Shaftesbury illustrate "the Religion of Philosophy" (140)?

d. How do the various secular moral philosophies Newman describes eventually tame Pride? How do they transform and redirect Pride into a kind of self-respect that overcomes many antisocial tendencies? What are the qualities Newman associates with "the Gentleman"? What is the relationship of the Gentleman to the Christian?

Discourse IX

a. Why does Newman contend that the Church must have active jurisdiction over the life of the Catholic University? How may Liberal Knowledge possibly lead to ignoring Religious Truth? How may Liberal Learning adulterate the Catholic Faith?

b. What are the complaints of practitioners of Theology and Physical Science against each other? Why is deduction the method of Theology and induction that of Physical Science? Why does Newman believe there should be no essential conflict between religion and science?

c. Why does Newman contend there cannot be "a Christian Literature" (158)? What are the moral dangers that students and faculty may encounter in the study of Literature? At the same time, why does he believe that Literature must be taught in the Catholic University? Could any of the dangers Newman describes be used as an argument to limit the kinds of literature students today encounter in universities? Are there issues today that would lead some people to use such arguments to impose boundaries on university study?

d. How does teaching pure doctrine in the Catholic University make it safe for the University "not to prohibit truth of any kind" within its walls (161)? Do universities today feel secure in not prohibiting discussion of any sort of truth?

University Subjects

I. Christianity and Letters

a. Why have Faculties of Arts remained at the core of most universities? Are there arguments why this situation might or should be challenged? In the course of this lecture, what subjects does Newman associate with the Liberal Education? Why does he exclude the physical sciences?

b. How does Newman define "Civilization"? Why did he not see "Civilization" extending over the entire earth? What is the relationship he draws between "Civilization" and Christianity? If one were offering a lecture on the same subject today, how might the definition of "Civilization" be changed? What are the chief social, political, religious, cultural, and intellectual traditions associated today with the concept of Western civilization?

c. What does Newman mean by calling Homer "the first Apostle of

Civilization" (171)? Why does Newman favor the study of the Greek and Roman classics over more modern literature? Could one use Newman's arguments to establish a different set of writings as the core of literary study? What arguments might be made for including non-ancient and non-Western writers in the curriculum?

d. Like many writers before him, Newman presents Athens and Jerusalem as the fountainheads of different traditions in Western civilization. What elements of the Western tradition does he associate with each? Are there other cities or areas of the world that, following Newman's example, one could use metaphorically to trace various aspects of Western civilization?

II. Catholic Literature in the English Tongue

a. What does Newman mean by a "Catholic Literature in the English Tongue"? Why does he distinguish it from Catholic Theology? Why does he see no need for such a literature in relation to science? What is the relationship Newman portrays between a Catholic University and the possible presence of non-Catholic scientists on its faculty?

b. Why is a literature "a national and historical fact" (185)? How do both a language and a literature develop over time? What is the association of literature with historical nations?

c. How do particular masters of composition, such as those Newman cites in connection with English, forge a literature and establish a language? How does Newman relate National Literatures to the development of natural man? Why does Newman view the literature of England as inherently a Protestant literature?

d. What does Newman mean by "the Classics of a national Literature" (193)? How does a classic work influence later literature in a nation? Are these influences positive or negative? What cultural, literary, and historical forces foster or inhibit the emergence of new Classics? Why does Newman think there may be no new English Classics?

e. Newman used his arguments about National Literatures to suggest that there would be no distinct Catholic Classics or Catholic Literature. He also premised his comments by limiting "Civilization" to the Mediterranean basin and Europe. How might his own arguments be used to expand the canon of National Literatures and of literary Classics beyond the geographical and cultural boundaries he established?

III. Christianity and Physical Science

a. How does Newman differentiate the realm of Science and the realm of Theology? How does this relate to his assigning the Physicist to trace efficient causes and the Theologian final causes? In what manner does his quotation from Macaulay lead him to contend that "Catholic Theology has nothing to fear from the progress of Physical Science" (206)?

b. How does Newman differentiate the methods of the Physical Sciences from those of Theology? Why has confusion over these methods and over spheres of intellectual investigation led to conflict between science and religion?

c. What are the criticisms Newman brings to bear against physical theology? Why does he think it a mistake to use physical theology either for or against Christianity? Why does Newman contend that physical theology is theologically inadequate? Why in Newman's opinion may the God of Physical Theology "very easily become a mere idol" (217)? Why is Newman more willing to see a person an outright Atheist than a professor of a pantheistic religion drawn from Physical Theology? How does Newman's skepticism toward Physical Theology allow him to have few fears of the impact of scientific discovery on religious truth? Would Newman's arguments have any relevance in the current debates over creationism or over medical ethics?

IV. Christianity and Scientific Investigation

a. How does Newman portray the University as an institution in which numerous disciplines are pursued? Why does he describe the University as a vast empire and its role in balancing the claims of the various disciplines as "an imperial intellect" (221)? Does his portrayal here of the University as a social system fully agree with his description of the University in the Nine Discourses? Does Newman provide any guidance as to how Universities might choose among the subjects to be brought into the empire or how the resources of the imperial intellect are to be divided?

b. Why is the person who holds to the Catholic faith unlikely to be nervous about new discoveries in science or in other areas of research? What is his attitude toward earlier instances, such as the case of Galileo, when the Catholic Church clashed with scientific investigators?

c. What is the basis for Newman's argument that investigators within universities should have a great deal of freedom for their investigations? Does he extend that freedom of thought and investigation to those concerned with Theology? What are the limits he draws for the publication and dispersion of theories and ideas that might have a negative religious impact? Who would decide which ideas are to be published and which withheld? Does Newman's attitude toward the publication of controversial scientific ideas have any parallel with the teaching and publication of controversial ideas in science or other disciplines in the present-day university? Can or should universities limit speech or publications by members of their communities? On what grounds, if any, might such limits be established? What are the costs of such limits? Who would have the right to decide upon them? In terms of Newman's opening contention, that a University is "a place of teaching universal knowledge," (3) can a University in his sense exist if it does not permit full freedom of speech and publication?

The
Idea
of a
University

---

*Defined and
Illustrated*

Preface.

The view taken of a University in these Discourses is the following: – That it is a place of *teaching* universal *knowledge*. This implies that its object is, on the one hand, intellectual, not moral; and, on the other, that it is the diffusion and extension of knowledge rather than the advancement. If its object were scientific and philosophical discovery, I do not see why a University should have students; if religious training, I do not see how it can be the seat of literature and science.

Such is a University in its *essence,* and independently of its relation to the Church. But, practically speaking, it cannot fulfil its object duly, such as I have described it, without the Church's assistance; or, to use the theological term, the Church is necessary for its *integrity.* Not that its main characters are changed by this incorporation: it still has the office of intellectual education; but the Church steadies it in the performance of that office.

Such are the main principles of the Discourses which follow; though it would be unreasonable for me to expect that I have treated so large and important a field of thought with the fulness and precision necessary to secure me from incidental misconceptions of my meaning on the part of the reader. It is true, there is nothing novel or singular in the argument which I have been pursuing, but this does not protect me from such misconceptions; for the very circumstance that the views I have been delineating are not original with me may lead to false notions as to my relations in opinion towards those from whom I happened in the first instance to learn them, and may cause me to be interpreted by the objects or sentiments of schools to which I should be simply opposed.

For instance, some persons may be tempted to complain, that I have servilely followed the English idea of a University, to the disparagement of that Knowledge which I profess to be so strenuously upholding; and they may anticipate that an academical system, formed upon my model, will result in nothing better or higher than in the production of that antiquated variety of human nature and remnant of feudalism, as they consider it, called "a gentleman."[1] Now, I have anticipated this charge in various parts of my discussion; if, however, any Catholic is found to prefer it (and to Catholics of course this Volume is primarily addressed), I would have him first of all ask himself the previous question, *what* he conceives to be the reason contemplated by the Holy See in recommending just now to the Irish Hierarchy the establishment of a Catholic University? Has the Supreme Pontiff recommended it for the sake of the Sciences, which are to be the matter, and not rather of the Students, who are to be the subjects, of its teaching? Has he any obligation or duty at all towards secular knowledge as such? Would it become his Apostolical Ministry, and his descent from the Fisherman, to have a zeal for the Baconian or other philosophy of man for its own sake? Is the Vicar of Christ bound by office or by vow to be the preacher of the theory of gravitation, or a martyr for electro-magnetism? Would he be acquitting himself of the dispensation committed to him if he were smitten with an abstract love of these matters, however true, or beautiful, or ingenious, or useful? Or rather, does he not contemplate such achievements of the intellect, as far as he contemplates them, solely and simply in their relation to the interests of Revealed Truth? Surely, what he does he does for the sake of Religion; if he looks with satisfaction on strong temporal governments, which promise perpetuity, it is for the sake of Religion; and if he encourages and patronizes art and science, it is for the sake of Religion. He rejoices in the widest and most philosophical systems of intellectual education, from an intimate conviction that Truth is his real ally, as it is his profession; and that Knowledge and Reason are sure ministers to Faith.

This being undeniable, it is plain that, when he suggests to the Irish Hierarchy the establishment of a University, his first and chief and direct object is, not science, art, professional skill, literature, the discovery of knowledge, but some benefit or other, to accrue, by means of literature and science, to his own children; not indeed their formation on any narrow or fantastic type, as, for instance, that of an "English Gentleman" may be called, but their exercise and growth in certain habits, moral or intellectual. Nothing short of this can be his aim, if, as becomes the Successor of the Apostles, he is to be able to say with St. Paul, "Non judicavi me scire aliquid inter vos, nisi Jesum Christum, et hunc crucifixum."[2] Just as a commander wishes to have tall and well-formed and vigorous soldiers, not from any abstract devotion to the military standard of height or age, but for the purposes of war, and no one thinks it any thing but natural and praiseworthy in him to be contemplating, not abstract qualities, but his own living and breathing men; so, in like manner, when the Church founds a University, she is not cherishing talent, genius, or knowledge, for their own sake, but for the sake of her children, with a view to their spiritual welfare and their religious influence and usefulness, with the object of training them to fill their respective posts in life better, and of making them more intelligent, capable, active members of society.

Nor can it justly be said that in thus acting she sacrifices Science, and, under a pretence of fulfilling the duties of her mission, perverts a University to ends not its own, as soon as it is taken into account that there are other institutions far more suited to act as instruments of stimulating philosophical inquiry, and extending the boundaries of our knowledge, than a University. Such, for instance, are the literary and scientific "Academies," which are so celebrated in Italy and France, and which have frequently been connected with Universities, as committees, or, as it were, congregations or delegacies subordinate to them. Thus the present Royal Society originated in Charles the Second's time, in Oxford; such just now are the Ashmolean and Architectural Societies in the same seat of learning, which have risen in our own time. Such, too, is the British Association, a migratory body, which at least at times is found in the halls of the Protestant Universities of the United Kingdom, and the faults of which lie, not in its exclusive devotion to science, but in graver matters which it is irrelevant here to enter upon. Such again is the Antiquarian Society, the Royal Academy for the Fine Arts, and others which might be mentioned. This, then, is the sort of institution, which primarily contemplates Science itself, and not students: and, in thus speaking, I am saying nothing of my own, being supported by no less an authority than Cardinal Gerdil. "Ce n'est pas," he says, "qu'il y ait aucune véritable opposition entre l'esprit des Académies et celui des Universités; ce sont seulement des vues différentes. Les Universités sont établies pour *enseigner* les sciences *aux élèves* qui veulent s'y former; les Académies se proposent *de nouvelles recherches* à faire dans la carrière des sciences. Les Universités d'Italie ont fourni des sujets qui ont fait honneur aux Académies; et celles-ci ont donné aux Universités des Professeurs, qui ont rempli les chaires avec la plus grande distinction."[3]

The nature of the case and the history of philosophy combine to recommend to us this division of intellectual labour between Academies and Universities. To discover and to teach are distinct functions; they are also distinct gifts, and are not commonly found united in the same person. He, too, who spends his day in dispensing his existing knowledge to all comers is unlikely to have either leisure or energy to acquire new. The common sense of mankind has associated the search after truth with seclusion and quiet. The greatest thinkers have been too intent on their subject to admit of interruption; they have been men of absent minds and idosyncratic habits, and have, more or less, shunned the lecture room and the public school. Pythagoras, the light of Magna Græcia, lived for a time in a cave. Thales, the light of Ionia, lived unmarried and in private, and refused the invitations of princes. Plato withdrew from Athens to the groves of Academus. Aristotle gave twenty years to a studious discipleship under him. Friar Bacon lived in his tower upon the Isis. Newton indulged in an intense severity of meditation which almost shook his reason. The great discoveries in chemistry and electricity were not made in Universities. Observatories are more frequently out of Universities than in them, and even when within their bounds need have no moral connexion with them. Porson had no classes; Elmsley lived a good part of his life in the country. I do not say that there are not great examples the other way, perhaps Socrates, certainly Lord Bacon; still I think it must be allowed on the whole that, while teaching involves external engagements, the natural home for experiment and speculation is retirement.

Returning, then, to the consideration of the question, from which I may seem to have digressed, thus much I think I have made good, – that, whether or no a Catholic University should put before it, as its great object, to make its students "gentlemen," still to make them something or other *is* its great object, and not simply to protect the interests and advance the dominion of Science. If, then, this may be taken for granted, as I think it may, the only point which remains to be settled is, whether I have formed a probable conception of the *sort of benefit* which the Holy See has intended to confer on Catholics who speak the English tongue by recommending to the Irish Hierarchy the establishment of a University; and this I now proceed to consider.

Here, then, it is natural to ask those who are interested in the question, whether any better interpretation of the recommendation of the Holy See can be given than that which I have suggested in this Volume. Certainly it does not seem to me rash to pronounce that, whereas Protestants have great advantages of education in the Schools, Colleges, and Universities of the United Kingdom, our ecclesiastical rulers have it in purpose that Catholics should enjoy the like advantages, whatever they are, to the full. I conceive they view it as prejudicial to the interests of Religion that there should be any cultivation of mind bestowed upon Protestants which is not given to their own youth also. As they wish their schools for the poorer and middle classes to be at least on a par with those of Protestants, they contemplate the same object also as regards that higher education which is given to comparatively the few. Protestant youths, who can spare the time, continue their studies till the age of twenty-one or twenty-two; thus they employ a time of life all-important and especially favourable to mental culture. I conceive that our Prelates are impressed with the fact and its consequences, that a youth who ends his education at seventeen is no match (*cæteris paribus*) for one who ends it at twenty-two.

All classes indeed of the community are impressed with a fact so obvious as this. The consequence is, that Catholics who aspire to be on a level with Protestants in discipline and refinement of intellect have recourse to Protestant Universities to obtain what they cannot find at home. Assuming (as the Rescripts from Propaganda allow me to do) that Protestant education is inexpedient for our youth, – we see here an additional reason why those advantages, whatever they are, which Protestant communities dispense through the medium of Protestantism should be accessible to Catholics in a Catholic form.

What are these advantages? I repeat, they are in one word the culture of the intellect. Robbed, oppressed, and thrust aside, Catholics in these islands have not been in a condition for centuries to attempt the sort of education which is necessary for the man of the world, the statesman, the landholder, or the opulent gentleman. Their legitimate stations, duties, employments, have been taken from them, and the qualifications withal, social and intellectual, which are necessary both for reversing the forfeiture and for availing themselves of the reversal. The time is come when this moral disability must be removed. Our desideratum is, not the manners and habits of gentlemen; – these can be, and are, acquired in various other ways, by good society, by foreign travel, by the innate grace and dignity of the Catholic mind; – but the force, the steadiness, the comprehensiveness and the versatility of intellect, the command over our own powers, the instinctive just estimate of things as they pass before us, which sometimes indeed is a natural gift, but commonly is not gained without much effort and the exercise of years.

This is real cultivation of mind; and I do not deny that the characteristic excellences of a gentleman are included in it. Nor need we be ashamed that they should be, since the poet long ago wrote, that "Ingenuas didicisse fideliter artes Emollit mores."[4] Certainly a liberal education does manifest itself in a courtesy, propriety, and polish of word and action, which is beautiful in itself, and acceptable to others; but it does much more. It brings the mind into form, – for the mind is like the body. Boys outgrow their shape and their strength; their limbs have to be knit together, and their constitution needs tone. Mistaking animal spirits for vigour, and over-confident in their health, ignorant what they can bear and how to manage themselves, they are immoderate and extravagant; and fall into sharp sicknesses. This is an emblem of their minds; at first they have no principles laid down within them as a foundation for the intellect to build upon; they have no discriminating convictions, and no grasp of consequences. And therefore they talk at random, if they talk much, and cannot help being flippant, or what is emphatically called "*young.*" They are merely dazzled by phenomena, instead of perceiving things as they are.

It were well if none remained boys all their lives; but what is more common than the sight of grown men, talking on political or moral or religious subjects, in that offhand, idle way, which we signify by the word *unreal?* "That they simply do not know what they are talking about" is the spontaneous silent remark of any man of sense who hears them. Hence such persons have no difficulty in contradicting themselves in successive sentences, without being conscious of it. Hence others, whose defect in intellectual training is more latent, have their most unfortunate crotchets, as they are called, or hobbies, which deprive them of the influence which their estimable qualities would otherwise secure. Hence others can never look straight before them, never see the point, and have no difficulties in the most difficult subjects. Others are hopelessly obstinate and prejudiced, and, after they have been driven from their opinions, return to them the next moment without even an attempt to explain why. Others are so intemperate and intractable that there is no greater calamity for a good cause than that they should get hold of it. It is very plain from the very particulars I have mentioned that, in this delineation of intellectual infirmities, I am drawing, not from Catholics, but from the world at large; I am referring to an evil which is forced upon us in every railway carriage, in every coffee-room or *table-d'hôte,* in every mixed company, an evil, however, to which Catholics are not less exposed than the rest of mankind.

When the intellect has once been properly trained and formed to have a connected view or grasp of things, it will display its powers with more or less effect according to its particular quality and capacity in the individual. In the case of most men it makes itself felt in the good sense, sobriety of thought, reasonableness, candour, self-command, and steadiness of view, which characterize it. In some it will have developed habits of business, power of influencing others, and sagacity. In others it will elicit the talent of philosophical speculation, and lead the mind forward to eminence in this or that intellectual department. In all it will be a faculty of entering with comparative ease into any subject of thought, and of taking up with aptitude any science or profession. All this it will be and will do in a measure, even when the mental formation be made after a model but partially true; for, as far as effectiveness goes, even false views of things have more influence and inspire more respect than no views at all. Men who fancy they see what is not are more energetic, and make their way better, than those who see nothing; and so the undoubting infidel, the fanatic, the heresiarch, are able to do much, while the mere hereditary Christian, who has never realized the truths which he holds, is unable to do any thing. But, if consistency of view can add so much strength even to error, what may it not be expected to furnish to the dignity, the energy, and the influence of Truth!

Some one, however, will perhaps object that I am but advocating that spurious philosophism, which shows itself in what, for want of a word, I may call "viewiness," when I speak so much of the formation, and consequent grasp, of the intellect. It may be said that the theory of University Education, which I have been delineating, if acted upon, would teach youths nothing soundly or thoroughly, and would dismiss them with nothing better than brilliant general views about all things whatever.

This indeed, if well founded, would be a most serious objection to what I have advanced in this Volume, and would demand my immediate attention, had I any reason to think that I could not remove it at once, by a simple explanation of what I consider the true *mode* of educating, were this the place to do so. But these Discourses are directed simply to the consideration of the *aims* and *principles* of Education. Suffice it, then, to say here, that I hold very strongly that the first step in intellectual training is to impress upon a boy's mind the idea of science, method, order, principle, and system; of rule and exception, of richness and harmony. This is commonly and excellently done by making him begin with Grammar; nor can too great accuracy, or minuteness and subtlety of teaching be used towards him, as his faculties expand, with this simple purpose. Hence it is that critical scholarship is so important a discipline for him when he is leaving school for the University. A second science is the Mathematics: this should follow Grammar, still with the same object, viz., to give him a conception of development and arrangement from and around a common centre. Hence it is that Chronology and Geography are so necessary for him, when he reads History, which is otherwise little better than a storybook. Hence, too, Metrical Composition, when he reads Poetry; in order to stimulate his powers into action in every practicable way, and to prevent a merely passive reception of images and ideas which in that case are likely to pass out of the mind as soon as they have entered it. Let him once gain this habit of method, of starting from fixed points, of making his ground good as he goes, of distinguishing what he knows from what he does not know, and I conceive he will be gradually initiated into the largest and truest philosophical views, and will feel nothing but impatience and disgust at the random theories and imposing sophistries and dashing paradoxes, which carry away half-formed and superficial intellects.

Such parti-coloured ingenuities are indeed one of the chief evils of the day, and men of real talent are not slow to minister to them. An intellectual man, as the world now conceives of him, is one who is full of "views" on all subjects of philosophy, on all matters of the day. It is almost thought a disgrace not to have a view at a moment's notice on any question from the Personal Advent to the Cholera or Mesmerism. This is owing in great measure to the necessities of periodical literature, now so much in request. Every quarter of a year, every month, every day, there must be a supply, for the gratification of the public, of new and luminous theories on the subjects of religion, foreign politics, home politics, civil economy, finance, trade, agriculture, emigration, and the colonies. Slavery, the gold fields, German philosophy, the French Empire, Wellington, Peel, Ireland, must all be practised on, day after day, by what are called original thinkers. As the great man's guest must produce his good stories or songs at the evening banquet, as the platform orator exhibits his telling facts at mid-day, so the journalist lies under the stern obligation of extemporizing his lucid views, leading ideas, and nutshell truths for the breakfast table. The very nature of periodical literature, broken into small wholes, and demanded punctually to an hour, involves the habit of this extempore philosophy. "Almost all the Ramblers," says Boswell of Johnson, "were written just as they were wanted for the press; he sent a certain portion of the copy of an essay, and wrote the remainder while the former part of it was printing." Few men have the gifts of Johnson, who to great vigour and resource of intellect, when it was fairly roused, united a rare common-sense and a conscientious regard for veracity, which preserved him from flippancy or extravagance in writing. Few men are Johnsons; yet how many men at this day are assailed by incessant demands on their mental powers, which only a productiveness like his could suitably supply! There is a demand for a reckless originality of thought, and a sparkling plausibility of argument, which he would have despised, even if he could have displayed; a demand for crude theory and unsound philosophy, rather than none at all. It is a sort of repetition of the "Quid novi?" of the Areopagus, and it must have an answer. Men must be found who can treat, where it is necessary, like the Athenian sophist, *de omni scibili,*

"Grammaticus, Rhetor, Geometres, Pictor, Aliptes,
Augur, Schœnobates, Medicus, Magus, omnia novit."[5]

I am speaking of such writers with a feeling of real sympathy for men who are under the rod of a cruel slavery. I have never indeed been in such circumstances myself, nor in the temptations which they involve; but most men who have had to do with composition must know the distress which at times it occasions them to have to write – a distress sometimes so keen and so specific that it resembles nothing else than bodily pain. That pain is the token of the wear and tear of mind; and, if works done comparatively at leisure involve such mental fatigue and exhaustion, what must be the toil of those whose intellects are to be flaunted daily before the public in full dress, and that dress ever new and varied, and spun, like the silkworm's, out of themselves! Still, whatever true sympathy we may feel for the ministers of this dearly purchased luxury, and whatever sense we may have of the great intellectual power which the literature in question displays, we cannot honestly close our eyes to its direct evil.

One other remark suggests itself, which is the last I shall think it necessary to make. The authority, which in former times was lodged in Universities, now resides in very great measure in that literary world, as it is called, to which I have been referring. This is not satisfactory, if, as no one can deny, its teaching be so off-hand, so ambitious, so changeable. It increases the seriousness of the mischief, that so very large a portion of its writers are anonymous, for irresponsible power never can be any thing but a great evil; and, moreover, that, even when they are known, they can give no better guarantee for the philosophical truth of their principles than their popularity at the moment, and their happy conformity in ethical character to the age which admires them. Protestants, however, may do as they will: it is a matter for their own consideration; but at least it concerns us that our own literary tribunals and oracles of moral duty should bear a graver character. At least it is a matter of deep solicitude to Catholic Prelates that their people should be taught a wisdom, safe from the excesses and vagaries of individuals, embodied in institutions which have stood the trial and received the sanction of ages, and administered by men who have no need to be anonymous, as being supported by their consistency with their predecessors and with each other.

November 21, 1852.

I

University Teaching

CONSIDERED IN NINE

DISCOURSES.

DISCOURSE I.

INTRODUCTORY.

I.

In addressing myself, Gentlemen, to the consideration of a question which has excited so much interest, and elicited so much discussion at the present day, as that of University Education, I feel some explanation is due from me for supposing, after such high ability and wide experience have been brought to bear upon it, that any field remains for the additional labours either of a disputant or of an inquirer. If, nevertheless, I still venture to ask permission to continue the discussion, already so protracted, it is because the subject of Liberal Education, and of the principles on which it must be conducted, has ever had a hold upon my own mind; and because I have lived the greater part of my life in a place which has all that time been occupied in a series of controversies both domestic and with strangers, and of measures, experimental or definitive, bearing upon it. About fifty years since, the English University, of which I was so long a member, after a century of inactivity, at length was roused, at a time when (as I may say) it was giving no education at all to the youth committed to its keeping, to a sense of the responsibilities which its profession and its station involved, and it presents to us the singular example of an heterogeneous and an independent body of men, setting about a work of self-reformation, not from any pressure of public opinion, but because it was fitting and right to undertake it. Its initial efforts, begun and carried on amid many obstacles, were met from without, as often happens in such cases, by ungenerous and jealous criticisms, which, at the very moment that they were urged, were beginning to be unjust. Controversy did but bring out more clearly to its own apprehension the views on which its reformation was proceeding, and throw them into a philosophical form. The course of beneficial change made progress, and what was at first but the result of individual energy and an act of the academical corporation, gradually became popular, and was taken up and carried out by the separate collegiate bodies, of which the University is composed. This was the first stage of the controversy. Years passed away, and then political adversaries arose against it, and the system of education which it had established was a second time assailed; but still, since that contest was conducted for the most part through the medium, not of political acts, but of treatises and pamphlets, it happened as before that the threatened dangers, in the course of their repulse, did but afford fuller development and more exact delineation to the principles of which the University was the representative.

In the former of these two controversies the charge brought against its studies was their remoteness from the occupations and duties of life, to which they are the formal introduction, or, in other words, their *inutility;* in the latter, it was their connexion with a particular form of belief, or, in other words, their *religious exclusiveness.*

Living then so long as a witness, though hardly as an actor, in these scenes of intellectual conflict, I am able to bear witness to views of University Education, without authority indeed in themselves, but not without value to a Catholic, and less familiar to him, as I conceive, than they deserve to be. And, while an argument originating in the controversies to which I have referred, may be serviceable at this season to that great cause in which we are here so especially interested, to me personally it will afford satisfaction of a peculiar kind; for, though it has been my lot for many years to take a prominent, sometimes a presumptuous, part in theological discussions, yet the natural turn of my mind carries me off to trains of thought like those which I am now about to open, which, important though they be for Catholic objects, and admitting of a Catholic treatment, are sheltered from the extreme delicacy and peril which attach to disputations directly bearing on the subject-matter of Divine Revelation.

2.

There are several reasons why I should open the discussion with a reference to the lessons with which past years have supplied me. One reason is this: It would concern me, Gentlemen, were I supposed to have got up my opinions for the occasion. This, indeed, would have been no reflection on me personally, supposing I were persuaded of their truth, when at length addressing myself to the inquiry; but it would have destroyed, of course, the force of my testimony, and deprived such arguments, as I might adduce, of that moral persuasiveness which attends on tried and sustained conviction. It would have made me seem the advocate, rather than the cordial and deliberate maintainer and witness, of the doctrines which I was to support; and, though it might be said to evidence the faith I reposed in the practical judgment of the Church, and the intimate concurrence of my own reason with the course she had authoritatively sanctioned, and the devotion with which I could promptly put myself at her disposal, it would have cast suspicion on the validity of reasonings and conclusions which rested on no independent inquiry, and appealed to no past experience. In that case it might have been plausibly objected by opponents that I was the serviceable expedient of an emergency, and never, after all, could be more than ingenious and adroit in the management of an argument which was not my own, and which I was sure to forget again as readily as I had mastered it. But this is not so. The views to which I have referred have grown into my whole system of thought, and are, as it were, part of myself. Many changes has my mind gone through: here it has known no variation or vacillation of opinion, and though this by itself is no proof of the truth of my principles, it puts a seal upon conviction and is a justification of earnestness and zeal. Those principles, which I am now to set forth under the sanction of the Catholic Church, were my profession at that early period of my life, when religion was to me more a matter of feeling and experience than of faith. They did but take greater hold upon me, as I was introduced to the records of Christian Antiquity, and approached in sentiment and desire to Catholicism; and my sense of their correctness has been increased with the events of every year since I have been brought within its pale.

And here I am brought to a second and more important reason for referring, on this occasion, to the conclusions at which Protestants have arrived on the subject of Liberal Education; and it is as follows: Let it be observed, then, that the principles on which I would conduct the inquiry are attainable, as I have already implied, by the mere experience of life. They do not come simply of theology; they imply no supernatural discernment; they have no special connexion with Revelation; they almost arise out of the nature of the case; they are dictated even by human prudence and wisdom, though a divine illumination be absent, and they are recognized by common sense, even where self-interest is not present to quicken it; and, therefore, though true, and just, and good in themselves, they imply nothing whatever as to the religious profession of those who maintain them. They may be held by Protestants as well as by Catholics; nay, there is reason to anticipate that in certain times and places they will be more thoroughly investigated, and better understood, and held more firmly by Protestants than by ourselves.

It is natural to expect this from the very circumstance that the philosophy of Education is founded on truths in the natural order. Where the sun shines bright, in the warm climate of the south, the natives of the place know little of safeguards against cold and wet. They have, indeed, bleak and piercing blasts; they have chill and pouring rain, but only now and then, for a day or a week; they bear the inconvenience as they best may, but they have not made it an art to repel it; it is not worth their while; the science of calefaction and ventilation is reserved for the north. It is in this way that Catholics stand relatively to Protestants in the science of Education; Protestants depending on human means mainly, are led to make the most of them: their sole resource is to use what they have; "Knowledge is" their "power" and nothing else; they are the anxious cultivators of a rugged soil. It is otherwise with us; "*funes ceciderunt mihi in præclaris.*"[6] We have a goodly inheritance. This is apt to cause us – I do not mean to rely too much on prayer, and the Divine Blessing, for that is impossible, but we sometimes forget that we shall please Him best, and get most from Him, when, according to the Fable, we "put our shoulder to the wheel," when we use what we have by nature to the utmost, at the same time that we look out for what is beyond nature in the confidence of faith and hope. However, we are sometimes tempted to let things take their course, as if they would in one way or another turn up right at last for certain; and so we go on, living from hand to mouth, getting into difficulties and getting out of them, succeeding certainly on the whole, but with failure in detail which might be avoided, and with much of imperfection or inferiority in our appointments and plans, and much disappointment, discouragement, and collision of opinion in consequence. If this be in any measure the state of the case, there is certainly so far a reason for availing ourselves of the investigations and experience of those who are not Catholics, when we have to address ourselves to the subject of Liberal Education.

Nor is there surely any thing derogatory to the position of a Catholic in such a proceeding. The Church has ever appealed and deferred to witnesses and authorities external to herself, in those matters in which she thought they had means of forming a judgment: and that on the principle, *Cuique in arte sua credendum.*[7] She has even used unbelievers and pagans in evidence of her truth, as far as their testimony went. She avails herself of scholars, critics, and antiquarians, who are not of her communion. She has worded her theological teaching in the phraseology of Aristotle; Aquila, Symmachus, Theodotion, Origen, Eusebius, and Apollinaris, all more or less heterodox, have supplied materials for primitive exegetics. St. Cyprian called Tertullian his master; St. Augustin refers to Ticonius; Bossuet, in modern times, complimented the labours of the Anglican Bull; the Benedictine editors of the Fathers are familiar with the labours of Fell, Ussher, Pearson, and Beveridge. Pope Benedict XIV. cites according to the occasion the works of Protestants without reserve, and the late French collection of Christian Apologists contains the writings of Locke, Burnet, Tillotson, and Paley. If, then, I come forward in any degree as borrowing the views of certain Protestant schools on the point which is to be discussed, I do so,

Gentlemen, as believing, first, that the Catholic Church has ever, in the plenitude of her divine illumination, made use of whatever truth or wisdom she has found in their teaching or their measures; and next, that in particular places or times her children are likely to profit from external suggestions or lessons, which have not been provided for them by herself.

3.

And here I may mention a third reason for appealing at the outset to the proceedings of Protestant bodies in regard to Liberal Education. It will serve to intimate the mode in which I propose to handle my subject altogether. Observe then, Gentlemen, I have no intention, in any thing I shall say, of bringing into the argument the authority of the Church, or any authority at all; but I shall consider the question simply on the grounds of human reason and human wisdom. I am investigating in the abstract, and am determining what is in itself right and true. For the moment I know nothing, so to say, of history. I take things as I find them; I have no concern with the past; I find myself here; I set myself to the duties I find here; I set myself to further, by every means in my power, doctrines and views, true in themselves, recognized by Catholics as such, familiar to my own mind; and to do this quite apart from the consideration of questions which have been determined without me and before me. I am here the advocate and the minister of a certain great principle; yet not merely advocate and minister, else had I not been here at all. It has been my previous keen sense and hearty reception of that principle, that has been at once the reason, as I must suppose, of my being selected for this office, and is the cause of my accepting it. I am told on authority that a principle is expedient, which I have ever felt to be true. And I argue in its behalf on its own merits, the authority, which brings me here, being my opportunity for arguing, but not the ground of my argument itself.

And a fourth reason is here suggested for consulting the history of Protestant institutions, when I am going to speak of the object and nature of University Education. It will serve to remind you, Gentleman, that I am concerned with questions, not simply of immutable truth, but of practice and expedience. It would ill have become me to undertake a subject, on which points of dispute have arisen among persons so far above me in authority and name, in relation to a state of society, about which I have so much to learn, if it involved an appeal to sacred truths, or the determination of some imperative rule of conduct. It would have been presumptuous in me so to have acted, nor am I so acting. Even the question of the union of

Theology with the secular Sciences, which is its religious side, simple as it is of solution in the abstract, has, according to difference of circumstances, been at different times differently decided. Necessity has no law, and expedience is often one form of necessity. It is no principle with sensible men, of whatever cast of opinion, to do always what is abstractedly best. Where no direct duty forbids, we may be obliged to do, as being best under circumstances, what we murmur and rise against, while we do it. We see that to attempt more is to effect less; that we must accept so much, or gain nothing; and so perforce we reconcile ourselves to what we would have far otherwise, if we could. Thus a system of what is called secular Education, in which Theology and the Sciences are taught separately, may, in a particular place or time, be the least of evils; it may be of long standing; it may be dangerous to meddle with; it may be professedly a temporary arrangement; it may be under a process of improvement; its disadvantages may be neutralized by the persons by whom, or the provisions under which, it is administered.

Hence it was, that in the early ages the Church allowed her children to attend the heathen schools for the acquisition of secular accomplishments, where, as no one can doubt, evils existed, at least as great as can attend on Mixed Education now. The gravest Fathers recommended for Christian youth the use of Pagan masters; the most saintly Bishops and most authoritative Doctors had been sent in their adolescence by Christian parents to Pagan lecture halls.[8] And, not to take other instances, at this very time, and in this very country, as regards at least the poorer classes of the community, whose secular acquirements ever must be limited, it has seemed best to the Irish Bishops, under the circumstances, to suffer the introduction into the country of a system of Mixed Education in the schools called National. Such a state of things, however, is passing away; as regards University education at least, the highest authority has now decided that the plan, which is abstractedly best, is in this time and country also most expedient.

4.

And here I have an opportunity of recognizing once for all that higher view of approaching the subject of these Discourses, which, after this formal recognition, I mean to dispense with. Ecclesiastical authority, not argument, is the supreme rule and the appropriate guide for Catholics in matters of religion. It has always the right to interpose, and sometimes, in the conflict of parties and opinions, it is called on to exercise that right. It has lately exercised it in our own instance: it has interposed in favour of a pure

University system for Catholic youth, forbidding compromise or accommodation of any kind. Of course its decision must be heartily accepted and obeyed, and that the more, because the decision proceeds, not simply from the Bishops of Ireland, great as their authority is, but the highest authority on earth, from the Chair of St. Peter.

Moreover, such a decision not only demands our submission, but has a claim upon our trust. It not only acts as a prohibition of any measures, but as an *ipso facto* confutation of any reasonings, inconsistent with it. It carries with it an earnest and an augury of its own expediency. For instance, I can fancy, Gentlemen, there may be some, among those who hear me, disposed to say that they are ready to acquit the principles of Education, which I am to advocate, of all fault whatever, except that of being impracticable. I can fancy them granting to me, that those principles are most correct and most obvious, simply irresistible on paper, but maintaining, nevertheless, that after all, they are nothing more than the dreams of men who live out of the world, and who do not see the difficulty of keeping Catholicism anyhow afloat on the bosom of this wonderful nineteenth century. Proved, indeed, those principles are, to demonstration, but they will not work. Nay, it was my own admission just now, that, in a particular instance, it might easily happen, that what is only second best is best practically, because what is actually best is out of the question.

This, I hear you say to yourselves, is the state of things at present. You recount in detail the numberless impediments, great and small, formidable or only vexatious, which at every step embarrass the attempt to carry out ever so poorly a principle in itself so true and ecclesiastical. You appeal in your defence to wise and sagacious intellects, who are far from enemies to Catholicism, or to the Irish Hierarchy, and you have no hope, or rather you absolutely disbelieve, that Education can possibly be conducted, here and now, on a theological principle, or that youths of different religions can, under the circumstances of the country, be educated apart from each other. The more you think over the state of politics, the position of parties, the feelings of classes, and the experience of the past, the more chimerical does it seem to you to aim at a University, of which Catholicity is the fundamental principle. Nay, even if the attempt could accidentally succeed, would not the mischief exceed the benefit of it? How great the sacrifices, in how many ways, by which it would be preceded and followed! how many wounds, open and secret, would it inflict upon the body politic! And, if it fails, which is to be expected, then a double mischief will ensue from its recognition of evils which it has been unable to remedy. These are your deep misgivings; and, in proportion to the force with which they come to you, is the concern and anxiety which you feel, that there should be those whom you love, whom you revere, who from one cause or other refuse to enter into them.

5.

This, I repeat, is what some good Catholics will say to me, and more than this. They will express themselves better than I can speak for them in their behalf, – with more earnestness and point, with more force of argument and fulness of detail; and I will frankly and at once acknowledge, that I shall insist on the high theological view of a University without attempting to give a direct answer to their arguments against its present practicability. I do not say an answer cannot be given; on the contrary, I have a confident expectation that, in proportion as those objections are looked in the face, they will fade away. But, however this may be, it would not become me to argue the matter with those who understand the circumstances of the problem so much better than myself. What do I know of the state of things in Ireland, that I should presume to put ideas of mine, which could not be right except by accident, by the side of theirs, who speak in the country of their birth and their home? No, Gentlemen, you are natural judges of the difficulties which beset us, and they are doubtless greater than I can even fancy or forbode. Let me, for the sake of argument, admit all you say against our enterprise, and a great deal more. Your proof of its intrinsic impossibility shall be to me as cogent as my own of its theological advisableness. Why, then, should I be so rash and perverse as to involve myself in trouble not properly mine? Why go out of my own place? Why so headstrong and reckless as to lay up for myself miscarriage and disappointment, as though I were not sure to have enough of personal trial anyhow without going about to seek for it?

Reflections such as these would be decisive even with the boldest and most capable minds, but for one consideration. In the midst of our difficulties I have one ground of hope, just one stay, but, as I think, a sufficient one, which serves me in the stead of all other argument whatever, which hardens me against criticism, which supports me if I begin to despond, and to which I ever come round, when the question of the possible and the expedient is brought into discussion. It is the decision of the Holy See; St. Peter has spoken, it is he who has enjoined that which seems to us so unpromising. He has spoken, and has a claim on us to trust him. He is no recluse, no solitary student, no dreamer about the past, no doter upon the dead and gone, no projector of the visionary. He for eighteen hundred years has lived in the world; he has seen all fortunes, he has encountered all adversaries, he has shaped himself for all emergencies. If ever there was a power on earth who had an eye for the times, who has confined himself to the practicable, and has been happy in his anticipations, whose words have been facts, and whose commands prophecies, such is he in the history of ages, who sits from generation to generation in the Chair of the Apostles, as the Vicar of Christ, and the Doctor of His Church.

6.

These are not the words of rhetoric, Gentlemen, but of history. All who take part with the Apostle, are on the winning side. He has long since given warrants for the confidence which he claims. From the first he has looked through the wide world, of which he has the burden; and, according to the need of the day, and the inspirations of his Lord, he has set himself now to one thing, now to another; but to all in season, and to nothing in vain. He came first upon an age of refinement and luxury like our own, and, in spite of the persecutor, fertile in the resources of his cruelty, he soon gathered, out of all classes of society, the slave, the soldier, the high-born lady, and the sophist, materials enough to form a people to his Master's honour. The savage hordes come down in torrents from the north, and Peter went out to meet them, and by his very eye he sobered them, and backed them in their full career. They turned aside and flooded the whole earth, but only to be more surely civilized by him, and to be made ten times more his children even than the older populations which they had overwhelmed. Lawless kings arose, sagacious as the Roman, passionate as the Hun, yet in him they found their match, and were shattered, and he lived on. The gates of the earth were opened to the east and west, and men poured out to take possession; but he went with them by his missionaries, to China, to Mexico, carried along by zeal and charity, as far as those children of men were led by enterprise, covetousness, or ambition. Has he failed in his successes up to this hour? Did he, in our fathers' day, fail in his struggle with Joseph of Germany and his confederates, with Napoleon, a greater name, and his dependent kings, that, though in another kind of fight, he should fail in ours? What grey hairs are on the head of Judah, whose youth is renewed like the eagle's, whose feet are like the feet of harts, and underneath the Everlasting arms?

In the first centuries of the Church all this practical sagacity of Holy Church was mere matter of faith, but every age, as it has come, has confirmed faith by actual sight; and shame on us, if, with the accumulated testimony of eighteen centuries, our eyes are too gross to see those victories which the Saints have ever seen by anticipation. Least of all can we, the Catholics of islands which have in the cultivation and diffusion of Knowledge heretofore been so singularly united under the auspices of the Apostolic See, least of all can we be the men to distrust its wisdom and to predict its failure, when it sends us on a similar mission now. I cannot forget that, at a time when Celt and Saxon were alike savage, it was the See of Peter that gave both of them, first faith, then civilization; and then again bound them together in one by the seal of a joint commission to convert and illuminate in their turn the pagan continent. I cannot forget how it was from Rome that the glorious St. Patrick was sent to Ireland, and did a work so great that he could not have a successor in it, the sanctity and learning and zeal and charity which followed on his death being but the result of the one impulse which he gave. I cannot forget how, in no long time, under the fostering breath of the Vicar of Christ, a country of heathen superstitions became the very wonder and asylum of all people, – the wonder by reason of its knowledge, sacred and profane, and the asylum of religion, literature and science, when chased away from the continent by the barbarian invaders. I recollect its hospitality, freely accorded to the pilgrim; its volumes munificently presented to the foreign student; and the prayers, the blessings, the holy rites, the solemn chants, which sanctified the while both giver and receiver.

Nor can I forget either, how my own England had meanwhile become the solicitude of the same unwearied eye: how Augustine was sent to us by Gregory; how he fainted in the way at the tidings of our fierceness, and, but for the Pope, would have shrunk as from an impossible expedition; how he was forced on "in weakness and in fear and in much trembling," until he had achieved the conquest of the island to Christ. Nor, again, how it came to pass that, when Augustine died and his work slackened, another Pope, unwearied still, sent three saints from Rome, to ennoble and refine the people Augustine had converted. Three holy men set out for England together, of different nations: Theodore, an Asiatic Greek, from Tarsus; Adrian, an African; Bennett alone a Saxon, for Peter knows no distinction of races in his ecumenical work. They came with theology and science in their train; with relics, with pictures, with manuscripts of the Holy Fathers and the Greek classics; and Theodore and Adrian founded schools, secular and monastic, all over England, while Bennett brought to the north the large library he had collected in foreign parts, and, with plans and ornamental work from France, erected a church of stone, under the invocation of St. Peter, after the Roman fashion, "which," says the historian, "he most affected."[9] I call to mind how St. Wilfrid, St. John of Beverley, St. Bede, and other saintly men, carried on the good work in the following generations, and how from that time forth the two islands, England and Ireland, in a dark and dreary age, were the two lights of Christendom, and had no claims on each other, and no thought of self, save in the interchange of kind offices and the rivalry of love.

7.

O memorable time, when St. Aidan and the Irish monks went up to Lindisfarne and Melrose, and taught the Saxon youth, and when a St. Cuthbert and a St. Eata repaid their charitable toil! O blessed days of peace and confidence, when the Celtic Mailduf penetrated to Malmesbury in the south, which has inherited his name, and founded there the famous school which gave birth to the great St. Aldhelm! O precious seal and testimony of Gospel unity, when, as Aldhelm in turn tells us, the English went to Ireland "numerous as bees;" when the Saxon St. Egbert and St. Willibrod, preachers to the heathen Frisons, made the voyage to Ireland to prepare themselves for their work; and when from Ireland went forth to Germany the two noble Ewalds, Saxons also, to earn the crown of martyrdom! Such a period, indeed, so rich in grace, in peace, in love, and in good works, could only last for a season; but, even when the light was to pass away from them, the sister islands were destined, not to forfeit, but to transmit it together. The time came when the neighbouring continental country was in turn to hold the mission which they had exercised so long and well; and when to it they made over their honourable office, faithful to the alliance of two hundred years, they made it a joint act. Alcuin was the pupil both of the English and of the Irish schools; and when Charlemagne would revive science and letters in his own France, it was Alcuin, the representative both of the Saxon and the Celt, who was the chief of those who went forth to supply the need of the great Emperor. Such was the foundation of the School of Paris, from which, in the course of centuries, sprang the famous University, the glory of the middle ages.

The past never returns; the course of events, old in its texture, is ever new in its colouring and fashion. England and Ireland are not what they once were, but Rome is where it was, and St. Peter is the same: his zeal, his charity, his mission, his gifts are all the same. He of old made the two islands one by giving them joint work of teaching; and now surely he is giving us a like mission, and we shall become one again, while we zealously and lovingly fulfil it.

DISCOURSE II.

THEOLOGY A BRANCH OF KNOWLEDGE.

There were two questions, to which I drew your attention, Gentlemen, in the beginning of my first Discourse, as being of especial importance and interest at this time: first, whether it is consistent with the idea of University teaching to exclude Theology from a place among the sciences which it embraces; next, whether it is consistent with that idea to make the useful arts and sciences its direct and principal concern, to the neglect of those liberal studies and exercises of mind, in which it has heretofore been considered mainly to consist. These are the questions which will form the subject of what I have to lay before you, and I shall now enter upon the former of the two.

I.

It is the fashion just now, as you very well know, to erect so-called Universities, without making any provision in them at all for Theological chairs. Institutions of this kind exist both here and in England. Such a procedure, though defended by writers of the generation just passed with much plausible argument and not a little wit, seems to me an intellectual absurdity; and my reason for saying so runs, with whatever abruptness, into the form of a syllogism: – A University, I should lay down, by its very name professes to teach universal knowledge: Theology is surely a branch of knowledge: how then is it possible for it to profess all branches of knowledge, and yet to exclude from the subjects of its teaching one which, to say the least, is as important and as large as any of them? I do not see that either premiss of this argument is open to exception.

As to the range of University teaching, certainly the very name of University is inconsistent with restrictions of any kind. Whatever was the original reason of the adoption of that term, which is unknown,[10] I am only putting on it its popular, its recognized sense, when I say that a University should teach universal knowledge. That there is a real necessity for this universal teaching in the highest schools of intellect, I will show by-and-by; here it is sufficient to say that such universality is considered by writers on the subject to be the very characteristic of a University, as contrasted with other seats of learning. Thus Johnson, in his Dictionary, defines it to be "a school where all arts and faculties are taught;" and Mosheim, writing as an historian, says that, before the rise of the University of Paris, – for instance, at Padua, or Salamanca, or Cologne, – "the whole circle of sciences then known was not taught;" but that the school of Paris, "which exceeded all others in various respects, as well as in the number of teachers and students, was the first to embrace all the arts and sciences, and therefore first became a University."[11]

If, with other authors, we consider the word to be derived from the invitation which is held out by a University to students of every kind, the result is the same; for, if certain branches of knowledge were excluded, those students of course would be excluded also, who desired to pursue them.

Is it, then, logically consistent in a seat of learning to call itself a University, and to exclude Theology from the number of its studies? And again, is it wonderful that Catholics, even in the view of reason, putting aside faith or religious duty, should be dissatisfied with existing institutions, which profess to be Universities, and refuse to teach Theology; and that they should in consequence desire to possess seats of learning, which are, not only more Christian, but more philosophical in their construction, and larger and deeper in their provisions?

But this, of course, is to assume that Theology *is* a science, and an important one: so I will throw my argument into a more exact form. I say, then, that if a University be, from the nature of the case, a place of instruction, where universal knowledge is professed, and if in a certain University, so called, the subject of Religion is excluded, one of two conclusions is inevitable, – either, on the one hand, that the province of Religion is very barren of real knowledge, or, on the other hand, that in such University one special and important branch of knowledge is omitted. I say, the advocate of such an institution must say *this,* or he must say *that;* he must own, either that little or nothing is known about the Supreme Being, or that his seat of learning calls itself what it is not. This is the thesis which I lay down, and on which I shall insist as the subject of this Discourse. I repeat, such a compromise between religious parties, as is involved in the establishment of a University which makes no religious profession, implies that those parties severally consider, – not indeed that their own respective opinions are trifles in a moral and practical point of view – of course not; but certainly as much as this, that they are not knowledge. Did they in their hearts believe that their private views of religion, whatever they are, were absolutely and objectively true, it is inconceivable that they would so insult them as to consent to their omission in an Institution which is bound, from the nature of the case – from its very idea and its name – to make a profession of all sorts of knowledge whatever.

2.

I think this will be found to be no matter of words. I allow then fully, that, when men combine together for any common object, they are obliged, as a matter of course, in order to secure the advantages accruing from united action, to sacrifice many of their private opinions and wishes, and to drop the minor differences, as they are commonly called, which exist between man and man. No two persons perhaps are to be found, however intimate, however congenial in tastes and judgments, however eager to have one heart and one soul, but must deny themselves, for the sake of each other, much which they like or desire, if they are to live together happily. Compromise, in a large sense of the word, is the first principle of combination; and any one who insists on enjoying his rights to the full, and his opinions without toleration for his neighbour's, and his own way in all things, will soon have all things altogether to himself, and no one to share them with him. But most true as this confessedly is, still there is an obvious limit, on the other hand, to these compromises, however necessary they be; and this is found in the *proviso,* that the differences surrendered should be *but* "minor," or that there should be no sacrifice of the main object of the combination, in the concessions which are mutually made. Any sacrifice which compromises that object is destructive of the principle of the combination, and no one who would be consistent can be a party to it.

Thus, for instance, if men of various religious denominations join together for the dissemination of what are called "evangelical" tracts, it is under the belief, that, the object of their uniting, as recognized on all hands, being the spiritual benefit of their neighbours, no religious exhortations, whatever be their character, can essentially interfere with that benefit, which faithfully insist upon the Lutheran doctrine of Justification. If, again, they agree together in printing and circulating the Protestant Bible, it is because they, one and all, hold to the principle, that, however serious be their differences of religious sentiment, such differences fade away before the one great principle, which that circulation symbolizes – that the Bible, the whole Bible, and nothing but the Bible, is the religion of Protestants. On the contrary, if the committee of some such association inserted tracts into the copies of the said Bible which they sold, and tracts in recommendation

of the Athanasian Creed or the merit of good works, I conceive any sub-
scribing member would have a just right to complain of a proceeding,
which compromised the principle of Private Judgment as the one true interpreter of Scripture. These instances are sufficient to illustrate my general
position, that coalitions and comprehensions for an object, have their life in
the prosecution of that object, and cease to have any meaning as soon as that
object is compromised or disparaged.

When, then, a number of persons come forward, not as politicians, not as
diplomatists, lawyers, traders, or speculators, but with the one object of
advancing Universal Knowledge, much we may allow them to sacrifice. –
ambition, reputation, leisure, comfort, party-interests, gold; one thing they
may not sacrifice, – Knowledge itself. Knowledge being their object, they
need not of course insist on their own private views about ancient or modern history, or national prosperity, or the balance of power; they need not of
course shrink from the co-operation of those who hold the opposite views;
but stipulate they must that Knowledge itself is not compromised; – and as
to those views, of whatever kind, which they do allow to be dropped, it is
plain they consider such to be opinions, and nothing more, however dear,
however important to themselves personally; opinions ingenious, admirable, pleasurable, beneficial, expedient, but not worthy the name of Knowledge or Science. Thus no one would insist on the Malthusian teaching being
a *sine quâ non* in a seat of learning, who did not think it simply ignorance
not to be a Malthusian; and no one would consent to drop the Newtonian
theory, who thought it to have been proved true, in the same sense as the
existence of the sun and moon is true. If, then, in an Institution which
professes all knowledge, nothing is professed, nothing is taught about the
Supreme Being, it is fair to infer that every individual in the number of
those who advocate that Institution, supposing him consistent, distinctly
holds that nothing is known for certain about the Supreme Being; nothing
such, as to have any claim to be regarded as a material addition to the stock
of general knowledge existing in the world. If on the other hand it turns out
that something considerable *is* known about the Supreme Being, whether
from Reason or Revelation, then the Institution in question professes every
science, and yet leaves out the foremost of them. In a word, strong as may
appear the assertion, I do not see how I can avoid making it, and bear with
me, Gentlemen, while I do so, viz., such an Institution cannot be what it
professes, if there be a God. I do not wish to declaim; but, by the very force
of the terms, it is very plain, that a Divine Being and a University so
circumstanced cannot co-exist.

3.

Still, however, this may seem to many an abrupt conclusion, and will not be acquiesced in: what answer, Gentlemen, will be made to it? Perhaps this: – It will be said, that there are different kinds or spheres of Knowledge, human, divine, sensible, intellectual, and the like; and that a University certainly takes in all varieties of Knowledge in its own line, but still that it has a line of its own. It contemplates, it occupies a certain order, a certain platform, of Knowledge. I understand the remark; but I own to you, I do not understand how it can be made to apply to the matter in hand. I cannot so construct my definition of the subject-matter of University Knowledge, and so draw my boundary lines around it, as to include therein the other sciences commonly studied at Universities, and to exclude the science of Religion. For instance, are we to limit our idea of University Knowledge by the evidence of our senses? then we exclude ethics; by intuition? we exclude history; by testimony? we exclude metaphysics; by abstract reasoning? we exclude physics. Is not the being of a God reported to us by testimony, handed down by history, inferred by an inductive process, brought home to us by metaphysical necessity, urged on us by the suggestions of our conscience? It is a truth in the natural order, as well as in the supernatural. So much for its origin; and, when obtained, what is it worth? Is it a great truth or a small one? Is it a comprehensive truth? Say that no other religious idea whatever were given but it, and you have enough to fill the mind; you have at once a whole dogmatic system. The word "God" is a Theology in itself, indivisibly one, inexhaustibly various, from the vastness and the simplicity of its meaning. Admit a God, and you introduce among the subjects of your knowledge, a fact encompassing, closing in upon, absorbing, every other fact conceivable. How can we investigate any part of any order of Knowledge, and stop short of that which enters into every order? All true principles run over with it, all phenomena converge to it; it is truly the First and the Last. In word indeed, and in idea, it is easy enough to divide Knowledge into human and divine, secular and religious, and to lay down that we will address ourselves to the one without interfering with the other; but it is impossible in fact. Granting that divine truth differs in kind from human, so do human truths differ in kind one from another. If the knowledge of the Creator is in a different order from knowledge of the creature, so, in like manner, metaphysical science is in a different order from physical, physics from history, history from ethics. You will soon break up into fragments the whole circle of secular knowledge, if you begin the mutilation with divine.

I have been speaking simply of Natural Theology; my argument of course is stronger when I go on to Revelation. Let the doctrine of the Incarnation be true: is it not at once of the nature of an historical fact, and of a metaphysical? Let it be true that there are Angels: how is not this a point of knowledge in the same sense as the naturalist's asseveration, that myriads of living things might co-exist on the point of a needle? That the Earth is to be burned by fire, is, if true, as large a fact as that huge monsters once played amid its depths; that Antichrist is to come, is as categorical a heading to a chapter of history, as that Nero or Julian was Emperor of Rome; that a divine influence moves the will, is a subject of thought not more mysterious than the result of volition on our muscles, which we admit as a fact in metaphysics.

I do not see how it is possible for a philosophical mind, first, to believe these religious facts to be true; next, to consent to ignore them; and thirdly, in spite of this, to go on to profess to be teaching all the while *de omni scibili.* No; if a man thinks in his heart that these religious facts are short of truth, that they are not true in the sense in which the general fact and the law of the fall of a stone to the earth is true, I understand his excluding Religion from his University, though he professes other reasons for its exclusion. In that case the varieties of religious opinion under which he shelters his conduct, are not only his apology for publicly disowning Religion, but a cause of his privately disbelieving it. He does not think that any thing is known or can be known for certain, about the origin of the world or the end of man.

4.

This, I fear, is the conclusion to which intellects, clear, logical, and consistent, have come, or are coming, from the nature of the case; and, alas! in addition to this *primâ-facie* suspicion, there are actual tendencies in the same direction in Protestantism, viewed whether in its original idea, or again in the so-called Evangelical movement in these islands during the last century. The religious world, as it is styled, holds, generally speaking, that Religion consists, not in knowledge, but in feeling or sentiment. The old Catholic notion, which still lingers in the Established Church, was, that Faith was an intellectual act, its object truth, and its result knowledge. Thus if you look into the Anglican Prayer Book, you will find definite *credenda,* as well as definite *agenda;* but in proportion as the Lutheran leaven spread, it became fashionable to say that Faith was, not an acceptance of revealed doctrine, not an act of the intellect, but a feeling, an emotion, an affection, an appetency; and, as this view of Faith obtained, so was the connexion of Faith with Truth and Knowledge more and more either forgotten or denied. At length the identity of this (so-called) spirituality of heart and the virtue of Faith was acknowledged on all hands. Some men indeed disapproved the pietism in question, others admired it; but whether they admired or disapproved, both the one party and the other found themselves in agreement on the main point, viz. – in considering that this really was in substance Religion, and nothing else; that Religion was based, not on argument, but on taste and sentiment, that nothing was objective, every thing subjective, in doctrine. I say, even those who saw through the affectation in which the religious school of which I am speaking clad itself, still came to think that Religion, as such, consisted in something short of intellectual exercises, viz., in the affections, in the imagination, in inward persuasions and consolations, in pleasurable sensations, sudden changes, and sublime fancies. They learned to believe and to take it for granted, that Religion was nothing beyond a *supply* of the wants of human nature, not an external fact and a work of God. There was, it appeared, a demand for Religion, and therefore there was a supply; human nature could not do without Religion, any more than it could do without bread; a supply was absolutely necessary, good or bad, and, as in the case of the articles of daily sustenance, an article which was really inferior was better than none at all. Thus Religion was useful, venerable, beautiful, the sanction of order, the stay of government, the curb of self-will and self-indulgence, which the laws cannot reach: but, after all, on what was it based? Why, that was a question delicate to ask, and imprudent to answer; but, if the truth must be spoken, however reluctantly, the long and the short of the matter was this, that Religion was based on custom, on prejudice, on law, on education, on habit, on loyalty, on feudalism, on enlightened expedience, on many, many things, but not at all on reason; reason was neither its warrant, nor its instrument, and science had as little connexion with it as with the fashions of the season, or the state of the weather.

You see, Gentlemen, how a theory or philosophy, which began with the religious changes of the sixteenth century, has led to conclusions, which the authors of those changes would be the first to denounce, and has been taken up by that large and influential body which goes by the name of Liberal or Latitudinarian; and how, where it prevails, it is as unreasonable of course to demand for Religion a chair in a University, as to demand one for fine feeling, sense of honour, patriotism, gratitude, maternal affection, or good companionship, proposals which would be simply unmeaning.

5.

Now, in illustration of what I have been saying, I will appeal, in the first place, to a statesman, but not merely so, to no mere politician, no trader in places, or in votes, or in the stock market, but to a philosopher, to an orator, to one whose profession, whose aim, has ever been to cultivate the fair, the noble, and the generous. I cannot forget the celebrated discourse of the celebrated man to whom I am referring; a man who is first in his peculiar walk; and who, moreover (which is much to my purpose), has had a share, as much as any one alive, in effecting the public recognition in these Islands of the principle of separating secular and religious knowledge. This brilliant thinker, during the years in which he was exerting himself in behalf of this principle, made a speech or discourse, on occasion of a public solemnity; and in reference to the bearing of general knowledge upon religious belief, he spoke as follows:

"As men," he said, "will no longer suffer themselves to be led blindfold in ignorance, so will they no more yield to the vile principle of judging and treating their fellow-creatures, not according to the intrinsic merit of their actions, but according to the accidental and involuntary coincidence of their opinions. The great truth has finally gone forth to all the ends of the earth," and he prints it in capital letters, "that man shall no more render account to man for his belief, over which he has himself no control. Henceforward, nothing shall prevail upon us to praise or to blame any one for that which he can no more change, than he can the hue of his skin or the height of his stature."[12] You see, Gentlemen, if this philosopher is to decide the matter, religious ideas are just as far from being real, or representing anything beyond themselves, are as truly peculiarities, idiosyncracies, accidents of the individual, as his having the stature of a Patagonian, or the features of a Negro.

But perhaps this was the rhetoric of an excited moment. Far from it, Gentlemen, or I should not have fastened on the words of a fertile mind, uttered so long ago. What Mr. Brougham laid down as a principle in 1825, resounds on all sides of us, with ever-growing confidence and success, in 1852. I open the Minutes of the Committee of Council on Education for the years 1848-50, presented to both Houses of Parliament by command of Her Majesty, and I find one of Her Majesty's Inspectors of Schools, at p. 467 of the second volume, dividing "the topics usually embraced in the better class of primary schools" into four: – the knowledge of *signs,* as reading and writing; of *facts,* as geography and astronomy; of *relations and laws,* as mathematics; and lastly *sentiment,* such as poetry and music. Now, on first catching sight of this division, it occurred to me to ask myself, before ascertaining the writer's own resolution of the matter, under which of these four heads would fall Religion, or whether it fell under any of them. Did he put it aside as a thing too delicate and sacred to be enumerated with earthly studies? or did he distinctly contemplate it when he made his division? Anyhow, I could really find a place for it under the first head, or the second, or the third; – for it has to do with facts, since it tells of the Self-subsisting; it has to do with relations, for it tells of the Creator; it has to do with signs, for it tells of the due manner of speaking of Him. There was just one head of the division to which I could not refer it, viz., to *sentiment;* for, I suppose, music and poetry, which are the writer's own examples of sentiment, have not much to do with Truth, which is the main object of Religion. Judge then my surprise, Gentlemen, when I found the fourth was the very head selected by the writer of the Report in question, as the special receptacle of religious topics. "The inculcation of *sentiment,*" he says, "embraces reading in its higher sense, poetry, music, together with moral and religious Education." I am far from introducing this writer for his own sake, because I have no wish to hurt the feelings of a gentleman, who is but exerting himself zealously in the discharge of anxious duties; but, taking him as an illustration of the widespreading school of thought to which he belongs, I ask what can more clearly prove than a candid avowal like this, that, in the view of his school, Religion is not knowledge, has nothing whatever to do with knowledge, and is excluded from a University course of instruction, not simply because the exclusion cannot be helped, from political or social obstacles, but because it has no business there at all, because it is to be considered a taste, sentiment, opinion, and nothing more?

The writer avows this conclusion himself, in the explanation into which he presently enters, in which he says: "According to the classification proposed, the *essential idea* of all religious Education will consist in the direct cultivation of the *feelings.*" What we contemplate, then, what we aim at, when we give a religious Education, is, it seems, not to impart any knowledge whatever, but to satisfy anyhow desires after the Unseen which will arise in our minds in spite of ourselves, to provide the mind with a means of self-command, to impress on it the beautiful ideas which saints and sages have struck out, to embellish it with the bright hues of a celestial piety, to teach it the poetry of devotion, the music of well-ordered affections, and the luxury of doing good. As for the intellect, its exercise happens to be unavoidable, whenever moral impressions are made, from the constitution of the human mind, but it varies in the results of that exercise, in the conclusions which it draws from our impressions, according to the peculiarities of the individual.

Something like this seems to be the writer's meaning, but we need not pry into its finer issues in order to gain a distinct view of its general bearing; and taking it, as I think we fairly may take it, as a specimen of the philosophy of the day, as adopted by those who are not conscious unbelievers, or open scoffers, I consider it amply explains how it comes to pass that this day's philosophy sets up a system of universal knowledge, and teaches of plants, and earths, and creeping things, and beasts, and gases, about the crust of the earth and the changes of the atmosphere, about sun, moon, and stars, about man and his doings, about the history of the world, about sensation, memory, and the passions, about duty, about cause and effect, about all things imaginable, except one – and that is, about Him that made all these things, about God. I say the reason is plain because they consider knowledge, as regards the creature, is illimitable, but impossible or hopeless as regards the being and attributes and works of the Creator.

6.

Here, however, it may be objected to me that this representation is certainly extreme, for the school in question does, in fact, lay great stress on the evidence afforded by the creation, to the Being and Attributes of the Creator. I may be referred, for instance, to the words of one of the speakers on a memorable occasion. At the very time of laying the first stone of the University of London, I confess it, a learned person, since elevated to the Protestant See of Durham, which he still fills, opened the proceedings with prayer. He addressed the Deity, as the authoritative Report informs us, "the whole surrounding assembly standing uncovered in solemn silence." "Thou," he said, in the name of all present, "thou hast constructed the vast fabric of the universe in so wonderful a manner, so arranged its motions, and so formed its productions, that the contemplation and study of thy works exercise at once the mind in the pursuit of human science, and lead it onwards to *Divine Truth.*" Here is apparently a distinct recognition that there is such a thing as Truth in the province of Religion; and, did the passage stand by itself, and were it the only means we possessed of ascertaining the sentiments of the powerful body whom this distinguished person there represented, it would, as far as it goes, be satisfactory. I admit it; and I admit also the recognition of the Being and certain Attributes of the Deity, contained in the writings of the gifted person whom I have already quoted, whose genius, versatile and multiform as it is, in nothing has been so constant, as in its devotion to the advancement of knowledge, scientific and literary. He then certainly, in his "Discourse of the objects, advantages, and

pleasures of science," after variously illustrating what he terms its "gratifying treats," crowns the catalogue with mention of "the *highest* of *all* our
gratifications in the contemplation of science," which he proceeds to explain thus:

"We are raised by them," says he, "to an understanding of the infinite
wisdom and goodness which the Creator has displayed in all His works. Not
a step can be taken in any direction," he continues, "without perceiving the
most extraordinary traces of design; and the skill, every where conspicuous,
is calculated in so vast a proportion of instances to promote the happiness of
living creatures, and especially of ourselves, that we can feel no hesitation
in concluding, that, if we knew the whole scheme of Providence, every part
would be in harmony with a plan of absolute benevolence. Independent,
however, of this most consoling inference, the delight is inexpressible, of
being able to follow, as it were, with our eyes, the marvellous works of the
Great Architect of Nature, to trace the unbounded power and exquisite skill
which are exhibited in the most minute, as well as the mightiest parts of His
system. The pleasure derived from this study is unceasing, and so various,
that it never tires the appetite. But it is unlike the low gratifications of sense
in another respect: it elevates and refines our nature, while those hurt the
health, debase the understanding, and corrupt the feelings; it teaches us to
look upon all earthly objects as insignificant and below our notice, except
the pursuit of knowledge and the cultivation of virtue, that is to say, the
strict performance of our duty in every relation of society; and it gives a
dignity and importance to the enjoyment of life, which the frivolous and the
grovelling cannot even comprehend."

Such are the words of this prominent champion of Mixed Education.[13] If
logical inference be, as it undoubtedly is, an instrument of truth, surely, it
may be answered to me, in admitting the possibility of inferring the Divine
Being and Attributes *from* the phenomena of nature, he distinctly admits a
basis of truth for the doctrines of Religion.

7.

I wish, Gentlemen, to give these representations their full weight, both from
the gravity of the question, and the consideration due to the persons whom I
am arraigning; but, before I can feel sure I understand them, I must ask an
abrupt question. When I am told, then, by the partisans of Universities
without Theological teaching, that human science leads to belief in a Supreme Being, without denying the fact, nay, as a Catholic, with full conviction of it, nevertheless I am obliged to ask what the statement means in *their*

mouths, what they, the speakers, understand by the word "God." Let me not be thought offensive, if I question, whether it means the same thing on the two sides of the controversy. With us Catholics, as with the first race of Protestants, as with Mahometans, and all Theists, the word contains, as I have already said, a theology in itself. At the risk of anticipating what I shall have occasion to insist upon in my next Discourse, let me say that, according to the teaching of Monotheism, God is an Individual, Self-dependent, All-perfect, Unchangeable Being; intelligent, living, personal, and present; almighty, all-seeing, all-remembering; between whom and His creatures there is an infinite gulf; who has no origin, who is all-sufficient for Himself; who created and upholds the universe; who will judge every one of us, sooner or later, according to that Law of right and wrong which He has written on our hearts. He is One who is sovereign over, operative amidst, independent of, the appointments which He has made; One in whose hands are all things, who has a purpose in every event, and a standard for every deed, and thus has relations of His own towards the subject-matter of each particular science which the book of knowledge unfolds; who has with an adorable, never-ceasing energy implicated Himself in all the history of creation, the constitution of nature, the course of the world, the origin of society, the fortunes of nations, the action of the human mind; and who thereby necessarily becomes the subject-matter of a science, far wider and more noble than any of those which are included in the circle of secular Education.

This is the doctrine which belief in a God implies in the mind of a Catholic: if it means any thing, it means all this, and cannot keep from meaning all this, and a great deal more; and, even though there were nothing in the religious tenets of the last three centuries to disparage dogmatic truth, still, even then, I should have difficulty in believing that a doctrine so mysterious, so peremptory, approved itself as a matter of course to educated men of this day, who gave their minds attentively to consider it. Rather, in a state of society such as ours, in which authority, prescription, tradition, habit, moral instinct, and the divine influences go for nothing, in which patience of thought, and depth and consistency of view, are scorned as subtle and scholastic, in which free discussion and fallible judgment are prized as the birthright of each individual, I must be excused if I exercise towards this age, as regards its belief in this doctrine, some portion of that scepticism which it exercises itself towards every received but unscrutinized assertion whatever. I cannot take it for granted, I must have it brought home to me by tangible evidence, that the spirit of the age means by the Supreme Being what Catholics mean. Nay, it would be a relief to my mind to gain some ground of assurance, that the parties influenced by that spirit had, I will not say, a true apprehension of God, but even so much as the idea of what a true apprehension is.

Nothing is easier than to use the word, and mean nothing by it. The heathens used to say, "God wills," when they meant "Fate;" "God provides," when they meant "Chance;" "God acts," when they meant "Instinct" or "Sense;" and "God is every where," when they meant "the Soul of Nature." The Almighty is something infinitely different from a principle, or a centre of action, or a quality, or a generalization of phenomena. If, then, by the word, you do but mean a Being who keeps the world in order, who acts in it, but only in the way of general Providence, who acts towards us but only through what are called laws of Nature, who is more certain not to act at all than to act independent of those laws, who is known and approached indeed, but only through the medium of those laws; such a God it is not difficult for any one to conceive, not difficult for any one to endure. If, I say, as you would revolutionize society, so you would revolutionize heaven, if you have changed the divine sovereignty into a sort of constitutional monarchy, in which the Throne has honour and ceremonial enough, but cannot issue the most ordinary command except through legal forms and precedents, and with the counter-signature of a minister, then belief in a God is no more than an acknowledgment of existing, sensible powers and phenomena, which none but an idiot can deny. If the Supreme Being is powerful or skilful, just so far forth as the telescope shows power, and the microscope shows skill, if His moral law is to be ascertained simply by the physical processes of the animal frame, or His will gathered from the immediate issues of human affairs, if His Essence is just as high and deep and broad and long as the universe, and no more; if this be the fact, then will I confess that there is no specific science about God, that theology is but a name, and a protest in its behalf an hypocrisy. Then is He but coincident with the laws of the universe; then is He but a function, or correlative, or subjective reflection and mental impression, of each phenomenon of the material or moral world, as it flits before us. Then, pious as it is to think of Him, while the pageant of experiment or abstract reasoning passes by, still, such piety is nothing more than a poetry of thought or an ornament of language, and has not even an infinitesimal influence upon philosophy or science, of which it is rather the parasitical production.

I understand, in that case, why Theology should require no specific teaching, for there is nothing to mistake about; why it is powerless against scientific anticipations, for it merely is one of them; why it is simply absurd in its denunciations of heresy, for heresy does not lie in the region of fact and experiment. I understand, in that case, how it is that the religious sense is but a "sentiment," and its exercise a "gratifying treat," for it is like the sense of the beautiful or the sublime. I understand how the contemplation of the universe "leads onwards to *divine* truth," for divine truth is not something separate from Nature, but it is Nature with a divine glow upon it. I understand the zeal expressed for Physical Theology, for this study is but a mode of looking at Physical Nature, a certain view taken of Nature, private and personal, which one man has, and another has not, which gifted minds strike out, which others see to be admirable and ingenious, and which all would be the better for adopting. It is but the theology of Nature, just as we talk of the *philosophy* or the *romance* of history, or the *poetry* of childhood, or the picturesque, or the sentimental, or the humorous, or any other abstract quality, which the genius or the caprice of the individual, or the fashion of the day, or the consent of the world, recognizes in any set of objects which are subjected to its contemplation.

8.

Such ideas of religion seem to me short of Monotheism; I do not impute them to this or that individual who belongs to the school which gives them currency; but what I read about the "gratification" of keeping pace in our scientific researches with "the Architect of Nature;" about the said gratification "giving a dignity and importance to the enjoyment of life," and teaching us that knowledge and our duties to society are the only earthly objects worth our notice, all this, I own it, Gentlemen, frightens me; nor is Dr. Maltby's address to the Deity sufficient to reassure me. I do not see much difference between avowing that there is no God, and implying that nothing definite can for certain be known about Him; and when I find Religious Education treated as the cultivation of sentiment, and Religious Belief as the accidental hue or posture of the mind, I am reluctantly but forcibly reminded of a very unpleasant page of Metaphysics, viz., of the relations between God and Nature insinuated by such philosophers as Hume. This acute, though most low-minded of speculators, in his inquiry concerning the Human Understanding, introduces, as is well known, Epicurus, that is, a teacher of atheism, delivering an harangue to the Athenian people, not indeed in defence, but in extenuation of that opinion. His object is to show that, whereas the atheistic view is nothing else than the repudiation of theory, and an accurate representation of phenomenon and fact, it cannot be dangerous, unless phenomenon and fact be dangerous. Epicurus is made to say, that the paralogism of philosophy has ever been that of arguing from Nature in behalf of something beyond Nature, greater than Nature; whereas, God, as he maintains, being known only through the visible world, our knowledge of Him is absolutely commensurate with our knowledge of it, – is nothing distinct from it, – is but a mode of viewing it. Hence it follows that, provided we admit, as we cannot help admitting, the phenomena of Nature and the world, it is only a question of words whether or not we go on to the hypothesis of a second Being, not visible but immaterial, parallel and coincident with Nature, to whom we give the name of God. "Allowing," he says, "the gods to be the authors of the existence or order of the universe, it follows that they possess that precise degree of power, intelligence, and benevolence, which appears in their workmanship; but nothing farther can be proved, except we call in the assistance of exaggeration and flattery to supply the defects of argument and reasoning. So far as the traces of any attributes, at present, appear, so far may we conclude these attributes to exist. The supposition of farther attributes is mere hypothesis; much more the supposition that, in distant periods of place and time, there has been, or will be, a more magnificent display of these attributes, and a scheme of administration more suitable to such imaginary virtues." [14]

Here is a reasoner, who would not hesitate to deny that there is any distinct science or philosophy possible concerning the Supreme Being; since every single thing we know of Him is this or that or the other phenomenon, material or moral, which already falls under this or that natural science. In him then it would be only consistent to drop Theology in a course of University Education: but how is it consistent in any one who shrinks from his companionship? I am glad to see that the author, several times mentioned, is in opposition to Hume, in one sentence of the quotation I have made from his Discourse upon Science, deciding, as he does, that the phenomena of the material world are insufficient for the full exhibition of the Divine Attributes, and implying that they require a supplemental process to complete and harmonize their evidence. But is not this supplemental process a science? and if so, why not acknowledge its existence? If God is more than Nature, Theology claims a place among the sciences: but, on the other hand, if you are not sure of as much as this, how do you differ from Hume or Epicurus?

9.

I end then as I began: religious doctrine is knowledge. This is the important truth, little entered into at this day, which I wish that all who have honoured me with their presence here would allow me to beg them to take away with them. I am not catching at sharp arguments, but laying down grave principles. Religious doctrine is knowledge, in as full a sense as Newton's doctrine is knowledge. University Teaching without Theology is simply unphilosophical. Theology has at least as good a right to claim a place there as Astronomy.

In my next Discourse it will be my object to show that its omission from the list of recognised sciences is not only indefensible in itself, but prejudicial to all the rest.

DISCOURSE III.

BEARING OF THEOLOGY ON OTHER BRANCHES OF KNOWLEDGE.

I.

When men of great intellect, who have long and intently and exclusively given themselves to the study or investigation of some one particular branch of secular knowledge, whose mental life is concentrated and hidden in their chosen pursuit, and who have neither eyes nor ears for any thing which does not immediately bear upon it, when such men are at length made to realize that there is a clamour all around them, which must be heard, for what they have been so little accustomed to place in the category of knowledge as Religion, and that they themselves are accused of disaffection to it, they are impatient at the interruption; they call the demand tyrannical, and the requisitionists bigots or fanatics. They are tempted to say, that their only wish is to be let alone; for themselves, they are not dreaming of offending any one, or interfering with any one; they are pursuing their own particular line, they have never spoken a word against any one's religion, whoever he may be, and never mean to do so. It does not follow that they deny the existence of a God, because they are not found talking of it, when the topic would be utterly irrelevant. All they say is, that there are other beings in the world besides the Supreme Being; their business is with them. After all, the creation is not the Creator, nor things secular religious. Theology and human science are two things, not one, and have their respective provinces, contiguous it may be and cognate to each other, but not identical.

When we are contemplating earth, we are not contemplating heaven; and when we are contemplating heaven, we are not contemplating earth. Separate subjects should be treated separately. As division of labour, so division of thought is the only means of successful application. "Let us go our own way," they say, "and you go yours. We do not pretend to lecture on Theology, and you have no claim to pronounce upon Science."

With this feeling they attempt a sort of compromise, between their opponents who claim for Theology a free introduction into the Schools of Science, and themselves who would exclude it altogether, and it is this: viz., that it should remain indeed excluded from the public schools, but that it should be permitted in private, wherever a sufficient number of persons is found to desire it. Such persons, they seem to say, may have it all their own way, when they are by themselves, so that they do not attempt to disturb a comprehensive system of instruction, acceptable and useful to all, by the intrusion of opinions peculiar to their own minds.

I am now going to attempt a philosophical answer to this representation, that is, to the project of teaching secular knowledge in the University Lecture Room, and remanding religious knowledge to the parish priest, the catechism, and the parlour; and in doing so, you must pardon me, Gentlemen, if my subject should oblige me to pursue a lengthy and careful course of thought, which may be wearisome to the hearer: – I begin then thus: –

2.

Truth is the object of Knowledge of whatever kind; and when we inquire what is meant by Truth, I suppose it is right to answer that Truth means facts and their relations, which stand towards each other pretty much as subjects and predicates in logic. All that exists, as contemplated by the human mind, forms one large system or complex fact, and this of course resolves itself into an indefinite number of particular facts, which, as being portions of a whole, have countless relations of every kind, one towards another. Knowledge is the apprehension of these facts, whether in themselves, or in their mutual positions and bearings. And, as all taken together form one integral subject for contemplation, so there are no natural or real limits between part and part; one is ever running into another; all, as viewed by the mind, are combined together, and possess a correlative character one with another, from the internal mysteries of the Divine Essence down to our own sensations and consciousness, from the most solemn appointments of the Lord of all down to what may be called the accident of the hour, from the most glorious seraph down to the vilest and most noxious of reptiles.

Now, it is not wonderful that, with all its capabilities, the human mind cannot take in this whole vast fact at a single glance, or gain possession of it at once. Like a short-sighted reader, its eye pores closely, and travels slowly, over the awful volume which lies open for its inspection. Or again, as we deal with some huge structure of many parts and sides, the mind goes round about it, noting down, first one thing, then another, as it best may, and viewing it under different aspects, by way of making progress towards mastering the whole. So by degrees and by circuitous advances does it rise aloft and subject to itself a knowledge of that universe into which it has been born.

These various partial views or abstractions, by means of which the mind looks out upon its object, are called sciences, and embrace respectively larger or smaller portions of the field of knowledge; sometimes extending far and wide, but superficially, sometimes with exactness over particular departments, sometimes occupied together on one and the same portion, sometimes holding one part in common, and then ranging on this side or that in absolute divergence one from the other. Thus Optics has for its subject the whole visible creation, so far forth as it is simply visible; Mental Philosophy has a narrower province, but a richer one. Astronomy, plane and physical, each has the same subject-matter, but views it or treats it differently; lastly, Geology and Comparative Anatomy have subject-matters partly the same, partly distinct. Now these views or sciences, as being abstractions, have far more to do with the relations of things than with things themselves. They tell us what things are, only or principally by telling us their relations, or assigning predicates to subjects; and therefore they never tell us all that can be said about a thing, even when they tell something, nor do they bring it before us, as the senses do. They arrange and classify facts; they reduce separate phenomena under a common law; they trace effects to a cause. Thus they serve to transfer our knowledge from the custody of memory to the surer and more abiding protection of philosophy, thereby providing both for its spread and its advance: – for, inasmuch as sciences are forms of knowledge, they enable the intellect to master and increase it; and, inasmuch as they are instruments, to communicate it readily to others. Still after all, they proceed on the principle of a division of labour, even though that division is an abstraction, not a literal separation into parts; and, as the maker of a bridle or an epaulet has not, on that account, any idea of the science of tactics or strategy, so in a parallel way, it is not every science which equally, nor any one which fully, enlightens the mind in the knowledge of things, as they are, or brings home to it the external object on which it wishes to gaze. Thus they differ in importance; and according to their importance will be their influence, not only on the mass of knowledge to which they all converge and contribute, but on each other.

Since then sciences are the results of mental processes about one and the same subject-matter, viewed under its various aspects, and are true results, as far as they go, yet at the same time separate and partial, it follows that on the one hand they need external assistance, one by one, by reason of their incompleteness, and on the other that they are able to afford it to each other, by reason, first, of their independence in themselves, and then of their connexion in their subject-matter. Viewed altogether, they approximate to a representation or subjective reflection of the objective truth, as nearly as is possible to the human mind, which advances towards the accurate apprehension of that object, in proportion to the number of sciences which it has mastered; and which, when certain sciences are away, in such a case has but a defective apprehension, in proportion to the value of the sciences which are thus wanting, and the importance of the field on which they are employed.

3.

Let us take, for instance, man himself as our object of contemplation; then at once we shall find we can view him in a variety of relations; and according to those relations are the sciences of which he is the subject-matter, and according to our acquaintance with them is our possession of a true knowledge of him. We may view him in relation to the material elements of his body, or to his mental constitution, or to his household and family, or to the community in which he lives, or to the Being who made him; and in consequence we treat of him respectively as physiologists, or as moral philosophers, or as writers of economics, or of politics, or as theologians. When we think of him in all these relations together, or as the subject at once of all the sciences I have named, then we may be said to reach unto and rest in the idea of man as an object or external fact, similar to that which the eye takes of his outward form. On the other hand, according as we are only physiologists, or only politicians, or only moralists, so is our idea of man more or less unreal; we do not take in the whole of him, and the defect is greater or less, in proportion as the relation is, or is not, important, which is omitted, whether his relation to God, or to his king, or to his children, or to his own component parts. And if there be one relation, about which we know nothing at all except that it exists, then is our knowledge of him, confessedly and to our own consciousness, deficient and partial, and that, I repeat, in proportion to the importance of the relation.

That therefore is true of sciences in general which we are apt to think applies only to pure mathematics, though to pure mathematics it applies especially, viz., that they cannot be considered as simple representations or informants of things as they are. We are accustomed to say, and say truly, that the conclusions of pure mathematics are applied, corrected, and adapted, by mixed; but so too the conclusions of Anatomy, Chemistry, Dynamics, and other sciences, are revised and completed by each other. Those several conclusions do not represent whole and substantive things, but views, true, so far as they go; and in order to ascertain how far they do go, that is, how far they correspond to the object to which they belong, we must compare them with the views taken out of that object by other sciences. Did we proceed upon the abstract theory of forces, we should assign a much more ample range to a projectile than in fact the resistance of the air allows it to accomplish. Let, however, that resistance be made the subject of scientific analysis, and then we shall have a new science, assisting, and to a certain point completing, for the benefit of questions of fact, the science of projection. On the other hand, the science of projection itself, considered as belonging to the forces it contemplates, is not more perfect, as such, by this supplementary investigation. And in like manner, as regards the whole circle of sciences, one corrects another for purposes of fact, and one without the other cannot dogmatize, except hypothetically and upon its own abstract principles. For instance, the Newtonian philosophy requires the admission of certain metaphysical postulates, if it is to be more than a theory or an hypothesis; as, for instance, that what happened yesterday will happen to-morrow; that there is such a thing as matter, that our senses are trustworthy, that there is a logic of induction, and so on. Now to Newton metaphysicians grant all that he asks; but, if so be, they may not prove equally accommodating to another who asks something else, and then all his most logical conclusions in the science of physics would remain hopelessly on the stocks, though finished, and never could be launched into the sphere of fact.

Again, did I know nothing about the movement of bodies, except what the theory of gravitation supplies, were I simply absorbed in that theory so as to make it measure all motion on earth and in the sky, I should indeed come to many right conclusions, I should hit off many important facts, ascertain many existing relations, and correct many popular errors: I should scout and ridicule with great success the old notion, that light bodies flew up and heavy bodies fell down; but I should go on with equal confidence to deny the phenomenon of capillary attraction. Here I should be wrong, but only because I carried out my science irrespectively of other sciences. In like manner, did I simply give myself to the investigation of the external action of body upon body, I might scoff at the very idea of chemical affinities and combinations, and reject it as simply unintelligible. Were I a mere chemist, I should deny the influence of mind upon bodily health; and so on, as regards the devotees of any science, or family of sciences, to the exclusion of others; they necessarily become bigots and quacks, scorning all principles and reported facts which do not belong to their own pursuit, and thinking to effect everything without aid from any other quarter. Thus, before now, chemistry has been substituted for medicine; and again, political economy, or intellectual enlightenment, or the reading of the Scriptures, has been cried up as a panacea against vice, malevolence, and misery.

4.

Summing up, Gentlemen, what I have said, I lay it down that all knowledge forms one whole, because its subject-matter is one; for the universe in its length and breadth is so intimately knit together, that we cannot separate off portion from portion, and operation from operation, except by a mental abstraction; and then again, as to its Creator, though He of course in His own Being is infinitely separate from it, and Theology has its departments towards which human knowledge has no relations, yet He has so implicated Himself with it, and taken it into His very bosom, by His presence in it, His providence over it, His impressions upon it, and His influences through it, that we cannot truly or fully contemplate it without in some main aspects contemplating Him. Next, sciences are the results of that mental abstraction, which I have spoken of, being the logical record of this or that aspect of the whole subject-matter of knowledge. As they all belong to one and the same circle of objects, they are one and all connected together; as they are but aspects of things, they are severally incomplete in their relation to the things themselves, though complete in their own idea and for their own respective purposes; on both accounts they at once need and subserve each other. And further, the comprehension of the bearings of one science on another, and the use of each to each, and the location and limitation and adjustment and due appreciation of them all, one with another, this belongs, I conceive, to a sort of science distinct from all of them, and in some sense a science of sciences, which is my own conception of what is meant by Philosophy, in the true sense of the word, and of a philosophical habit of mind, and which in these Discourses I shall call by that name. This is what I have to say about knowledge and philosophical knowledge generally; and now I proceed to apply it to the particular science, which has led me to draw it out.

I say, then, that the systematic omission of any one science from the catalogue prejudices the accuracy and completeness of our knowledge altogether, and that, in proportion to its importance. Not even Theology itself, though it comes from heaven, though its truths were given once for all at the first, though they are more certain on account of the Giver than those of mathematics, not even Theology, so far as it is relative to us, or is the Science of Religion, do I exclude from the law to which every mental exercise is subject, viz., from that imperfection, which ever must attend the abstract, when it would determine the concrete. Nor do I speak only of Natural Religion; for even the teaching of the Catholic Church, in certain of its aspects, that is, its religious teaching, is variously influenced by the other sciences. Not to insist on the introduction of the Aristotelic philosophy into its phraseology, its explanation of dogmas is influenced by ecclesiastical acts or events; its interpretations of prophecy are directly affected by the issues of history; its comments upon Scripture by the conclusions of the astronomer and the geologist; and its casuistical decisions by the various experience, political, social, and psychological, with which times and places are ever supplying it.

What Theology gives, it has a right to take; or rather, the interests of Truth oblige it to take. If we would not be beguiled by dreams, if we would ascertain facts as they are, then, granting Theology is a real science, we cannot exclude it, and still call ourselves philosophers. I have asserted nothing as yet as to the pre-eminent dignity of Religious Truth; I only say, if there be Religious Truth at all, we cannot shut our eyes to it without prejudice to truth of every kind, physical, metaphysical, historical, and moral; for it bears upon all truth. And thus I answer the objection with which I opened this Discourse. I supposed the question put to me by a philosopher of the day, "Why cannot you go your way, and let us go ours?" I answer, in the name of the Science of Religion, "When Newton can dispense with the metaphysician, then may you dispense with us." So much at first sight; now I am going on to claim a little more for Theology, by classing it with branches of knowledge which may with greater decency be compared to it.

5.

Let us see, then, how this supercilious treatment of so momentous a science, for momentous it must be, if there be a God, runs in a somewhat parallel case. The great philosopher of antiquity, when he would enumerate the causes of the things that take place in the world, after making mention of those which he considered to be physical and material, adds, "and the mind and everything which is by means of man."[15] Certainly; it would have been a preposterous course, when he would trace the effects he saw around him to their respective sources, had he directed his exclusive attention upon some one class or order of originating principles, and ascribed to these everything which happened anywhere. It would indeed have been unworthy a genius so curious, so penetrating, so fertile, so analytical as Aristotle's, to have laid it down that everything on the face of the earth could be accounted for by the material sciences, without the hypothesis of moral agents. It is incredible that in the investigation of physical results he could ignore so influential a being as man, or forget that, not only brute force and elemental movement, but knowledge also is power. And this so much the more, inasmuch as moral and spiritual agents belong to another, not to say a higher, order than physical; so that the omission supposed would not have been merely an oversight in matters of detail, but a philosophical error, and a fault in division.

However, we live in an age of the world when the career of science and literature is little affected by what was done, or would have been done, by this venerable authority; so, we will suppose, in England or Ireland, in the middle of the nineteenth century, a set of persons of name and celebrity to meet together, in spite of Aristotle, in order to adopt a line of proceeding which they conceive the circumstances of the time render imperative. We will suppose that a difficulty just now besets the enunciation and discussion of all matters of science, in consequence of the extreme sensitiveness of large classes of the community, clergy and laymen, on the subjects of necessity, responsibility, the standard of morals, and the nature of virtue. Parties run so high, that the only way of avoiding constant quarrelling in defence of this or that side of the question is, in the judgment of the persons I am supposing, to shut up the subject of anthropology altogether. This is accordingly done. Henceforth man is to be as if he were not, in the general course of Education; the moral and mental sciences are to have no professorial chairs, and the treatment of them is to be simply left as a matter of private judgment, which each individual may carry out as he will. I can just fancy such a prohibition abstractedly possible; but one thing I cannot fancy possible, viz., that the parties in question, after this sweeping act of exclusion, should forthwith send out proposals on the basis of such exclusion for publishing an Encyclopædia, or erecting a National University.

It is necessary, however, Gentlemen, for the sake of the illustration which I am setting before you, to imagine what cannot be. I say, let us imagine a project for organizing a system of scientific teaching, in which the agency of man in the material world cannot allowably be recognized, and may allowably be denied. Physical and mechanical causes are exclusively to be treated of; volition is a forbidden subject. A prospectus is put out, with a list of sciences, we will say, Astronomy, Optics, Hydrostatics, Galvanism, Pneumatics, Statics, Dynamics, Pure Mathematics, Geology, Botany, Physiology, Anatomy, and so forth; but not a word about the mind and its powers, except what is said in explanation of the omission. That explanation is to the effect that the parties concerned in the undertaking have given long and anxious thought to the subject, and have been reluctantly driven to the conclusion that it is simply impracticable to include in the list of University Lectures the Philosophy of Mind. What relieves, however, their regret is the reflection, that domestic feelings and polished manners are best cultivated in the family circle and in good society, in the observance of the sacred ties which unite father, mother, and child, in the correlative claims and duties of citizenship, in the exercise of disinterested loyalty and enlightened patriotism. With this apology, such as it is, they pass over the consideration of the human mind and its powers and works, "in solemn silence," in their scheme of University Education.

Let a charter be obtained for it; let professors be appointed, lectures given, examinations passed, degrees awarded: – what sort of exactness or trustworthiness, what philosophical largeness, will attach to views formed in an intellectual atmosphere thus deprived of some of the constituent elements of daylight? What judgment will foreign countries and future times pass on the labours of the most acute and accomplished of the philosophers who have been parties to so portentous an unreality? Here are professors gravely lecturing on medicine, or history, or political economy, who, so far from being bound to acknowledge, are free to scoff at the action of mind upon matter, or of mind upon mind, or the claims of mutual justice and charity. Common sense indeed and public opinion set bounds at first to so intolerable a licence; yet, as time goes on, an omission which was originally but a matter of expedience, commends itself to the reason; and at length a professor is found, more hardy than his brethren, still however, as he himself maintains, with sincere respect for domestic feelings and good manners, who takes on him to deny psychology *in toto,* to pronounce the influence of mind in the visible world a superstition, and to account for every effect which is found in the world by the operation of physical causes. Hitherto intelligence and volition were accounted real powers; the muscles act, and their action cannot be represented by any scientific expression; a stone flies out of the hand and the propulsive force of the muscle resides in the will; but there has been a revolution, or at least a new theory in philosophy, and our Professor, I say, after speaking with the highest admiration of

the human intellect, limits its independent action to the region of speculation, and denies that it can be a motive principle, or can exercise a special
interference, in the material world. He ascribes every work, every external
act of man, to the innate force or soul of the physical universe. He observes
that spiritual agents are so mysterious and unintelligible, so uncertain in
their laws, so vague in their operation, so sheltered from experience, that a
wise man will have nothing to say to them. They belong to a different order
of causes, which he leaves to those whose profession it is to investigate
them, and he confines himself to the tangible and sure. Human exploits,
human devices, human deeds, human productions, all that comes under the
scholastic terms of "genius" and "art," and the metaphysical ideas of
"duty," "right," and "heroism," it is his office to contemplate all these
merely in their place in the eternal system of physical cause and effect. At
length he undertakes to show how the whole fabric of material civilization
has arisen from the constructive powers of physical elements and physical laws. He descants upon palaces, castles, temples, exchanges, bridges,
causeways, and shows that they never could have grown into the imposing
dimensions which they present to us, but for the laws of gravitation and the
cohesion of part with part. The pillar would come down, the loftier the more
speedily, did not the centre of gravity fall within its base; and the most
admired dome of Palladio or of Sir Christopher would give way, were it not
for the happy principle of the arch. He surveys the complicated machinery
of a single day's arrangements in a private family; our dress, our furniture,
our hospitable board; what would become of them, he asks, but for the laws
of physical nature? Those laws are the causes of our carpets, our furniture,
our travelling, and our social intercourse. Firm stitches have a natural
power, in proportion to the toughness of the material adopted, to keep
together separate portions of cloth; sofas and chairs could not turn upside
down, even if they would; and it is a property of caloric to relax the fibres of
animal matter, acting through water in one way, through oil in another, and
this is the whole mystery of the most elaborate *cuisine:* – but I should be
tedious if I continued the illustration.

6.

Now, Gentlemen, pray understand how it is to be here applied. I am not
supposing that the principles of Theology and Psychology are the same, or
arguing from the works of man to the works of God, which Paley has done,
which Hume has protested against. I am not busying myself to prove the
existence and attributes of God, by means of the Argument from design. I

am not proving anything at all about the Supreme Being. On the contrary, I am assuming His existence, and I do but say this: – that, man existing, no University Professor, who had suppressed in physical lectures the idea of volition, who did not take volition for granted, could escape a one-sided, a radically false view of the things which he discussed; not indeed that his own definitions, principles, and laws would be wrong, or his abstract statements, but his considering his own study to be the key of everything that takes place on the face of the earth, and his passing over anthropology, this would be his error. I say, it would not be his science which was untrue, but his so-called knowledge which was unreal. He would be deciding on facts by means of theories. The various busy world, spread out before our eyes, is physical, but it is more than physical; and, in making its actual system identical with his scientific analysis, formed on a particular aspect, such a Professor as I have imagined was betraying a want of philosophical depth, and an ignorance of what an University Teaching ought to be. He was no longer a teacher of liberal knowledge, but a narrow-minded bigot. While his doctrines professed to be conclusions formed upon an hypothesis or partial truth, they were undeniable; not so if they professed to give results in facts which he could grasp and take possession of. Granting, indeed, that a man's arm is moved by a simple physical cause, then of course we may dispute about the various external influences which, when it changes its position, sway it to and fro, like a scarecrow in a garden; but to assert that the motive cause *is* physical, this is an assumption in a case, when our question is about a matter of fact, not about the logical consequences of an assumed premiss. And, in like manner, if a people prays, and the wind changes, the rain ceases, the sun shines, and the harvest is safely housed, when no one expected it, our Professor may, if he will, consult the barometer, discourse about the atmosphere, and throw what has happened into an equation, ingenious, even though it be not true; but, should he proceed to rest the phenomenon, in matter of fact, simply upon a physical cause, to the exclusion of a divine, and to say that the given case actually belongs to his science because other like cases do, I must tell him, *Ne sutor ultra crepidam:* he is making his particular craft usurp and occupy the universe.[16] This then is the drift of my illustration. If the creature is ever setting in motion an endless series of physical causes and effects, much more is the Creator; and as our excluding volition from our range of ideas is a denial of the soul, so our ignoring Divine Agency is a virtual denial of God. Moreover, supposing man can will and act of himself in spite of physics, to shut up this great truth, though one, is to put our whole encyclopædia of knowledge out of joint; and supposing God can will and act of Himself in this world which He has made, and we deny or slur it over, then we are throwing the circle of universal science into a like, or a far worse confusion.

Worse incomparably, for the idea of God, if there be a God, is infinitely higher than the idea of man, if there be man. If to blot out man's agency is to deface the book of knowledge, on the supposition of that agency existing, what must it be, supposing it exists, to blot out the agency of God? I have hitherto been engaged in showing that all the sciences come to us as one, that they all relate to one and the same integral subject-matter, that each separately is more or less an abstraction, wholly true as an hypothesis, but not wholly trustworthy in the concrete, conversant with relations more than with facts, with principles more than with agents, needing the support and guarantee of its sister sciences, and giving in turn while it takes: – from which it follows that none can safely be omitted, if we would obtain the exactest knowledge possible of things as they are, and that the omission is more or less important, in proportion to the field which each covers, and the depth to which it penetrates, and the order to which it belongs; for its loss is a positive privation of an influence which exerts itself in the correction and completion of the rest. This is a general statement; but now as to Theology in particular, what, in matter of fact, are its pretensions, what its importance, what its influence upon other branches of knowledge, supposing there be a God, which it would not become me to set about proving? Has it vast dimensions, or does it lie in a nutshell? Will its omission be imperceptible, or will it destroy the equilibrium of the whole system of Knowledge? This is the inquiry to which I proceed.

7.

Now what is Theology? First, I will tell you what it is not. And here, in the first place (though of course I speak on the subject as a Catholic), observe that, strictly speaking, I am not assuming that Catholicism is true, while I make myself the champion of Theology. Catholicism has not formally entered into my argument hitherto, nor shall I just now assume any principle peculiar to it, for reasons which will appear in the sequel, though of course I shall use Catholic language. Neither, secondly, will I fall into the fashion of the day, of identifying Natural Theology with Physical Theology; which said Physical Theology is a most jejune study, considered as a science, and really is no science at all, for it is ordinarily nothing more than a series of pious or polemical remarks upon the physical world viewed religiously, whereas the word "Natural" properly comprehends man and society, and all that is involved therein, as the great Protestant writer, Dr. Butler, shows us.[17] Nor, in the third place, do I mean by Theology polemics of any kind; for instance, what are called "the Evidences of Religion," or "the Christian Evidences;" for, though these constitute a science supplemental to Theology and are necessary in their place, they are not Theology itself, unless an army is synonymous with the body politic. Nor, fourthly, do I mean by Theology that vague thing called "Christianity," or "our common Christianity," or "Christianity the law of the land," if there is any man alive who can tell what it is. I discard it, for the very reason that it cannot throw itself into a proposition. Lastly, I do not understand by Theology, acquaintance with the Scriptures; for, though no person of religious feelings can read Scripture but he will find those feelings roused, and gain much knowledge of history into the bargain, yet historical reading and religious feeling are not science. I mean none of these things by Theology, I simply mean the Science of God, or the truths we know about God put into system; just as we have a science of the stars, and call it astronomy, or of the crust of the earth, and call it geology.

For instance, I mean, for this is the main point, that, as in the human frame there is a living principle, acting upon it and through it by means of volition, so, behind the veil of the visible universe, there is an invisible, intelligent Being, acting on and through it, as and when He will. Further, I mean that this invisible Agent is in no sense a soul of the world, after the analogy of human nature, but, on the contrary, is absolutely distinct from the world, as being its Creator, Upholder, Governor, and Sovereign Lord. Here we are at once brought into the circle of doctrines which the idea of God embodies. I mean then by the Supreme Being, one who is simply self-dependent, and the only Being who is such; moreover, that He is without beginning or Eternal, and the only Eternal; that in consequence He has lived a whole eternity by Himself; and hence that He is all-sufficient, sufficient for His own blessedness, and all-blessed, and ever-blessed. Further, I mean a Being, who, having these prerogatives, has the Supreme Good, or rather is the Supreme Good, or has all the attributes of Good in infinite intenseness; all wisdom, all truth, all justice, all love, all holiness, all beautifulness; who is omnipotent, omniscient, omnipresent; ineffably one, absolutely perfect; and such, that what we do not know and cannot even imagine of Him, is far more wonderful than what we do and can. I mean One who is sovereign over His own will and actions, though always according to the eternal Rule of right and wrong, which is Himself. I mean, moreover, that He created all things out of nothing, and preserves them every moment, and could destroy them as easily as He made them; and that, in consequence, He is separated from them by an abyss, and is incommunicable in all His attributes. And further, He has stamped upon all things in the hour of their creation, their respective natures, and has given them their work and mission and their length of days, greater or less, in their appointed place. I mean, too, that He is ever present with His works, one by one, and confronts every thing He has made by His particular and most loving Providence, and manifests Himself to each according to its needs; and has on rational beings imprinted the moral law, and given them power to obey it, imposing on them the duty of worship and service, searching and scanning them through and through with His omniscient eye, and putting before them a present trial and a judgment to come.

Such is what Theology teaches about God, a doctrine, as the very idea of its subject-matter presupposes, so mysterious as in its fulness to lie beyond any system, and in particular aspects to be simply external to nature, and to seem in parts even to be irreconcileable with itself, the imagination being unable to embrace what the reason determines. It teaches of a Being infinite, yet personal; all-blessed, yet ever operative; absolutely separate from the creature, yet in every part of the creation at every moment; above all things, yet under every thing. It teaches of a Being who, though the highest, yet in the work of creation, conservation, government, retribution, makes Himself, as it were, the minister and servant of all; who, though inhabiting eternity, allows Himself to take an interest, and to have a sympathy, in the matters of space and time. His are all beings, visible and invisible, the noblest and the vilest of them. His are the substance, and the operation, and the results of that system of physical nature into which we are born. His too are the powers and achievements of the intellectual essences, on which He has bestowed an independent action and the gift of origination. The laws of the universe, the principles of truth, the relation of one thing to another, their qualities and virtues, the order and harmony of the whole, all that exists, is from Him; and, if evil is not from Him, as assuredly it is not, this is because evil has no substance of its own, but is only the defect, excess, perversion, or corruption of that which has substance. All we see, hear, and touch, the remote sidereal firmament, as well as our own sea and land, and the elements which compose them, and the ordinances they obey, are His. The primary atoms of matter, their properties, their mutual action, their disposition and collocation, electricity, magnetism, gravitation, light, and whatever other subtle principles or operations the wit of man is detecting or shall detect, are the work of His hands. From Him has been every movement which has convulsed and re-fashioned the surface of the earth. The most insignificant or unsightly insect is from Him, and good in its kind; the ever-teeming, inexhaustible swarms of animalculæ, the myriads of living motes invisible to the naked eye, the restless ever-spreading vegetation which creeps like a garment over the whole earth, the lofty cedar, the umbrageous banana, are His. His are the tribes and families of birds and beasts, their graceful forms, their wild gestures, and their passionate cries.

And so in the intellectual, moral, social, and political world. Man, with his motives and works, his languages, his propagation, his diffusion, is from Him. Agriculture, medicine, and the arts of life, are His gifts. Society, laws, government, He is their sanction. The pageant of earthly royalty has the semblance and the benediction of the Eternal King. Peace and civilization, commerce and adventure, wars when just, conquest when humane and necessary, have His co-operation, and His blessing upon them. The course of events, the revolution of empires, the rise and fall of states, the periods and eras, the progresses and the retrogressions of the world's history, not indeed the incidental sin, over-abundant as it is, but the great outlines and the results of human affairs, are from His disposition. The elements and types and seminal principles and constructive powers of the moral world, in ruins though it be, are to be referred to Him. He "enlighteneth every man that cometh into this world." His are the dictates of the moral sense, and the retributive reproaches of conscience. To Him must be ascribed the rich endowments of the intellect, the irradiation of genius, the imagination of the poet, the sagacity of the politician, the wisdom (as Scripture calls it), which now rears and decorates the Temple, now manifests itself in proverb or in parable. The old saws of nations, the majestic precepts of philosophy, the luminous maxims of law, the oracles of individual wisdom, the traditionary rules of truth, justice, and religion, even though imbedded in the corruption, or alloyed with the pride, of the world, betoken His original agency, and His long-suffering presence. Even where there is habitual rebellion against Him, or profound far-spreading social depravity, still the undercurrent, or the heroic outburst, of natural virtue, as well as the yearnings of the heart after what it has not, and its presentiment of its true remedies, are to be ascribed to the Author of all good. Anticipations or reminiscences of His glory haunt the mind of the self-sufficient sage, and of the pagan devotee; His writing is upon the wall, whether of the Indian fane, or of the porticoes of Greece. He introduces Himself, He all but concurs, according to His good pleasure, and in His selected season, in the issues of unbelief, superstition, and false worship, and He changes the character of acts by His overruling operation. He condescends, though He gives no sanction, to the altars and shrines of imposture, and He makes His own fiat the substitute for its sorceries. He speaks amid the incantations of Balaam, raises Samuel's spirit in the witch's cavern, prophesies of the Messias by the tongue of the Sibyl, forces Python to recognize His ministers, and baptizes by the hand of the misbeliever. He is with the heathen dramatist in his denunciations of injustice and tyranny, and his auguries of divine vengeance upon crime. Even on the unseemly legends of a popular mythology He casts His shadow, and is dimly discerned in the ode or the epic, as in troubled water or in fantastic dreams. All that is good, all that is true, all that is beautiful, all that is beneficent, be it great or small, be it perfect or fragmentary, natural as well as supernatural, moral as well as material, comes from Him.

8.

If this be a sketch, accurate in substance and as far as it goes, of the doctrines proper to Theology, and especially of the doctrine of a particular Providence, which is the portion of it most on a level with human sciences, I cannot understand at all how, supposing it to be true, it can fail, considered as knowledge, to exert a powerful influence on philosophy, literature, and every intellectual creation or discovery whatever. I cannot understand how it is possible, as the phrase goes, to blink the question of its truth or false-hood. It meets us with a profession and a proffer of the highest truths of which the human mind is capable; it embraces a range of subjects the most diversified and distant from each other. What science will not find one part or other of its province traversed by its path? What results of philosophic speculation are unquestionable, if they have been gained without inquiry as to what Theology had to say to them? Does it cast no light upon history? has it no influence upon the principles of ethics? is it without any sort of bearing on physics, metaphysics, and political science? Can we drop it out of the circle of knowledge, without allowing, either that that circle is thereby mutilated, or on the other hand, that Theology is really no science?

And this dilemma is the more inevitable, because Theology is so precise and consistent in its intellectual structure. When I speak of Theism or Monotheism, I am not throwing together discordant doctrines; I am not merging belief, opinion, persuasion, of whatever kind, into a shapeless aggregate, by the help of ambiguous words, and dignifying this medley by the name of Theology. I speak of one idea unfolded in its just proportions, carried out upon an intelligible method, and issuing in necessary and immu-table results; understood indeed at one time and place better than at another, held here and there with more or less of inconsistency, but still, after all, in all times and places, where it is found, the evolution, not of half-a-dozen ideas, but of one.

9.

And here I am led to another and most important point in the argument in its behalf, – I mean its wide reception. Theology, as I have described it, is no accident of particular minds, as are certain systems, for instance, of prophetical interpretation. It is not the sudden birth of a crisis, as the Lutheran or Wesleyan doctrine.[18] It is not the splendid development of some uprising philosophy, as the Cartesian or Platonic. It is not the fashion of a season, as certain medical treatments may be considered. It has had a place, if not possession, in the intellectual world from time immemorial; it has been received by minds the most various, and in systems of religion the most hostile to each other. It has *primâ facie* claims upon us, so imposing, that it can only be rejected on the ground of those claims being nothing more than imposing, that is, being false. As to our own countries, it occupies our language, it meets us at every turn in our literature, it is the secret assumption, too axiomatic to be distinctly professed, of all our writers; nor can we help assuming it ourselves, except by the most unnatural vigilance. Whoever philosophizes, starts with it, and introduces it, when he will, without any apology. Bacon, Hooker, Taylor, Cudworth, Locke, Newton, Clarke, Berkeley, and Butler, and it would be as easy to find more, as difficult to find greater names among English authors, inculcate or comment upon it. Men the most opposed, in creed or cast of mind, Addison and Johnson, Shakespeare and Milton, Lord Herbert and Baxter, herald it forth. Nor is it an English or a Protestant notion only; you track it across the Continent, you pursue it into former ages. When was the world without it? Have the systems of Atheism or Pantheism, as sciences, prevailed in the literature of nations, or received a formation or attained a completeness such as Monotheism? We find it in old Greece, and even in Rome, as well as in Judea and the East. We find it in popular literature, in philosophy, in poetry, as a positive and settled teaching, differing not at all in the appearance it presents, whether in Protestant England, or in schismatical Russia, or in the Mahometan populations, or in the Catholic Church. If ever there was a subject of thought, which had earned by prescription to be received among the studies of a University, and which could not be rejected except on the score of convicted imposture, as astrology or alchemy; if there be a science anywhere, which at least could claim not to be ignored, but to be entertained, and either distinctly accepted or distinctly reprobated, or rather, which cannot be passed over in a scheme of universal instruction, without involving a positive denial of its truth, it is this ancient, this far-spreading philosophy.

10.

And now, Gentlemen, I may bring a somewhat tedious discussion to a close. It will not take many words to sum up what I have been urging. I say then, if the various branches of knowledge, which are the matter of teaching in a University, so hang together, that none can be neglected without prejudice to the perfection of the rest, and if Theology be a branch of knowledge, of wide reception, of philosophical structure, of unutterable importance, and of supreme influence, to what conclusion are we brought from these two premises but this? that to withdraw Theology from the public schools is to impair the completeness and to invalidate the trustworthiness of all that is actually taught in them.

But I have been insisting simply on Natural Theology, and that, because I wished to carry along with me those who were not Catholics, and, again, as being confident, that no one can really set himself to master and to teach the doctrine of an intelligent Creator in its fulness, without going on a great deal farther than he at present dreams. I say, then, secondly: – if this Science, even as human reason may attain to it, has such claims on the regard, and enters so variously into the objects, of the Professor of Universal Knowledge, how can any Catholic imagine that it is possible for him to cultivate Philosophy and Science with due attention to their ultimate end, which is Truth, supposing that system of revealed facts and principles, which constitutes the Catholic Faith, which goes so far beyond nature, and which he knows to be most true, be omitted from among the subjects of his teaching?

In a word, Religious Truth is not only a portion, but a condition of general knowledge. To blot it out is nothing short, if I may so speak, of unravelling the web of University Teaching. It is, according to the Greek proverb, to take the Spring from out of the year; it is to imitate the preposterous proceeding of those tragedians who represented a drama with the omission of its principal part.

DISCOURSE IV.

BEARING OF OTHER BRANCHES OF KNOWLEDGE ON THEOLOGY.

I.

Nothing is more common in the world at large than to consider the resistance, made on the part of religious men, especially Catholics, to the separation of Secular Education from Religion, as a plain token that there is some real contrariety between human science and Revelation. To the multitude who draw this inference, it matters not whether the protesting parties avow their belief in this contrariety or not; it is borne in upon the many, as if it were self-evident, that religious men would not thus be jealous and alarmed about Science, did they not feel instinctively, though they may not recognize it, that knowledge is their born enemy, and that its progress, if it is not arrested, will be certain to destroy all that they hold venerable and dear. It looks to the world like a misgiving on our part similar to that which is imputed to our refusal to educate by means of the Bible only; why should you dread the sacred text, men say, if it be not against you? And in like manner, why should you dread secular education, except that it is against you? Why impede the circulation of books which take religious views opposite to your own? Why forbid your children and scholars the free perusal of poems or tales or essays or other light literature which you fear would unsettle their minds? Why oblige them to know these persons and to shun those, if you think that your friends have reason on their side as fully as your opponents? Truth is bold and unsuspicious; want of self-reliance is the mark of falsehood.

Now, as far as this objection relates to any supposed opposition between secular science and divine, which is the subject on which I am at present engaged, I made a sufficient answer to it in my foregoing Discourse. In it I said, that, in order to have possession of truth at all, we must have the whole truth; and no one science, no two sciences, no one family of sciences, nay, not even all secular science, is the whole truth; that revealed truth enters to a very great extent into the province of science, philosophy, and literature, and that to put it on one side, in compliment to secular science, is simply, under colour of a compliment, to do science a great damage. I do not say that every science will be equally affected by the omission; pure mathematics will not suffer at all; chemistry will suffer less than politics, politics than history, ethics, or metaphysics; still, that the various branches of science are intimately connected with each other, and form one whole, which whole is impaired, and to an extent which it is difficult to limit, by any considerable omission of knowledge, of whatever kind, and that revealed knowledge is very far indeed from an inconsiderable department of knowledge, this I consider undeniable. As the written and unwritten word of God make up Revelation as a whole, and the written, taken by itself, is but a part of that whole, so in turn Revelation itself may be viewed as one of the constituent parts of human knowledge, considered as a whole, and its omission is the omission of one of those constituent parts. Revealed Religion furnishes facts to the other sciences, which those sciences, left to themselves, would never reach; and it invalidates apparent facts, which, left to themselves, they would imagine. Thus, in the science of history, the preservation of our race in Noah's ark is an historical fact, which history never would arrive at without Revelation; and, in the province of physiology and moral philosophy, our race's progress and perfectibility is a dream, because Revelation contradicts it, whatever may be plausibly argued in its behalf by scientific inquirers. It is not then that Catholics are afraid of human knowledge, but that they are proud of divine knowledge, and that they think the omission of any kind of knowledge whatever, human or divine, to be, as far as it goes, not knowledge, but ignorance.

2.

Thus I anticipated the objection in question last week: now I am going to make it the introduction to a further view of the relation of secular knowledge to divine. I observe, then, that, if you drop any science out of the circle of knowledge, you cannot keep its place vacant for it; that science is forgotten; the other sciences close up, or, in other words, they exceed their proper bounds, and intrude where they have no right. For instance, I suppose, if ethics were sent into banishment, its territory would soon disappear, under a treaty of partition, as it may be called, between law, political economy, and physiology; what, again, would become of the province of experimental science, if made over to the Antiquarian Society; or of history, if surrendered out and out to Metaphysicians? The case is the same with the subject-matter of Theology; it would be the prey of a dozen various sciences, if Theology were put out of possession; and not only so, but those sciences would be plainly exceeding their rights and their capacities in seizing upon it. They would be sure to teach wrongly, where they had no mission to teach at all. The enemies of Catholicism ought to be the last to deny this: – for they have never been blind to a like usurpation, as they have called it, on the part of theologians; those who accuse us of wishing, in accordance with Scripture language, to make the sun go round the earth, are not the men to deny that a science which exceeds its limits falls into error.

I neither then am able nor care to deny, rather I assert the fact, and to-day I am going on to account for it, that any secular science cultivated exclusively, may become dangerous to Religion; and I account for it on this broad principle, that no science whatever, however comprehensive it may be, but will fall largely into error, if it be constituted the sole exponent of all things in heaven and earth, and that, for the simple reason that it is encroaching on territory not its own, and undertaking problems which it has no instruments to solve. And I set off thus:

3.

One of the first acts of the human mind is to take hold of and appropriate what meets the senses, and herein lies a chief distinction between man's and a brute's use of them. Brutes gaze on sights, they are arrested by sounds; and what they see and what they hear are mainly sights and sounds only. The intellect of man, on the contrary, energizes as well as his eye or ear, and perceives in sights and sounds something beyond them. It seizes and unites what the senses present to it; it grasps and forms what need not have been seen or heard except in its constituent parts. It discerns in lines and colours, or in tones, what is beautiful and what is not. It gives them a meaning, and invests them with an idea. It gathers up a succession of notes into the expression of a whole, and calls it a melody; it has a keen sensibility towards angles and curves, lights and shadows, tints and contours. It distinguishes between rule and exception, between accident and design. It assigns phenomena to a general law, qualities to a subject, acts to a principle, and effects to a cause. In a word, it philosophizes; for I suppose Science and Philosophy, in their elementary idea, are nothing else but this habit of *viewing,* as it may be called, the objects which sense conveys to the mind, of throwing them into system, and uniting and stamping them with one form.

This method is so natural to us, as I have said, as to be almost spontaneous; and we are impatient when we cannot exercise it, and in consequence we do not always wait to have the means of exercising it aright, but we often put up with insufficient or absurd views or interpretations of what we meet with, rather than have none at all. We refer the various matters which are brought home to us, material or moral, to causes which we happen to know of, or to such as are simply imaginary, sooner than refer them to nothing; and according to the activity of our intellect do we feel a pain and begin to fret, if we are not able to do so. Here we have an explanation of the multitude of off-hand sayings, flippant judgments, and shallow generalizations, with which the world abounds. Not from self-will only, nor from malevolence, but from the irritation which suspense occasions, is the mind forced on to pronounce, without sufficient data for pronouncing. Who does not form some view or other, for instance, of any public man, or any public event, nay, even so far in some cases as to reach the mental delineation of his appearance or of its scene? yet how few have a right to form any view. Hence the misconceptions of character, hence the false impressions and reports of words or deeds, which are the rule, rather than the exception, in the world at large; hence the extravagances of undisciplined talent, and the narrowness of conceited ignorance; because, though it is no easy matter to view things correctly, nevertheless the busy mind will ever be viewing. We cannot do without a view, and we put up with an illusion, when we cannot get a truth.

4.

Now, observe how this impatience acts in matters of research and speculation. What happens to the ignorant and hotheaded, will take place in the case of every person whose education or pursuits are contracted, whether they be merely professional, merely scientific, or of whatever other peculiar complexion. Men, whose life lies in the cultivation of one science, or the exercise of one method of thought, have no more right, though they have often more ambition, to generalize upon the basis of their own pursuit but beyond its range, than the schoolboy or the ploughman to judge of a Prime Minister. But they must have something to say on every subject; habit, fashion, the public require it of them: and, if so, they can only give sentence according to their knowledge. You might think this ought to make such a person modest in his enunciations; not so: too often it happens that, in proportion to the narrowness of his knowledge, is, not his distrust of it, but the deep hold it has upon him, his absolute conviction of his own conclusions, and his positiveness in maintaining them. He has the obstinacy of the bigot, whom he scorns, without the bigot's apology, that he has been taught, as he thinks, his doctrine from heaven. Thus he becomes, what is commonly called, a man of one idea; which properly means a man of one science, and of the view, partly true, but subordinate, partly false, which is all that can proceed out of any thing so partial. Hence it is that we have the principles of utility, of combination, of progress, of philanthropy, or, in material sciences, comparative anatomy, phrenology, electricity, exalted into leading ideas, and keys, if not of all knowledge, at least of many things more than belong to them, – principles, all of them true to a certain point, yet all degenerating into error and quackery, because they are carried to excess, viz., at the point where they require interpretation and restraint from other quarters, and because they are employed to do what is simply too much for them, inasmuch as a little science is not deep philosophy.

Lord Bacon has set down the abuse, of which I am speaking, among the impediments to the Advancement of the Sciences, when he observes that "men have used to infect their meditations, opinions, and doctrines, with some conceits which they have most admired, or *some Sciences which they have most applied;* and give all things else a *tincture* according to them *utterly untrue and improper.* . . . So have the alchemists made a philosophy out of a few experiments of the furnace; and Gilbertus, our countryman, hath made a philosophy out of the observations of a lodestone. So Cicero, when, reciting the several opinions of the nature of the soul, he found a musician that held the soul was but a harmony, saith pleasantly, 'hic ab arte suâ non recessit,' 'he was true to his art.' But of these conceits Aristotle speaketh seriously and wisely when he saith, 'Qui respiciunt ad pauca, de facili pronunciant,' 'they who contemplate a few things have no difficulty in deciding.' "[19]

5.

And now I have said enough to explain the inconvenience which I conceive necessarily to result from a refusal to recognize theological truth in a course of Universal Knowledge; – it is not only the loss of Theology, it is the perversion of other sciences. What it unjustly forfeits, others unjustly seize. They have their own department, and, in going out of it, attempt to do what they really cannot do; and that the more mischievously, because they do teach what in its place is true, though when out of its place, perverted or carried to excess, it is not true. And, as every man has not the capacity of separating truth from falsehood, they persuade the world of what is false by urging upon it what is true. Nor is it open enemies alone who encounter us here, sometimes it is friends, sometimes persons who, if not friends, at least have no wish to oppose Religion, and are not conscious they are doing so; and it will carry out my meaning more fully if I give some illustrations of it.

As to friends, I may take as an instance the cultivation of the Fine Arts, Painting, Sculpture, Architecture, to which I may add Music. These high ministers of the Beautiful and the Noble are, it is plain, special attendants and handmaids of Religion; but it is equally plain that they are apt to forget their place, and, unless restrained with a firm hand, instead of being servants, will aim at becoming principals. Here lies the advantage, in an ecclesiastical point of view, of their more rudimental state, I mean of the ancient style of architecture, of Gothic sculpture and painting, and of what is called Gregorian music, that these inchoate sciences have so little innate vigour and life in them, that they are in no danger of going out of their place, and giving the law to Religion. But the case is very different when genius has breathed upon their natural elements, and has developed them into what I may call intellectual powers. When Painting, for example, grows into the fulness of its function as a simply imitative art, it at once ceases to be a dependant on the Church. It has an end of its own, and that of earth: Nature is its pattern, and the object it pursues is the beauty of Nature, even till it becomes an ideal beauty, but a natural beauty still. It cannot imitate that beauty of Angels and Saints which it has never seen. At first, indeed, by outlines and emblems it shadowed out the Invisible, and its want of skill became the instrument of reverence and modesty; but as time went on and it attained its full dimensions as an art, it rather subjected Religion to its own ends than ministered to the ends of Religion, and in its long galleries and stately chambers, did but mingle adorable figures and sacred histories with a multitude of earthly, not to say unseemly forms, which the Art had created, borrowing withal a colouring and a character from that bad company. Not content with neutral ground for its development, it was attracted by the sublimity of divine subjects to ambitious and hazardous essays. Without my saying a word more, you will clearly understand, Gentlemen, that under these circumstances Religion was bound to exert itself, that the world might not gain an advantage over it. Put out of sight the severe teaching of Catholicism in the schools of Painting, as men now would put it aside in their philosophical studies, and in no long time you would have the hierarchy of the Church, the Anchorite and Virgin-martyr, the Confessor and the Doctor, the Angelic Hosts, the Mother of God, the Crucifix, the Eternal Trinity, supplanted by a sort of pagan mythology in the guise of sacred names, by a creation indeed of high genius, of intense, and dazzling, and soul-absorbing beauty, in which, however, there was nothing which subserved the cause of Religion, nothing on the other hand which did not directly or indirectly minister to corrupt nature and the powers of darkness.

6.

The art of Painting, however, is peculiar: Music and Architecture are more ideal, and their respective archetypes, even if not supernatural, at least are abstract and unearthly; and yet what I have been observing about Painting, holds, I think, analogously, in the marvellous development which Musical Science has undergone in the last century. Doubtless here too the highest genius may be made subservient to Religion; here too, still more simply than in the case of Painting, the Science has a field of its own, perfectly innocent, into which Religion does not and need not enter; on the other hand here also, in the case of Music as of Painting, it is certain that Religion must be alive and on the defensive, for, if its servants sleep, a potent enchantment will steal over it. Music, I suppose, though this is not the place to enlarge upon it, has an object of its own; as mathematical science also, it is the expression of ideas greater and more profound than any in the visible world, ideas, which centre indeed in Him whom Catholicism manifests, who is the seat of all beauty, order, and perfection whatever, still ideas after all which are not those on which Revelation directly and principally fixes our gaze. If then a great master in this mysterious science (if I may speak of matters which seem to lie out of my own province) throws himself on his own gift, trusts its inspirations, and absorbs himself in those thoughts which, though they come to him in the way of nature, belong to things above nature, it is obvious he will neglect everything else. Rising in his strength, he will break through the trammels of words, he will scatter human voices, even the sweetest, to the winds; he will be borne upon nothing less than the fullest flood of sounds which art has enabled him to draw from mechanical contrivances; he will go forth as a giant, as far as ever his instruments can reach, starting from their secret depths fresh and fresh elements of beauty and grandeur as he goes, and pouring them together into still more marvellous and rapturous combinations; – and well indeed and lawfully, while he keeps to that line which is his own, but, should he happen to be attracted, as he well may, by the sublimity, so congenial to him, of the Catholic doctrine and ritual, should he engage in sacred themes, should he resolve by means of his art to do honour to the Mass, or the Divine Office, – (he cannot have a more pious, a better purpose, and Religion will gracefully accept what he gracefully offers; but) – is it not certain, from the circumstances of the case, that he will be carried on rather to use Religion than to minister to it, unless Religion is strong on its own ground, and reminds him that, if he would do honour to the highest of subjects, he must make himself its scholar, must humbly follow the thoughts given him, and must aim at the glory, not of his own gift, but of the Great Giver?

7.

As to Architecture, it is a remark, if I recollect aright, both of Fénelon and Berkeley, men so different, that it carries more with it even than the names of those celebrated men, that the Gothic style is not as *simple* as befits ecclesiastical structures. I understand this to be a similar judgment to that which I have been passing on the cultivation of Painting and Music. For myself, certainly I think that that style which, whatever be its origin, is called Gothic, is endowed with a profound and a commanding beauty, such as no other style possesses with which we are acquainted, and which probably the Church will not see surpassed till it attain to the Celestial City. No other architecture, now used for sacred purposes, seems to be the growth of an idea, whereas the Gothic style is as harmonious and as intellectual as it is graceful. But this feeling should not blind us, rather it should awaken us, to the danger lest what is really a divine gift be incautiously used as an end rather than as a means. It is surely quite within the bounds of possibility, that, as the *renaissance* three centuries ago carried away its own day, in spite of the Church, into excesses in literature and art, so that revival of an almost forgotten architecture, which is at present taking place in our own countries, in France, and in Germany, may in some way or other run away with us into this or that error, unless we keep a watch over its course. I am not speaking of Ireland; but to English Catholics at least it would be a serious evil, if it came as the emblem and advocate of a past ceremonial or an extinct nationalism. We are not living in an age of wealth and loyalty, of pomp and stateliness, of time-honoured establishments, of pilgrimage and penance, of hermitages and convents in the wild, and of fervent populations supplying the want of education by love, and apprehending in form and symbol what they cannot read in books. Our rules and our rubrics have been altered now to meet the times, and hence an obsolete discipline may be a present heresy.

8.

I have been pointing out how the Fine Arts may prejudice Religion, by laying down the law in cases where they should be subservient. The illustration is analogous rather than strictly proper to my subject, yet I think it is to the point. If then the most loyal and dutiful children of the Church must deny themselves, and do deny themselves, when they would sanctify to a heavenly purpose sciences as sublime and as divine as any which are cultivated by fallen man, it is not wonderful, when we turn to sciences of a different character, of which the object is tangible and material, and the principles belong to the Reason, not to the Imagination, that we should find their disciples, if disinclined to the Catholic Faith, acting the part of opponents to it, and that, as may often happen, even against their will and intention. Many men there are, who, devoted to one particular subject of thought, and making its principles the measure of all things, become enemies to Revealed Religion before they know it, and, only as time proceeds, are aware of their own state of mind. These, if they are writers or lecturers, while in this state of unconscious or semi-conscious unbelief, scatter infidel principles under the garb and colour of Christianity; and this, simply because they have made their own science, whatever it is, Political Economy, or Geology, or Astronomy, to the neglect of Theology, the centre of all truth, and view every part or the chief parts of knowledge as if developed from it, and to be tested and determined by its principles. Others, though conscious to themselves of their anti-Christian opinions, have too much good feeling and good taste to obtrude them upon the world. They neither wish to shock people, nor to earn for themselves a confessorship which brings with it no gain. They know the strength of prejudice, and the penalty of innovation; they wish to go through life quietly; they scorn polemics; they shrink, as from a real humiliation, from being mixed up in religious controversy; they are ashamed of the very name. However, they have had occasion at some time to publish on some literary or scientific subject; they have wished to give no offence; but after all, to their great annoyance, they find when they least expect it, or when they have taken considerable pains to avoid it, that they have roused by their publication what they would style the bigoted and bitter hostility of a party. This misfortune is easily conceivable, and has befallen many a man. Before he knows where he is, a cry is raised on all sides of him; and so little does he know what we may call the *lie* of the land, that his attempts at apology perhaps only make matters worse. In other words, an exclusive line of study has led him, whether he will or no, to run counter to the principles of Religion; which principles he has never made his landmarks, and which, whatever might be their effect upon himself, at least would have warned him against practising upon the faith of others, had they been authoritatively held up before him.

9.

Instances of this kind are far from uncommon. Men who are old enough, will remember the trouble which came upon a person, eminent as a professional man in London even at that distant day, and still more eminent since, in consequence of his publishing a book in which he so treated the subject of Comparative Anatomy as to seem to deny the immateriality of the soul. I speak here neither as excusing nor reprobating sentiments about which I have not the means of forming a judgment; all indeed I have heard of him makes me mention him with interest and respect; anyhow of this I am sure, that if there be a calling which feels its position and its dignity to lie in abstaining from controversy and in cultivating kindly feelings with men of all opinions, it is the medical profession, and I cannot believe that the person in question would purposely have raised the indignation and incurred the censure of the religious public. What then must have been his fault or mistake, but that he unsuspiciously threw himself upon his own particular science, which is of a material character, and allowed it to carry him forward into a subject-matter, where it had no right to give the law, viz., that of spiritual beings, which directly belongs to the science of Theology?

Another instance occurred at a later date. A living dignitary of the Established Church wrote a History of the Jews; in which, with what I consider at least bad judgment, he took an external view of it, and hence was led to assimilate it as nearly as possible to secular history. A great sensation was the consequence among the members of his own communion, from which he still suffers. Arguing from the dislike and contempt of polemical demonstrations which that accomplished writer has ever shown, I must conclude that he was simply betrayed into a false step by the treacherous fascination of what is called the Philosophy of History, which is good in its place, but can scarcely be applied in cases where the Almighty has superseded the natural laws of society and history. From this he would have been saved, had he been a Catholic; but in the Establishment he knew of no teaching, to which he was bound to defer, which might rule that to be false which attracted him by its speciousness.

10.

I will now take an instance from another science, and will use more words about it. Political Economy is the science, I suppose, of wealth, – a science simply lawful and useful, for it is no sin to make money, any more than it is a sin to seek honour; a science at the same time dangerous and leading to occasions of sin, as is the pursuit of honour too; and in consequence, if studied by itself, and apart from the control of Revealed Truth, sure to conduct a speculator to unchristian conclusions. Holy Scripture tells us distinctly, that "covetousness," or more literally the love of money, "is the root of all evils;" and that "they that would become rich fall into temptation;" and that "hardly shall they that have riches enter into the kingdom of God;" and after drawing the picture of a wealthy and flourishing people, it adds, "They have called the people happy that hath these things; but happy is that people whose God is the Lord:" – while on the other hand it says with equal distinctness, "If any will not work, neither let him eat;" and, "If any man have not care of his own, and especially of those of his house, he hath denied the faith, and is worse than an infidel." These opposite injunctions are summed up in the wise man's prayer, who says, "Give me neither beggary nor riches, give me only the necessaries of life." With this most precise view of a Christian's duty, viz., to labour indeed, but to labour for a competency for himself and his, and to be jealous of wealth, whether personal or national, the holy Fathers are, as might be expected, in simple accordance. "Judas," says St. Chrysostom, "was with Him who knew not where to lay His head, yet could not restrain himself; and how canst thou hope to escape the contagion without anxious effort?" "It is ridiculous," says St. Jerome, "to call it idolatry to offer to the creature the grains of incense that are due to God, and not to call it so, to offer the whole service of one's life to the creature." "There is not a trace of justice in that heart," says St. Leo, "in which the love of gain has made itself a dwelling." The same thing is emphatically taught us by the counsels of perfection, and by every holy monk and nun anywhere, who has ever embraced them; but it is needless to collect testimonies, when Scripture is so clear.

Now, observe, Gentlemen, my drift in setting Scripture and the Fathers over against Political Economy. Of course if there is a science of wealth, it must give rules for gaining wealth and disposing of wealth, and can do nothing more; it cannot itself declare that it is a subordinate science, that its end is not the ultimate end of all things, and that its conclusions are only hypothetical, depending on its premisses, and liable to be overruled by a higher teaching. I do not then blame the Political Economist for anything which follows from the very idea of his science, from the very moment that it is recognized as a science. He must of course direct his inquiries towards his end; but then at the same time it must be recollected, that so far he is not practical, but only pursues an abstract study, and is busy himself in establishing logical conclusions from indisputable premisses. Given that wealth is to be sought, this and that is the method of gaining it. This is the extent to which a Political Economist has a right to go; he has no right to determine that wealth is at any rate to be sought, or that it is the way to be virtuous and the price of happiness; I say, this is to pass the bounds of his science, independent of the question whether he be right or wrong in so determining, for he is only concerned with an hypothesis.

To take a parallel case: – a physician may tell you, that if you are to preserve your health, you must give up your employment and retire to the country. He distinctly says "if;" that is all in which he is concerned, he is no judge whether there are objects dearer to you, more urgent upon you, than the preservation of your health; he does not enter into your circumstances, your duties, your liabilities, the persons dependent on you, he knows nothing about what is advisable or what is not; he only says, "I speak *as* a physician; if you would be well, give up your profession, your trade, your office, whatever it is." However he may wish it, it would be impertinent in him to say more, unless indeed he spoke, not as a physician but as a friend; and it would be extravagant, if he asserted that bodily health was the *summum bonum,* and that no one could be virtuous whose animal system was not in good order.

II.

But now let us turn to the teaching of the actual Political Economist, in his present fashionable shape. I will take a very favourable instance of him: he shall be represented by a gentleman of high character, whose religious views are sufficiently guaranteed to us by his being the special choice, in this department of science, of a University removed more than any other Protestant body of the day from sordid or unchristian principles on the subject of money-making. I say, if there be a place where Political Economy would be kept in order, and would not be suffered to leave the high road and ride across the pastures and the gardens dedicated to other studies, it is the University of Oxford. And if a man could anywhere be found who would have too much good taste to offend the religious feeling of the place, or to say any thing which he would himself allow to be inconsistent with Revelation, I conceive it is the person whose temperate and well-considered composition, as it would be generally accounted, I am going to offer to your notice. Nor did it occasion any excitement whatever on the part of the academical or the religious public, as did the instances which I have hitherto been adducing. I am representing then the science of Political Economy, in its independent or unbridled action, to great advantage, when I select, as its specimen, the Inaugural Lecture upon it, delivered in the University in question, by its first Professor. Yet with all these circumstances in its favour, you will soon see, Gentlemen, into what extravagance, for so I must call it, a grave lawyer is led in praise of his chosen science, merely from the circumstance that he has fixed his mind upon it, till he has forgotten there are subjects of thought higher and more heavenly than it. You will find beyond mistake, that it is his object to recommend the science of wealth, by claiming for it an *ethical* quality, viz., by extolling it as the road to virtue and happiness, whatever Scripture and holy men may say to the contrary.

He begins by predicting of Political Economy, that in the course of a very few years, "it will rank in public estimation among the first of *moral* sciences in interest and in utility." Then he explains most lucidly its objects and duties, considered as "the science which teaches in what wealth consists, by what agents it is produced, and according to what laws it is distributed, and what are the institutions and customs by which production may be facilitated and distribution regulated, so as to give the largest possible amount of wealth to each individual." And he dwells upon the interest which attaches to the inquiry, "whether England has run her full career of wealth and improvement, but stands safe where she is, or whether to remain stationary is impossible." After this he notices a certain objection, which I shall set before you in his own words, as they will furnish me with the illustration I propose.

This objection, he says, is, that, "as the pursuit of wealth is one of the humblest of human occupations, far inferior to the pursuit of virtue, or of knowledge, or even of reputation, and as the possession of wealth is not necessarily joined, – perhaps it will be said, is not conducive, – to happiness, a science, of which the only subject is wealth, cannot claim to rank as the first, or nearly the first, of moral sciences."[20] Certainly, to an enthusiast in behalf of any science whatever, the temptation is great to meet an objection urged against its dignity and worth; however, from the very form of it, such an objection cannot receive a satisfactory answer by means of the science itself. It is an objection external to the science, and reminds us of the truth of Lord Bacon's remark, "No perfect discovery can be made upon a flat or a level; neither is it possible to discover the more remote and deeper parts of any science, if you stand upon the level of the science, and ascend not to a higher science."[21] The objection that Political Economy is inferior to the science of virtue, or does not conduce to happiness, is an ethical or theological objection; the question of its "rank" belongs to that Architectonic Science or Philosophy, whatever it be, which is itself the arbiter of all truth, and which disposes of the claims and arranges the places of all the departments of knowledge which man is able to master. I say, when an opponent of a particular science asserts that it does not conduce to happiness, and much more when its champion contends in reply that it certainly does conduce to virtue, as this author proceeds to contend, the obvious question which occurs to one to ask is, what does Religion, what does Revelation, say on the point? Political Economy must not be allowed to give judgment in its own favour, but must come before a higher tribunal. The objection is an appeal to the Theologian; however, the Professor does not so view the matter; he does not consider it a question for Philosophy; nor indeed on the other hand a question for Political Economy; not a question for Science at all; but for Private Judgment, – so he answers it himself, and as follows:

12.

"My answer," he says, "is, first, that the pursuit of wealth, that is, the endeavour to accumulate the means of future subsistence and enjoyment, is, to the mass of mankind, the great source of *moral* improvement." Now observe, Gentlemen, how exactly this bears out what I have been saying. It is just so far true, as to be able to instil what is false, far as the author was from any such design. I grant, then, that, ordinarily, beggary is not the means of moral improvement; and that the orderly habits which attend upon the hot pursuit of gain, not only may effect an external decency, but may at least shelter the soul from the temptations of vice. Moreover, these habits of good order guarantee regularity in a family or household, and thus are accidentally the means of good; moreover, they lead to the education of its younger branches, and they thus accidentally provide the rising generation with a virtue or a truth which the present has not: but without going into these considerations, further than to allow them generally, and under circumstances, let us rather contemplate what the author's direct assertion is. He says, "the endeavour to *accumulate,*" the words should be weighed, and for what? "for *enjoyment;*" – "to accumulate the means of future subsistence and enjoyment, is, to the mass of mankind, *the great* source," not merely *a* source, but *the great* source, and of what? of social and political progress? – such an answer would have been more within the limits of his art, – no, but of something individual and personal, "of *moral improvement.*" The soul, in the case of "the mass of mankind," improves in moral excellence from this more than any thing else, viz., from heaping up the means of enjoying this world in time to come! I really should on every account be sorry, Gentlemen, to exaggerate, but indeed one is taken by surprise, one is startled, on meeting with so very categorical a contradiction of our Lord, St. Paul, St. Chrysostom, St. Leo, and all Saints.

"No institution," he continues, "could be more beneficial to the morals of the lower orders, that is, to at least nine-tenths of the whole body of any people, than one which should increase their power and their wish to accumulate; none more mischievous than one which should diminish their motives and means to save." No institution more beneficial than one which should increase the *wish to accumulate!* then Christianity is not one of such beneficial institutions, for it expressly says, "*Lay not up to* yourselves *treasures* on earth . . . for where thy treasure is, there is thy heart also;" – no institution more mischievous than one which should diminish the *motives to save!* then Christianity is one of such mischiefs, for the inspired text proceeds, "Lay up to yourselves treasures *in heaven, where* neither the rust nor the moth doth consume, and where thieves do not dig through, nor steal."[22]

But it is not enough that morals and happiness are made to depend on gain and accumulation; the practice of Religion is ascribed to these causes also, and in the following way. Wealth depends upon the pursuit of wealth; education depends upon wealth; knowledge depends on education; and Religion depends on knowledge; therefore Religion depends on the pursuit of wealth. He says, after speaking of a poor and savage people, "Such a population must be grossly ignorant. The desire of knowledge is one of the last results of refinement; it requires in general to have been implanted in the mind during childhood; and it is absurd to suppose that persons thus situated would have the power or the will to devote much to the education of their children. A further consequence is the *absence of all real religion;* for the religion of the grossly ignorant, if they have any, scarcely ever amounts to more than a debasing superstition." The pursuit of gain then is the basis of virtue, religion, happiness; though it is all the while, as a Christian knows, the "root of all evils," and the "poor on the contrary are blessed, for theirs is the kingdom of God."

As to the argument contained in the logical *Sorites* which I have been drawing out, I anticipated just now what I should say to it in reply. I repeat, doubtless "beggary," as the wise man says, is not desirable; doubtless, if men will not work, they should not eat; there is doubtless a sense in which it may be said that mere social or political virtue tends to moral and religious excellence; but the sense needs to be defined and the statement to be kept within bounds. This is the very point on which I am all along insisting. I am not denying, I am granting, I am assuming, that there is reason and truth in the "leading ideas," as they are called, and "large views" of scientific men;

I only say that, though they speak truth, they do not speak the whole truth; that they speak a narrow truth, and think it a broad truth; that their deductions must be compared with other truths, which are acknowledged to be truths, in order to verify, complete, and correct them. They say what is true, *exceptis excipiendis;* what is true, but requires guarding; true, but must not be ridden too hard, or made what is called a *hobby;* true, but not the measure of all things; true, but if thus inordinately, extravagantly, ruinously carried out, in spite of other sciences, in spite of Theology, sure to become but a great bubble, and to burst.

13.

I am getting to the end of this Discourse, before I have noticed one tenth part of the instances with which I might illustrate the subject of it. Else I should have wished especially to have dwelt upon the not unfrequent perversion which occurs of antiquarian and historical research, to the prejudice of Theology. It is undeniable that the records of former ages are of primary importance in determining Catholic doctrine; it is undeniable also that there is a silence or a contrariety abstractedly conceivable in those records, as to an alleged portion of that doctrine, which would be sufficient to invalidate its claims on our acceptance; but it is quite as undeniable that the existing documentary testimony to Catholicism and Christianity may be so unduly valued as to be made the absolute measure of Revelation, as if no part of theological teaching were true which cannot bring its express text, as it is called, from Scripture, and authorities from the Fathers or profane writers, – whereas there are numberless facts in past times which we cannot deny, for they are indisputable, though history is silent about them. I suppose, on this score, we ought to deny that the round towers of this country had any origin, because history does not disclose it; or that any individual came from Adam who cannot produce the table of his ancestry. Yet Gibbon argues against the darkness at the Passion, from the accident that it is not mentioned by Pagan historians: – as well might he argue against the existence of Christianity itself in the first century, because Seneca, Pliny, Plutarch, the Jewish Mishna, and other authorities are silent about it. Protestants argue in a parallel way against Transubstantiation, and Arians against our Lord's Divinity, viz., on the ground that extant writing of certain Fathers do not witness those doctrines to their satisfaction: – as well might they say that Christianity was not spread by the Twelve Apostles, because we know so little of their labours. The evidence of History, I say, is invaluable in its place; but, if it assumes to be the sole means of gaining Religious Truth, it goes beyond its place. We are putting it to a larger office than it can undertake, if we countenance the usurpation; and we are turning a true guide and blessing into a source of inexplicable difficulty and interminable doubt.

And so of other sciences: just as Comparative Anatomy, Political Economy, the Philosophy of History, and the Science of Antiquities may be and are turned against Religion, by being taken by themselves, as I have been showing, so a like mistake may befall any other. Grammar, for instance, at first sight does not appear to admit of a perversion; yet Horne Tooke made it the vehicle of his peculiar scepticism. Law would seem to have enough to do with its own clients, and their affairs; and yet Mr. Bentham made a treatise on Judicial Proofs a covert attack upon the miracles of Revelation. And in like manner Physiology may deny moral evil and human responsibility; Geology may deny Moses; and Logic may deny the Holy Trinity;[23] and other sciences, now rising into notice, are or will be victims of a similar abuse.

14.

And now to sum up what I have been saying in a few words. My object, it is plain, has been – not to show that Secular Science in its various departments may take up a position hostile to Theology; – this is rather the basis of the objection with which I opened this Discourse; – but to point out the cause of an hostility to which all parties will bear witness. I have been insisting then on this, that the hostility in question, when it occurs, is coincident with an evident deflection or exorbitance of Science from its proper course; and that this exorbitance is sure to take place, almost from the necessity of the case, if Theology be not present to defend its own boundaries and to hinder the encroachment. The human mind cannot keep from speculating and systematizing; and if Theology is not allowed to occupy its own territory, adjacent sciences, nay, sciences which are quite foreign to Theology, will take possession of it. And this occupation is proved to be a usurpation by this circumstance, that these foreign sciences will assume certain principles as true, and act upon them, which they neither have authority to lay down themselves, nor appeal to any other higher science to lay down for them. For example, it is a mere unwarranted assumption if the Antiquarian says, "Nothing has ever taken place but is to be found in historical documents;" or if the Philosophic Historian says, "There is nothing in Judaism different from other political institutions;" or if the Anatomist, "There is no soul beyond the brain;" or if the Political Economist, "Easy circumstances make men virtuous." These are enunciations, not of Science, but of Private Judgment; and it is Private Judgment that infects every science which it touches with a hostility to Theology, a hostility which properly attaches to no science in itself whatever.

If then, Gentlemen, I now resist such a course of acting as unphilosophical, what is this but to do as men of Science do when the interests of their own respective pursuits are at stake? If they certainly would resist the divine who determined the orbit of Jupiter by the Pentateuch, why am I to be accused of cowardice or illiberality, because I will not tolerate their attempt in turn to theologize by means of astronomy? And if experimentalists would be sure to cry out, did I attempt to install the Thomist philosophy in the schools of astronomy and medicine, why may not I, when Divine Science is ostracized, and La Place, or Buffon, or Humboldt, sits down in its chair, why may not I fairly protest against their exclusiveness, and demand the emancipation of Theology?

15.

And now I consider I have said enough in proof of the first point, which I undertook to maintain, viz., the claim of Theology to be represented among the Chairs of a University. I have shown, I think, that exclusiveness really attaches, not to those who support that claim, but to those who dispute it. I have argued in its behalf, first, from the consideration that, whereas it is the very profession of a University to teach all sciences, on this account it cannot exclude Theology without being untrue to its profession. Next, I have said that, all sciences being connected together, and having bearings one on another, it is impossible to teach them all thoroughly, unless they all are taken into account, and Theology among them. Moreover, I have insisted on the important influence, which Theology in matter of fact does and must exercise over a great variety of sciences, completing and correcting them; so that, granting it to be a real science occupied upon truth, it cannot be omitted without great prejudice to the teaching of the rest. And lastly, I have urged that, supposing Theology be not taught, its province will not simply be neglected, but will be actually usurped by other sciences, which will teach, without warrant, conclusions of their own in a subject-matter which needs its own proper principles for its due formation and disposition.

Abstract statements are always unsatisfactory; these, as I have already observed, could be illustrated at far greater length than the time allotted to me for the purpose has allowed. Let me hope that I have said enough upon the subject to suggest thoughts, which those who take an interest in it may pursue for themselves.

DISCOURSE V.

KNOWLEDGE ITS OWN END.

A University may be considered with reference either to its Students or to its Studies; and the principle, that all Knowledge is a whole and the separate Sciences parts of one, which I have hitherto been using in behalf of its studies, is equally important when we direct our attention to its students. Now then I turn to the students, and shall consider the education which, by virtue of this principle, a University will give them; and thus I shall be introduced, Gentlemen, to the second question, which I proposed to discuss, viz., whether and in what sense its teaching, viewed relatively to the taught, carries the attribute of Utility along with it.

I.

I have said that all branches of knowledge are connected together, because the subject-matter of knowledge is intimately united in itself, as being the acts and the work of the Creator. Hence it is that the Sciences, into which our knowledge may be said to be cast, have multiplied bearings one on another, and an internal sympathy, and admit, or rather demand, comparison and adjustment. They complete, correct, balance each other. This consideration, if well-founded, must be taken into account, not only as regards the attainment of truth, which is their common end, but as regards the influence which they exercise upon those whose education consists in the study of them. I have said already, that to give undue prominence to one is to be unjust to another; to neglect or supersede these is to divert those from their proper object. It is to unsettle the boundary lines between science and science, to disturb their action, to destroy the harmony which binds them together. Such a proceeding will have a corresponding effect when introduced into a place of education. There is no science but tells a different tale, when viewed as a portion of a whole, from what it is likely to suggest when taken by itself, without the safeguard, as I may call it, of others.

Let me make use of an illustration. In the combination of colours, very different effects are produced by a difference in their selection and juxtaposition; red, green, and white, change their shades, according to the contrast to which they are submitted. And, in like manner, the drift and meaning of a branch of knowledge varies with the company in which it is introduced to the student. If his reading is confined simply to one subject, however such division of labour may favour the advancement of a particular pursuit, a point into which I do not here enter, certainly it has a tendency to contract his mind. If it is incorporated with others, it depends on those others as to the kind of influence which it exerts upon him. Thus the Classics, which in England are the means of refining the taste, have in France subserved the spread of revolutionary and deistical doctrines. In Metaphysics, again, Butler's Analogy of Religion, which has had so much to do with the conversion to the Catholic faith of members of the University of Oxford, appeared to Pitt and others, who had received a different training, to operate only in the direction of infidelity. And so again, Watson, Bishop of Llandaff, as I think he tells us in the narrative of his life, felt the science of Mathematics to indispose the mind to religious belief, while others see in its investigations the best parallel, and thereby defence, of the Christian Mysteries. In like manner, I suppose, Arcesilas would not have handled logic as Aristotle, nor Aristotle have criticized poets as Plato; yet reasoning and poetry are subject to scientific rules.

It is a great point then to enlarge the range of studies which a University professes, even for the sake of the students; and, though they cannot pursue every subject which is open to them, they will be the gainers by living among those and under those who represent the whole circle. This I conceive to be the advantage of a seat of universal learning, considered as a place of education. An assemblage of learned men, zealous for their own sciences, and rivals of each other, are brought, by familiar intercourse and for the sake of intellectual peace, to adjust together the claims and relations of their respective subjects of investigation. They learn to respect, to consult, to aid each other. Thus is created a pure and clear atmosphere of thought, which the student also breathes, though in his own case he only pursues a few sciences out of the multitude. He profits by an intellectual tradition, which is independent of particular teachers, which guides him in his choice of subjects, and duly interprets for him those which he chooses. He apprehends the great outlines of knowledge, the principles on which it rests, the scale of its parts, its lights and its shades, its great points and its little, as he otherwise cannot apprehend them. Hence it is that his education is called "Liberal." A habit of mind is formed which lasts through life, of which the attributes are, freedom, equitableness, calmness, moderation, and wisdom; or what in a former Discourse I have ventured to call a philosophical habit. This then I would assign as the special fruit of the education furnished at a University, as contrasted with other places of teaching or modes of teaching. This is the main purpose of a University in its treatment of its students.

And now the question is asked me, What is the *use* of it? and my answer will constitute the main subject of the Discourses which are to follow.

2.

Cautious and practical thinkers, I say, will ask of me, what, after all, is the gain of this Philosophy, of which I make such account, and from which I promise so much. Even supposing it to enable us to exercise the degree of trust exactly due to every science respectively, and to estimate precisely the value of every truth which is anywhere to be found, how are we better for this master view of things, which I have been extolling? Does it not reverse the principle of the division of labour? will practical objects be obtained better or worse by its cultivation? to what then does it lead? where does it end? what does it do? how does it profit? what does it promise? Particular sciences are respectively the basis of definite arts, which carry on to results tangible and beneficial the truths which are the subjects of the knowledge attained; what is the Art of this science of sciences? what is the fruit of such a Philosophy? what are we proposing to effect, what inducements do we hold out to the Catholic community, when we set about the enterprise of founding a University?

I am asked what is the end of University Education, and of the Liberal or Philosophical Knowledge which I conceive it to impart: I answer, that what I have already said has been sufficient to show that it has a very tangible, real, and sufficient end, though the end cannot be divided from that knowledge itself. Knowledge is capable of being its own end. Such is the constitution of the human mind, that any kind of knowledge, if it be really such, is its own reward. And if this is true of all knowledge, it is true also of that special Philosophy, which I have made to consist in a comprehensive view of truth in all its branches, of the relations of science to science, of their mutual bearings, and their respective values. What the worth of such an acquirement is, compared with other objects which we seek, – wealth or power or honour or the conveniences and comforts of life, I do not profess here to discuss; but I would maintain, and mean to show, that it is an object, in its own nature so really and undeniably good, as to be the compensation of a great deal of thought in the compassing, and a great deal of trouble in the attaining.

Now, when I say that Knowledge is, not merely a means to something beyond it, or the preliminary of certain arts into which it naturally resolves, but an end sufficient to rest in and to pursue for its own sake, surely I am uttering no paradox, for I am stating what is both intelligible in itself, and has ever been the common judgment of philosophers and the ordinary feeling of mankind. I am saying what at least the public opinion of this day ought to be slow to deny, considering how much we have heard of late years, in opposition to Religion, of entertaining, curious, and various knowledge. I am but saying what whole volumes have been written to illustrate, viz., by a "selection from the records of Philosophy, Literature, and Art, in all ages and countries, of a body of examples, to show how the most unpropitious circumstances have been unable to conquer an ardent desire for the acquisition of knowledge."[24] That further advantages accrue to us and redound to others by its possession, over and above what it is in itself, I am very far indeed from denying; but, independent of these, we are satisfying a direct need of our nature in its very acquisition; and, whereas our nature, unlike that of the inferior creation, does not at once reach its perfection, but depends, in order to it, on a number of external aids and appliances, Knowledge, as one of the principal of these, is valuable for what its very presence in us does for us after the manner of a habit, even though it be turned to no further account, nor subserve any direct end.

3.

Hence it is that Cicero, in enumerating the various heads of mental excellence, lays down the pursuit of Knowledge for its own sake, as the first of them. "This pertains most of all to human nature," he says, "for we are all of us drawn to the pursuit of Knowledge; in which to excel we consider excellent, whereas to mistake, to err, to be ignorant, to be deceived, is both an evil and a disgrace."[25] And he considers Knowledge the very first object to which we are attracted, after the supply of our physical wants. After the calls and duties of our animal existence, as they may be termed, as regards ourselves, our family, and our neighbours, follows, he tells us, "the search after truth. Accordingly, as soon as we escape from the pressure of necessary cares, forthwith we desire to see, to hear, and to learn; and consider the knowledge of what is hidden or is wonderful a condition of our happiness."

This passage, though it is but one of many similar passages in a multitude of authors, I take for the very reason that it is so familiarly known to us; and I wish you to observe, Gentlemen, how distinctly it separates the pursuit of Knowledge from those ulterior objects to which certainly it can be made to conduce, and which are, I suppose, solely contemplated by the persons who would ask of me the use of a University or Liberal Education. So far from dreaming of the cultivation of Knowledge directly and mainly in order to our physical comfort and enjoyment, for the sake of life and person, of health, of the conjugal and family union, of the social tie and civil security, the great Orator implies, that it is only after our physical and political needs are supplied, and when we are "free from necessary duties and cares," that we are in a condition for "desiring to see, to hear, and to learn." Nor does he contemplate in the least degree the reflex or subsequent action of Knowledge, when acquired, upon those material goods which we set out by securing before we seek it; on the contrary, he expressly denies its bearing upon social life altogether, strange as such a procedure is to those who live after the rise of the Baconian philosophy, and he cautions us against such a cultivation of it as will interfere with our duties to our fellow-creatures. "All these methods," he says, "are engaged in the investigation of truth; by the pursuit of which to be carried off from public occupations is a transgression of duty. For the praise of virtue lies altogether in action; yet intermissions often occur, and then we recur to such pursuits; not to say that the incessant activity of the mind is vigorous enough to carry us on in the pursuit of knowledge, even without any exertion of our own." The idea of benefiting society by means of "the pursuit of science and knowledge" did not enter at all into the motives which he would assign for their cultivation.

This was the ground of the opposition which the elder Cato made to the introduction of Greek Philosophy among his countrymen, when Carneades and his companions, on occasion of their embassy, were charming the Roman youth with their eloquent expositions of it. The fit representative of a practical people, Cato estimated every thing by what it produced; whereas the Pursuit of Knowledge promised nothing beyond Knowledge itself. He despised that refinement or enlargement of mind of which he had no experience.

4.

Things, which can bear to be cut off from every thing else and yet persist in living, must have life in themselves; pursuits, which issue in nothing, and still maintain their ground for ages, which are regarded as admirable, though they have not as yet proved themselves to be useful, must have their sufficient end in themselves, whatever it turn out to be. And we are brought to the same conclusion by considering the force of the epithet, by which the knowledge under consideration is popularly designated. It is common to speak of "*liberal* knowledge," of the "*liberal* arts and studies," and of a "*liberal* education," as the especial characteristic or property of a University and of a gentleman; what is really meant by the word? Now, first, in its grammatical sense it is opposed to *servile;* and by "servile work" is understood, as our catechisms inform us, bodily labour, mechanical employment, and the like, in which the mind has little or no part. Parallel to such servile works are those arts, if they deserve the name, of which the poet speaks,[26] which owe their origin and their method to hazard, not to skill; as, for instance, the practice and operations of an empiric. As far as this contrast may be considered as a guide into the meaning of the word, liberal education and liberal pursuits are exercises of mind, of reason, of reflection.

But we want something more for its explanation, for there are bodily exercises which are liberal, and mental exercises which are not so. For instance, in ancient times the practitioners in medicine were commonly slaves; yet it was an art as intellectual in its nature, in spite of the pretence, fraud, and quackery with which it might then, as now, be debased, as it was heavenly in its aim. And so in like manner, we contrast a liberal education with a commercial education or a professional; yet no one can deny that commerce and the professions afford scope for the highest and most diversified powers of mind. There is then a great variety of intellectual exercises, which are not technically called "liberal;" on the other hand, I say, there are exercises of the body which do receive that appellation. Such, for instance, was the palæstra, in ancient times; such the Olympic games, in which strength and dexterity of body as well as of mind gained the prize. In Xenophon we read of the young Persian nobility being taught to ride on horseback and to speak the truth; both being among the accomplishments of a gentleman. War, too, however rough a profession, has ever been accounted liberal, unless in cases when it becomes heroic, which would introduce us to another subject.

Now comparing these instances together, we shall have no difficulty in determining the principle of this apparent variation in the application of the term which I am examining. Manly games, or games of skill, or military prowess, though bodily, are, it seems, accounted liberal; on the other hand, what is merely professional, though highly intellectual, nay, though liberal in comparison of trade and manual labour, is not simply called liberal, and mercantile occupations are not liberal at all. Why this distinction? because that alone is liberal knowledge, which stands on its own pretensions, which is independent of sequel, expects no complement, refuses to be *informed* (as it is called) by any end, or absorbed into any art, in order duly to present itself to our contemplation. The most ordinary pursuits have this specific character, if they are self-sufficient and complete; the highest lose it, when they minister to something beyond them. It is absurd to balance, in point of worth and importance, a treatise on reducing fractures with a game of cricket or a fox-chase; yet of the two the bodily exercise has that quality which we call "liberal," and the intellectual has it not. And so of the learned professions altogether, considered merely as professions; although one of them be the most popularly beneficial, and another the most politically important, and the third the most intimately divine of all human pursuits, yet the very greatness of their end, the health of the body, or of the commonwealth, or of the soul, diminishes, not increases, their claim to the appellation "liberal," and that still more, if they are cut down to the strict exigencies of that end. If, for instance, Theology, instead of being cultivated as a contemplation, be limited to the purposes of the pulpit or be represented by the catechism, it loses, – not its usefulness, not its divine character, not its meritoriousness (rather it gains a claim upon these titles by such charitable condescension), – but it does lose the particular attribute which I am illustrating; just as a face worn by tears and fasting loses its beauty, or a labourer's hand loses its delicateness; – for Theology thus exercised is not simple knowledge, but rather is an art or a business making use of Theology. And thus it appears that even what is supernatural need not be liberal, nor need a hero be a gentleman, for the plain reason that one idea is not another idea. And in like manner the Baconian Philosophy, by using its physical sciences in the service of man, does thereby transfer them from the order of Liberal Pursuits to, I do not say the inferior, but the distinct class of the Useful. And, to take a different instance, hence again, as is evident, whenever personal gain is the motive, still more distinctive an effect has it upon the character of a given pursuit; thus racing, which was a liberal exercise in Greece, forfeits its rank in times like these, so far as it is made the occasion of gambling.

All that I have been now saying is summed up in a few characteristic words of the great Philosopher. "Of possessions," he says, "those rather are useful, which bear fruit; those *liberal, which tend to enjoyment.* By fruitful, I mean, which yield revenue; by enjoyable, where *nothing accrues of consequence beyond the using.*"[27]

5.

Do not suppose, that in thus appealing to the ancients, I am throwing back the world two thousand years, and fettering Philosophy with the reasonings of paganism. While the world lasts, will Aristotle's doctrine on these matters last, for he is the oracle of nature and of truth. While we are men, we cannot help, to a great extent, being Aristotelians, for the great Master does but analyze the thoughts, feelings, views, and opinions of human kind. He has told us the meaning of our own words and ideas, before we were born.

In many subject-matters, to think correctly, is to think like Aristotle; and we are his disciples whether we will or no, though we may not know it. Now, as to the particular instance before us, the word "liberal" as applied to Knowledge and Education, expresses a specific idea, which ever has been, and ever will be, while the nature of man is the same, just as the idea of the Beautiful is specific, or of the Sublime, or of the Ridiculous, or of the Sordid. It is in the world now, it was in the world then; and, as in the case of the dogmas of faith, it is illustrated by a continuous historical tradition, and never was out of the world, from the time it came into it. There have indeed been differences of opinion from time to time, as to what pursuits and what arts came under that idea, but such differences are but an additional evidence of its reality. That idea must have a substance in it, which has maintained its ground amid these conflicts and changes, which has ever served as a standard to measure things withal, which has passed from mind to mind unchanged, when there was so much to colour, so much to influence any notion or thought whatever, which was not founded in our very nature. Were it a mere generalization, it would have varied with the subjects from which it was generalized; but though its subjects vary with the age, it varies not itself. The palæstra may seem a liberal exercise to Lycurgus, and illiberal to Seneca; coach-driving and prize-fighting may be recognized in Elis, and be condemned in England; music may be despicable in the eyes of certain moderns, and be in the highest place with Aristotle and Plato, – (and the case is the same in the particular application of the idea of Beauty, or of Goodness, or of Moral Virtue, there is a difference of tastes, a difference of judgments) – still these variations imply, instead of discrediting, the archetypal idea, which is but a previous hypothesis or condition, by means of which issue is joined between contending opinions, and without which there would be nothing to dispute about.

I consider, then, that I am chargeable with no paradox, when I speak of a Knowledge which is its own end, when I call it liberal knowledge, or a gentleman's knowledge, when I educate for it, and make it the scope of a University. And still less am I incurring such a charge, when I make this acquisition consist, not in Knowledge in a vague and ordinary sense, but in that Knowledge which I have especially called Philosophy or, in an extended sense of the word, Science; for whatever claims Knowledge has to be considered as a good, these it has in a higher degree when it is viewed not vaguely, not popularly, but precisely and transcendently as Philosophy. Knowledge, I say, is then especially liberal, or sufficient for itself, apart from every external and ulterior object, when and so far as it is philosophical, and this I proceed to show.

6.

Now bear with me, Gentlemen, if what I am about to say, has at first sight a fanciful appearance. Philosopy, then, or Science, is related Knowledge in this way: – Knowledge is called by the name of Science or Philosophy, when it is acted upon, informed, or if I may use a strong figure, impregnated by Reason. Reason is the principle of that intrinsic fecundity of Knowledge, which, to those who possess it, is its especial value, and which dispenses with the necessity of their looking abroad for any end to rest upon external to itself. Knowledge, indeed, when thus exalted into a scientific form, is also power; not only is it excellent in itself, but whatever such excellence may be, it is something more, it has a result beyond itself. Doubtless; but that is a further consideration, with which I am not concerned. I only say that, prior to its being a power, it is a good; that it is, not only an instrument, but an end. I know well it may resolve itself into an art, and terminate in a mechanical process, and in tangible fruit; but it also may fall back upon that Reason which informs it, and resolve itself into Philosophy. In one case it is called Useful Knowledge, in the other Liberal. The same person may culti-vate it in both ways at once; but this again is a matter foreign to my subject; here I do but say that there are two ways of using Knowledge, and in matter of fact those who use it in one way are not likely to use it in the other, or at least in a very limited measure. You see, then, here are two methods of Education; the end of the one is to be philosophical, of the other to be mechanical; the one rises towards general ideas, the other is exhausted upon what is particular and external. Let me not be thought to deny the necessity, or to decry the benefit, of such attention to what is particular and practical, as belongs to the useful or mechanical arts; life could not go on without them; we owe our daily welfare to them; their exercise is the duty of the many, and we owe to the many a debt of gratitude for fulfilling that duty. I only say that Knowledge, in proportion as it tends more and more to be particular, ceases to be Knowledge. It is a question whether Knowledge can in any proper sense be predicated of the brute creation; without pretending to metaphysical exactness of phraseology, which would be unsuitable to an occasion like this, I say, it seems to me improper to call that passive sensa-tion, or perception of things, which brutes seem to possess, by the name of Knowledge. When I speak of Knowledge, I mean something intellectual, something which grasps what it perceives through the senses; something which takes a view of things; which sees more than the senses convey; which reasons upon what it sees, and while it sees; which invests it with an idea. It expresses itself, not in a mere enunciation, but by an enthymeme: it is of the nature of science from the first, and in this consists its dignity. The principle of real dignity in Knowledge, its worth, its desirableness, considered irrespectively of its results, is this germ within it of a scientific or a philosophical process. This is how it comes to be an end in itself; this is why it admits of being called Liberal. Not to know the relative disposition of things is the state of slaves or children; to have mapped out the Universe is the boast, or at least the ambition, of Philosophy.

Moreover, such knowledge is not a mere extrinsic or accidental advantage, which is ours to-day and another's to-morrow, which may be got up from a book, and easily forgotten again, which we can command or communicate at our pleasure, which we can borrow for the occasion, carry about in our hand, and take into the market; it is an acquired illumination, it is a habit, a personal possession, and an inward endowment. And this is the reason, why it is more correct, as well as more usual, to speak of a University as a place of education, than of instruction, though, when knowledge is concerned, instruction would at first sight have seemed the more appropriate word. We are instructed, for instance, in manual exercises, in the fine and useful arts, in trades, and in ways of business; for these are methods, which have little or no effect upon the mind itself, are contained in rules committed to memory, to tradition, or to use, and bear upon an end external to themselves. But education is a higher word; it implies an action upon our mental nature, and the formation of a character; it is something individual and permanent, and is commonly spoken of in connexion with religion and virtue. When, then, we speak of the communication of Knowledge as being Education, we thereby really imply that that Knowledge is a state or condition of mind; and since cultivation of mind is surely worth seeking for its own sake, we are thus brought once more to the conclusion, which the word "Liberal" and the word "Philosophy" have already suggested, that there is a Knowledge, which is desirable, though nothing come of it, as being of itself a treasure, and a sufficient remuneration of years of labour.

7.

This, then, is the answer which I am prepared to give to the question with which I opened this Discourse. Before going on to speak of the object of the Church in taking up Philosophy, and the uses to which she puts it, I am prepared to maintain that Philosophy is its own end, and, as I conceive, I have now begun the proof of it. I am prepared to maintain that there is a knowledge worth possessing for what it is, and not merely for what it does; and what minutes remain to me to-day I shall devote to the removal of some portion of the indistinctness and confusion with which the subject may in some minds be surrounded.

It may be objected then, that, when we profess to seek Knowledge for some end or other beyond itself, whatever it be, we speak intelligibly; but that, whatever men may have said, however obstinately the idea may have kept its ground from age to age, still it is simply unmeaning to say that we seek Knowledge for its own sake, and for nothing else; for that it ever leads to something beyond itself, which therefore is its end, and the cause why it is desirable; – moreover, that this end is twofold, either of this world or of the next; that all knowledge is cultivated either for secular objects or for eternal; that if it is directed to secular objects, it is called Useful Knowledge, if to eternal, Religious or Christian Knowledge; – in consequence, that if, as I have allowed, this Liberal Knowledge does not benefit the body or estate, it ought to benefit the soul; but if the fact be really so, that it is neither a physical or a secular good on the one hand, nor a moral good on the other, it cannot be a good at all, and is not worth the trouble which is necessary for its acquisition.

And then I may be reminded that the professors of this Liberal or Philosophical Knowledge have themselves, in every age, recognized this exposition of the matter, and have submitted to the issue in which it terminates; for they have ever been attempting to make men virtuous; or, if not, at least have assumed that refinement of mind was virtue, and that they themselves were the virtuous portion of mankind. This they have professed on the one hand; and on the other, they have utterly failed in their professions, so as ever to make themselves a proverb among men, and a laughing-stock both to the grave and the dissipated portion of mankind, in consequence of them. Thus they have furnished against themselves both the ground and the means of their own exposure, without any trouble at all to any one else. In a word, from the time that Athens was the University of the world, what has Philosophy taught men, but to promise without practising, and to aspire without attaining? What has the deep and lofty thought of its disciples ended in but eloquent words? Nay, what has its teaching ever meditated, when it was boldest in its remedies for human ill, beyond charming us to sleep by its lessons, that we might feel nothing at all? like some melodious air, or rather like those strong and transporting perfumes, which at first spread their sweetness over every thing they touch, but in a little while do but offend in proportion as they once pleased us. Did Philosophy support Cicero under the disfavour of the fickle populace, or nerve Seneca to oppose an imperial tyrant? It abandoned Brutus, as he sorrowfully confessed, in his greatest need, and it forced Cato, as his panegyrist strangely boasts, into the false position of defying heaven. How few can be counted among its professors, who, like Polemo, were thereby converted from a profligate course, or like Anaxagoras, thought the world well lost in exchange for its possession? The philosopher in Rasselas taught a superhuman doctrine, and then succumbed without an effort to a trial of human affection.

"He discoursed," we are told, "with great energy on the government of the passions. His look was venerable, his action graceful, his pronunciation clear, and his diction elegant. He showed, with great strength of sentiment and variety of illustration, that human nature is degraded and debased, when the lower faculties predominate over the higher. He communicated the various precepts given, from time to time, for the conquest of passion, and displayed the happiness of those who had obtained the important victory, after which man is no longer the slave of fear, nor the fool of hope . . . He enumerated many examples of heroes immoveable by pain or pleasure, who looked with indifference on those modes or accidents to which the vulgar give the names of good and evil."

Rasselas in a few days found the philosopher in a room half darkened, with his eyes misty, and his face pale. "Sir," said he, "you have come at a time when all human friendship is useless; what I suffer cannot be remedied, what I have lost cannot be supplied. My daughter, my only daughter, from whose tenderness I expected all the comforts of my age, died last night of a fever." "Sir," said the prince, "mortality is an event by which a wise man can never be surprised; we know that death is always near, and it should therefore always be expected." "Young man," answered the philosopher, "you speak like one who has never felt the pangs of separation." "Have you, then, forgot the precept," said Rasselas, "which you so powerfully enforced? . . . consider that external things are naturally variable, but truth and reason are always the same." "What comfort," said the mourner, "can truth and reason afford me? Of what effect are they now, but to tell me that my daughter will not be restored?"

8.

Better, far better, to make no professions, you will say, than to cheat others with what we are not, and to scandalize them with what we are. The sensualist, or the man of the world, at any rate is not the victim of fine words, but pursues a reality and gains it. The Philosophy of Utility, you will say, Gentlemen, has at least done its work; and I grant it, – it aimed low, but it has fulfilled its aim. If that man of great intellect who has been its Prophet in the conduct of life played false to his own professions, he was not bound by his philosophy to be true to his friend or faithful in his trust. Moral virtue was not the line in which he undertook to instruct men; and though, as the poet calls him, he were the "meanest" of mankind, he was so in what may be called his private capacity and without any prejudice to the theory of induction. He had a right to be so, if he chose, for any thing that the Idols of the den or the theatre had to say to the contrary. His mission was the increase of physical enjoyment and social comfort;[28] and most wonderfully, most awfully has he fulfilled his conception and his design. Almost day by day have we fresh and fresh shoots, and buds, and blossoms, which are to ripen into fruit, on that magical tree of Knowledge which he planted, and to which none of us perhaps, except the very poor, but owes, if not his present life, at least his daily food, his health, and general well-being. He was the divinely provided minister of temporal benefits to all of us so great, that, whatever I am forced to think of him as a man, I have not the heart, from mere gratitude, to speak of him severely. And, in spite of the tendencies of his philosophy, which are, as we see at this day, to depreciate, or to trample on Theology, he has himself, in his writings, gone out of his way, as if with a prophetic misgiving of those tendencies, to insist on it as the instrument of that beneficent Father, who, when He came on earth in visible form, took on Him first and most prominently the office of assuaging the bodily wounds of human nature.[29] And truly, like the old mediciner in the tale, "he sat diligently at his work, and hummed, with cheerful countenance, a pious song;" and then in turn "went out singing into the meadows so gaily, that those who had seen him from afar might well have thought it was a youth gathering flowers for his beloved, instead of an old physician gathering healing herbs in the morning dew."[30]

Alas, that men, in the action of life or in their heart of hearts, are not what they seem to be in their moments of excitement, or in their trances or intoxications of genius, – so good, so noble, so serene! Alas, that Bacon too in his own way should after all be but the fellow of those heathen philosophers who in their disadvantages had some excuse for their inconsistency, and who surprise us rather in what they did say than in what they did not do! Alas, that he too, like Socrates or Seneca, must be stripped of his holy-day coat, which looks so fair, and should be but a mockery amid his most majestic gravity of phrase; and, for all his vast abilities, should, in the littleness of his own moral being, but typify the intellectual narrowness of his school! However, granting all this, heroism after all was not his philosophy: – I cannot deny he has abundantly achieved what he proposed. His is simply a Method whereby bodily discomforts and temporal wants are to be most effectually removed from the greatest number; and already, before it has shown any signs of exhaustion, the gifts of nature, in their most artificial shapes and luxurious profusion and diversity, from all quarters of the earth, are, it is undeniable, by its means brought even to our doors, and we rejoice in them.

9.

Useful Knowledge then, I grant, has done its work; and Liberal Knowledge as certainly has not done its work; – that is, supposing, as the objectors assume, its direct end, like Religious Knowledge, is to make men better; but this I will not for an instant allow, and, unless I allow it, those objectors have said nothing to the purpose. I admit, rather I maintain, what they have been urging, for I consider Knowledge to have its end in itself. For all its friends, or its enemies, may say, I insist upon it, that it is as real a mistake to burden it with virtue or religion as with the mechanical arts. Its direct business is not to steel the soul against temptation or to console it in affliction, any more than to set the loom in motion, or to direct the steam carriage; be it ever so much the means or the condition of both material and moral advancement, still, taken by and in itself, it as little mends our hearts as it improves our temporal circumstances. And if its eulogists claim for it such a power, they commit the very same kind of encroachment on a province not their own as the political economist who should maintain that his science educated him for casuistry or diplomacy. Knowledge is one thing, virtue is another; good sense is not conscience, refinement is not humility, nor is largeness and justness of view faith. Philosophy, however enlightened, however profound, gives no command over the passions, no influential motives, no vivifying principles. Liberal Education makes not the Christian, not the Catholic, but the gentleman. It is well to be a gentleman, it is well to have a cultivated intellect, a delicate taste, a candid, equitable, dispassionate mind, a noble and courteous bearing in the conduct of life; – these are the connatural qualities of a large knowledge; they are the objects of a University; I am advocating, I shall illustrate and insist upon them; but still, I repeat, they are no guarantee for sanctity or even for conscientiousness, they may attach to the man of the world, to the profligate, to the heartless, – pleasant, alas, and attractive as he shows when decked out in them. Taken by themselves, they do but seem to be what they are not; they look like virtue at a distance, but they are detected by close observers, and on the long run; and hence it is that they are popularly accused of pretence and hypocrisy, not, I repeat, from their own fault, but because their professors and their admirers persist in taking them for what they are not, and are officious in arrogating for them a praise to which they have no claim. Quarry the granite rock with razors, or moor the vessel with a thread of silk; then may you hope with such keen and delicate instruments as human knowledge and human reason to contend against those giants, the passion and the pride of man.

Surely we are not driven to theories of this kind, in order to vindicate the value and dignity of Liberal Knowledge. Surely the real grounds on which its pretensions rest are not so very subtle or abstruse, so very strange or improbable. Surely it is very intelligible to say, and that is what I say here, that Liberal Education, viewed in itself, is simply the cultivation of the intellect, as such, and its object is nothing more or less than intellectual excellence. Every thing has its own perfection, be it higher or lower in the scale of things; and the perfection of one is not the perfection of another. Things animate, inanimate, visible, invisible, all are good in their kind, and have a *best* of themselves, which is an object of pursuit. Why do you take such pains with your garden or your park? You see to your walks and turf and shrubberies; to your trees and drives; not as if you meant to make an orchard of the one, or corn or pasture land of the other, but because there is a special beauty in all that is goodly in wood, water, plain, and slope, brought all together by art into one shape, and grouped into one whole. Your cities are beautiful, your palaces, your public buildings, your territorial mansions, your churches; and their beauty leads to nothing beyond itself. There is a physical beauty and a moral: there is a beauty of person, there is a beauty of our moral being, which is natural virtue; and in like manner there is a beauty, there is a perfection, of the intellect. There is an ideal perfection in these various subject-matters, towards which individual instances are seen to rise, and which are the standards for all instances whatever. The Greek divinities and demigods, as the statuary has moulded them, with their symmetry of figure, and their high forehead and their regular features, are the perfection of physical beauty. The heroes, of whom history tells, Alexander, or Cæsar, or Scipio, or Saladin, are the representatives of that magnanimity or self-mastery which is the greatness of human nature. Christianity too has its heroes, and in the supernatural order, and we call them Saints. The artist puts before him beauty of feature and form; the poet, beauty of mind; the preacher, the beauty of grace: then intellect too, I repeat, has its beauty, and it has those who aim at it. To open the mind, to correct it, to refine it, to enable it to know, and to digest, master, rule, and use its knowledge, to give it power over its own faculties, application, flexibility, method, critical exactness, sagacity, resource, address, eloquent expression, is an object as intelligible (for here we are inquiring, not what the object of a Liberal

Education is worth, nor what use the Church makes of it, but what it is in itself), I say, an object as intelligible as the cultivation of virtue, while, at the same time, it is absolutely distinct from it.

10.

This indeed is but a temporal object, and a transitory possession; but so are other things in themselves which we make much of and pursue. The moralist will tell us that man, in all his functions, is but a flower which blossoms and fades, except so far as a higher principle breathes upon him, and makes him and what he is immortal. Body and mind are carried on into an eternal state of being by the gifts of Divine Munificence; but at first they do but fail in a failing world; and if the powers of intellect decay, the powers of the body have decayed before them, and, as an Hospital or an Almshouse, though its end be ephemeral, may be sanctified to the service of religion, so surely may a University, even were it nothing more than I have as yet described it. We attain to heaven by using this world well, though it is to pass away; we perfect our nature, not by undoing it, but by adding to it what is more than nature, and directing it towards aims higher than its own.

DISCOURSE VI

KNOWLEDGE VIEWED IN RELATION
TO LEARNING.

1.

It were well if the English, like the Greek language, possessed some definite word to express, simply and generally, intellectual proficiency or perfection, such as "health," as used with reference to the animal frame, and "virtue," with reference to our moral nature. I am not able to find such a term; – talent, ability, genius belong distinctly to the raw material, which is the subject-matter, not to that excellence which is the result of exercise and training. When we turn, indeed, to the particular kinds of intellectual perfection, words are forthcoming for our purpose, as, for instance, judgment, taste, and skill; yet even these belong, for the most part, to powers or habits bearing upon practice or upon art, and not to any perfect condition of the intellect, considered in itself. Wisdom, again, is certainly a more comprehensive word than any other, but it has a direct relation to conduct, and to human life. Knowledge, indeed, and Science express purely intellectual ideas, but still not a state or quality of the intellect; for knowledge, in its ordinary sense, is but one of its circumstances, denoting a possession or a habit; and science has been appropriated to the subject-matter of the intellect, instead of belonging in English, as it ought to do, to the intellect itself. The consequence is that, on an occasion like this, many words are necessary, in order, first, to bring out and convey what surely is no difficult idea in itself, – that of the cultivation of the intellect as an end; next, in order to recommend what surely is no unreasonable object; and lastly, to describe and make the mind realize the particular perfection in which that object consists. Every one knows practically what are the constituents of health or of virtue; and every one recognizes health and virtue as ends to be pursued; it is otherwise with intellectual excellence, and this must be my excuse, if I seem to any one to be bestowing a good deal of labour on a preliminary matter.

In default of a recognized term, I have called the perfection or virtue of the intellect by the name of philosophy, philosophical knowledge, enlargement of mind, or illumination; terms which are not uncommonly given to it by writers of this day: but, whatever name we bestow on it, it is, I believe, as a matter of history, the business of a University to make this intellectual culture its direct scope, or to employ itself in the education of the intellect, – just as the work of a Hospital lies in healing the sick or wounded, of a Riding or Fencing School, or of a Gymnasium, in exercising the limbs, of an Almshouse, in aiding and solacing the old, of an Orphanage, in protecting innocence, of a Penitentiary, in restoring the guilty. I say, a University, taken in its bare idea, and before we view it as an instrument of the Church, has this object and this mission; it contemplates neither moral impression nor mechanical production; it professes to exercise the mind neither in art nor in duty; its function is intellectual culture; here it may leave its scholars, and it has done its work when it has done as much as this. It educates the intellect to reason well in all matters, to reach out towards truth, and to grasp it.

2.

This, I said in my foregoing Discourse, was the object of a University, viewed in itself, and apart from the Catholic Church, or from the State, or from any other power which may use it; and I illustrated this in various ways. I said that the intellect must have an excellence of its own, for there was nothing which had not its specific good; that the word "educate" would not be used of intellectual culture, as it is used, had not the intellect had an end of its own; that, had it not such an end, there would be no meaning in calling certain intellectual exercises "liberal," in contrast with "useful," as is commonly done; that the very notion of a philosophical temper implied it, for it threw us back upon research and system as ends in themselves, distinct from effects and works of any kind; that a philosophical scheme of knowledge, or system of sciences, could not, from the nature of the case, issue in any one definite art or pursuit, as its end; and that, on the other hand, the discovery and contemplation of truth, to which research and systematizing led, were surely sufficient ends, though nothing beyond them were added, and that they had ever been accounted sufficient by mankind.

Here then I take up the subject; and, having determined that the cultivation of the intellect is an end distinct and sufficient in itself, and that, so far as words go it is an enlargement or illumination, I proceed to inquire what this mental breadth, or power, or light, or philosophy consists in. A Hospital heals a broken limb or cures a fever: what does an Institution effect, which professes the health, not of the body, not of the soul, but of the intellect? What is this good, which in former times, as well as our own, has been found worth the notice, the appropriation, of the Catholic Church?

I have then to investigate, in the Discourses which follow, those qualities and characteristics of the intellect in which its cultivation issues or rather consists; and, with a view of assisting myself in this undertaking, I shall recur to certain questions which have already been touched upon. These questions are three: viz., the relation of intellectual culture, first, to *mere* knowledge; secondly, to *professional* knowledge; and thirdly, to *religious* knowledge. In other words, are *acquirements* and *attainments* the scope of a University Education? or *expertness in particular arts and pursuits?* or *moral and religious proficiency?* or something besides these three? These questions I shall examine in succession, with the purpose I have mentioned; and I hope to be excused, if, in this anxious undertaking, I am led to repeat what, either in these Discourses or elsewhere, I have already put upon paper. And first, of *Mere Knowledge,* or Learning, and its connexion with intellectual illumination or Philosophy.

3.

I suppose the *primâ-facie* view which the public at large would take of a University, considering it as a place of Education, is nothing more or less than a place for acquiring a great deal of knowledge on a great many subjects. Memory is one of the first developed of the mental faculties; a boy's business when he goes to school is to learn, that is, to store up things in his memory. For some years his intellect is little more than an instrument for taking in facts, or a receptacle for storing them; he welcomes them as fast as they come to him; he lives on what is without; he has his eyes ever about him; he has a lively susceptibility of impressions; he imbibes information of every kind; and little does he make his own in a true sense of the word, living rather upon his neighbours all around him. He has opinions, religious, political, and literary, and, for a boy, is very positive in them and sure about them; but he gets them from his schoolfellows, or his masters, or his parents, as the case may be. Such as he is in his other relations, such also is he in his school exercises; his mind is observant, sharp, ready, retentive; he is almost passive in the acquisition of knowledge. I say this in no disparagement of the idea of a clever boy. Geography, chronology, history, language, natural history, he heaps up the matter of these studies as treasures for a future day. It is the seven years of plenty with him: he gathers in by handfuls, like the Egyptians, without counting; and though, as time goes on, there is exercise for his argumentative powers in the Elements of Mathematics, and for his taste in the Poets and Orators, still, while at school, or at least, till quite the last years of his time, he acquires, and little more; and when he is leaving for the University, he is mainly the creature of foreign influences and circumstances, and made up of accidents, homogeneous or not, as the case may be. Moreover, the moral habits, which are a boy's praise, encourage and assist this result; that is, diligence, assiduity, regularity, despatch, persevering application; for these are the direct conditions of acquisition, and naturally lead to it. Acquirements, again, are emphatically producible, and at a moment; they are a something to show, both for master and scholar; an audience, even though ignorant themselves of the subjects of an examination, can comprehend when questions are answered and when they are not. Here again is a reason why mental culture is in the minds of men identified with the acquisition of knowledge.

The same notion possesses the public mind, when it passes on from the thought of a school to that of a University: and with the best of reasons so far as this, that there is no true culture without acquirements, and that philosophy presupposes knowledge. It requires a great deal of reading, or a wide range of information, to warrant us in putting forth our opinions on any serious subject; and without such learning the most original mind may be able indeed to dazzle, to amuse, to refute, to perplex, but not to come to any useful result or any trustworthy conclusion. There are indeed persons who profess a different view of the matter, and even act upon it. Every now and then you will find a person of vigorous or fertile mind, who relies upon his own resources, despises all former authors, and gives the world, with the utmost fearlessness, his views upon religion, or history, or any other popular subject. And his works may sell for a while; he may get a name in his day; but this will be all. His readers are sure to find on the long run that his doctrines are mere theories, and not the expression of facts, that they are chaff instead of bread, and then his popularity drops as suddenly as it rose.

Knowledge then is the indispensable condition of expansion of mind, and the instrument of attaining to it; this cannot be denied, it is ever to be insisted on; I begin with it as a first principle; however, the very truth of it carries men too far, and confirms to them the notion that it is the whole of the matter. A narrow mind is thought to be that which contains little knowledge; and an enlarged mind, that which holds a great deal; and what seems to put the matter beyond dispute is, the fact of the great number of studies which are pursued in a University, by its very profession. Lectures are given on every kind of subject; examinations are held; prizes awarded. There are moral, metaphysical, physical Professors; Professors of languages, of history, of mathematics, of experimental science. Lists of questions are published, wonderful for their range and depth, variety and difficulty; treatises are written, which carry upon their very face the evidence of extensive reading or multifarious information; what then is wanting for mental culture to a person of large reading and scientific attainments? what is grasp of mind but acquirement? where shall philosophical repose be found, but in the consciousness and enjoyment of large intellectual possessions?

And yet this notion is, I conceive, a mistake, and my present business is to show that it is one, and that the end of a Liberal Education is not mere knowledge, or knowledge considered in its *matter;* and I shall best attain my object, by actually setting down some cases, which will be generally granted to be instances of the process of enlightenment or enlargement of mind, and others which are not, and thus, by the comparison, you will be able to judge for yourselves, Gentlemen, whether Knowledge, that is, acquirement, is after all the real principle of the enlargement, or whether that principle is not rather something beyond it.

4.

For instance,[31] let a person, whose experience has hitherto been confined to the more calm and unpretending scenery of these islands, whether here or in England, go for the first time into parts where physical nature puts on her wilder and more awful forms, whether at home or abroad, as into mountainous districts; or let one, who has ever lived in a quiet village, go for the first time to a great metropolis, – then I suppose he will have a sensation which perhaps he never had before. He has a feeling not in addition or increase of former feelings, but of something different in its nature. He will perhaps be borne forward, and find for a time that he has lost his bearings. He has made a certain progress, and he has a consciousness of mental enlargement; he does not stand where he did, he has a new centre, and a range of thoughts to which he was before a stranger.

Again, the view of the heavens which the telescope opens upon us, if allowed to fill and possess the mind, may almost whirl it round and make it dizzy. It brings in a flood of ideas, and is rightly called an intellectual enlargement, whatever is meant by the term.

And so again, the sight of beasts of prey and other foreign animals, their strangeness, the originality (if I may use the term) of their forms and gestures and habits and their variety and independence of each other, throw us out of ourselves into another creation, and as if under another Creator, if I may so express the temptation which may come on the mind. We seem to have new faculties, or a new exercise for our faculties, by this addition to our knowledge; like a prisoner, who, having been accustomed to wear manacles or fetters, suddenly finds his arms and legs free.

Hence Physical Science generally, in all its departments, as bringing before us the exuberant riches and resources, yet the orderly course, of the Universe, elevates and excites the student, and at first, I may say, almost takes away his breath, while in time it exercises a tranquilizing influence upon him.

Again, the study of history is said to enlarge and enlighten the mind, and why? because, as I conceive, it gives it a power of judging of passing events, and of all events, and a conscious superiority over them, which before it did not possess.

And in like manner, what is called seeing the world, entering into active life, going into society, travelling, gaining acquaintance with the various classes of the community, coming into contact with the principles and modes of thought of various parties, interests, and races, their views, aims, habits and manners, their religious creeds and forms of worship, – gaining experience how various yet how alike men are, how low-minded, how bad, how opposed, yet how confident in their opinions; all this exerts a perceptible influence upon the mind, which it is impossible to mistake, be it good or be it bad, and is popularly called its enlargement.

And then again, the first time the mind comes across the arguments and speculations of unbelievers, and feels what a novel light they cast upon what he has hitherto accounted sacred; and still more, if it gives in to them and embraces them, and throws off as so much prejudice what it has hitherto held, and, as if waking from a dream, begins to realize to its imagination that there is now no such thing as law and the transgression of law, that sin is a phantom, and punishment a bugbear, that it is free to sin, free to enjoy the world and the flesh; and still further, when it does enjoy them, and reflects that it may think and hold just what it will, that "the world is all before it where to choose," and what system to build up as its own private persuasion; when this torrent of wilful thoughts rushes over and inundates it, who will deny that the fruit of the tree of knowledge, or what the mind takes for knowledge, has made it one of the gods, with a sense of expansion and elevation, – an intoxication in reality, still, so far as the subjective state of the mind goes, an illumination? Hence the fanaticism of individuals or nations, who suddenly cast off their Maker. Their eyes are opened; and, like the judgment-stricken king in the Tragedy, they see two suns, and a magic universe, out of which they look back upon their former state of faith and innocence with a sort of contempt and indignation, as if they were then but fools, and the dupes of imposture.

On the other hand, Religion has its own enlargement, and an enlargement, not of tumult, but of peace. It is often remarked of uneducated persons, who have hitherto thought little of the unseen world, that, on their turning to God, looking into themselves, regulating their hearts, reforming their conduct, and meditating on death and judgment, heaven and hell, they seem to become, in point of intellect, different beings from what they were. Before, they took things as they came, and thought no more of one thing than another. But now every event has a meaning; they have their own estimate of whatever happens to them; they are mindful of times and seasons, and compare the present with the past; and the world, no longer dull, monotonous, unprofitable, and hopeless, is a various and complicated drama, with parts and an object, and an awful moral.

5.

Now from these instances, to which many more might be added, it is plain, first, that the communication of knowledge certainly is either a condition or the means of that sense of enlargement or enlightenment, of which at this day we hear so much in certain quarters: this cannot be denied; but next, it is equally plain, that such communication is not the whole of the process. The enlargement consists, not merely in the passive reception into the mind of a number of ideas hitherto unknown to it, but in the mind's energetic and simultaneous action upon and towards and among those new ideas, which are rushing in upon it. It is the action of a formative power, reducing to order and meaning the matter of our acquirements; it is a making the objects of our knowledge subjectively our own, or, to use a familiar word, it is a digestion of what we receive, into the substance of our previous state of thought; and without this no enlargement is said to follow. There is no enlargement, unless there be a comparison of ideas one with another, as they come before the mind, and a systematizing of them. We feel our minds to be growing and expanding *then,* when we not only learn, but refer what we learn to what we know already. It is not the mere addition to our knowledge that is the illumination; but the locomotion, the movement onwards, of that mental centre, to which both what we know, and what we are learning, the accumulating mass of our acquirements, gravitates. And therefore a truly great intellect, and recognized to be such by the common opinion of mankind, such as the intellect of Aristotle, or of St. Thomas, or of Newton, or of Goethe, (I purposely take instances within and without the Catholic pale, when I would speak of the intellect as such,) is one which takes a connected view of old and new, past and present, far and near, and which has an insight into the influence of all these one on another; without which there is no whole, and no centre. It possesses the knowledge, not only of things, but also of their mutual and true relations; knowledge, not merely considered as acquirement, but as philosophy.

Accordingly, when this analytical, distributive, harmonizing process is away, the mind experiences no enlargement, and is not reckoned as enlightened or comprehensive, whatever it may add to its knowledge. For instance, a great memory, as I have already said, does not make a philosopher, any more than a dictionary can be called a grammar. There are men who embrace in their minds a vast multitude of ideas, but with little sensibility about their real relations towards each other. These may be antiquarians, annalists, naturalists; they may be learned in the law; they may be versed in statistics; they are most useful in their own place; I should shrink from speaking disrespectfully of them; still, there is nothing in such attainments to guarantee the absence of narrowness of mind. If they are nothing more than well-read men, or men of information, they have not what specially deserves the name of culture of mind, or fulfils the type of Liberal Education.

In like manner, we sometimes fall in with persons who have seen much of the world, and of the men who, in their day, have played a conspicuous part in it, but who generalize nothing, and have no observation, in the true sense of the word. They abound in information in detail, curious and entertaining, about men and things; and, having lived under the influence of no very clear or settled principles, religious or political, they speak of every one and every thing, only as so many phenomena, which are complete in themselves, and lead to nothing, not discussing them, or teaching any truth, or instructing the hearer, but simply talking. No one would say that these persons, well informed as they are, had attained to any great culture of intellect or to philosophy.

The case is the same still more strikingly where the persons in question are beyond dispute men of inferior powers and deficient education. Perhaps they have been much in foreign countries, and they receive, in a passive, otiose, unfruitful way, the various facts which are forced upon them there. Seafaring men, for example, range from one end of the earth to the other; but the multiplicity of external objects, which they have encountered, forms no symmetrical and consistent picture upon their imagination; they see the tapestry of human life, as it were on the wrong side, and it tells no story. They sleep, and they rise up, and they find themselves, now in Europe, now in Asia; they see visions of great cities and wild regions; they are in the marts of commerce, or amid the islands of the South; they gaze on Pompey's Pillar, or on the Andes; and nothing which meets them carries them forward or backward, to any idea beyond itself. Nothing has a drift or relation; nothing has a history or a promise. Every thing stands by itself, and comes and goes in its turn, like the shifting scenes of a show, which leave the spectator where he was. Perhaps you are near such a man on a particular occasion, and expect him to be shocked or perplexed at something which occurs; but one thing is much the same to him as another, or, if he is perplexed, it is as not knowing what to say, whether it is right to admire, or to ridicule, or to disapprove, while conscious that some expression of opinion is expected from him; for in fact he has no standard of judgment at all, and no landmarks to guide him to a conclusion. Such is mere acquisition, and, I repeat, no one would dream of calling it philosophy.

6.

Instances, such as these, confirm, by the contrast, the conclusion I have already drawn from those which preceded them. That only is true enlargement of mind which is the power of viewing many things at once as one whole, of referring them severally to their true place in the universal system, of understanding their respective values, and determining their mutual dependence. Thus is that form of Universal Knowledge, of which I have on a former occasion spoken, set up in the individual intellect, and constitutes its perfection. Possessed of this real illumination, the mind never views any part of the extended subject-matter of Knowledge without recollecting that it is but a part, or without the associations which spring from this recollection. It makes every thing in some sort lead to every thing else; it would communicate the image of the whole to every separate portion, till that whole becomes in imagination like a spirit, every where pervading and penetrating its component parts, and giving them one definite meaning. Just as our bodily organs, when mentioned, recall their function in the body, as the word "creation" suggests the Creator, and "subjects" a sovereign, so, in the mind of the Philosopher, as we are abstractedly conceiving of him, the elements of the physical and moral world, sciences, arts, pursuits, ranks, offices, events, opinions, individualities, are all viewed as one, with correlative functions, and as gradually by successive combinations converging, one and all, to the true centre.

To have even a portion of this illuminative reason and true philosophy is the highest state to which nature can aspire, in the way of intellect; it puts the mind above the influences of chance and necessity, above anxiety, suspense, unsettlement, and superstition, which is the lot of the many. Men, whose minds are possessed with some one object, take exaggerated views of its importance, are feverish in the pursuit of it, make it the measure of things which are utterly foreign to it, and are startled and despond if it happens to fail them. They are ever in alarm or in transport. Those on the other hand who have no object or principle whatever to hold by, lose their way, every step they take. They are thrown out, and do not know what to think or say, at every fresh juncture; they have no view of persons, or occurrences, or facts, which come suddenly upon them, and they hang upon the opinion of others, for want of internal resources. But the intellect, which has been disciplined to the perfection of its powers, which knows, and thinks while it knows, which has learned to leaven the dense mass of facts and events with the elastic force of reason, such an intellect cannot be partial, cannot be exclusive, cannot be impetuous, cannot be at a loss, cannot but be patient, collected, and majestically calm, because it discerns the end in every beginning, the origin in every end, the law in every interruption, the limit in each delay; because it ever knows where it stands, and and how its path lies from one point to another. It is the τετράγωνος of the Peripatetic, and has the "nil admirari" of the Stoic, –

> Felix qui potuit rerum cognoscere causas,
> Atque metus omnes, et inexorabile fatum
> Subjecit pedibus, strepitumque Acherontis avari.[32]

There are men who, when in difficulties, originate at the moment vast ideas or dazzling projects; who, under the influence of excitement, are able to cast a light, almost as if from inspiration, on a subject or course of action which comes before them; who have a sudden presence of mind equal to any emergency, rising with the occasion, and an undaunted magnanimous bearing, and an energy and keenness which is but made intense by opposition. This is genius, this is heroism; it is the exhibition of a natural gift, which no culture can teach, at which no Institution can aim; here, on the contrary, we are concerned, not with mere nature, but with training and teaching. That perfection of the Intellect, which is the result of Education, and its *beau ideal,* to be imparted to individuals in their respective measures, is the clear, calm, accurate vision and comprehension of all things, as far as the finite mind can embrace them, each in its place, and with its own characteristics upon it. It is almost prophetic from its knowledge of history; it is almost heart-searching from its knowledge of human nature; it has almost supernatural charity from its freedom from littleness and prejudice; it has almost the repose of faith, because nothing can startle it; it has almost the beauty and harmony of heavenly contemplation, so intimate is it with the eternal order of things and the music of the spheres.

7·

And now, if I may take for granted that the true and adequate end of intellectual training and of a University is not Learning or Acquirement, but rather, is Thought or Reason exercised upon Knowledge, or what may be called Philosophy, I shall be in a position to explain the various mistakes which at the present day beset the subject of University Education.

I say then, if we would improve the intellect, first of all, we must ascend; we cannot gain real knowledge on a level; we must generalize, we must reduce to method, we must have a grasp of principles, and group and shape our acquisitions by means of them. It matters not whether our field of operation be wide or limited; in every case, to command it, is to mount above it. Who has not felt the irritation of mind and impatience created by a deep, rich country, visited for the first time, with winding lanes, and high hedges, and green steeps, and tangled woods, and every thing smiling indeed, but in a maze? The same feeling comes upon us in a strange city, when we have no map of its streets. Hence you hear of practised travellers, when they first come into a place, mounting some high hill or church tower, by way of reconnoitring its neighbourhood. In like manner, you must be above your knowledge, not under it, or it will oppress you; and the more you have of it, the greater will be the load. The learning of a Salmasius or a Burman, unless you are its master, will be your tyrant. "Imperat aut servit;"[33] if you can wield it with a strong arm, it is a great weapon; otherwise,

> Vis consili expers
> Mole ruit suâ.[34]

You will be overwhelmed, like Tarpeia, by the heavy wealth which you have exacted from tributary generations.

Instances abound; there are authors who are as pointless as they are inexhaustible in their literary resources. They measure knowledge by bulk, as it lies in the rude block, without symmetry, without design. How many commentators are there on the Classics, how many on Holy Scripture, from whom we rise up, wondering at the learning which has passed before us, and wondering why it passed! How many writers are there of Ecclesiastical History, such as Mosheim or Du Pin, who, breaking up their subject into details, destroy its life, and defraud us of the whole by their anxiety about the parts! The Sermons, again, of the English Divines in the seventeenth century, how often are they mere repertories of miscellaneous and officious learning! Of course Catholics also may read without thinking; and in their case, equally as with Protestants, it holds good, that such knowledge is unworthy of the name, knowledge which they have not thought through, and thought out. Such readers are only possessed by their knowledge, not possessed of it; nay, in matter of fact they are often even carried away by it, without any volition of their own. Recollect, the Memory can tyrannize, as well as the Imagination. Derangement, I believe, has been considered as a loss of control over the sequence of ideas. The mind, once set in motion, is henceforth deprived of the power of initiation, and becomes the victim of a train of associations, one thought suggesting another, in the way of cause and effect, as if by a mechanical process, or some physical necessity. No one, who has had experience of men of studious habits, but must recognize the existence of a parallel phenomenon in the case of those who have overstimulated the Memory. In such persons Reason acts almost as feebly and as impotently as in the madman; once fairly started on any subject whatever, they have no power of self-control; they passively endure the succession of impulses which are evolved out of the original exciting cause; they are passed on from one idea to another and go steadily forward, plodding along one line of thought in spite of the amplest concessions of the hearer, or wandering from it in endless digression in spite of his remonstrances. Now, if, as is very certain, no one would envy the madman the glow and originality of his conceptions, why must we extol the cultivation of that intellect, which is the prey, not indeed of barren fancies but of barren facts, of random intrusions from without, though not of morbid imaginations from within? And in thus speaking, I am not denying that a strong and ready memory is in itself a real treasure; I am not disparaging a well-stored mind, though it be nothing besides, provided it be sober, any more than I would despise a bookseller's shop: – it is of great value to others, even when not so to the owner. Nor am I banishing, far from it, the possessors of deep and multifarious learning from my ideal University; they adorn it in the eyes of men; I do but say that they constitute no type of the results at which it aims; that it is no great gain to the intellect to have enlarged the memory at the expense of faculties which are indisputably higher.

8.

Nor indeed am I supposing that there is any great danger, at least in this day, of over-education; the danger is on the other side. I will tell you, Gentlemen, what has been the practical error of the last twenty years, – not to load the memory of the student with a mass of undigested knowledge, but to force upon him so much that he has rejected all. It has been the error of distracting and enfeebling the mind by an unmeaning profusion of subjects; of implying that a smattering in a dozen branches of study is not shallowness, which it really is, but enlargement, which it is not; of considering an acquaintance with the learned names of things and persons, and the possession of clever duodecimos, and attendance on eloquent lecturers, and membership with scientific institutions, and the sight of the experiments of a platform and the specimens of a museum, that all this was not dissipation of mind, but progress. All things now are to be learned at once, not first one thing, then another, not one well, but many badly. Learning is to be without exertion, without attention, without toil; without grounding, without advance, without finishing. There is to be nothing individual in it; and this, forsooth, is the wonder of the age. What the steam engine does with matter, the printing press is to do with mind; it is to act mechanically, and the population is to be passively, almost unconsciously enlightened, by the mere multiplication and dissemination of volumes. Whether it be the school boy, or the school girl, or the youth at college, or the mechanic in the town, or the politician in the senate, all have been the victims in one way or other of this most preposterous and pernicious of delusions. Wise men have lifted up their voices in vain; and at length, lest their own institutions should be outshone and should disappear in the folly of the hour, they have been obliged, as far as they could with a good conscience, to humour a spirit which they could not withstand, and make temporizing concessions at which they could not but inwardly smile.

It must not be supposed that, because I so speak, therefore I have some sort of fear of the education of the people: on the contrary, the more education they have, the better, so that it is really education. Nor am I an enemy to the cheap publication of scientific and literary works, which is now in vogue: on the contrary, I consider it a great advantage, convenience, and gain; that is, to those to whom education has given a capacity for using them. Further, I consider such innocent recreations as science and literature are able to furnish will be a very fit occupation of the thoughts and the leisure of young persons, and may be made the means of keeping them from bad employments and bad companions. Moreover, as to that superficial acquaintance with chemistry, and geology, and astronomy, and political economy, and modern history, and biography, and other branches of knowledge, which periodical literature and occasional lectures and scientific institutions diffuse through the community, I think it a graceful accomplishment, and a suitable, nay, in this day a necessary accomplishment, in the case of educated men. Nor, lastly, am I disparaging or discouraging the thorough acquisition of any one of these studies, or denying that, as far as it goes, such thorough acquisition is a real education of the mind. All I say is, call things by their right names, and do not confuse together ideas which are essentially different. A thorough knowledge of one science and a superficial acquaintance with many, are not the same thing; a smattering of a hundred things or a memory for detail, is not a philosophical or comprehensive view. Recreations are not education; accomplishments are not education. Do not say, the people must be educated, when, after all, you only mean, amused, refreshed, soothed, put into good spirits and good humour, or kept from vicious excesses. I do not say that such amusements, such occupations of mind, are not a great gain; but they are not education. You may as well call drawing and fencing education, as a general knowledge of botany or conchology. Stuffing birds or playing stringed instruments is an elegant pastime, and a resource to the idle, but it is not education; it does not form or cultivate the intellect. Education is a high word; it is the preparation for knowledge, and it is the imparting of knowledge in proportion to that preparation. We require intellectual eyes to know withal, as bodily eyes for sight. We need both objects and organs intellectual; we cannot gain them without setting about it; we cannot gain them in our sleep, or by hap-hazard. The best telescope does not dispense with eyes; the printing press or the lecture room will assist us greatly, but we must be true to ourselves, we must be parties in the work. A University is, according to the usual designation, an Alma Mater, knowing her children one by one, not a foundry, or a mint, or a treadmill.

9.

I protest to you, Gentlemen, that if I had to choose between a so-called University, which dispensed with residence and tutorial superintendence, and gave its degrees to any person who passed an examination in a wide range of subjects, and a University which had no professors or examinations at all, but merely brought a number of young men together for three or four years, and then sent them away as the University of Oxford is said to have done some sixty years since, if I were asked which of these two methods was the better discipline of the intellect, – mind, I do not say which is *morally* the better, for it is plain that compulsory study must be a good and idleness an intolerable mischief, – but if I must determine which of the two courses was the more successful in training, moulding, enlarging the mind, which sent out men the more fitted for their secular duties, which produced better public men, men of the world, men whose names would descend to posterity, I have no hesitation in giving the preference to that University which did nothing, over that which exacted of its members an acquaintance with every science under the sun. And, paradox as this may seem, still if results be the test of systems, the influence of the public schools and colleges of England, in the course of the last century, at least will bear out one side of the contrast as I have drawn it. What would come, on the other hand, of the ideal systems of education which have fascinated the imagination of this age, could they ever take effect, and whether they would not produce a generation frivolous, narrow-minded, and resourceless, intellectually considered, is a fair subject for debate; but so far is certain, that the Universities and scholastic establishments, to which I refer, and which did little more than bring together first boys and then youths in large numbers, these institutions, with miserable deformities on the side of morals, with a hollow profession of Christianity, and a heathen code of ethics, – I say, at least they can boast of a succession of heroes and statesmen, of literary men and philosophers, of men conspicuous for great natural virtues, for habits of business, for knowledge of life, for practical judgment, for cultivated tastes, for accomplishments, who have made England what it is, – able to subdue the earth, able to domineer over Catholics.

How is this to be explained? I suppose as follows: When a multitude of young men, keen, open-hearted, sympathetic, and observant, as young men are, come together and freely mix with each other, they are sure to learn one from another, even if there be no one to teach them; the conversation of all is a series of lectures to each, and they gain for themselves new ideas and views, fresh matter of thought, and distinct principles for judging and acting, day by day. An infant has to learn the meaning of the information which its senses convey to it, and this seems to be its employment. It fancies all that the eye presents to it to be close to it, till it actually learns the contrary, and thus by practice does it ascertain the relations and uses of those first elements of knowledge which are necessary for its animal existence. A parallel teaching is necessary for our social being, and it is secured by a large school or a college; and this effect may be fairly called in its own department an enlargement of mind. It is seeing the world on a small field with little trouble; for the pupils or students come from very different places, and with widely different notions, and there is much to generalize, much to adjust, much to eliminate, there are inter-relations to be defined, and conventional rules to be established, in the process, by which the whole assemblage is moulded together, and gains one tone and one character.

Let it be clearly understood, I repeat it, that I am not taking into account moral or religious considerations; I am but saying that that youthful community will constitute a whole, it will embody a specific idea, it will represent a doctrine, it will administer a code of conduct, and it will furnish principles of thought and action. It will give birth to a living teaching, which in course of time will take the shape of a self-perpetuating tradition, or a *genius loci,* as it is sometimes called; which haunts the home where it has been born, and which imbues and forms, more or less, and one by one, every individual who is successively brought under its shadow. Thus it is that, independent of direct instruction on the part of Superiors, there is a sort of self-education in the academic institutions of Protestant England; a characteristic tone of thought, a recognized standard of judgment is found in them, which, as developed in the individual who is submitted to it, becomes a twofold source of strength to him, both from the distinct stamp it impresses on his mind, and from the bond of union which it creates between him and others, – effects which are shared by the authorities of the place, for they themselves have been educated in it, and at all times are exposed to the influence of its ethical atmosphere. Here then is a real teaching, whatever be its standards and principles, true or false; and it at least tends towards cultivation of the intellect; it at least recognizes that knowledge is something more than a sort of passive reception of scraps and details; it is a something, and it does a something, which never will issue from the most strenuous efforts of a set of teachers, with no mutual sympathies and no intercommunion, of a set of examiners with no opinions which they dare profess, and with no common principles, who are teaching or questioning a set of youths who do not know them, and do not know each other, on a large number of subjects, different in kind, and connected by no wide philosophy, three times a week, or three times a year, or once in three years, in chill lecture-rooms or on a pompous anniversary.

10.

Nay, self-education in any shape, in the most restricted sense, is preferable to a system of teaching which, professing so much, really does so little for the mind. Shut your College gates against the votary of knowledge, throw him back upon the searchings and the efforts of his own mind; he will gain by being spared an entrance into your Babel. Few indeed there are who can dispense with the stimulus and support of instructors, or will do anything at all, if left to themselves. And fewer still (though such great minds are to be found), who will not, from such unassisted attempts, contract a self-reliance and a self-esteem, which are not only moral evils, but serious hindrances to the attainment of truth. And next to none, perhaps, or none, who will not be reminded from time to time of the disadvantage under which they lie, by their imperfect grounding, by the breaks, deficiencies, and irregularities of their knowledge, by the eccentricity of opinion and the confusion of principle which they exhibit. They will be too often ignorant of what every one knows and takes for granted, of that multitude of small truths which fall upon the mind like dust, impalpable and ever accumulating; they may be unable to converse, they may argue perversely, they may pride themselves on their worst paradoxes or their grossest truisms, they may be full of their own mode of viewing things, unwilling to be put out of their way, slow to enter into the minds of others; – but, with these and whatever other liabilities upon their heads, they are likely to have more thought, more mind, more philosophy, more true enlargement, than those earnest but ill-used persons, who are forced to load their minds with a score of subjects against an examination, who have too much on their hands to indulge themselves in thinking or investigation, who devour premiss and conclusion together with indiscriminate greediness, who hold whole sciences on faith, and commit demonstrations to memory, and who too often, as might be expected, when their period of education is passed, throw up all they have learned in disgust, having gained nothing really by their anxious labours, except perhaps the habit of application.

Yet such is the better specimen of the fruit of that ambitious system which has of late years been making way among us: for its result on ordinary minds, and on the common run of students, is less satisfactory still; they leave their place of education simply dissipated and relaxed by the multiplicity of subjects, which they have never really mastered, and so shallow as not even to know their shallowness. How much better, I say, is it for the active and thoughtful intellect, where such is to be found, to eschew the College and the University altogether, than to submit to a drudgery so ignoble, a mockery so contumelious! How much more profitable for the independent mind, after the mere rudiments of education, to range through a library at random, taking down books as they meet him, and pursuing the trains of thought which his mother wit suggests! How much healthier to wander into the fields, and there with the exiled Prince to find "tongues in the trees, books in the running brooks!"[35] How much more genuine an education is that of the poor boy in the Poem[36] – a Poem, whether in conception or in execution, one of the most touching in our language – who, not in the wide world, but ranging day by day around his widowed mother's home, "a dexterous gleaner" in a narrow field, and with only such slender outfit

> "as the village school and books a few
> Supplied,"

contrived from the beach, and the quay, and the fisher's boat, and the inn's fireside, and the tradesman's shop, and the shepherd's walk, and the smuggler's hut, and the mossy moor, and the screaming gulls, and the restless waves, to fashion for himself a philosophy and a poetry of his own!

But in a large subject, I am exceeding my necessary limits. Gentlemen, I must conclude abruptly; and postpone any summing up of my argument, should that be necessary, to another day.

DISCOURSE VII.

KNOWLEDGE VIEWED IN RELATION
TO PROFESSIONAL SKILL.

I.

I have been insisting, in my two preceding Discourses, first, on the cultivation of the intellect, as an end which may reasonably be pursued for its own sake; and next, on the nature of that cultivation, or what that cultivation consists in. Truth of whatever kind is the proper object of the intellect; its cultivation then lies in fitting it to apprehend and contemplate truth. Now the intellect in its present state, with exceptions which need not here be specified, does not discern truth intuitively, or as a whole. We know, not by a direct and simple vision, not at a glance, but, as it were, by piecemeal and accumulation, by a mental process, by going round an object, by the comparison, the combination, the mutual correction, the continual adaptation, of many partial notions, by the employment, concentration, and joint action of many faculties and exercises of mind. Such a union and concert of the intellectual powers, such an enlargement and development, such a comprehensiveness, is necessarily a matter of training. And again, such a training is a matter of rule; it is not mere application, however exemplary, which introduces the mind to truth, nor the reading many books, nor the getting up many subjects, nor the witnessing many experiments, nor the attending many lectures. All this is short of enough; a man may have done it all, yet be lingering in the vestibule of knowledge: – he may not realize what his mouth utters; he may not see with his mental eye what confronts him; he may have no grasp of things as they are; or at least he may have no power at all of advancing one step forward of himself, in consequence of what he has already acquired, no power of discriminating between truth and falsehood, of sifting out the grains of truth from the mass, of arranging things according to their real value, and, if I may use the phrase, of building up ideas. Such a power is the result of a scientific formation of mind; it is an acquired faculty of judgment, of clear-sightedness, of sagacity, of wisdom, of philosophical reach of mind, and of intellectual self-possession and repose, – qualities which do not come of mere acquirement. The bodily eye, the organ for apprehending material objects, is provided by nature; the eye of the mind, of which the object is truth, is the work of discipline and habit.

This process of training, by which the intellect, instead of being formed or sacrificed to some particular or accidental purpose, some specific trade or profession, or study or science, is disciplined for its own sake, for the perception of its own proper object, and for its own highest culture, is called Liberal Education; and though there is no one in whom it is carried as far as is conceivable, or whose intellect would be a pattern of what intellects should be made, yet there is scarcely any one but may gain an idea of what real training is, and at least look towards it, and make its true scope and result, not something else, his standard of excellence; and numbers there are who may submit themselves to it, and secure it to themselves in good measure. And to set forth the right standard, and to train according to it, and to help forward all students towards it according to their various capacities, this I conceive to be the business of a University.

2.

Now this is what some great men are very slow to allow; they insist that Education should be confined to some particular and narrow end, and should issue in some definite work, which can be weighed and measured. They argue as if every thing, as well as every person, had its price; and that where there has been a great outlay, they have a right to expect a return in kind. This they call making Education and Instruction "useful," and "Utility" becomes their watchword. With a fundamental principle of this nature, they very naturally go on to ask, what there is to show for the expense of a University; what is the real worth in the market of the article called "a Liberal Education," on the supposition that it does not teach us definitely how to advance our manufactures, or to improve our lands, or to better our civil economy; or again, if it does not at once make this man a lawyer, that an engineer, and that a surgeon; or at least if it does not lead to discoveries in chemistry, astronomy, geology, magnetism, and science of every kind.

This question, as might have been expected, has been keenly debated in the present age, and formed one main subject of the controversy, to which I referred in the Introduction to the present Discourses, as having been sustained in the first decade of this century by a celebrated Northern Review on the one hand, and defenders of the University of Oxford on the other. Hardly had the authorities of that ancient seat of learning, waking from their long neglect, set on foot a plan for the education of the youth committed to them, than the representatives of science and literature in the city, which has sometimes been called the Northern Athens, remonstrated, with their gravest arguments and their most brilliant satire, against the direction and shape which the reform was taking. Nothing would content them, but that the University should be set to rights on the basis of the philosophy of Utility; a philosophy, as they seem to have thought, which needed but to be proclaimed in order to be embraced. In truth, they were little aware of the depth and force of the principles on which the academical authorities were proceeding, and, this being so, it was not to be expected that they would be allowed to walk at leisure over the field of controversy which they had selected. Accordingly they were encountered in behalf of the University by two men of great name and influence in their day, of very different minds, but united, as by Collegiate ties, so in the clear-sighted and large view which they took of the whole subject of Liberal Education; and the defence thus provided for the Oxford studies has kept its ground to this day.

3.

Let me be allowed to devote a few words to the memory of distinguished persons, under the shadow of whose name I once lived, and by whose doctrine I am now profiting. In the heart of Oxford there is a small plot of ground, hemmed in by public thoroughfares, which has been the possession and the home of one Society for above five hundred years. In the old time of Boniface the Eighth and John the Twenty-second, in the age of Scotus and Occam and Dante, before Wiclif or Huss had kindled those miserable fires which are still raging to the ruin of the highest interests of man, an unfortunate king of England, Edward the Second, flying from the field of Bannockburn, is said to have made a vow to the Blessed Virgin to found a religious house in her honour, if he got back in safety. Prompted and aided by his Almoner, he decided on placing this house in the city of Alfred; and the Image of our Lady, which is opposite its entrance-gate, is to this day the token of the vow and its fulfilment. King and Almoner have long been in the dust, and strangers have entered into their inheritance, and their creed has been forgotten, and their holy rites disowned; but day by day a memento is still made in the holy Sacrifice by at least one Catholic Priest, once a member of that College, for the souls of those Catholic benefactors who fed him there for so many years. The visitor, whose curiosity has been excited by its present fame, gazes perhaps with something of disappointment on a collection of buildings which have with them so few of the circumstances of dignity or wealth. Broad quadrangles, high halls and chambers, ornamented cloisters, stately walks, or umbrageous gardens, a throng of students, ample revenues, or a glorious history, none of these things were the portion of that old Catholic foundation; nothing in short which to the common eye sixty years ago would have given tokens of what it was to be. But it had at that time a spirit working within it, which enabled its inmates to do, amid its seeming insignificance, what no other body in the place could equal; not a very abstruse gift or extraordinary boast, but a rare one, the honest purpose to administer the trust committed to them in such a way as their conscience pointed out as best. So, whereas the Colleges of Oxford are self-electing bodies, the fellows in each perpetually filling up for themselves the vacancies which occur in their number, the members of this foundation determined, at a time when, either from evil custom or from ancient statute, such a thing was not known elsewhere, to throw open their fellowships to the competition of all comers, and, in the choice of associates henceforth, to cast to the winds every personal motive and feeling, family connexion, and friendship, and patronage, and political interest, and local claim, and prejudice, and party jealousy, and to elect solely on public and patriotic grounds. Nay, with a remarkable independence of mind, they resolved that even the table of honours, awarded to literary merit by the University in its new system of examination for degrees, should not fetter their judgment as electors; but that at all risks, and whatever criticism it might cause, and whatever odium they might incur, they would select the men, whoever they were, to be children of their Founder, whom they thought in their consciences to be most likely from their intellectual and moral qualities to please him, if (as they expressed it) he were still upon earth, most likely to do honour to his College, most likely to promote the objects which they believed he had at heart. Such persons did not promise to be the disciples of a low Utilitarianism; and consequently, as their collegiate reform synchronized with that reform of the Academical body, in which they bore a principal part, it was not unnatural that, when the storm broke upon the University from the North, their Alma Mater, whom they loved, should have found her first defenders within the walls of that small College, which had first put itself into a condition to be her champion.

These defenders, I have said, were two, of whom the more distinguished was the late Dr. Copleston, then a Fellow of the College, successively its Provost, and Protestant Bishop of Llandaff. In that Society, which owes so much to him, his name lives, and ever will live, for the distinction which his talents bestowed on it, for the academical importance to which he raised it, for the generosity of spirit, the liberality of sentiment, and the kindness of heart, with which he adorned it, and which even those who had least sympathy with some aspects of his mind and character could not but admire and love. Men come to their meridian at various periods of their lives; the last years of the eminent person I am speaking of were given to duties which, I am told, have been the means of endearing him to numbers, but which afforded no scope for that peculiar vigour and keenness of mind which enabled him, when a young man, single-handed, with easy gallantry, to encounter and overthrow the charge of three giants of the North combined against him. I believe I am right in saying that, in the progress of the controversy, the most scientific, the most critical, and the most witty, of that literary company, all of them now, as he himself, removed from this visible scene, Professor Playfair, Lord Jeffrey, and the Rev. Sydney Smith, threw together their several efforts into one article of their Review, in order to crush and pound to dust the audacious controvertist who had come out against them in defence of his own Institutions.[37] To have even contended with such men was a sufficient voucher for his ability, even before we open his pamphlets, and have actual evidence of the good sense, the spirit, the scholar-like taste, and the purity of style, by which they are distinguished.

He was supported in the controversy, on the same general principles, but with more of method and distinctness, and, I will add, with greater force and beauty and perfection, both of thought and of language, by the other distinguished writer, to whom I have already referred, Mr. Davison; who, though not so well known to the world in his day, has left more behind him than the Provost of Oriel, to make his name remembered by posterity. This thoughtful man, who was the admired and intimate friend of a very remarkable person, whom, whether he wish it or not, numbers revere and love as the first author of the subsequent movement in the Protestant Church towards Catholicism,[38] this grave and philosophical writer, whose works I can never look into without sighing that such a man was lost to the Catholic Church, as Dr. Butler before him, by some early bias or some fault of self-education – he, in a review of a work by Mr. Edgeworth on Professional Education, which attracted a good deal of attention in its day, goes leisurely over the same ground, which had already been rapidly traversed by Dr. Copleston, and, though professedly employed upon Mr. Edgeworth, is really replying to the northern critic who had brought that writer's work into notice, and to a far greater author than either of them, who in a past age had argued on the same side.

4.

The author to whom I allude is no other than Locke. That celebrated philosopher has preceded the Edinburgh Reviewers in condemning the ordinary subjects in which boys are instructed at school, on the ground that they are not needed by them in after life; and before quoting what his disciples have said in the present century, I will refer to a few passages of the master.[39] " 'Tis matter of astonishment," he says in his work on Education, "that men of quality and parts should suffer themselves to be so far misled by custom and implicit faith. Reason, if consulted with, would advise, that their children's time should be spent in acquiring what might be *useful* to them, when they come to be men, rather than that their heads should be stuffed with a deal of trash, a great part whereof they usually never do ('tis certain they never need to) think on again as long as they live; and so much of it as does stick by them they are only the worse for."

And so again, speaking of verse-making, he says, "I know not what reason a father can have to wish his son a poet, who does not desire him to *bid defiance to all other callings and business;* which is not yet the worst of the case; for, if he proves a successful rhymer, and gets once the reputation of a wit, I desire it to be considered, what company and places he is likely to spend his time in, nay, and estate too; for it is very seldom seen that any one discovers *mines of gold or silver in Parnassus.* 'Tis a pleasant air, but a barren soil."

In another passage he distinctly limits utility in education to its bearing on the future profession or trade of the pupil, that is, he scorns the idea of any education of the intellect, simply as such. "Can there be any thing more ridiculous," he asks, "than that a father should waste his own money, and his son's time, in setting him to *learn the Roman language,* when at the same time he *designs him for a trade,* wherein he, having no use of Latin, fails not to forget that little which he brought from school, and which 'tis ten to one he abhors for the ill-usage it procured him? Could it be believed, unless we have every where amongst us examples of it, that a child should be forced to learn the rudiments of a language, which *he is never to use in the course of life that he is designed to,* and neglect all the while the writing a good hand, and casting accounts, which are of great advantage in all conditions of life, and to most trades indispensably necessary?" Nothing of course can be more absurd than to neglect in education those matters which are necessary for a boy's future calling; but the tone of Locke's remarks evidently implies more than this, and is condemnatory of any teaching which tends to the general cultivation of the mind.

Now to turn to his modern disciples. The study of the Classics had been made the basis of the Oxford education, in the reforms which I have spoken of, and the Edinburgh Reviewers protested, after the manner of Locke, that no good could come of a system which was not based upon the principle of Utility.[40]

"Classical Literature," they said, "is the great object at Oxford. Many minds, so employed, have produced many works and much fame in that department; but if all liberal arts and sciences, *useful to human life,* had been taught there, if *some* had dedicated themselves to *chemistry, some* to *mathematics, some* to *experimental philosophy,* and if *every* attainment had been honoured in the mixt ratio of its difficulty and *utility,* the system of such a University would have been much more valuable, but the splendour of its name something less."

Utility may be made the end of education, in two respects: either as regards the individual educated, or the community at large. In which light do these writers regard it? in the latter. So far they differ from Locke, for they consider the advancement of science as the supreme and real end of a University. This is brought into view in the sentences which follow.

"When a University has been doing *useless* things for a long time, it appears at first degrading to them to be *useful.* A set of Lectures on Political Economy would be discouraged in Oxford, probably despised, probably not permitted. To discuss the inclosure of commons, and to dwell upon imports and exports, to come so near to common life, would seem to be undignified and contemptible. In the same manner, the Parr or the Bentley of the day would be scandalized, in a University, to be put on a level with the discoverer of a neutral salt; and yet, *what other measure is there of dignity in intellectual labour but usefulness?* And what ought the term University to mean, but a place where every science is taught which is liberal, and at the same time useful to mankind? Nothing would so much tend to bring classical literature within proper bounds as *a steady and invariable appeal to utility* in our appreciation of all human knowledge. . . . *Looking always to real utility as our guide,* we should see, with equal pleasure, a studious and inquisitive mind arranging the productions of nature, investigating the qualities of bodies, or mastering the difficulties of the learned languages. We should not care whether he was chemist, naturalist, or scholar, because we know it to be as *necessary* that matter should be studied and subdued *to the use of man,* as that taste should be gratified, and imagination inflamed."

Such then is the enunciation, as far as words go, of the theory of Utility in Education; and both on its own account, and for the sake of the able men who have advocated it, it has a claim on the attention of those whose principles I am here representing. Certainly it is specious to contend that nothing is worth pursuing but what is useful; and that life is not long enough to expend upon interesting, or curious, or brilliant trifles. Nay, in one sense, I will grant it is more than specious, it is true; but, if so, how do I propose directly to meet the objection? Why, Gentlemen, I have really met it already, viz., in laying down, that intellectual culture is its own end; for what has its *end* in itself, has its *use* in itself also. I say, if a Liberal Education consists in the culture of the intellect, and if that culture be in itself a good, here, without going further, is an answer to Locke's question; for if a healthy body is a good in itself, why is not a healthy intellect? and if a College of Physicians is a useful institution, because it contemplates bodily health, why is not an Academical Body, though it were simply and solely engaged in imparting vigour and beauty and grasp to the intellectual portion of our nature? And the Reviewers I am quoting seem to allow this in their better moments, in a passage which, putting aside the question of its justice in fact, is sound and true in the principles to which it appeals: –

"The present state of classical education," they say, "cultivates the *imagination* a great deal too much, and other *habits of mind* a great deal too little, and trains up many young men in a style of elegant imbecility, utterly unworthy of the talents with which nature has endowed them. . . . The matter of fact is, that a classical scholar of twenty-three or twenty-four is a man principally conversant with works of imagination. His feelings are quick, his fancy lively, and his taste good. Talents for *speculation* and *original inquiry* he has none, nor has he formed the invaluable *habit of pushing things up to their first principles,* or of collecting dry and unamusing facts as the materials for reasoning. All the solid and masculine parts of his *understanding* are left wholly without *cultivation;* he hates the pain of thinking, and suspects every man whose boldness and originality call upon him to defend his opinions and prove his assertions."

5.

Now, I am not at present concerned with the specific question of classical education; else, I might reasonably question the justice of calling an intellectual discipline, which embraces the study of Aristotle, Thucydides, and Tacitus, which involves Scholarship and Antiquities, *imaginative;* still so far I readily grant, that the cultivation of the "understanding," of a "talent for speculation and original inquiry," and of "the habit of pushing things up to their first principles," is a principal portion of a *good* or *liberal* education. If then the Reviewers consider such cultivation the characteristic of a *useful* education, as they seem to do in the foregoing passage, it follows, that what they mean by "useful" is just what I mean by "good" or "liberal:" and Locke's question becomes a verbal one. Whether youths are to be taught Latin or verse-making will depend on the *fact,* whether these studies tend to mental culture; but, however this is determined, so far is clear, that in that mental culture consists what I have called a liberal or non-professional, and what the Reviewers call a useful education.

This is the obvious answer which may be made to those who urge upon us the claims of Utility in our plans of Education; but I am not going to leave the subject here: I mean to take a wider view of it. Let us take "useful," as Locke takes it, in its proper and popular sense, and then we enter upon a large field of thought, to which I cannot do justice in one Discourse, though to-day's is all the space that I can give to it. I say, let us take "useful" to mean, not what is simply good, but what *tends* to good, or is the *instrument* of good; and in this sense also, Gentlemen, I will show you how a liberal education is truly and fully a useful, though it be not a professional, education. "Good" indeed means one thing, and "useful" means another; but I lay it down as a principle, which will save us a great deal of anxiety, that, though the useful is not always good, the good is always useful. Good is not only good, but reproductive of good; this is one of its attributes; nothing is excellent, beautiful, perfect, desirable for its own sake, but it overflows, and spreads the likeness of itself all around it. Good is prolific; it is not only good to the eye, but to the taste; it not only attracts us, but it communicates itself; it excites first our admiration and love, then our desire and our gratitude, and that, in proportion to its intenseness and fulness in particular instances. A great good will impart great good. If then the intellect is so excellent a portion of us, and its cultivation so excellent, it is not only beautiful, perfect, admirable, and noble in itself, but in a true and high sense it must be useful to the possessor and to all around him; not useful in any low, mechanical, mercantile sense, but as diffusing good, or as a blessing, or a gift, or power, or a treasure, first to the owner, then through him to the world. I say then, if a liberal education be good, it must necessarily be useful too.

6.

You will see what I mean by the parallel of bodily health. Health is a good in itself, though nothing came of it, and is especially worth seeking and cherishing; yet, after all, the blessings which attend its presence are so great, while they are so close to it and so redound back upon it and encircle it, that we never think of it except as useful as well as good, and praise and prize it for what it does, as well as for what it is, though at the same time we cannot point out any definite and distinct work or production which it can be said to effect. And so as regards intellectual culture, I am far from denying utility in this large sense as the end of Education, when I lay it down, that the culture of the intellect is a good in itself and its own end; I do not exclude from the idea of intellectual culture what it cannot but be, from the very nature of things; I only deny that we must be able to point out, before we have any right to call it useful, some art, or business, or profession, or trade, or work, as resulting from it, and as its real and complete end. The parallel is exact: – As the body may be sacrificed to some manual or other toil, whether moderate or oppressive, so may the intellect be devoted to some specific profession; and I do not call *this* the culture of the intellect. Again, as some member or organ of the body may be inordinately used and developed, so may memory, or imagination, or the reasoning faculty; and *this* again is not intellectual culture. On the other hand, as the body may be tended, cherished, and exercised with a simple view to its general health, so may the intellect also be generally exercised in order to its perfect state; and this *is* its cultivation.

Again, as health ought to precede labour of the body, and as a man in health can do what an unhealthy man cannot do, and as of this health the properties are strength, energy, agility, graceful carriage and action, manual dexterity, and endurance of fatigue, so in like manner general culture of mind is the best aid to professional and scientific study, and educated men can do what illiterate cannot; and the man who has learned to think and to reason and to compare and to discriminate and to analyze, who has refined his taste, and formed his judgment, and sharpened his mental vision, will not indeed at once be a lawyer, or a pleader, or an orator, or a statesman, or a physician, or a good landlord, or a man of business, or a soldier, or an engineer, or a chemist, or a geologist, or an antiquarian, but he will be placed in that state of intellect in which he can take up any one of the sciences or callings I have referred to, or any other for which he has a taste or special talent, with an ease, a grace, a versatility, and a success, to which another is a stranger. In this sense then, and as yet I have said but a very few words on a large subject, mental culture is emphatically *useful.*

If then I am arguing, and shall argue, against Professional or Scientific knowledge as the sufficient end of a University Education, let me not be supposed, Gentlemen, to be disrespectful towards particular studies, or arts, or vocations, and those who are engaged in them. In saying that Law or Medicine is not the end of a University course, I do not mean to imply that the University does not teach Law or Medicine. What indeed can it teach at all, if it does not teach something particular? It teaches *all* knowledge by teaching all *branches* of knowledge, and in no other way. I do but say that there will be this distinction as regards a Professor of Law, or of Medicine, or of Geology, or of Political Economy, in a University and out of it, that out of a University he is in danger of being absorbed and narrowed by his pursuit, and of giving Lectures which are the Lectures of nothing more than a lawyer, physician, geologist, or political economist; whereas in a University he will just know where he and his science stand, he has come to it, as it were, from a height, he has taken a survey of all knowledge, he is kept from extravagance by the very rivalry of other studies, he has gained from them a special illumination and largeness of mind and freedom and self-possession, and he treats his own in consequence with a philosophy and a resource, which belongs not to the study itself, but to his liberal education.

This then is how I should solve the fallacy, for so I must call it, by which

Locke and his disciples would frighten us from cultivating the intellect, under the notion that no education is useful which does not teach us some temporal calling, or some mechanical art, or some physical secret. I say that a cultivated intellect, because it is a good in itself, brings with it a power and a grace to every work and occupation which it undertakes, and enables us to be more useful, and to a greater number. There is a duty we owe to human society as such, to the state to which we belong, to the sphere in which we move, to the individuals towards whom we are variously related, and whom we successively encounter in life; and that philosophical or liberal education, as I have called it, which is the proper function of a University, if it refuses the foremost place to professional interests, does but postpone them to the formation of the citizen, and, while it subserves the larger interests of philanthropy, prepares also for the successful prosecution of those merely personal objects, which at first sight it seems to disparage.

7.

And now, Gentlemen, I wish to be allowed to enforce in detail what I have been saying, by some extracts from the writings to which I have already alluded, and to which I am so greatly indebted.[41]

"It is an undisputed maxim in Political Economy," says Dr. Copleston, "that the separation of professions and the division of labour tend to the perfection of every art, to the wealth of nations, to the general comfort and well-being of the community. This principle of division is in some instances pursued so far as to excite the wonder of people to whose notice it is for the first time pointed out. There is no saying to what extent it may not be carried; and the more the powers of each individual are concentrated in one employment, the greater skill and quickness will he naturally display in performing it. But, while he thus contributes more effectually to the accumulation of national wealth, he becomes himself more and more degraded as a rational being. In proportion as his sphere of action is narrowed his mental powers and habits become contracted; and he resembles a subordinate part of some powerful machinery, useful in its place, but insignificant and worthless out of it. If it be necessary, as it is beyond all question necessary, that society should be split into divisions and subdivisions, in order that its several duties may be well performed, yet we must be careful not to yield up ourselves wholly and exclusively to the guidance of this system; we must observe what its evils are, and we should modify and restrain it, by bringing into action other principles, which may serve as a check and counterpoise to the main force.

"There can be no doubt that every art is improved by confining the professor of it to that single study. But, *although the art itself is advanced by this concentration of mind in its service, the individual who is confined to it goes back.* The advantage of the community is nearly in an inverse ratio with his own.

"Society itself requires some other contribution from each individual, besides the particular duties of his profession. And, if no such liberal intercourse be established, it is the common failing of human nature, to be engrossed with petty views and interests, to underrate the importance of all in which we are not concerned, and to carry our partial notions into cases where they are inapplicable, to act, in short, as so many unconnected units, displacing and repelling one another.

"In the cultivation of literature is found that common link, which, among the higher and middling departments of life, unites the jarring sects and subdivisions into one interest, which supplies common topics, and kindles common feelings, unmixed with those narrow prejudices with which all professions are more or less infected. The knowledge, too, which is thus acquired, expands and enlarges the mind, excites its faculties, and calls those limbs and muscles into freer exercise which, by too constant use in one direction, not only acquire an illiberal air, but are apt also to lose somewhat of their native play and energy. And thus, without directly qualifying a man for any of the employments of life, it enriches and ennobles all. Without teaching him the peculiar business of any one office or calling, it enables him to act his part in each of them with better grace and more elevated carriage; and, if happily planned and conducted, is a main ingredient in that complete and generous education which fits a man 'to perform justly, skilfully, and magnanimously, all the offices, both private and public, of peace and war.' "[42]

8.

The view of Liberal Education, advocated in these extracts, is expanded by Mr. Davison in the Essay to which I have already referred.[43] He lays more stress on the "usefulness" of Liberal Education in the larger sense of the word than his predecessor in the controversy. Instead of arguing that the Utility of knowledge to the individual varies inversely with its Utility to the public, he chiefly employs himself on the suggestions contained in Dr. Copleston's last sentences. He shows, first, that a Liberal Education is something far higher, even in the scale of Utility, than what is commonly called a Useful Education, and next, that it is necessary or useful for the purposes even of that Professional Education which commonly engrosses the title of Useful. The former of these two theses he recommends to us in an argument from which the following passages are selected: –

"It is to take a very contracted view of life," he says, "to think with great anxiety how persons may be educated to superior skill in their department, comparatively neglecting or excluding the more liberal and enlarged cultivation. In his (Mr. Edgeworth's) system, the value of every attainment is to be measured by its subserviency to a calling. The specific duties of that calling are exalted at the cost of those free and independent tastes and virtues which come in to sustain the common relations of society, and raise the individual in them. In short, a man is to be usurped by his profession. He is to be clothed in its garb from head to foot. His virtues, his science, and his ideas are all to be put into a gown or uniform, and the whole man to be shaped, pressed, and stiffened, in the exact mould of his technical character. Any interloping accomplishments, or a faculty which cannot be taken into public pay, if they are to be indulged in him at all, must creep along under the cloak of his more serviceable privileged merits. Such is the state of perfection to which the spirit and general tendency of this system would lead us.

"But the professional character is not the only one which a person engaged in a profession has to support. He is not always upon duty. There are services he owes, which are neither parochial, nor forensic, nor military, nor to be described by any such epithet of civil regulation, and yet are in no wise inferior to those that bear these authoritative titles; inferior neither in their intrinsic value, nor their moral import, nor their impression upon society. As a friend, as a companion, as a citizen at large; in the connections of domestic life; in the improvement and embellishment of his leisure, he has a sphere of action, revolving, if you please, within the sphere of his profession, but not clashing with it; in which if he can show none of the advantages of an improved understanding, whatever may be his skill or proficiency in the other, he is no more than an ill-educated man.

"There is a certain faculty in which all nations of any refinement are great practitioners. It is not taught at school or college as a distinct science; though it deserves that what is taught there should be made to have some reference to it; nor is it endowed at all by the public; everybody being obliged to exercise it for himself in person, which he does to the best of his skill. But in nothing is there a greater difference than in the manner of doing it. The advocates of professional learning will smile when we tell them that this same faculty which we would have encouraged, is simply that of speaking good sense in English, without fee or reward, in common conversation.

They will smile when we lay some stress upon it; but in reality it is no such trifle as they imagine. Look into the huts of savages, and see, for there is nothing to listen to, the dismal blank of their stupid hours of silence; their professional avocations of war and hunting are over; and, having nothing to do, they have nothing to say. Turn to improved life, and you find conversation in all its forms the medium of something more than an idle pleasure; indeed, a very active agent in circulating and forming the opinions, tastes, and feelings of a whole people. It makes of itself a considerable affair. Its topics are the most promiscuous – all those which do not belong to any particular province. As for its power and influence, we may fairly say that it is of just the same consequence to a man's immediate society, how he talks, as how he acts. Now of all those who furnish their share to rational conversation, a mere adept in his own art is universally admitted to be the worst. The sterility and uninstructiveness of such a person's social hours are quite proverbial. Or if he escape being dull, it is only by launching into ill-timed, learned loquacity. We do not desire of him lectures or speeches; and he has nothing else to give. Among benches he may be powerful; but seated on a chair he is quite another person. On the other hand, we may affirm, that one of the best companions is a man who, to the accuracy and research of a profession, has joined a free excursive acquaintance with various learning, and caught from it the spirit of general observation."

9.

Having thus shown that a liberal education is a real benefit to the subjects of it, as members of society, in the various duties and circumstances and accidents of life, he goes on, in the next place, to show that, over and above those direct services which might fairly be expected of it, it actually subserves the discharge of those particular functions, and the pursuit of those particular advantages, which are connected with professional exertion, and to which Professional Education is directed.

"We admit," he observes, "that when a person makes a business of one pursuit, he is in the right way to eminence in it; and that divided attention will rarely give excellence in many. But our assent will go no further. For, to think that the way to prepare a person for excelling in any one pursuit (and that is the only point in hand), is to fetter his early studies, and cramp the first development of his mind, by a reference to the exigencies of that pursuit barely, is a very different notion, and one which, we apprehend, deserves to be exploded rather than received. Possibly a few of the abstract, insulated kinds of learning might be approached in that way. The exceptions to be made are very few, and need not be recited. But for the acquisition of professional and practical ability such maxims are death to it. The main ingredients of that ability are requisite knowledge and cultivated faculties; but, of the two, the latter is by far the chief. A man of well improved faculties has the command of another's knowledge. A man without them, has not the command of his own.

"Of the intellectual powers, the judgment is that which takes the foremost lead in life. How to form it to the two habits it ought to possess, of exactness and vigour, is the problem. It would be ignorant presumption so much as to hint at any routine of method by which these qualities may with certainty be imparted to every or any understanding. Still, however, we may safely lay it down that they are not to be got 'by a gatherer of simples,' but are the combined essence and extracts of many different things, drawn from much varied reading and discipline, first, and observation afterwards. For if there be a single intelligible point on this head, it is that a man who has been trained to think upon one subject or for one subject only, will never be a good judge even in that one: whereas the enlargement of his circle gives him increased knowledge and power in a rapidly increasing ratio. So much do ideas act, not as solitary units, but by grouping and combination; and so clearly do all the things that fall within the proper province of the same faculty of the mind, intertwine with and support each other. Judgment lives as it were by comparison and discrimination. Can it be doubted, then, whether the range and extent of that assemblage of things upon which it is practised in its first essays are of use to its power?

"To open our way a little further on this matter, we will define what we mean by the power of judgment; and then try to ascertain among what kind of studies the improvement of it may be expected at all.

"Judgment does not stand here for a certain homely, useful quality of intellect, that guards a person from committing mistakes to the injury of his fortunes or common reputation; but for that master-principle of business, literature, and talent, which gives him strength in any subject he chooses to grapple with, and enables him to *seize the strong point* in it. Whether this definition be metaphysically correct or not, it comes home to the substance of our inquiry. It describes the power that every one desires to possess when he comes to act in a profession, or elsewhere; and corresponds with our best idea of a cultivated mind.

"Next, it will not be denied, that in order to do any good to the judgment, the mind must be employed upon such subjects as come within the cognizance of that faculty, and give some real exercise to its perceptions. Here we have a rule of selection by which the different parts of learning may be classed for our purpose. Those which belong to the province of the judgment are religion (in its evidences and interpretation), ethics, history, eloquence, poetry, theories of general speculation, the fine arts, and works of wit. Great as the variety of these large divisions of learning may appear, they are all held in union by two capital principles of connexion. First, they are all quarried out of one and the same great subject of man's moral, social, and feeling nature. And secondly, they are all under the control (more or less strict) of the same power of moral reason."

"If these studies," he continues, "be such as give a direct play and exercise to the faculty of the judgment, then they are the true basis of education for the active and inventive powers, whether destined for a profession or any other use. Miscellaneous as the assemblage may appear, of history, eloquence, poetry, ethics, etc., blended together, they will all conspire in an union of effect. They are necessary mutually to explain and interpret each other. The knowledge derived from them all will amalgamate, and the habits of a mind versed and practised in them by turns will join to produce a richer vein of thought and of more general and practical application than could be obtained of any single one, as the fusion of the metals into Corinthian brass gave the artist his most ductile and perfect material. Might we venture to imitate an author (whom indeed it is much safer to take as an authority than to attempt to copy), Lord Bacon, in some of his concise illustrations of the comparative utility of the different studies, we should say that history would give fulness, moral philosophy strength, and poetry elevation to the understanding. Such in reality is the natural force and tendency of the studies; but there are few minds susceptible enough to derive from them any sort of virtue adequate to those high expressions. We must be contented therefore to lower our panegyric to this, that a person cannot avoid receiving some infusion and tincture, at least, of those several qualities, from that course of diversified reading. One thing is unquestionable, that the elements of general reason are not to be found fully and truly expressed in any one kind of study; and that he who would wish to know her idiom, must read it in many books.

"If different studies are useful for aiding, they are still more useful for correcting each other; for as they have their particular merits severally, so they have their defects, and the most extensive acquaintance with one can produce only an intellect either too flashy or too jejune, or infected with some other fault of confined reading. History, for example, shows things as they are, that is, the morals and interests of men disfigured and perverted by all their imperfections of passion, folly, and ambition; philosophy strips the picture too much; poetry adorns it too much; the concentrated lights of the three correct the false peculiar colouring of each, and show us the truth. The right mode of thinking upon it is to be had from them taken all together, as every one must know who has seen their united contributions of thought and feeling expressed in the masculine sentiment of our immortal states-man, Mr. Burke, whose eloquence is inferior only to his more admirable wisdom. If any mind improved like his, is to be our instructor, we must go to the fountain head of things as he did, and study not his works but his method; by the one we may become feeble imitators, by the other arrive at some ability of our own. But, as all biography assures us, he, and every other able thinker, has been formed, not by a parsimonious admeasurement of studies to some definite future object (which is Mr. Edgeworth's maxim), but by taking a wide and liberal compass, and thinking a great deal on many subjects with no better end in view than because the exercise was one which made them more rational and intelligent beings."

10.

But I must bring these extracts to an end. To-day I have confined myself to saying that that training of the intellect, which is best for the individual himself, best enables him to discharge his duties to society. The Philoso-pher, indeed, and the man of the world differ in their very notion, but the methods, by which they are respectively formed, are pretty much the same. The Philosopher has the same command of matters of thought, which the true citizen and gentleman has of matters of business and conduct. If then a practical end must be assigned to a University course, I say it is that of training good members of society. Its art is the art of social life, and its end is fitness for the world. It neither confines its views to particular professions on the one hand, nor creates heroes or inspires genius on the other. Works indeed of genius fall under no art; heroic minds come under no rule; a University is not a birthplace of poets or of immortal authors, of founders of schools, leaders of colonies, or conquerors of nations. It does not promise a generation of Aristotles or Newtons, of Napoleons or Washingtons, of Raphaels or Shakespeares, though such miracles of nature it has before now contained within its precincts. Nor is it content on the other hand with forming the critic or the experimentalist, the economist or the engineer, though such too it includes within its scope. But a University training is the great ordinary means to a great but ordinary end; it aims at raising the intellectual tone of society, at cultivating the public mind, at purifying the national taste, at supplying true principles to popular enthusiasm and fixed aims to popular aspiration, at giving enlargement and sobriety to the ideas of the age, at facilitating the exercise of political power, and refining the intercourse of private life. It is the education which gives a man a clear conscious view of his own opinions and judgments, a truth in developing them, an eloquence in expressing them, and a force in urging them. It teaches him to see things as they are, to go right to the point, to disentangle a skein of thought, to detect what is sophistical, and to discard what is irrelevant. It prepares him to fill any post with credit, and to master any subject with facility. It shows him how to accommodate himself to others, how to throw himself into their state of mind, how to bring before them his own, how to influence them, how to come to an understanding with them, how to bear with them. He is at home in any society, he has common ground with every class; he knows when to speak and when to be silent; he is able to converse, he is able to listen; he can ask a question pertinently, and gain a lesson seasonably, when he has nothing to impart himself; he is ever ready, yet never in the way; he is a pleasant companion, and a comrade you can depend upon; he knows when to be serious and when to trifle, and he has a sure tact which enables him to trifle with gracefulness and to be serious with effect. He has the repose of a mind which lives in itself, while it lives in the world, and which has resources for its happiness at home when it cannot go abroad. He has a gift which serves him in public, and supports him in retirement, without which good fortune is but vulgar, and with which failure and disappointment have a charm. The art which tends to make a man all this, is in the object which it pursues as useful as the art of wealth or the art of health, though it is less susceptible of method, and less tangible, less certain, less complete in its result.

DISCOURSE VIII.

KNOWLEDGE VIEWED IN RELATION TO RELIGION.

I.

We shall be brought, Gentlemen, to-day, to the termination of the investigation which I commenced three Discourses back, and which, I was well aware, from its length, if for no other reason, would make demands upon the patience even of indulgent hearers.

First I employed myself in establishing the principle that Knowledge is its own reward; and I showed that, when considered in this light, it is called Liberal Knowledge, and is the scope of Academical Institutions.

Next, I examined what is meant by Knowledge, when it is said to be pursued for its own sake; and I showed that, in order satisfactorily to fulfil this idea, Philosophy must be its *form;* or, in other words, that its matter must not be admitted into the mind passively, as so much acquirement, but must be mastered and appropriated as a system consisting of parts, related one to the other, and interpretative of one another in the unity of a whole.

Further, I showed that such a philosophical contemplation of the field of Knowledge as a whole, leading, as it did, to an understanding of its separate departments, and an appreciation of them respectively, might in consequence be rightly called an illumination; also, it was rightly called an enlargement of mind, because it was a distinct location of things one with another, as if in space; while it was moreover its proper cultivation and its best condition, both because it secured to the intellect the sight of things as they are, or of truth, in opposition to fancy, opinion, and theory; and again, because it presupposed and involved the perfection of its various powers.

Such, I said, was that Knowledge, which deserves to be sought for its own sake, even though it promised no ulterior advantage. But, when I had got as far as this, I went farther, and observed that, from the nature of the case, what was so good in itself could not but have a number of external uses, though it did not promise them, simply because it *was* good; and that it was necessarily the source of benefits to society, great and diversified in proportion to its own intrinsic excellence. Just as in morals, honesty is the best policy, as being profitable in a secular aspect, though such profit is not the measure of its worth, so too as regards what may be called the virtues of the Intellect, their very possession indeed is a substantial good, and is enough, yet still that substance has a shadow, inseparable from it, viz., its social and political usefulness. And this was the subject to which I devoted the preceding Discourse.

One portion of the subject remains: - this intellectual culture, which is so exalted in itself, not only has a bearing upon social and active duties, but upon Religion also. The educated mind may be said to be in a certain sense religious; that is, it has what may be considered a religion of its own, independent of Catholicism, partly cooperating with it, partly thwarting it; at once a defence yet a disturbance to the Church in Catholic countries, - and in countries beyond her pale, at one time in open warfare with her, at another in defensive alliance. The history of Schools and Academies, and of

Literature and Science generally, will, I think, justify me in thus speaking. Since, then, my aim in these Discourses is to ascertain the function and the action of a University, viewed in itself, and its relations to the various instruments of teaching and training which are round about it, my survey of it would not be complete unless I attempted, as I now propose to do, to exhibit its general bearings upon Religion.

2.

Right Reason, that is, Reason rightly exercised, leads the mind to the Catholic Faith, and plants it there, and teaches it in all its religious speculations to act under its guidance. But Reason, considered as a real agent in the world, and as an operative principle in man's nature, with an historical course and with definite results, is far from taking so straight and satisfactory a direction. It considers itself from first to last independent and supreme; it requires no external authority; it makes a religion for itself. Even though it accepts Catholicism, it does not go to sleep; it has an action and development of its own, as the passions have, or the moral sentiments, or the principle of self-interest. Divine grace, to use the language of Theology, does not by its presence supersede nature; nor is nature at once brought into simple concurrence and coalition with grace. Nature pursues its course, now coincident with that of grace, now parallel to it, now across, now divergent, now counter, in proportion to its own imperfection and to the attraction and influence which grace exerts over it. And what takes place as regards other principles of our nature and their developments is found also as regards the Reason. There is, we know, a Religion of enthusiasm, of superstitious ignorance of statecraft; and each has that in it which resembles Catholicism, and that again which contradicts Catholicism. There is the Religion of a warlike people, and of a pastoral people; there is a Religion of rude times, and in like manner there is a Religion of civilized times, of the cultivated intellect, of the philosopher, scholar, and gentleman. This is that Religion of Reason, of which I speak. Viewed in itself, however near it comes to Catholicism, it is of course simply distinct from it; for Catholicism is one whole, and admits of no compromise or modification. Yet this is to view it in the abstract; in matter of fact, and in reference to individuals, we can have no difficulty in conceiving this philosophical Religion present in a Catholic country, as a spirit influencing men to a certain extent, for good or for bad or for both, - a spirit of the age, which again may be found, as among Catholics, so with still greater sway and success in a country not Catholic,

yet specifically the same in such a country as it exists in a Catholic community. The problem then before us to-day, is to set down some portions of the
outline, if we can ascertain them, of the Religion of Civilization, and to
determine how they lie relatively to those principles, doctrines, and rules,
which Heaven has given us in the Catholic Church.

And here again, when I speak of Revealed Truth, it is scarcely necessary
to say that I am not referring to the main articles and prominent points of
faith, as contained in the Creed. Had I undertaken to delineate a philosophy,
which directly interfered with the Creed, I could not have spoken of it as
compatible with the profession of Catholicism. The philosophy I speak of,
whether it be viewed within or outside the Church, does not necessarily take
cognizance of the Creed. Where the country is Catholic, the educated mind
takes its articles for granted, by a sort of implicit faith; where it is not, it
simply ignores them and the whole subject-matter to which they relate, as
not affecting social and political interests. Truths about God's Nature, about
His dealings towards the human race, about the Economy of Redemption, -
in the one case it humbly accepts them, and passes on; in the other it passes
them over, as matters of simple opinion, which never can be decided, and
which can have no power over us to make us morally better or worse. I am
not speaking then of belief in the great objects of faith, when I speak of
Catholicism, but I am contemplating Catholicism chiefly as a system of
pastoral instruction and moral duty; and I have to do with its doctrines
mainly as they are subservient to its direction of the conscience and the
conduct. I speak of it, for instance, as teaching the ruined state of man; his
utter inability to gain Heaven by any thing he can do himself; the moral
certainty of his losing his soul if left to himself; the simple absence of all
rights and claims on the part of the creature in the presence of the Creator;
the illimitable claims of the Creator on the service of the creature; the
imperative and obligatory force of the voice of conscience; and the inconceivable evil of sensuality. I speak of it as teaching, that no one gains
Heaven except by the free grace of God, or without a regeneration of
nature; that no one can please Him without faith; that the heart is the seat
both of sin and of obedience; that charity is the fulfilling of the Law; and
that incorporation into the Catholic Church is the ordinary instrument of
salvation. These are the lessons which distinguish Catholicism as a popular
religion, and these are the subjects to which the cultivated intellect will
practically be turned: – I have to compare and contrast, not the doctrinal,
but the moral and social teaching of Philosophy on the one hand, and
Catholicism on the other.

3.

Now, on opening the subject, we see at once a momentous benefit which the philosopher is likely to confer on the pastors of the Church. It is obvious that the first step which they have to effect in the conversion of man and the renovation of his nature, is his rescue from that fearful subjection to sense which is his ordinary state. To be able to break through the meshes of that thraldom, and to disentangle and to disengage its ten thousand holds upon the heart, is to bring it, I might almost say, half way to Heaven. Here, even divine grace, to speak of things according to their appearances, is ordinarily baffled, and retires, without expedient or resource, before this giant fascination. Religion seems too high and unearthly to be able to exert a continued influence upon us: its effort to rouse the soul, and the soul's effort to co-operate, are too violent to last. It is like holding out the arm at full length, or supporting some great weight, which we manage to do for a time, but soon are exhausted and succumb. Nothing can act beyond its own nature; when then we are called to what is supernatural, though those extraordinary aids from Heaven are given us, with which obedience becomes possible, yet even with them it is of transcendent difficulty. We are drawn down to earth every moment with the ease and certainty of a natural gravitation, and it is only by sudden impulses and, as it were, forcible plunges that we attempt to mount upwards. Religion indeed enlightens, terrifies, subdues; it gives faith, it inflicts remorse, it inspires resolutions, it draws tears, it inflames devotion, but only for the occasion. I repeat, it imparts an inward power which ought to effect more than this; I am not forgetting either the real sufficiency of its aids, nor the responsibility of those in whom they fail. I am not discussing theological questions at all, I am looking at phenomena as they lie before me, and I say that, in matter of fact, the sinful spirit repents, and protests it will never sin again, and for a while is protected by disgust and abhorrence from the malice of its foe. But that foe knows too well that such seasons of repentance are wont to have their end: he patiently waits, till nature faints with the effort of resistance, and lies passive and hopeless under the next access of temptation. What we need then is some expedient or instrument, which at least will obstruct and stave off the approach of our spiritual enemy, and which is sufficiently congenial and level with our nature to maintain as firm a hold upon us as the inducements of sensual gratification. It will be our wisdom to employ nature against itself. Thus sorrow, sickness, and care are providential antagonists to our inward disorders; they come upon us as years pass on, and generally produce their natural effects on us, in proportion as we are subjected to their influence.

These, however, are God's instruments, not ours; we need a similar remedy, which we can make our own, the object of some legitimate faculty, or the aim of some natural affection, which is capable of resting on the mind, and taking up its familiar lodging with it, and engrossing it, and which thus becomes a match for the besetting power of sensuality, and a sort of homœopathic medicine for the disease. Here then I think is the important aid which intellectual cultivation furnishes to us in rescuing the victims of passion and self-will. It does not supply religious motives; it is not the cause or proper antecedent of any thing supernatural; it is not meritorious of heavenly aid or reward; but it does a work, at least *materially* good (as theologians speak), whatever be its real and formal character. It expels the excitements of sense by the introduction of those of the intellect.

This then is the *primâ facie* advantage of the pursuit of Knowledge; it is the drawing the mind off from things which will harm it to subjects which are worthy a rational being; and, though it does not raise it above nature, nor has any tendency to make us pleasing to our Maker, yet is it nothing to substitute what is in itself harmless for what is, to say the least, inexpressibly dangerous? is it a little thing to exchange a circle of ideas which are certainly sinful, for others which are certainly not so? You will say, perhaps, in the words of the Apostle, "Knowledge puffeth up:" and doubtless this mental cultivation, even when it is successful for the purpose for which I am applying it, may be from the first nothing more than the substitution of pride for sensuality. I grant it, I think I shall have something to say on this point presently; but this is not a necessary result, it is but an incidental evil, a danger which may be realized or may be averted, whereas we may in most cases predicate guilt, and guilt of a heinous kind, where the mind is suffered to run wild and indulge its thoughts without training or law of any kind; and surely to turn away a soul from mortal sin is a good and a gain so far, whatever comes of it. And therefore, if a friend in need is twice a friend, I conceive that intellectual employments, though they do no more than occupy the mind with objects naturally noble or innocent, have a special claim upon our consideration and gratitude.

4.

Nor is this all: Knowledge, the discipline by which it is gained, and the tastes which it forms, have a natural tendency to refine the mind, and to give it an indisposition, simply natural, yet real, nay, more than this, a disgust and abhorrence, towards excesses and enormities of evil, which are often or ordinarily reached at length by those who are not careful from the first to set themselves against what is vicious and criminal. It generates within the mind a fastidiousness, analogous to the delicacy or daintiness which good nurture or a sickly habit induces in respect of food; and this fastidiousness, though arguing no high principle, though no protection in the case of violent temptation, nor sure in its operation, yet will often or generally be lively enough to create an absolute loathing of certain offences, or a detestation and scorn of them as ungentlemanlike, to which ruder natures, nay, such as have far more of real religion in them, are tempted, or even betrayed. Scarcely can we exaggerate the value, in its place, of a safeguard such as this, as regards those multitudes who are thrown upon the open field of the world, or are withdrawn from its eye and from the restraint of public opinion. In many cases, where it exists, sins, familiar to those who are otherwise circumstanced, will not even occur to the mind: in others, the sense of shame and the quickened apprehension of detection will act as a sufficient obstacle to them, when they do present themselves before it. Then, again, the fastidiousness I am speaking of will create a simple hatred of that miserable tone of conversation which, obtaining as it does in the world, is a constant fuel of evil, heaped up round about the soul: moreover, it will create an irresolution and indecision in doing wrong, which will act as a *remora* till the danger is past away. And though it has no tendency, I repeat, to mend the heart, or to secure it from the dominion in other shapes of those very evils which it repels in the particular modes of approach by which they prevail over others, yet cases may occur when it gives birth, after sins have been committed, to so keen a remorse and so intense a self-hatred, as are even sufficient to cure the particular moral disorder, and to prevent its accesses ever afterwards; – as the spendthrift in the story, who, after gazing on his lost acres from the summit of an eminence, came down a miser, and remained a miser to the end of his days.

And all this holds good in a special way, in an age such as ours, when, although pain of body and mind may be rife as heretofore, yet other counteractions of evil, of a penal character, which are present at other times, are away. In rude and semi-barbarous periods, at least in a climate such as our own, it is the daily, nay, the principal business of the senses, to convey feelings of discomfort to the mind, as far as they convey feelings at all. Exposure to the elements, social disorder and lawlessness, the tyranny of the powerful, and the inroads of enemies, are a stern discipline, allowing brief intervals, or awarding a sharp penance, to sloth and sensuality. The rude food, the scanty clothing, the violent exercise, the vagrant life, the military constraint, the imperfect pharmacy, which now are the trials of only particular classes of the community, were once the lot more or less of all. In the deep woods or the wild solitudes of the medieval era, feelings of religion or superstition were naturally present to the population, which in various ways co-operated with the missionary or pastor, in retaining it in a noble simplicity of manners. But, when in the advancement of society men congregate in towns, and multiply in contracted spaces, and law gives them security, and art gives them comforts, and good government robs them of courage and manliness, and monotony of life throws them back upon themselves, who does not see that diversion or protection from evil they have none, that vice is the mere reaction of unhealthy toil, and sensual excess the holyday of resourceless ignorance? This is so well understood by the practical benevolence of the day, that it has especially busied itself in plans for supplying the masses of our town population with intellectual and honourable recreations. Cheap literature, libraries of useful and entertaining knowledge, scientific lectureships, museums, zoological collections, buildings and gardens to please the eye and to give repose to the feelings, external objects of whatever kind, which may take the mind off itself, and expand and elevate it in liberal contemplations, these are the human means, wisely suggested, and good as far as they go, for at least parrying the assaults of moral evil, and keeping at bay the enemies, not only of the individual soul, but of society at large.

Such are the instruments by which an age of advanced civilization combats those moral disorders, which Reason as well as Revelation denounces; and I have not been backward to express my sense of their serviceableness to Religion. Moreover, they are but the foremost of a series of influences, which intellectual culture exerts upon our moral nature, and all upon the type of Christianity, manifesting themselves in veracity, probity, equity, fairness, gentleness, benevolence, and amiableness; so much so, that a character more noble to look at, more beautiful, more winning, in the various relations of life and in personal duties, is hardly conceivable, than may, or might be, its result, when that culture is bestowed upon a soil naturally adapted to virtue. If you would obtain a picture for contemplation which may seem to fulfil the ideal, which the Apostle has delineated under the name of charity, in its sweetness and harmony, its generosity, its courtesy to others, and its depreciation of self, you could not have recourse to a better furnished *studio* than to that of Philosophy, with the specimens of it, which with greater or less exactness are scattered through society in a civilized age. It is enough to refer you, Gentlemen, to the various Biographies and Remains of contemporaries and others, which from time to time issue from the press, to see how striking is the action of our intellectual upon our moral nature, where the moral material is rich, and the intellectual cast is perfect. Individuals will occur to all of us, who deservedly attract our love and admiration, and whom the world almost worships as the work of its own hands. Religious principle, indeed, – that is, faith, – is, to all appearance, simply away; the work is as certainly not supernatural as it is certainly noble and beautiful. This must be insisted on, that the Intellect may have its due; but it also must be insisted on for the sake of conclusions to which I wish to conduct our investigation. The radical difference indeed of this mental refinement from genuine religion, in spite of its seeming relationship, is the very cardinal point on which my present discussion turns; yet, on the other hand, such refinement may readily be assigned to a Christian origin by hasty or distant observers, or by those who view it in a particular light. And as this is the case, I think it advisable, before proceeding with the delineation of its characteristic features, to point out to you distinctly the elementary principles on which its morality is based.

5.

You will bear in mind then, Gentlemen, that I spoke just now of the scorn and hatred which a cultivated mind feels for some kinds of vice, and the utter disgust and profound humiliation which may come over it, if it should happen in any degree to be betrayed into them. Now this feeling may have its root in faith and love, but it may not; there is nothing really religious in it, considered by itself. Conscience indeed is implanted in the breast by nature, but it inflicts upon us fear as well as shame; when the mind is simply angry with itself and nothing more, surely the true import of the voice of nature and the depth of its intimations have been forgotten, and a false philosophy has misinterpreted emotions which ought to lead to God. Fear implies the transgression of a law, and a law implies a lawgiver and judge; but the tendency of intellectual culture is to swallow up the fear in the self-reproach, and self-reproach is directed and limited to our mere sense of what is fitting and becoming. Fear carries us out of ourselves, whereas shame may act upon us only within the round of our own thoughts. Such, I say, is the danger which awaits a civilized age; such is its besetting sin (not inevitable, God forbid! or we must abandon the use of God's own gifts), but still the ordinary sin of the Intellect; conscience tends to become what is called a moral sense; the command of duty is a sort of taste; sin is not an offence against God, but against human nature.

The less amiable specimens of this spurious religion are those which we meet not unfrequently in my own country. I can use with all my heart the poet's words,

"England, with all thy faults, I love thee still;"[44]

but to those faults no Catholic can be blind. We find there men possessed of many virtues, but proud, bashful, fastidious, and reserved. Why is this? it is because they think and act as if there were really nothing objective in their religion; it is because conscience to them is not the word of a lawgiver, as it ought to be, but the dictate of their own minds and nothing more; it is because conscience to them is not the word of a lawgiver, as it ought to be, but the dictate of their own minds and nothing more; it is because they do not look out of themselves, because they do not look through and beyond their own minds to their Maker, but are engrossed in notions of what is due to themselves, to their own dignity and their own consistency. Their conscience has become a mere self-respect. Instead of doing one thing and then another, as each is called for, in faith and obedience, careless of what may be called the *keeping* of deed with deed, and leaving Him who gives the command to blend the portions of their conduct into a whole, their one object, however unconscious to themselves, is to paint a smooth and perfect surface, and to be able to say to themselves that they have done their duty. When they do wrong, they feel, not contrition, of which God is the object, but remorse, and a sense of degradation. They call themselves fools, not sinners; they are angry and impatient, not humble. They shut themselves up in themselves; it is misery to them to think or to speak of their own feelings; it is misery to suppose that others see them, and their shyness and sensitiveness often becomes morbid. As to confession, which is so natural to the Catholic, to them it is impossible; unless indeed, in cases where they have been guilty, an apology is due to their own character, is expected of them, and will be satisfactory to look back upon. They are victims of an intense self-contemplation.

There are, however, far more pleasing and interesting forms of this moral malady than that which I have been depicting: I have spoken of the effect of intellectual culture on proud natures; but it will show to greater advantage, yet with as little approximation to religious faith, in amiable and unaffected minds. Observe, Gentlemen, the heresy, as it may be called, of which I speak, is the substitution of a moral sense or taste for conscience in the true meaning of the word; now this error may be the foundation of a character of far more elasticity and grace than ever adorned the persons whom I have been describing. It is especially congenial to men of an imaginative and poetical cast of mind, who will readily accept the notion that virtue is nothing more than the graceful in conduct. Such persons, far from tolerating fear, as a principle, in their apprehension of religious and

moral truth, will not be slow to call it simply gloom and superstition. Rather
a philosopher's, a gentleman's religion, is of a liberal and generous character; it is based upon honour; vice is evil, because it is unworthy, despicable,
and odious. This was the quarrel of the ancient heathen with Christianity,
that, instead of simply fixing the mind on the fair and the pleasant, it
intermingled other ideas with them of a sad and painful nature; that it spoke
of tears before joy, a cross before a crown; that it laid the foundation of
heroism in penance; that it made the soul tremble with the news of Purgatory and Hell; that it insisted on views and a worship of the Deity, which to
their minds was nothing else than mean, servile, and cowardly. The notion
of an All-perfect, Ever-present God, in whose sight we are less than atoms,
and who, while He deigns to visit us, can punish as well as bless, was
abhorrent to them; they made their own minds their sanctuary, their own
ideas their oracle, and conscience in morals was but parallel to genius in art,
and wisdom in philosophy.

6.

Had I room for all that might be said upon the subject I might illustrate this
intellectual religion from the history of the Emperor Julian, the apostate
from Christian Truth, the foe of Christian education. He, in whom every
Catholic sees the shadow of the future Anti-Christ, was all but the pattern-
man of philosophical virtue. Weak points in his character he had, it is true,
even in a merely poetical standard; but, take him all in all, and I cannot but
recognize in him a specious beauty and nobleness of moral deportment,
which combines in it the rude greatness of Fabricius or Regulus with the
accomplishments of Pliny or Antoninus. His simplicity of manners, his
frugality, his austerity of life, his singular disdain of sensual pleasure,
his military heroism, his application to business, his literary diligence, his
modesty, his clemency, his accomplishments, as I view them, go to make
him one of the most eminent specimens of pagan virtue which the world has
ever seen.[45] Yet how shallow, how meagre, nay, how unamiable is that
virtue after all, when brought upon its critical trial by his sudden summons
into the presence of his Judge! His last hours form a *unique* passage in
history, both as illustrating the helplessness of philosophy under the stern
realities of our being, and as being reported to us on the evidence of an eyewitness. "Friends and fellow-soldiers," he said, to use the words of a writer,
well fitted, both from his literary tastes and from his hatred of Christianity,
to be his panegyrist, "the seasonable period of my departure is now arrived,
and I discharge, with the cheerfulness of a ready debtor, the demands of

nature. . . . I die without remorse, as I have lived without guilt. I am pleased to reflect on the innocence of my private life; and I can affirm with confidence that the supreme authority, that emanation of the divine Power, has been preserved in my hands pure and immaculate . . . I now offer my tribute of gratitude to the Eternal Being, who has not suffered me to perish by the cruelty of a tyrant, by the secret dagger of conspiracy, or by the slow tortures of lingering disease. He has given me, in the midst of an honourable career, a splendid and glorious departure from this world, and I hold it equally absurd, equally base, to solicit, or to decline, the stroke of fate . . .

"He reproved the immoderate grief of the spectators, and conjured them not to disgrace, by unmanly tears, the fate of a prince who in a few moments would be united with Heaven and with the stars. The spectators were silent; and Julian entered into a metaphysical argument with the philosophers Priscus and Maximus on the nature of the soul. The efforts which he made, of mind as well as body, most probably hastened his death. His wound began to bleed with great violence; his respiration was embarrassed by the swelling of the veins; he called for a draught of cold water, and as soon as he had drank it expired without pain, about the hour of midnight."[46] Such, Gentlemen, is the final exhibition of the Religion of Reason: in the insensibility of conscience, in the ignorance of the very idea of sin, in the contemplation of his own moral consistency, in the simple absence of fear, in the cloudless self-confidence, in the serene self-possession, in the cold self-satisfaction, we recognize the mere Philosopher.

7.

Gibbon paints with pleasure what, conformably with the sentiments of a godless intellectualism, was an historical fulfilment of his own idea of moral perfection; Lord Shaftesbury had already drawn out that idea in a theoretical form, in his celebrated collection of Treatises which he has called "Characteristics of men, manners, opinions, views;" and it will be a further illustration of the subject before us, if you will allow me, Gentlemen, to make some extracts from this work."[47]

One of his first attacks is directed against the doctrine of reward and punishment, as if it introduced a notion into religion inconsistent with the true apprehension of the beauty of virtue, and with the liberality and nobleness of spirit in which it should be pursued. "Men have not been content," he says, "to show the natural advantages of honesty and virtue. They have rather lessened these, the better, as they thought, to advance another foundation. They have made virtue so mercenary a thing, and have talked so much of its rewards, that one can hardly tell what there is in it, after all, which can be worth rewarding. For to be *bribed* only or *terrified* into an honest practice, bespeaks little of real honesty or worth." "If," he says elsewhere, insinuating what he dare not speak out, "if through hope merely of reward, or fear of punishment, the creature be inclined to do the good he hates, or restrained from doing the ill to which he is not otherwise in the least degree averse, there is in this case no virtue or goodness whatever. There is no more of rectitude, piety, or sanctity, in a creature thus reformed, than there is meekness or gentleness in a tiger strongly chained, or innocence and sobriety in a monkey under the discipline of the whip. . . . While the will is neither gained, nor the inclination wrought upon, but awe alone prevails and forces obedience, the obedience is servile, and all which is done through it merely servile." That is, he says that Christianity is the enemy of moral virtue, as influencing the mind by fear of God, not by love of good.

The motives then of hope and fear being, to say the least, put far into the background, and nothing being morally good but what springs simply or mainly from a love of virtue for its own sake, this love-inspiring quality in virtue is its beauty, while a bad conscience is not much more than the sort of feeling which makes us shrink from an instrument out of tune. "Some by mere nature," he says, "others by art and practice, are masters of an ear in music, an eye in painting, a fancy in the ordinary things of ornament and grace, a judgment in proportions of all kinds, and a general good taste in most of those subjects which make the amusement and delight of the ingenious people of the world. Let such gentlemen as these be as extravagant as they please, or as irregular in their morals, they must at the same time discover their *inconsistency,* live at *variance* with themselves, and in *contradiction* to that principle on which they ground their highest pleasure and entertainment. Of all other *beauties* which virtuosos pursue, poets celebrate, musicians sing, and architects or artists of whatever kind describe or form, the most delightful, the most engaging and pathetic, is that which is drawn from real life and from the passions. Nothing affects the heart like that which is purely from itself, and of its own nature: such as the beauty of sentiments, the grace of actions, the turn of characters, and the *proportions and features* of a human mind. This lesson of philosophy, even a romance, a poem, or a play may teach us. . . . Let poets or the men of harmony deny, if they can, this force of nature, or withstand this *moral magic.* . . . Every one is a virtuoso of a higher or lower degree; every one pursues a grace . . . of one kind or other. The *venustum,* the *honestum,* the *decorum* of things will force its way. . . . The most natural beauty in the world is honesty and moral truth; for all beauty is truth."

Accordingly, virtue being only one kind of beauty, the principle which determines what is virtuous is, not conscience, but *taste*. "Could we once convince ourselves," he says, "of what is in itself so evident, viz., that in the very nature of things there must of necessity be the foundation of a right and wrong *taste,* as well in respect of inward character of features as of outward person, behaviour, and action, we should be far more ashamed of ignorance and wrong judgment in the former than in the latter of these subjects. . . . One who aspires to the character of a man of breeding and politeness is careful to form his judgment of arts and sciences upon right models of perfection. . . . He takes particular care to turn his eye from every thing which is gaudy, luscious, and of false taste. Nor is he less careful to turn his ear from every sort of music, besides that which is of the best manner and truest harmony. 'Twere to be wished we had the same regard to a *right taste in life and manners.* . . . If civility and humanity be a taste; if brutality, insolence, riot, be in the same manner a taste, ... who would not endeavour to force nature as well in this respect as in what relates to a taste or judgment in other arts and sciences?"

Sometimes he distinctly contrasts this taste with principle and conscience, and gives it the preference over them. "After all," he says, " *'tis not merely what we call principle,* but *a taste,* which governs men. They may think for certain, 'This is right,' or 'that wrong;' they may believe 'this is a virtue,' or 'that a sin;' 'this is punishable by man,' or 'that by God;' yet if the savour of things lies cross to honesty, if the fancy be florid, and the appetite high towards the subaltern beauties and lower orders of worldly symmetries and proportions, the conduct will infallibly turn this latter way." Thus, somewhat like a Jansenist, he makes the superior pleasure infallibly conquer, and implies that, neglecting principle, we have but to train the taste to a kind of beauty higher than sensual. He adds: "*Even conscience,* I fear, such as is owing to religious discipline, will make but a slight figure, when this taste is set amiss."

And hence the well-known doctrine of this author, that ridicule is the test of truth; for truth and virtue being beauty, and falsehood and vice deformity, and the feeling inspired by deformity being that of derision, as that inspired by beauty is admiration, it follows that vice is not a thing to weep about, but to laugh at. "Nothing is ridiculous," he says, "but what is deformed; nor is any thing proof against raillery but what is handsome and just. And therefore 'tis the hardest thing in the world to deny fair honesty the use of this weapon, which can never bear an edge against herself, and bears against every thing contrary."

And hence again, conscience, which intimates a Lawgiver, being superseded by a moral taste or sentiment, which has no sanction beyond the constitution of our nature, it follows that our great rule is to contemplate ourselves, if we would gain a standard of life and morals. Thus he has entitled one of his Treatises a "Soliloquy," with the motto, "Nec te quæsiveris extra;"[48] and he observes, "The chief interest of ambition, avarice, corruption, and every sly insinuating vice, is to prevent this interview and familiarity of discourse, which is consequent upon close retirement and inward recess. 'Tis the grand artifice of villainy and lewdness, *as well as of superstition and bigotry,* to put us upon terms of greater distance and formality with ourselves, and evade our *proving* method of soliloquy. . . . A passionate lover, whatever solitude he may affect, can never be truly by himself. . . . 'Tis the same reason which keeps the imaginary saint or mystic from being capable of this entertainment. Instead of looking narrowly into his own nature and mind, that he may be no longer a mystery to himself, he is taken up with *the contemplation of other mysterious natures,* which he never can explain or comprehend."

8.

Taking these passages as specimens of what I call the Religion of Philosophy, it is obvious to observe that there is no doctrine contained in them which is not in a certain sense true; yet, on the other hand, that almost every statement is perverted and made false, because it is not the whole truth. They are exhibitions of truth under one aspect, and therefore insufficient; conscience is most certainly a moral sense, but it is more; vice again, is a deformity, but it is worse. Lord Shaftesbury may insist, if he will, that simple and solitary fear cannot effect a moral conversion, and we are not concerned to answer him; but he will have a difficulty in proving that any real conversion follows from a doctrine which makes virtue a mere point of good taste, and vice vulgar and ungentlemanlike.

Such a doctrine is essentially superficial, and such will be its effects. It has no better measure of right and wrong than that of visible beauty and tangible fitness. Conscience indeed inflicts an acute pang, but that pang, forsooth, is irrational, and to reverence it is an illiberal superstition. But, if we will make light of what is deepest within us, nothing is left but to pay homage to what is more upon the surface. To *seem* becomes to *be;* what looks fair will be good, what causes offence will be evil; virtue will be what pleases, vice what pains. As well may we measure virtue by utility as by such a rule. Nor is this an imaginary apprehension; we all must recollect the celebrated sentiment into which a great and wise man was betrayed, in the glowing eloquence of his valediction to the spirit of chivalry. "It is gone," cries Mr. Burke; "that sensibility of principle, that chastity of honour, which felt a stain like a wound; which inspired courage, while it mitigated ferocity; which ennobled whatever it touched, and under which *vice lost half its evil by losing all its grossness.*"[49] In the last clause of this beautiful sentence we have too apt an illustration of the ethical temperament of a civilized age. It is detection, not the sin, which is the crime; private life is sacred, and inquiry into it is intolerable; and decency is virtue. Scandals, vulgarities, whatever shocks, whatever disgusts, are offences of the first order. Drinking and swearing, squalid poverty, improvidence, laziness, slovenly disorder, make up the idea of profligacy: poets may say any thing, however wicked, with impunity; works of genius may be read without danger or shame, whatever their principles; fashion, celebrity, the beautiful, the heroic, will suffice to force any evil upon the community. The splendours of a court, and the charms of good society, wit, imagination, taste, and high breeding, the *prestige* of rank, and the resources of wealth, are a screen, an instrument, and an apology for vice and irreligion. And thus at length we find, surprising as the change may be, that that very refinement of Intellectualism, which began by repelling sensuality, ends by excusing it. Under the shadow indeed of the Church, and in its due development, Philosophy does service to the cause of morality; but, when it is strong enough to have a will of its own, and is lifted up with an idea of its own importance, and attempts to form a theory, and to lay down a principle, and to carry out a system of ethics, and undertakes the moral education of the man, then it does but abet evils to which at first it seemed instinctively opposed. True Religion is slow in growth, and, when once planted, is difficult of dislodgement; but its intellectual counterfeit has no root in itself: it springs up suddenly, it suddenly withers. It appeals to what is in nature, and it falls under the dominion of the old Adam. Then, like dethroned princes, it keeps up a state and majesty, when it has lost the real power. Deformity is its abhorrence; accordingly, since it cannot dissuade men from vice, therefore in order to escape the sight of its deformity, it embellishes it. It "skins and films the ulcerous place," which it cannot probe or heal,

> "Whiles rank corruption, mining all within,
> Infects unseen."[50]

And from this shallowness of philosophical Religion it comes to pass that its disciples seem able to fulfil certain precepts of Christianity more readily and exactly than Christians themselves. St. Paul, as I have said, gives us a pattern of evangelical perfection; he draws the Christian character in in its most graceful form, and its most beautiful hues. He discourses of that charity which is patient and meek, humble and single-minded, disinterested, contented, and persevering. He tells us to prefer each the other before himself, to give way to each other, to abstain from rude words and evil speech, to avoid self-conceit, to be calm and grave, to be cheerful and happy, to observe peace with all men, truth and justice, courtesy and gentleness, all that is modest, amiable, virtuous, and of good repute. Such is St. Paul's exemplar of the Christian in his external relations; and, I repeat, the school of the world seems to send out living copies of this typical excellence with greater success than the Church. At this day the "gentleman" is the creation, not of Christianity, but of civilization. But the reason is obvious. The world is content with setting right the surface of things; the Church aims at regenerating the very depths of the heart. She ever begins with the beginning; and, as regards the multitude of her children, is never able to get beyond the beginning, but is continually employed in laying the foundation. She is engaged with what is essential, as previous and as introductory to the ornamental and the attractive. She is curing men and keeping them clear of mortal sin; she is "treating of justice and chastity, and the judgment to come:" she is insisting on faith and hope, and devotion, and honesty, and the elements of charity; and has so much to do with precept, that she almost leaves it to inspirations from Heaven to suggest what is of counsel and perfection. She aims at what is necessary rather than at what is desirable. She is for the many as well as for the few. She is putting souls in the way of salvation, that they may then be in a condition, if they shall be called upon, to aspire to the heroic, and to attain the full proportions, as well as the rudiments, of the beautiful.

9.

Such is the method, or the policy (so to call it), of the Church; but Philosophy looks at the matter from a very different point of view: what have Philosophers to do with the terror of judgment or the saving of the soul? Lord Shaftesbury calls the former a sort of "panic fear." Of the latter he scoffingly complains that "the saving of souls is now the heroic passion of exalted spirits."[51] Of course he is at liberty, on his principles, to pick and choose out of Christianity what he will; he discards the theological, the mysterious, the spiritual; he makes selection of the morally or esthetically beautiful. To him it matters not at all that he begins his teaching where he should end it; it matters not that, instead of planting the tree, he merely crops its flowers for his banquet; he only aims at the present life, his philosophy dies with him; if his flowers do but last to the end of his revel, he has nothing more to seek. When night comes, the withered leaves may be mingled with his own ashes; he and they will have done their work, he and they will be no more. Certainly, it costs little to make men virtuous on conditions such as these; it is like teaching them a language or an accomplishment, to write Latin or to play on an instrument, – the profession of an artist, not the commission of an Apostle.

This embellishment of the exterior is almost the beginning and the end of philosophical morality. This is why it aims at being modest rather than humble; this is how it can be proud at the very time that it is unassuming. To humility indeed it does not even aspire; humility is one of the most difficult of virtues both to attain and to ascertain. It lies close upon the heart itself, and its tests are exceedingly delicate and subtle. Its counterfeits abound; however, we are little concerned with them here, for, I repeat, it is hardly professed even by name in the code of ethics which we are reviewing. As has been often observed, ancient civilization had not the idea, and had no word to express it: or rather, it had the idea, and considered it a defect of mind, not a virtue, so that the word which denoted it conveyed a reproach. As to the modern world, you may gather its ignorance of it by its perversion of the somewhat parallel term "condescension." Humility or condescension, viewed as a virtue of conduct, may be said to consist, as in other things, so in our placing ourselves in our thoughts on a level with our inferiors; it is not only a voluntary relinquishment of the privileges of our own station, but an actual participation or assumption of the condition of those to whom we stoop. This is true humility, to feel and to behave as if we were low; not, to cherish a notion of our importance, while we affect a low position. Such was St. Paul's humility, when he called himself "the least of the saints;" such the humility of those many holy men who have considered themselves the greatest of sinners. It is an abdication, as far as their own thoughts are concerned, of those prerogatives or privileges to which others deem them entitled. Now it is not a little instructive to contrast with this idea, Gentlemen, – with this theological meaning of the word "condescension," – its proper English sense; put them in juxta-position, and you will at once see the difference between the world's humility and the humility of the Gospel. As the world uses the word, "condescension" is a stooping indeed of the person, but a bending forward, unattended with any the slightest effort to leave by a single inch the seat in which it is so firmly established. It is the act of a superior, who protests to himself, while he commits it, that he is superior still, and that he is doing nothing else but an act of grace towards those on whose level, in theory, he is placing himself. And this is the nearest idea which the philosopher can form of the virtue of self-abasement; to do more than this is to his mind a meanness or an hypocrisy, and at once excites his suspicion and disgust. What the world is, such it has ever been; we know the contempt which the educated pagans had for the martyrs and confessors of the Church; and it is shared by the anti-Catholic bodies of this day.

Such are the ethics of Philosophy, when faithfully represented; but an age like this, not pagan, but professedly Christian, cannot venture to reprobate humility in set terms, or to make a boast of pride. Accordingly, it looks out for some expedient by which it may blind itself to the real state of the case. Humility, with its grave and self-denying attributes, it cannot love; but what is more beautiful, what more winning, than modesty? what virtue, at first sight, simulates humility so well? though what in fact is more radically distinct from it? In truth, great as is its charm, modesty is not the deepest or the most religious of virtues. Rather it is the advanced guard or sentinel of the soul militant, and watches continually over its nascent intercourse with the world about it. It goes the round of the senses; it mounts up into the countenance; it protects the eye and ear; it reigns in the voice and gesture. Its province is the outward deportment, as other virtues have relation to matters theological, others to society, and others to the mind itself. And being more superficial than other virtues, it is more easily disjoined from their company; it admits of being associated with principles or qualities naturally foreign to it, and is often made the cloak of feelings or ends for which it was never given to us. So little is it the necessary index of humility, that it is even compatible with pride. The better for the purpose of Philosophy; humble it cannot be, so forthwith modesty becomes its humility.

Pride, under such training, instead of running to waste in the education of the mind, is turned to account; it gets a new name; it is called self-respect; and ceases to be the disagreeable, uncompanionable quality which it is in itself. Though it be the motive principle of the soul, it seldom comes to view; and when it shows itself, then delicacy and gentleness are its attire, and good sense and sense of honour direct its motions. It is no longer a restless agent, without definite aim; it has a large field of exertion assigned to it, and it subserves those social interests which it would naturally trouble. It is directed into the channel of industry, frugality, honesty, and obedience; and it becomes the very staple of the religion and morality held in honour in a day like our own. It becomes the safeguard of chastity, the guarantee of veracity, in high and low; it is the very household god of society, as at present constituted, inspiring neatness and decency in the servant girl, propriety of carriage and refined manners in her mistress, uprightness, manliness, and generosity in the head of the family. It diffuses a light over town and country; it covers the soil with handsome edifices and smiling gardens; it tills the field, it stocks and embellishes the shop. It is the stimulating principle of providence on the one hand, and of free expenditure on the other; of an honourable ambition, and of elegant enjoyment. It breathes upon the face of the community, and the hollow sepulchre is forthwith beautiful to look upon.

Refined by the civilization which has brought it into activity, this self-respect infuses into the mind an intense horror of exposure, and a keen sensitiveness of notoriety and ridicule. It becomes the enemy of extravagances of any kind; it shrinks from what are called scenes; it has no mercy on the mock-heroic, on pretence or egotism, on verbosity in language, or what is called prosiness in conversation. It detests gross adulation; not that it tends at all to the eradication of the appetite to which the flatterer ministers, but it sees the absurdity of indulging it, it understands the annoyance thereby given to others, and if a tribute must be paid to the wealthy or the powerful, it demands greater subtlety and art in the preparation. Thus vanity is changed into a more dangerous self-conceit, as being checked in its natural eruption. It teaches men to suppress their feelings, and to control their tempers, and to mitigate both the severity and the tone of their judgments. As Lord Shaftesbury would desire, it prefers playful wit and satire in putting down what is objectionable, as a more refined and good-natured, as well as a more effectual method, than the expedient which is natural to uneducated minds. It is from this impatience of the tragic and the bombastic that it is now quietly but energetically opposing itself to the unchristian practice of duelling, which it brands as simply out of taste, and as the remnant of a barbarous age; and certainly it seems likely to effect what Religion has aimed at abolishing in vain.

10.

Hence it is that it is almost a definition of a gentleman to say he is one who never inflicts pain. This description is both refined and, as far as it goes, accurate. He is mainly occupied in merely removing the obstacles which hinder the free and unembarrassed action of those about him; and he concurs with their movements rather than takes the initiative himself. His benefits may be considered as parallel to what are called comforts or conveniences in arrangements of a personal nature: like an easy chair or a good fire, which do their part in dispelling cold and fatigue, though nature provides both means of rest and animal heat without them. The true gentleman in like manner carefully avoids whatever may cause a jar or a jolt in the minds of those with whom he is cast; – all clashing of opinion, or collision of feeling, all restraint, or suspicion, or gloom, or resentment; his great concern being to make every one at their ease and at home. He has his eyes on all his company; he is tender towards the bashful, gentle towards the distant, and merciful towards the absurd; he can recollect to whom he is speaking; he guards against unseasonable allusions, or topics which may irritate; he is seldom prominent in conversation, and never wearisome. He makes light of favours while he does them, and seems to be receiving when he is conferring. He never speaks of himself except when compelled, never defends himself by a mere retort, he has no ears for slander or gossip, is scrupulous in imputing motives to those who interfere with him, and interprets every thing for the best. He is never mean or little in his disputes, never takes unfair advantage, never mistakes personalities or sharp sayings for arguments, or insinuates evil which he dare not say out. From a long-sighted prudence, he observes the maxim of the ancient sage, that we should ever conduct ourselves towards our enemy as if he were one day to be our friend. He has too much good sense to be affronted at insults, he is too well employed to remember injuries, and too indolent to bear malice. He is patient, forbearing, and resigned, on philosophical principles; he submits to pain, because it is inevitable, to bereavement, because it is irreparable, and to death, because it is his destiny. If he engages in controversy of any kind, his disciplined intellect preserves him from the blundering discourtesy of better, perhaps, but less educated minds; who, like blunt weapons, tear and hack instead of cutting clean, who mistake the point in argument, waste their strength on trifles, misconceive their adversary, and leave the question more involved than they find it. He may be right or wrong in his opinion, but he is too clear-headed to be unjust; he is as simple as he is forcible, and as brief as he is decisive. Nowhere shall we find greater candour, consideration, indulgence: he throws himself into the minds of his opponents, he accounts for their mistakes. He knows the weakness of human reason as well as its strength, its province and its limits. If he be an unbeliever, he will be too profound and large-minded to ridicule religion or to act against it; he is too wise to be a dogmatist or fanatic in his infidelity. He respects piety and devotion; he even supports institutions as venerable, beautiful, or useful, to which he does not assent; he honours the ministers of religion, and it contents him to decline its mysteries without assailing or denouncing them. He is a friend of religious toleration, and that, not only because his philosophy has taught him to look on all forms of faith with an impartial eye, but also from the gentleness and effeminacy of feeling, which is the attendant on civilization.

Not that he may not hold a religion too, in his own way, even when he is not a Christian. In that case his religion is one of imagination and sentiment; it is the embodiment of those ideas of the sublime, majestic, and beautiful, without which there can be no large philosophy. Sometimes he acknowledges the being of God, sometimes he invests an unknown principle or quality with the attributes of perfection. And this deduction of his reason, or creation of his fancy, he makes the occasion of such excellent thoughts, and the starting-point of so varied and systematic a teaching, that he even seems like a disciple of Christianity itself. From the very accuracy and steadiness of his logical powers, he is able to see what sentiments are consistent in those who hold any religious doctrine at all, and he appears to others to feel and to hold a whole circle of theological truths, which exist in his mind no otherwise than as a number of deductions.

Such are some of the lineaments of the ethical character, which the cultivated intellect will form, apart from religious principle. They are seen within the pale of the Church and without it, in holy men, and in profligate; they form the *beau-ideal* of the world; they partly assist and partly distort the development of the Catholic. They may subserve the education of a St. Francis de Sales or a Cardinal Pole; they may be the limits of the contemplation of a Shaftesbury or a Gibbon. Basil and Julian were fellow-students at the schools of Athens; and one became the Saint and Doctor of the Church, the other her scoffing and relentless foe.

DISCOURSE IX.

DUTIES OF THE CHURCH TOWARDS KNOWLEDGE.

I.

I have to congratulate myself, Gentlemen, that at length I have accomplished, with whatever success, the difficult and anxious undertaking to which I have been immediately addressing myself. Difficult and anxious it has been in truth, though the main subject of University Teaching has been so often and so ably discussed already; for I have attempted to follow out a line of thought more familiar to Protestants just now than to Catholics, upon Catholic grounds. I declared my intention, when I opened the subject, of treating it as a philosophical and practical, rather than as a theological question, with an appeal to common sense, not to ecclesiastical rules; and for this very reason, while my argument has been less ambitious, it has been deprived of the lights and supports which another mode of handling it would have secured.

No anxiety, no effort of mind is more severe than his, who in a difficult matter has it seriously at heart to investigate without error and to instruct without obscurity as to myself, if the past discussion has at any time tried the patience of the kind persons who have given it their attention, I can assure them that on no one can it have inflicted so great labour and fatigue as on myself. Happy they who are engaged in provinces of thought, so familiarly traversed and so thoroughly explored, that they see every where the footprints, the paths, the landmarks, and the remains of former travellers, and can never step wrong; but for myself, Gentlemen, I have felt like a navigator on a strange sea, who is out of sight of land, is surprised by night, and has to trust mainly to the rules and instruments of his science for reaching the port. The everlasting mountains, the high majestic cliffs, of the opposite coast, radiant in the sunlight, which are our ordinary guides, fail us in an excursion such as this; the lessons of antiquity, the determinations of authority, are here rather the needle, chart, and plummet, than great objects, with distinct and continuous outlines and completed details, which stand up and confront and occupy our gaze, and relieve us from the tension and suspense of our personal observation. And thus, in spite of the pains we may take to consult others and avoid mistakes, it is not till the morning comes and the shore greets us, and we see our vessel making straight for harbour, that we relax our jealous watch, and consider anxiety irrational. Such in a measure has been my feeling in the foregoing inquiry; in which indeed I have been in want neither of authoritative principles nor distinct precedents, but of treatises *in extenso* on the subject on which I have written, – the finished work of writers, who, by their acknowledged judgment and erudition, might furnish me for my private guidance with a running instruction on each point which successively came under review.

I have spoken of the arduousness of my "immediate" undertaking, because what I have been attempting has been of a preliminary nature, not contemplating the duties of the Church towards a University, nor the characteristics of a University which is Catholic, but inquiring what a University is, what is its aim, what its nature, what its bearings. I have accordingly laid down first, that all branches of knowledge are, at least implicitly, the subject-matter of its teaching; that these branches are not isolated and independent one of another, but form together a whole or system; that they run into each other, and complete each other, and that, in proportion to our view of them as a whole, is the exactness and trustworthiness of the knowledge which they separately convey; that the process of imparting knowledge to the intellect in this philosophical way is its true culture; that such culture is a good in itself; that the knowledge which is both its instrument and result is called Liberal Knowledge; that such culture, together with the knowledge which effects it, may fitly be sought for its own sake; that it is, however, in addition, of great secular utility, as constituting the best and highest formation of the intellect for social and political life; and lastly, that, considered in a religious aspect, it concurs with Christianity a certain way, and then diverges from it; and consequently proves in the event, sometimes its serviceable ally, sometimes, from its very resemblance to it, an insidious and dangerous foe.

Though, however, these Discourses have only professed to be preliminary, being directed to the investigation of the object and nature of the Education which a University professes to impart, at the same time I do not like to conclude without making some remarks upon the duties of the Church towards it, or rather on the ground of those duties. If the Catholic Faith is true, a University cannot exist externally to the Catholic pale, for it cannot teach Universal Knowledge if it does not teach Catholic theology. This is certain; but still, though it had ever so many theological Chairs, that would not suffice to make it a Catholic University; for theology would be included in its teaching only as a branch of knowledge, only as one out of many constituent portions, however important a one, of what I have called Philosophy. Hence a direct and active jurisdiction of the Church over it and in it is necessary, lest it should become the rival of the Church with the community at large in those theological matters which to the Church are exclusively committed, – acting as the representative of the intellect, as the Church is the representative of the religious principle. The illustration of this proposition shall be the subject of my concluding Discourse.

2.

I say then, that, even though the case could be so that the whole system of Catholicism was recognized and professed, without the direct presence of the Church, still this would not at once make such a University a Catholic Institution, nor be sufficient to secure the due weight of religious considerations in its philosophical studies. For it may easily happen that a particular bias or drift may characterize an Institution, which no rules can reach, nor officers remedy, nor professions or promises counteract. We have an instance of such a case in the Spanish Inquisition; – here was a purely

Catholic establishment, devoted to the maintenance, or rather the ascendancy of Catholicism, keenly zealous for theological truth, the stern foe of every anti-Catholic idea, and administered by Catholic theologians; yet it in no proper sense belonged to the Church. It was simply and entirely a State institution, it was an expression of that very Church-and-King spirit which has prevailed in these islands; nay, it was an instrument of the State, according to the confession of the acutest Protestant historians, in its warfare against the Holy See. Considered "*materially*," it was nothing but Catholic; but its spirit and form were earthly and secular, in spite of whatever faith and zeal and sanctity and charity were to be found in the individuals who from time to time had a share in its administration. And in like manner, it is no sufficient security for the Catholicity of a University, even that the whole of Catholic theology should be professed in it, unless the Church breathes her own pure and unearthly spirit into it, and fashions and moulds its organization, and watches over its teaching, and knits together its pupils, and superintends its action. The Spanish Inquisition came into collision with the supreme Catholic authority, and that, from the fact that its immediate end was of a secular character; and for the same reason, whereas Academical Institutions (as I have been so long engaged in showing) are in their very nature directed to social, national, temporal objects in the first instance, and since they are living and energizing bodies, if they deserve the name of University at all, and of necessity have some one formal and definite ethical character, good or bad, and do of a certainty imprint that character on the individuals who direct and who frequent them, it cannot but be that, if left to themselves, they will, in spite of their profession of Catholic Truth, work out results more or less prejudicial to its interests.

Nor is this all: such Institutions may become hostile to Revealed Truth, in consequence of the circumstances of their teaching as well as of their end. They are employed in the pursuit of Liberal Knowledge, and Liberal Knowledge has a special tendency, not necessary or rightful, but a tendency in fact, when cultivated by beings such as we are, to impress us with a mere philosophical theory of life and conduct, in the place of Revelation. I have said much on this subject already. Truth has two attributes – beauty and power; and while Useful Knowledge is the possession of truth as powerful, Liberal Knowledge is the apprehension of it as beautiful. Pursue it, either as beauty or as power, to its furthest extent and its true limit, and you are led by either road to the Eternal and Infinite, to the intimations of conscience and the announcements of the Church. Satisfy yourself with what is only visibly or intelligibly excellent, as you are likely to do, and you will make present utility and natural beauty the practical test of truth, and the sufficient object of the intellect. It is not that you will at once reject Catholicism, but you will measure and proportion it by an earthly standard. You will throw its highest and most momentous disclosures into the background, you will deny its principles, explain away its doctrines, re-arrange its precepts, and make light of its practices, even while you profess it. Knowledge, viewed as Knowledge, exerts a subtle influence in throwing us back on ourselves, and making us our own centre, and our minds the measure of all things. This then is the tendency of that Liberal Education, of which a University is the school, viz., to view Revealed Religion from an aspect of its own, – to fuse and recast it, – to tune it, as it were, to a different key, and to reset its harmonies, – to circumscribe it by a circle which unwarrantably amputates here, and unduly developes there; and all under the notion, conscious or unconscious, that the human intellect, self-educated and self-supported, is more true and perfect in its ideas and judgments than that of Prophets and Apostles, to whom the sights and sounds of Heaven were immediately conveyed. A sense of propriety, order, consistency, and completeness gives birth to a rebellious stirring against miracle and mystery, against the severe and the terrible.

This Intellectualism first and chiefly comes into collision with precept, then with doctrine, then with the very principle of dogmatism; – a perception of the Beautiful becomes the substitute for faith. In a country which does not profess the faith, it at once runs, if allowed, into scepticism or infidelity; but even within the pale of the Church, and with the most unqualified profession of her Creed, it acts, if left to itself, as an element of corruption and debility. Catholicism, as it has come down to us from the first, seems to be mean and illiberal; it is a mere popular religion; it is the religion of illiterate ages or servile populations or barbarian warriors; it must be treated with discrimination and delicacy, corrected, softened, improved, if it is to satisfy an enlightened generation. It must be stereotyped as the patron of arts, or the pupil of speculation, or the protégé of science; it must play the literary academician, or the empirical philanthropist, or the political partisan; it must keep up with the age; some or other expedient it must devise, in order to explain away, or to hide, tenets under which the intellect labours and of which it is ashamed – its doctrine, for instance, of grace, its mystery of the Godhead, its preaching of the Cross, its devotion to the Queen of Saints, or its loyalty to the Apostolic See. Let this spirit be freely evolved out of that philosophical condition of mind, which in former Discourses I have so highly, so justly extolled, and it is impossible but, first indifference, then laxity of belief, then even heresy will be the successive results.

Here then are two injuries which Revelation is likely to sustain at the hands of the Masters of human reason unless the Church, as in duty bound, protects the sacred treasure which is in jeopardy. The first is a simple ignoring of Theological Truth altogether, under the pretence of not recognising differences of religious opinion; – which will only take place in countries or under governments which have abjured Catholicism. The second, which is of a more subtle character, is a recognition indeed of Catholicism, but (as if in pretended mercy to it) an adulteration of its spirit. I will now proceed to describe the dangers I speak of more distinctly, by a reference to the general subject-matter of instruction which a University undertakes.

There are three great subjects on which Human Reason employs itself: – God, Nature, and Man: and theology being put aside in the present argument, the physical and social worlds remain. These, when respectively subjected to Human Reason, form two books: the book of nature is called Science, the book of man is called Literature. Literature and Science, thus considered, nearly constitute the subject-matter of Liberal Education; and, while Science is made to subserve the former of the two injuries, which Revealed Truth sustains, – its exclusion, Literature subserves the latter, – its corruption. Let us consider the influence of each upon Religion separately.

3.

I. As to Physical Science, of course there can be no real collision between it and Catholicism. Nature and Grace, Reason and Revelation, come from the same Divine Author, whose works cannot contradict each other. Nevertheless, it cannot be denied that, in matter of fact, there always has been a sort of jealousy and hostility between Religion and physical philosophers. The name of Galileo reminds us of it at once. Not content with investigating and reasoning in his own province, it is said, he went out of his way directly to insult the received interpretation of Scripture; theologians repelled an attack which was wanton and arrogant; and Science, affronted in her minister, has taken its full revenge upon Theology since. A vast multitude of its teachers, I fear it must be said, have been either unbelievers or sceptics, or at least have denied to Christianity any teaching, distinctive or special, over the Religion of Nature. There have indeed been most illustrious exceptions; some men protected by their greatness of mind, some by their religious profession, some by the fear of public opinion; but I suppose the run of experimentalists, external to the Catholic Church, have more or less inherited the positive or negative unbelief of Laplace, Buffon, Franklin,

Priestley, Cuvier, and Humboldt. I do not of course mean to say that there need be in every case a resentful and virulent opposition made to Religion on the part of scientific men; but their emphatic silence or phlegmatic inadvertence as to its claims have implied, more eloquently than any words, that in their opinion it had no voice at all in the subject-matter, which they had appropriated to themselves. The same antagonism shows itself in the middle ages. Friar Bacon was popularly regarded with suspicion as a dealer in unlawful arts; Pope Sylvester the Second has been accused of magic for his knowledge of natural secrets; and the geographical ideas of St. Virgil, Bishop of Saltzburg, were regarded with anxiety by the great St. Boniface, the glory of England, the Martyr-Apostle of Germany. I suppose, in matter of fact, magical superstition and physical knowledge did commonly go together in those ages: however, the hostility between experimental science and theology is far older than Christianity. Lord Bacon traces it to an era prior to Socrates; he tells us that, among the Greeks, the atheistic was the philosophy most favourable to physical discoveries, and he does not hesitate to imply that the rise of the religious schools was the ruin of science.

Now, if we would investigate the reason of this opposition between Theology and Physics, I suppose we must first take into account Lord Bacon's own explanation of it. It is common in judicial inquiries to caution the parties on whom the verdict depends to put out of their minds whatever they have heard out of court on the subject to which their attention is to be directed. They are to judge by the evidence; and this is a rule which holds in other investigations as far as this, that nothing of an adventitious nature ought to be introduced into the process. In like manner, from religious investigations, as such, physics must be excluded, and from physical, as such, religion; and if we mix them, we shall spoil both. The theologian, speaking of Divine Omnipotence, for the time simply ignores the laws of nature as existing restraints upon its exercise; and the physical philosopher, on the other hand, in his experiments upon natural phenomena, is simply ascertaining those laws, putting aside the question of that Omnipotence. If the theologian, in tracing the ways of Providence, were stopped with objections grounded on the impossibility of physical miracles, he would justly protest against the interruption; and were the philosopher, who was determining the motion of the heavenly bodies, to be questioned about their Final or their First Cause, he too would suffer an illogical interruption. The latter asks the cause of volcanoes, and is impatient at being told it is "the divine vengeance;" the former asks the cause of the overthrow of the guilty cities, and is preposterously referred to the volcanic action still visible in their neighbourhood. The inquiry into final causes for the moment passes over the existence of established laws; the inquiry into physical, passes over for the moment the existence of God. In other words, physical science is in a certain sense atheistic, for the very reason it is not theology.

This is Lord Bacon's justification, and an intelligible one, for considering that the fall of atheistic philosophy in ancient times was a blight upon the hopes of physical science. "Aristotle," he says, "Galen, and others frequently introduce such causes as these: – the hairs of the eyelids are for a fence to the sight; the bones for pillars whence to build the bodies of animals; the leaves of trees are to defend the fruit from the sun and wind; the clouds are designed for watering the earth. All which are properly alleged in metaphysics; but in physics, are impertinent, and as *remoras* to the ship, that hinder the sciences from holding on their course of improvement, and as introducing a neglect of searching after physical causes."[52] Here then is one reason for the prejudice of physical philosophers against Theology: – on the one hand, their deep satisfaction in the laws of nature indisposes them towards the thought of a Moral Governor, and makes them sceptical of His interposition; on the other hand, the occasional interference of religious criticism in a province not religious, has made them sore, suspicious, and resentful.

4.

Another reason of a kindred nature is to be found in the difference of method by which truths are gained in theology and in physical science. Induction is the instrument of Physics, and deduction only is the instrument of Theology. There the simple question is, What is revealed? all doctrinal knowledge flows from one fountain head. If we are able to enlarge our view and multiply our propositions, it must be merely by the comparison and adjustment of the original truths; if we would solve new questions, it must be by consulting old answers. The notion of doctrinal knowledge absolutely novel, and of simple addition from without, is intolerable to Catholic ears, and never was entertained by any one who was even approaching to an understanding of our creed. Revelation is all in all in doctrine; the Apostles its sole depository, the inferential method its sole instrument, and ecclesiastical authority its sole sanction. The Divine Voice has spoken once for all, and the only question is about its meaning. Now this process, as far as it was reasoning, was the very mode of reasoning which, as regards physical knowledge, the school of Bacon has superseded by the inductive method: –

no wonder, then, that that school should be irritated and indignant to find that a subject-matter remains still, in which their favourite instrument has no office; no wonder that they rise up against this memorial of an antiquated system, as an eyesore and an insult; and no wonder that the very force and dazzling success of their own method in its own departments should sway or bias unduly the religious sentiments of any persons who come under its influence. They assert that no new truth can be gained by deduction; Catholics assent, but add that, as regards religious truth, they have not to seek at all, for they have it already. Christian Truth is purely of revelation; that revelation we can but explain, we cannot increase, except relatively to our own apprehensions; without it we should have known nothing of its contents, with it we know just as much as its contents, and nothing more. And, as it was given by a divine act independent of man, so will it remain in spite of man. Niebuhr may revolutionize history, Lavoisier chemistry, Newton astronomy; but God Himself is the author as well as the subject of theology. When Truth can change, its Revelation can change; when human reason can outreason the Omniscient, then may it supersede His work.

Avowals such as these fall strange upon the ear of men whose first principle is the search after truth, and whose starting-points of search are things material and sensible. They scorn any process of inquiry not founded on experiment; the Mathematics indeed they endure, because that science deals with ideas, not with facts, and leads to conclusions hypothetical rather than real; "Metaphysics" they even use as a by-word of reproach; and Ethics they admit only on condition that it gives up conscience as its scientific ground, and bases itself on tangible utility: but as to Theology, they cannot deal with it, they cannot master it, and so they simply outlaw it and ignore it. Catholicism, forsooth, "confines the intellect," because it holds that God's intellect is greater than theirs, and that what He has done, man cannot improve. And what in some sort justifies them to themselves in this extravagance is the circumstance that there is a religion close at their doors which, discarding so severe a tone, has actually adopted their own principle of inquiry. Protestantism treats Scripture just as they deal with Nature; it takes the sacred text as a large collection of phenomena, from which, by an inductive process, each individual Christian may arrive at just those religious conclusions which approve themselves to his own judgment. It considers faith a mere modification of reason, as being an acquiescence in certain probable conclusions till better are found. Sympathy, then, if no other reason, throws experimental philosophers into alliance with the enemies of Catholicism.

5.

I have another consideration to add, not less important than any I have hitherto adduced. The physical sciences, Astronomy, Chemistry, and the rest, are doubtless engaged upon divine works, and cannot issue in untrue religious conclusions. But at the same time it must be recollected that Revelation has reference to circumstances which did not arise till after the heavens and the earth were made. They were made before the introduction of moral evil into the world: whereas the Catholic Church is the instrument of a remedial dispensation to meet that introduction. No wonder then that her teaching is simply distinct, though not divergent, from the theology which Physical Science suggests to its followers. She sets before us a number of attributes and acts on the part of the Divine Being, for which the material and animal creation gives no scope; power, wisdom, goodness are the burden of the physical world, but it does not and could not speak of mercy, long-suffering, and the economy of human redemption, and but partially of the moral law and moral goodness. "Sacred Theology," says Lord Bacon, "must be drawn from the words and the oracles of God: not from the light of nature or the dictates of reason. It is written, that 'the Heavens declare the glory of God;' but we nowhere find it that the Heavens declare the will of God; which is pronounced a law and a testimony, that men should do according to it. Nor does this hold only in the great mysteries of the Godhead, of the creation, of the redemption. . . . We cannot doubt that a large part of the moral law is too sublime to be attained by the light of nature; though it is still certain that men, even with the light and law of nature, have some notions of virtue, vice, justice, wrong, good, and evil."[53] That the new and further manifestations of the Almighty, made by Revelation, are in perfect harmony with the teaching of the natural world, forms indeed one subject of the profound work of the Anglican Bishop Butler; but they cannot in any sense be gathered from nature, and the silence of nature concerning them may easily seduce the imagination, though it has no force to persuade the reason, to revolt from doctrines which have not been authenticated by facts, but are enforced by authority. In a scientific age, then, there will naturally be a parade of what is called Natural Theology, a widespread profession of the Unitarian creed, an impatience of mystery, and a scepticism about miracles.

And to all this must be added the ample opportunity which physical science gives to the indulgence of those sentiments of beauty, order, and congruity, of which I have said so much, as the ensigns and colours (as they may be called) of a civilized age in its warfare against Catholicism.

It being considered, then, that Catholicism differs from physical science, in drift, in method of proof, and in subject-matter, how can it fail to meet with unfair usage from the philosophers of any Institution in which there is no one to take its part? That Physical Science itself will be ultimately the loser by such ill treatment of Theology, I have insisted on at great length in some preceding Discourses; for to depress unduly, to encroach upon any science, and much more on an important one, is to do an injury to all. However, this is not the concern of the Church; the Church has no call to watch over and protect Science: but towards Theology she has a distinct duty: it is one of the special trusts committed to her keeping. Where Theology is, there she must be; and if a University cannot fulfil its name and office without the recognition of Revealed Truth, she must be there to see that it is a *bonâ fide* recognition, sincerely made and consistently acted on.

6.

II. And if the interposition of the Church is necessary in the Schools of Science, still more imperatively is it demanded in the other main constituent portion of the subject-matter of Liberal Education, – Literature. Literature stands related to Man as Science stands to Nature; it is his history. Man is composed of body and soul; he thinks and he acts; he has appetites, passions, affections, motives, designs; he has within him the lifelong struggle of duty with inclination; he has an intellect fertile and capacious; he is formed for society, and society multiplies and diversifies in endless combinations his personal characteristics, moral and intellectual. All this constitutes his life; of all this Literature is the expression; so that Literature is to man in some sort what autobiography is to the individual; it is his Life and Remains. Moreover, he is this sentient, intelligent, creative, and operative being, quite independent of any extraordinary aid from Heaven, or any definite religious belief; and *as such,* as he is in himself, does Literature represent him; it is the Life and Remains of the *natural* man, innocent or guilty. I do not mean to say that it is impossible in its very notion that Literature should be tinctured by a religious spirit; Hebrew Literature, as far as it can be called Literature, certainly is simply theological, and has a character imprinted on it which is above nature; but I am speaking of what is to be expected without any extraordinary dispensation; and I say that, in matter of fact, as Science is the reflection of Nature, so is Literature also – the one, of Nature physical, the other, of Nature moral and social. Circumstances, such as locality, period, language, seem to make little or no difference in the character of Literature, as such; on the whole, all Literatures are one; they are the voices of the natural man.

I wish this were all that had to be said to the disadvantage of Literature; but while Nature physical remains fixed in its laws, Nature moral and social has a will of its own, is self-governed, and never remains any long while in that state from which it started into action. Man will never continue in a mere state of innocence; he is sure to sin, and his literature will be the expression of his sin, and this whether he be heathen or Christian. Christianity has thrown gleams of light on him and his literature; but as it has not converted him, but only certain choice specimens of him, so it has not changed the characters of his mind or of his history; his literature is either what it was, or worse than what it was, in proportion as there has been an abuse of knowledge granted and a rejection of truth. On the whole, then, I think it will be found, and ever found, as a matter of course, that Literature, as such, no matter of what nation, is the science or history, partly and at best of the natural man, partly of man in rebellion.

7.

Here then, I say, you are involved in a difficulty greater than that which besets the cultivation of Science; for, if Physical Science be dangerous, as I have said, it is dangerous, because it necessarily ignores the idea of moral evil; but Literature is open to the more grievous imputation of recognizing and understanding it too well. Some one will say to me perhaps: "Our youth shall not be corrupted. We will dispense with all general or national Literature whatever, if it be so exceptionable; we will have a Christian Literature of our own, as pure, as true, as the Jewish." You cannot have it: – I do not say you cannot form a select literature for the young, nay, even for the middle or lower classes; this is another matter altogether: I am speaking of University Education, which implies an extended range of reading, which has to deal with standard works of genius, or what are called the *classics* of a language: and I say, from the nature of the case, if Literature is to be made a study of human nature, you cannot have a Christian Literature. It is a contradiction in terms to attempt a sinless Literature of sinful man. You may gather together something very great and high, something higher than any Literature ever was; and when you have done so, you will find that it is not Literature at all. You will have simply left the delineation of man, as such, and have substituted for it, as far as you have had any thing to substitute, that of man, as he is or might be, under certain special advantages. Give up the study of man, as such, if so it must be; but say you do so. Do not say you are studying him, his history, his mind and his heart, when you are studying something else. Man is a being of genius, passion, intellect, conscience, power. He exercises these various gifts in various ways, in great deeds, in great thoughts, in heroic acts, in hateful crimes. He founds states, he fights battles, he builds cities, he ploughs the forest, he subdues the elements, he rules his kind. He creates vast ideas, and influences many generations. He takes a thousand shapes, and undergoes a thousand fortunes. Literature records them all to the life,

> Quicquid agunt homines, votum, timor, ira, voluptas,
> Gaudia, discursus.[54]

He pours out his fervid soul in poetry; he sways to and fro, he soars, he dives, in his restless speculations; his lips drop eloquence; he touches the canvas, and it glows with beauty; he sweeps the strings, and they thrill with an ecstatic meaning. He looks back into himself, and he reads his own thoughts, and notes them down; he looks out into the universe, and tells over and celebrates the elements and principles of which it is the product.

Such is man: put him aside, keep him before you; but, whatever you do, do not take him for what he is not, for something more divine and sacred, for man regenerate. Nay, beware of showing God's grace and its work at such disadvantage as to make the few whom it has thoroughly influenced compete in intellect with the vast multitude who either have it not, or use it ill. The elect are few to choose out of, and the world is inexhaustible. From the first, Jabel and Tubalcain, Nimrod "the stout hunter," the learning of the Pharaohs, and the wisdom of the East country, are of the world. Every now and then they are rivalled by a Solomon or a Beseleel, but the *habitat* of natural gifts is the natural man. The Church may use them, she cannot at her will originate them. Not till the whole human race is made new will its literature be pure and true. Possible of course it is in idea, for nature, inspired by heavenly grace, to exhibit itself on a large scale, in an originality of thought or action, even far beyond what the world's literature has recorded or exemplified; but, if you would in fact have a literature of saints, first of all have a nation of them.

What is a clearer proof of the truth of all this than the structure of the Inspired Word itself? It is undeniably *not* the reflection or picture of the many, but of the few; it is no picture of life, but an anticipation of death and judgment. Human literature is about all things, grave or gay, painful or pleasant; but the Inspired Word views them only in one aspect, and as they tend to one scope. It gives us little insight into the fertile developments of mind; it has no terms in its vocabulary to express with exactness the intellect and its separate faculties: it knows nothing of genius, fancy, wit, invention, presence of mind, resource. It does not discourse of empire, commerce, enterprise, learning, philosophy, or the fine arts. Slightly too does it touch on the more simple and innocent courses of nature and their reward. Little does it say of those temporal blessings which rest upon our worldly occupations, and make them easy; of the blessings which we derive from the sunshine day and the serene night, from the succession of the seasons, and the produce of the earth.[55] Little about our recreations and our daily domestic comforts; little about the ordinary occasions of festivity and mirth, which sweeten human life; and nothing at all about various pursuits or amusements, which it would be going too much into detail to mention. We read indeed of the feast when Isaac was weaned, and of Jacob's court-ship, and of the religious merry-makings of holy Job; but exceptions, such as these, do but remind us what might be in Scripture, and is not. If then by Literature is meant the manifestation of human nature in human language, you will seek for it in vain except in the world. Put up with it, as it is, or do not pretend to cultivate it; take things as they are, not as you could wish them.

8.

Nay, I am obliged to go further still; even if we could, still we should be shrinking from our plain duty, Gentlemen, did we leave out Literature from Education. For why do we educate, except to prepare for the world? Why do we cultivate the intellect of the many beyond the first elements of knowl-edge, except for this world? Will it be much matter in the world to come whether our bodily health or whether our intellectual strength was more or less, except of course as this world is in all its circumstances a trial for the next? If then a University is a direct preparation for this world, let it be what it professes. It is not a Convent, it is not a Seminary; it is a place to fit men of the world for the world. We cannot possibly keep them from plunging into the world, with all its ways and principles and maxims, when their time comes; but we can prepare them against what is inevitable; and it is not the way to learn to swim in troubled waters, never to have gone into them. Proscribe (I do not merely say particular authors, particular works, particu-lar passages) but Secular Literature as such; cut out from your class books all broad manifestations of the natural man; and those manifestations are waiting for your pupil's benefit at the very doors of your lecture room in living and breathing substance. They will meet him there in all the charm of novelty, and all the fascination of genius or of amiableness. To-day a pupil, to-morrow a member of the great world: to-day confined to the Lives of the Saints, to-morrow thrown upon Babel; – thrown on Babel, without the honest indulgence of wit and humour and imagination having ever been permitted to him, without any fastidiousness of taste wrought into him, without any rule given him for discriminating "the precious from the vile," beauty from sin, the truth from the sophistry of nature, what is innocent from what is poison. You have refused him the masters of human thought, who would in some sense have educated him, because of their incidental corruption: you have shut up from him those whose thoughts strike home to our hearts, whose words are proverbs, whose names are indigenous to all the world, who are the standard of their mother tongue, and the pride and boast of their countrymen, Homer, Ariosto, Cervantes, Shakespeare, because the old Adam smelt rank in them; and for what have you reserved him? You have given him "a liberty unto" the multitudinous blasphemy of his day; you have made him free of its newspapers, its reviews, its magazines, its novels, its controversial pamphlets, of its Parliamentary debates, its law proceedings, its platform speeches, its songs, its drama, its theatre, of its enveloping, stifling atmosphere of death. You have succeeded but in this, – in making the world his University.

Difficult then as the question may be, and much as it may try the judgments and even divide the opinions of zealous and religious Catholics, I cannot feel any doubt myself, Gentlemen, that the Church's true policy is not to aim at the exclusion of Literature from Secular Schools, but at her own admission into them. Let her do for Literature in one way what she does for Science in another; each has its imperfection, and she has her remedy for each. She fears no knowledge, but she purifies all; she represses no element of our nature, but she cultivates the whole. Science is grave, methodical, logical; with Science then she argues, and opposes reason to reason. Literature does not argue, but declaims and insinuates; it is multiform and versatile: it persuades instead of convincing, it seduces, it carries captive; it appeals to the sense of honour, or to the imagination, or to the stimulus of curiosity; it makes its way by means of gaiety, satire, romance, the beautiful, the pleasurable. Is it wonderful that with an agent like this the Church should claim to deal with a vigour corresponding to its restlessness, to interfere in its proceedings with a higher hand, and to wield an authority in the choice of its studies and of its books which would be tyrannical, if reason and fact were the only instruments of its conclusions? But, any how, her principle is one and the same throughout: not to prohibit truth of any kind, but to see that no doctrines pass under the name of Truth but those which claim it rightfully.

9.

Such at least is the lesson which I am taught by all the thought which I have been able to bestow upon the subject; such is the lesson which I have gained from the history of my own special Father and Patron, St. Philip Neri. He lived in an age as traitorous to the interests of Catholicism as any that preceded it, or can follow it. He lived at a time when pride mounted high, and the senses held rule; a time when kings and nobles never had more of state and homage, and never less of personal responsibility and peril; when medieval winter was receding, and the summer sun of civilization was bringing into leaf and flower a thousand forms of luxurious enjoyment; when a new world of thought and beauty had opened upon the human mind, in the discovery of the treasures of classic literature and art. He saw the great and the gifted, dazzled by the Enchantress, and drinking in the magic of her song; he saw the high and the wise, the student and the artist, painting, and poetry, and sculpture, and music, and architecture, drawn within her range, and circling round the abyss: he saw heathen forms mounting thence, and forming in the thick air: – all this he saw, and he perceived that the mischief was to be met, not with argument, not with science, not with protests and warnings, not by the recluse or the preacher, but by means of the great counter-fascination of purity and truth. He was raised up to do a work almost peculiar in the Church, – not to be a Jerome Savonarola, though Philip had a true devotion towards him and a tender memory of his Florentine house; not to be a St. Charles, though in his beaming countenance Philip had recognized the aureole of a saint; not to be a St. Ignatius, wrestling with the foe, though Philip was termed the Society's bell of call, so many subjects did he send to it; not to be a St. Francis Xavier, though Philip had longed to shed his blood for Christ in India with him; not to be a St. Cajetan, or hunter, of souls, for Philip preferred, as he expressed it, tranquilly to cast in his net to gain them; he preferred to yield to the stream, and direct the current, which he could not stop, of science, literature, art, and fashion, and to sweeten and to sanctify what God had made very good and man had spoilt.

And so he contemplated as the idea of his mission, not the propogation of the faith, nor the exposition of doctrine, nor the catechetical schools; whatever was exact and systematic pleased him not; he put from him monastic rule and authoritative speech, as David refused the armour of his king. No; he would be but an ordinary individual priest as others: and his weapons should be but unaffected humility and unpretending love. All He did was to be done by the light, and fervour, and convincing eloquence of his personal character and his easy conversation. He came to the Eternal City and he sat himself down there, and his home and his family gradually grew up around him, by the spontaneous accession of materials from without. He did not so much seek his own as draw them to him. He sat in his small room, and they in their gay worldly dresses, the rich and the wellborn, as well as the simple and the illiterate, crowded into it. In the mid-heats of summer, in the frosts of winter, still was he in that low and narrow cell at San Girolamo, reading the hearts of those who came to him, and curing their souls' maladies by the very touch of his hand. It was a vision of the Magi worshipping the infant Saviour, so pure and innocent, so sweet and beautiful was he; and so loyal and so dear to the gracious Virgin Mother. And they who came remained gazing and listening, till at length, first one and then another threw off their bravery, and took his poor cassock and girdle instead: or, if they kept it, it was to put haircloth under it, or to take on them a rule of life, while to the world they looked as before.

In the words of his biographer, "he was all things to all men. He suited himself to noble and ignoble, young and old, subjects and prelates, learned and ignorant; and received those who were strangers to him with singular benignity, and embraced them with as much love and charity as if he had been a long while expecting them. When he was called upon to be merry he was so; if there was a demand upon his sympathy he was equally ready. He gave the same welcome to all: caressing the poor equally with the rich, and wearying himself to assist all to the utmost limits of his power. In consequence of his being so accessible and willing to receive all comers, many went to him every day, and some continued for the space of thirty, nay forty years, to visit him very often both morning and evening, so that his room went by the agreeable nickname of the Home of Christian mirth. Nay, people came to him, not only from all parts of Italy, but from France, Spain, Germany, and all Christendom; and even the infidels and Jews, who had ever any communication with him, revered him as a holy man."[56] The first families of Rome, the Massimi, the Aldobrandini, the Colonnas, the Altieri, the Vitelleschi, were his friends and his penitents. Nobles of Poland, Grandees of Spain, Knights of Malta, could not leave Rome without coming to him. Cardinals, Archbishops, and Bishops were his intimates; Federigo Borromeo haunted his room and got the name of "Father Philip's soul." The Cardinal-Archbishops of Verona and Bologna wrote books in his honour. Pope Pius the Fourth died in his arms. Lawyers, painters, musicians, physicians, it was the same too with them. Baronius, Zazzara, and Ricci, left the law at his bidding, and joined his congregation, to do its work, to write the annals of the Church, and to die in the odour of sanctity. Palestrina had

Father Philip's ministrations in his last moments. Animuccia hung about him during life, sent him a message after death, and was conducted by him through Purgatory to Heaven. And who was he, I say, all the while, but an humble priest, a stranger in Rome, with no distinction of family or letters, no claim of station or of office, great simply in the attraction with which a Divine Power had gifted him? and yet thus humble, thus unennobled, thus empty-handed, he has achieved the glorious title of Apostle of Rome.

10.

Well were it for his clients and children, Gentlemen, if they could promise themselves the very shadow of his special power, or could hope to do a miserable fraction of the sort of work in which he was pre-eminently skilled. But so far at least they may attempt, – to take his position, and to use his method, and to cultivate the arts of which he was so bright a pattern. For me, if it be God's blessed will that in the years now coming I am to have a share in the great undertaking, which has been the occasion and the subject of these Discourses, so far I can say for certain that, whether or not I can do any thing at all in St. Philip's way, at least I can do nothing in any other. Neither by my habits of life, nor by vigour of age, am I fitted for the task of authority, or of rule, or of initiation. I do but aspire, if strength is given me, to be your minister in a work which must employ younger minds and stronger lives than mine. I am but fit to bear my witness, to proffer my suggestions, to express my sentiments, as has in fact been my occupation in these discussions; to throw such light upon general questions, upon the choice of objects, upon the import of principles, upon the tendency of measures, as past reflection and experience enable me to contribute. I shall have to make appeals to your consideration, your friendliness, your confidence, of which I have had so many instances, on which I so tranquilly repose; and after all, neither you nor I must even be surprised, should it so happen that the Hand of Him, with whom are the springs of life and death, weighs heavy on me, and makes me unequal to anticipations in which you have been too kind, and to hopes in which I may have been too sanguine.

II

University Subjects

DISCUSSED IN OCCASIONAL

LECTURES AND ESSAYS

Four Selections

I.

CHRISTIANITY AND LETTERS.

A LECTURE IN THE SCHOOL OF PHILOSOPHY
AND LETTERS.

I.

It seems but natural, Gentlemen, now that we are opening the School of Philosophy and Letters, or, as it was formerly called, of Arts, in this new University, that we should direct our attention to the question, what are the subjects generally included under that name, and what place they hold, and how they come to hold that place, in a University, and in the education which a University provides. This would be natural on such an occasion, even though the Faculty of Arts held but a secondary place in the academical system; but it seems to be even imperative on us, considering that the studies which that Faculty embraces are almost the direct subject-matter and the staple of the mental exercises proper to a University.

It is indeed not a little remarkable that, in spite of the special historical connexion of University Institutions with the Sciences of Theology, Law, and Medicine, a University, after all, should be formally based (as it really is), and should emphatically live in, the Faculty of Arts; but such is the deliberate decision of those who have most deeply and impartially considered the subject.[57] Arts existed before other Faculties; the Masters of Arts were the ruling and directing body; the success and popularity of the Faculties of Law and Medicine were considered to be in no slight measure an encroachment and a usurpation, and were met with jealousy and resistance. When Colleges arose and became the medium and instrument of University action, they did but confirm the ascendency of the Faculty of Arts; and thus, even down to this day, in those academical corporations which have more than others retained the traces of their medieval origin, – I mean the Universities of Oxford and Cambridge, – we hear little of Theology, Medicine, or Law, and almost exclusively of Arts.

Now, considering the reasonable association, to which I have already referred, which exists in our minds between Universities and the three learned professions, here is a phenomenon which has to be contemplated for its own sake and accounted for, as well as a circumstance enhancing the significance and importance of the act in which we have been for some weeks engaged; and I consider that I shall not be employing our time unprofitably, if I am able to make a suggestion, which, while it illustrates the fact, is able to explain the difficulty.

2.

Here I must go back, Gentlemen, a very great way, and ask you to review the course of Civilization since the beginning of history. When we survey the stream of human affairs for the last three thousand years, we find it to run thus: – At first sight there is so much fluctuation, agitation, ebbing and flowing, that we may despair to discern any law in its movements, taking the earth as its bed, and mankind as its contents; but, on looking more closely and attentively, we shall discern, in spite of the heterogeneous materials and the various histories and fortunes which are found in the race of man during the long period I have mentioned, a certain formation amid the chaos, – one and one only, – and extending, though not over the whole earth, yet through a very considerable portion of it. Man is a social being and can hardly exist without society, and in matter of fact societies have ever existed all over the habitable earth. The greater part of these associations have been political or religious, and have been comparatively limited in extent, and temporary. They have been formed and dissolved by the force of accidents or by inevitable circumstances; and, when we have enumerated them one by one, we have made of them all that can be made. But there is one remarkable association which attracts the attention of the philosopher, not political nor religious, or at least only partially and not essentially such, which began in the earliest times and grew with each succeeding age, till it reached its complete development, and then continued on, vigorous and unwearied, and which still remains as definite and as firm as ever it was. Its bond is a common civilization; and, though there are other civilizations in the world, as there are other societies, yet this civilization, together with the society which is its creation and its home, is so distinctive and luminous in its character, so imperial in its extent, so imposing in its duration, and so utterly without rival upon the face of the earth, that the association may fitly assume to itself the title of "Human Society," and its civilization the abstract term "Civilization."

There are indeed great outlying portions of mankind which are not, perhaps never have been, included in this Human Society; still they are outlying portions and nothing else, fragmentary, unsociable, solitary, and unmeaning, protesting and revolting against the grand central formation of which I am speaking, but not uniting with each other into a second whole. I am not denying of course the civilization of the Chinese, for instance, though it be not our civilization; but it is a huge, stationary, unattractive, morose civilization. Nor do I deny a civilization to the Hindoos, nor to the ancient Mexicans, nor to the Saracens, nor (in a certain sense) to the Turks; but each of these races has its own civilization, as separate from one another as from ours. I do not see how they can be all brought under one idea. Each stands by itself, as if the other were not; each is local; many of them are temporary; none of them will bear a comparison with the Society and the Civilization which I have described as alone having a claim to those names, and on which I am going to dwell.

Gentlemen, let me here observe that I am not entering upon the question of races, or upon their history. I have nothing to do with ethnology. I take things as I find them on the surface of history, and am but classing phenomena. Looking, then, at the countries which surround the Mediterranean Sea as a whole, I see them to be, from time immemorial, the seat of an association of intellect and mind, such as to deserve to be called the Intellect and the Mind of the Human Kind. Starting as it does and advancing from certain centres, till their respective influences intersect and conflict, and then at length intermingle and combine, a common Thought has been generated, and a common Civilization defined and established. Egypt is one such starting point, Syria another, Greece a third, Italy a fourth, and North Africa a fifth, – afterwards France and Spain. As time goes on, and as colonization and conquest work their changes, we see a great association of nations formed, of which the Roman empire is the maturity and the most intelligible expression; an association, however, not political, but mental, based on the same intellectual ideas, and advancing by common intellectual methods. And this association or social commonwealth, with whatever reverses, changes, and momentary dissolutions, continues down to this day; not, indeed, precisely on the same territory, but with such only partial and local disturbances, and on the other hand, with so combined and harmonious a movement, and such a visible continuity, that it would be utterly unreasonable to deny that it is throughout all that interval but one and the same.

In its earliest age it included far more of the eastern world than it has since; in these later times it has taken into its compass a new hemisphere; in the middle ages it lost Africa, Egypt, and Syria, and extended itself to Germany, Scandinavia, and the British Isles. At one time its territory was flooded by strange and barbarous races, but the existing civilization was vigorous enough to vivify what threatened to stifle it, and to assimilate to the old social forms what came to expel them; and thus the civilization of modern times remains what it was of old, not Chinese, or Hindoo, or Mexican, or Saracenic, or of any new description hitherto unknown, but the lineal descendant, or rather the continuation, *mutatis mutandis,* of the civilization which began in Palestine and Greece.

Considering, then, the characteristics of this great civilized Society, which I have already insisted on, I think it has a claim to be considered as the representative Society and Civilization of the human race, as its perfect result and limit, in fact; – those portions of the race which do not coalesce with it being left to stand by themselves as anomalies, unaccountable indeed, but for that very reason not interfering with what on the contrary has been turned to account and has grown into a whole. I call then this commonwealth pre-eminently and emphatically Human Society, and its intellect the Human Mind, and its decisions the sense of mankind, and its disciplined and cultivated state Civilization in the abstract, and the territory on which it lies the *orbis terrarum,* or the World. For, unless the illustration be fanciful, the object which I am contemplating is like the impression of a seal upon the wax; which rounds off and gives form to the greater portion of the soft material, and presents something definite to the eye, and preoccupies the space against any second figure, so that we overlook and leave out of our thoughts the jagged outline or unmeaning lumps outside of it, intent upon the harmonious circle which fills the imagination within it.

3.

Now, before going on to speak of the education, and the standards of education, which the Civilized World, as I may now call it, has enjoined and requires, I wish to draw your attention, Gentlemen, to the circumstance that this same *orbis terrarum,* which has been the seat of Civilization, will be found, on the whole, to be the seat also of that supernatural society and system which our Maker has given us directly from Himself, the Christian Polity. The natural and divine associations are not indeed exactly coincident, nor ever have been. As the territory of Civilization has varied with itself in different ages, while on the whole it has been the same, so, in like manner, Christianity has fallen partly outside Civilization, and Civilization partly outside Christianity; but, on the whole, the two have occupied one and the same *orbis terrarum.* Often indeed they have even moved *pari passu,* and at all times there has been found the most intimate connexion between them. Christianity waited till the *orbis terrarum* attained its most perfect form before it appeared; and it soon coalesced, and has ever since co-operated, and often seemed identical, with the Civilization which is its companion.

There are certain analogies, too, which hold between Civilization and Christianity. As Civilization does not cover the whole earth, neither does Christianity; but there is nothing else like the one, and nothing else like the other. Each is the only thing of its kind. Again, there are, as I have already said, large outlying portions of the world in a certain sense cultivated and educated, which, if they could exist together in one, would go far to constitute a second *orbis terrarum,* the home of a second distinct civilization; but every one of these is civilized on its own principle and idea, or at least they are separated from each other, and have not run together, while the Civilization and Society which I have been describing is one organized whole. And, in like manner, Christianity coalesces into one vast body, based upon common ideas; yet there are large outlying organizations of religion independent of each other and of it. Moreover, Christianity, as is the case in the parallel instance of Civilization, continues on in the world without interruption from the date of its rise, while other religious bodies, huge, local, and isolated, are rising and falling, or are helplessly stationary, from age to age, on all sides of it.

There is another remarkable analogy between Christianity and Civilization, and the mention of it will introduce my proper subject, to which what I have hitherto said is merely a preparation. We know that Christianity is built upon definite ideas, principles, doctrines, and writings, which were given at the time of its first introduction, and have never been superseded, and admit of no addition. I am not going to parallel any thing which is the work of man, and in the natural order, with what is from heaven, and in consequence infallible, and irreversible, and obligatory; but, after making this reserve, lest I should possibly be misunderstood, still I would remark that, in matter of fact, looking at the state of the case historically, Civilization too has its common principles, and views, and teaching, and especially its books, which have more or less been given from the earliest times, and are, in fact, in equal esteem and respect, in equal use now, as they were when they were received in the beginning. In a word, the Classics, and the subjects of thought and the studies to which they give rise, or, to use the term most to our present purpose, the Arts, have ever, on the whole, been the instruments of education which the civilized *orbis terrarum* has adopted; just as inspired works, and the lives of saints, and the articles of faith, and the catechism, have ever been the instrument of education in the case of Christianity. And this consideration, you see, Gentlemen (to drop down at once upon the subject proper to the occasion which has brought us together), invests the opening of the School in Arts with a solemnity and moment of a peculiar kind, for we are but reiterating an old tradition, and carrying on those august methods of enlarging the mind, and cultivating the intellect, and refining the feelings, in which the process of Civilization has ever consisted.

4.

In the country which has been the fountain head of intellectual gifts, in the age which preceded or introduced the first formations of Human Society, in an era scarcely historical, we may dimly discern an almost mythical personage, who, putting out of consideration the actors in Old Testament history, may be called the first Apostle of Civilization. Like an Apostle in a higher order of things, he was poor and a wanderer, and feeble in the flesh, though he was to do such great things, and to live in the mouths of a hundred generations and a thousand tribes. A blind old man; whose wanderings were such that, when he became famous, his birth-place could not be ascertained, so that it was said, –

> "Seven famous towns contend for Homer dead,
> Through which the living Homer begged his bread."[58]

Yet he had a name in his day; and, little guessing in what vast measures his wish would be answered, he supplicated, with a tender human sentiment, as he wandered over the islands of the Ægean and the Asian coasts, that those who had known and loved him would cherish his memory when he was away. Unlike the proud boast of the Roman poet, if he spoke it in earnest, "Exegi monumentum ære perennius," he did but indulge the hope that one, whose coming had been expected with pleasure, might excite regret when he had departed, and be rewarded by the sympathy and praise of his friends even in the presence of other minstrels.[59] A set of verses remains, which is ascribed to him, in which he addresses the Delian women in the tone of feeling which I have described. "Farewell to you all," he says, "and remember me in time to come, and when any one of men on earth, a stranger from far, shall inquire of you, O maidens, who is the sweetest of minstrels here about, and in whom do you most delight? then make answer modestly, It is a blind man, and he lives in steep Chios."

The great poet remained unknown for some centuries, – that is, unknown to what we call fame. His verses were cherished by his countrymen, they might be the secret delight of thousands, but they were not collected into a volume, nor viewed as a whole, nor made a subject of criticism. At length an Athenian Prince took upon him the task of gathering together the scattered fragments of a genius which had not aspired to immortality, of reducing them to writing, and of fitting them to be the text-book of ancient education. Henceforth the vagrant ballad-singer, as he might be thought, was submitted, to his surprise, to a sort of literary canonization, and was invested with the office of forming the young mind of Greece to noble thoughts and bold deeds. To be read in Homer soon became the education of a gentleman; and a rule, recognized in her free age, remained as a tradition even in the times of her degradation. Xenophon introduces to us a youth who knew both Iliad and Odyssey by heart; Dio witnesses that they were some of the first books put into the hands of boys; and Horace decided that they taught the science of life better than Stoic or Academic. Alexander the Great nourished his imagination by the scenes of the Iliad. As time went on, other poets were associated with Homer in the work of education, such as Hesiod and the Tragedians. The majestic lessons concerning duty and religion, justice and providence, which occur in Æschylus and Sophocles, belong to a higher school than that of Homer; and the verses of Euripides, even in his lifetime, were so familiar to Athenian lips and so dear to foreign ears, that, as is reported, the captives of Syracuse gained their freedom at the price of reciting them to their conquerors.

Such poetry may be considered oratory also, since it has so great a power of persuasion; and the alliance between these two gifts had existed from the time that the verses of Orpheus had, according to the fable, made woods and streams and wild animals to follow him about. Soon, however, Oratory became the subject of a separate art, which was called Rhetoric, and of which the Sophists were the chief masters. Moreover, as Rhetoric was especially political in its nature, it presupposed or introduced the cultivation of History; and thus the pages of Thucydides became one of the special studies by which Demosthenes rose to be the first orator of Greece.

But it is needless to trace out further the formation of the course of liberal education; it is sufficient to have given some specimens in illustration of it. The studies, which it was found to involve, were four principal ones, Grammar, Rhetoric, Logic, and Mathematics; and the science of Mathematics, again, was divided into four, Geometry, Arithmetic, Astronomy, and Music; making in all seven, which are known by the name of the Seven Liberal Arts. And thus a definite school of intellect was formed, founded on ideas and methods of a distinctive character, and (as we may say) of the highest and truest character, as far as they went, and which gradually associated in one, and assimilated, and took possession of, that multitude of nations which I have considered to represent mankind, and to possess the *orbis terrarum.*

When we pass from Greece to Rome, we are met with the common remark, that Rome produced little that was original, but borrowed from Greece. It is true; Terence copied from Menander, Virgil from Homer, Hesiod, and Theocritus; and Cicero professed merely to reproduce the philosophy of Greece. But, granting its truth ever so far, I do but take it as a proof of the sort of instinct which has guided the course of Civilization. The world was to have certain intellectual teachers, and no others; Homer and Aristotle, with the poets and philosophers who circle round them, were to be the schoolmasters of all generations, and therefore the Latins, falling into the law on which the world's education was to be carried on, so added to the classical library as not to reverse or interfere with what had already been determined. And there was the more meaning in this arrangement, when it is considered that Greek was to be forgotten during many centuries, and the tradition of intellectual training to be conveyed through Latin; for thus the world was secured against the consequences of a loss which would have changed the character of its civilization. I think it very remarkable, too, how soon the Latin writers became text-books in the boys' schools. Even to this day Shakespeare and Milton are not studied in our course of education; but the poems of Virgil and Horace, as those of Homer and the Greek authors in an earlier age, were in schoolboys' satchels not much more than a hundred years after they were written.

I need not go on to show at length that they have preserved their place in the system of education in the *orbis terrarum,* and the Greek writers with them or through them, down to this day. The induction of centuries has often been made. Even in the lowest state of learning the tradition was kept up. St. Gregory the Great, whose era, not to say whose influence, is often considered especially unfavourable to the old literature, was himself well versed in it, encouraged purity of Latinity in his court, and is said figuratively by the contemporary historian of his life to have supported the hall of the Apostolic See upon the columns of the Seven Liberal Arts. In the ninth century, when the dark age was close at hand, we still hear of the cultivation, with whatever success (according of course to the opportunities of the times, but I am speaking of the nature of the studies, not of the proficiency of the students), the cultivation of Music, Dialectics, Rhetoric, Grammar, Mathematics, Astronomy, Physics, and Geometry; of the supremacy of Horace in the schools, "and the great Virgil, Sallust, and Statius." In the thirteenth or following centuries, of "Virgil, Lucian, Statius, Ovid, Livy, Sallust, Cicero, and Quintilian;" and after the revival of literature in the commencement of the modern era, we find St. Carlo Borromeo enjoining the use of works of Cicero, Ovid, Virgil, and Horace.[60]

5.

I pass thus cursorily over the series of informations which history gives us on the subject, merely with a view of recalling to your memory, Gentlemen, and impressing upon you the fact, that the literature of Greece, continued into, and enriched by, the literature of Rome, together with the studies which it involves, has been the instrument of education, and the food of civilization, from the first times of the world down to this day; – and now we are in a condition to answer the question which thereupon arises, when we turn to consider, by way of contrast, the teaching which is characteristic of Universities. How has it come to pass that, although the genius of Universities is so different from that of the schools which preceded them, nevertheless the course of study pursued in those schools was not superseded in the middle ages by those more brilliant sciences which Universities introduced? It might have seemed as if Scholastic Theology, Law, and Medicine would have thrown the Seven Liberal Arts into the shade, but in the event they failed to do so. I consider the reason to be, that the authority and function of the monastic and secular schools, as supplying to the young the means of education, lay deeper than in any appointment of Charlemagne, who was their nominal founder, and were based in the special character of that civilization which is so intimately associated with Christianity, that it may even be called the soil out of which Christianity grew. The medieval sciences, great as is their dignity and utility, were never intended to supersede that more real and proper cultivation of the mind which is effected by the study of the liberal Arts; and, when certain of these sciences did in fact go out of their province and did attempt to prejudice the traditional course of education, the encroachment was in matter of fact resisted. There were those in the middle age, as John of Salisbury, who vigorously protested against the extravagances and usurpations which ever attend the introduction of any great good whatever, and which attended the rise of the peculiar sciences of which Universities were the seat; and, though there were times when the old traditions seemed to be on the point of failing, somehow it has happened that they have never failed; for the instinct of Civilization and the common sense of Society prevailed, and the danger passed away, and the studies which seemed to be going out gained their ancient place, and were acknowledged, as before, to be the best instruments of mental cultivation, and the best guarantees for intellectual progress.

And this experience of the past we may apply to the circumstances in which we find ourselves at present; for, as there was a movement against the Classics in the middle age, so has there been now. The truth of the Baconian method for the purposes for which it was created, and its inestimable services and inexhaustible applications in the interests of our material well-being, have dazzled the imaginations of men, somewhat in the same way as certain new sciences carried them away in the age of Abelard; and since that method does such wonders in its own province, it is not unfrequently supposed that it can do as much in any other province also. Now, Bacon himself never would have so argued; he would not have needed to be reminded that to advance the useful arts is one thing, and to cultivate the mind another. The simple question to be considered is, how best to strengthen, refine, and enrich the intellectual powers; the perusal of the poets, historians, and philosophers of Greece and Rome will accomplish this purpose, as long experience has shown; but that the study of the experimental sciences will do the like, is proved to us as yet by no experience whatever.

Far indeed am I from denying the extreme attractiveness, as well as the practical benefit to the world at large, of the sciences of Chemistry, Electricity, and Geology; but the question is not what department of study contains the more wonderful facts, or promises the more brilliant discoveries, and which is in the higher and which in an inferior rank; but simply which out of all provides the most robust and invigorating discipline for the unformed mind. And I conceive it is as little disrespectful to Lord Bacon to prefer the Classics in this point of view to the sciences which have grown out of his philosophy as it would be disrespectful to St. Thomas in the middle ages to have hindered the study of the Summa from doing prejudice to the Faculty of Arts. Accordingly, I anticipate that, as in the middle ages both the teaching and the government of the University remained in the Faculty of Arts, in spite of the genius which created or illustrated Theology and Law, so now too, whatever be the splendour of the modern philosophy, the marvellousness of its disclosures, the utility of its acquisitions, and the talent of its masters, still it will not avail in the event, to detrude classical literature and the studies connected with it from the place which they have held in all ages in education.

Such, then, is the course of reflection obviously suggested by the act in which we have been lately engaged, and which we are now celebrating. In the nineteenth century, in a country which looks out upon a new world, and anticipates a coming age, we have been engaged in opening the Schools dedicated to the studies of polite literature and liberal science, or what are called the Arts, as a first step towards the establishment on Catholic ground of a Catholic University. And while we thus recur to Greece and Athens with pleasure and affection, and recognize in that famous land the source and the school of intellectual culture, it would be strange indeed if we forgot to look further south also, and there to bow before a more glorious luminary, and a more sacred oracle of truth, and the source of another sort of knowledge, high and supernatural, which is seated in Palestine. Jerusalem is the fountain-head of religious knowledge, as Athens is of secular. In the ancient world we see two centres of illumination, acting independently of each other, each with its own movement, and at first apparently without any promise of convergence. Greek civilization spreads over the East, conquering in the conquests of Alexander, and, when carried captive into the West, subdues the conquerors who brought it thither. Religion, on the other hand, is driven from its own aboriginal home to the North and West by reason of the sins of the people who were in charge of it, in a long course of judgments and plagues and persecutions. Each by itself pursues its career and fulfils its mission; neither of them recognizes, nor is recognized by the other. At length the Temple of Jerusalem is rooted up by the armies of Titus, and the effete schools of Athens are stifled by the edict of Justinian. So pass away the ancient Voices of religion and learning; but they are silenced only to revive more gloriously and perfectly elsewhere. Hitherto they came from separate sources, and performed separate works. Each leaves an heir and successor in the West, and that heir and successor is one and the same. The grace stored in Jerusalem, and the gifts which radiate from Athens, are made over and concentrated in Rome. This is true as a matter of history. Rome has inherited both sacred and profane learning; she has perpetuated and dispensed the traditions of Moses and David in the supernatural order, and of Homer and Aristotle in the natural. To separate those distinct teachings, human and divine, which meet in Rome, is to retrograde; it is to rebuild the Jewish Temple and to plant anew the groves of Academus.

6.

On this large subject, however, on which I might say much, time does not allow me to enter. To show how sacred learning and profane are dependent on each other, correlative and mutually complementary, how faith operates by means of reason, and reason is directed and corrected by faith, is really the subject of a distinct lecture. I would conclude, then, with merely congratulating you, Gentlemen, on the great undertaking which we have so auspiciously commenced. Whatever be its fortunes, whatever its difficulties, whatever its delays, I cannot doubt at all that the encouragement which it has already received, and the measure of success which it has been allotted, are but a presage and an anticipation of a gradual advance towards its completion, in such times and such manner as Providence shall appoint. For myself, I have never had any misgiving about it, because I had never known anything of it before the time when the Holy See had definitely decided upon its prosecution. It is my happiness to have no cognizance of the anxieties and perplexities of venerable and holy prelates, or the discussions of experienced and prudent men, which preceded its definitive recognition on the part of the highest ecclesiastical authority. It is my happiness to have no experience of the time when good Catholics despaired of its success, distrusted its expediency, or even felt an obligation to oppose it. It has been my happiness that I have never been in controversy with persons in this country external to the Catholic Church, nor have been forced into any direct collision with institutions or measures which rest on a foundation hostile to Catholicism. No one can accuse me of any disrespect towards those whose principles or whose policy I disapprove; nor am I conscious of any other aim than that of working in my own place, without going out of my way to offend others. If I have taken part in the undertaking which has now brought us together, it has been because I believed it was a great work, great in its conception, great in its promise, and great in the authority from which it proceeds. I felt it to be so great that I did not dare to incur the responsibility of refusing to take part in it.

How far indeed, and how long, I am to be connected with it, is another matter altogether. It is enough for one man to lay only one stone of so noble and grand an edifice; it is enough, more than enough for me, if I do so much as merely begin, what others may more hopefully continue. One only among the sons of men has carried out a perfect work, and satisfied and exhausted the mission on which He came. One alone has with His last breath said "Consummatum est." But all who set about their duties in faith and hope and love, with a resolute heart and a devoted will, are able, weak though they be, to do what, though incomplete, is imperishable. Even their failures become successes, as being necessary steps in a course, and as terms (so to say) in a long series, which will at length fulfil the object which they propose. And they will unite themselves in spirit, in their humble degree, with those real heroes of Holy Writ and ecclesiastical history, Moses, Elias, and David, Basil, Athanasius, and Chrysostom, Gregory the Seventh, St. Thomas of Canterbury, and many others, who did most when they fancied themselves least prosperous, and died without being permitted to see the fruit of their labours.

ENGLISH CATHOLIC LITERATURE.

One of the special objects which a Catholic University would promote is that of the formation of a Catholic Literature in the English language. It is an object, however, which must be understood before it can be suitably prosecuted; and which will not be understood without some discussion and investigation. First ideas on the subject must almost necessarily be crude. The real state of the case, what is desirable, what is possible, has to be ascertained; and then what has to be done, and what is to be expected. We have seen in public matters, for half a year past, to what mistakes, and to what disappointments, the country has been exposed, from not having been able distinctly to put before it what was to be aimed at by its fleets and armies, what was practicable, what was probable, in operations of war: and so, too, in the field of literature, we are sure of falling into a parallel perplexity and dissatisfaction, if we start with a vague notion of doing something or other imporant by means of a Catholic University, without having the caution to examine what is feasible, and what is unnecessary or hopeless. Accordingly, it is natural I should wish to direct attention to this subject, even though it be too difficult to handle in any exact or complete way, and though my attempt must be left for others to bring into a more perfect shape, who are more fitted for the task.

Here I shall chiefly employ myself in investigating what the object is *not*.

§. 1. In its relation to Religious Literature.

When a "Catholic Literature in the English tongue" is spoken of as a *desideratum,* no reasonable person will mean by "Catholic works" much more than the "works of Catholics." The phrase does not mean a *religious* literature. "Religious Literature" indeed would mean much more than "the Literature of religious men;" it means over and above this, that the subject-matter of the Literature is religious; but by "Catholic Literature" is not to be understood a literature which treats exclusively or primarily of Catholic matters, of Catholic doctrine, controversy, history, persons, or politics; but it includes all subjects of literature whatever, treated as a Catholic would treat them, and as he only can treat them. Why it is important to have them treated by Catholics hardly need be explained here, though something will be incidentally said on the point as we proceed: meanwhile I am drawing attention to the distinction between the two phrases in order to avoid a serious misapprehension. For it is evident that, if by a Catholic Literature were meant nothing more or less than a religious literature, its writers would be mainly ecclesiastics; just as writers on Law are mainly lawyers, and writers on Medicine are mainly physicians or surgeons. And if this be so, a Catholic Literature is no object special to a University, unless a University is to be considered identical with a Seminary or a Theological School.

I am not denying that a University might prove of the greatest benefit even to our religious literature; doubtless it would, and in various ways; still it is concerned with Theology only as one great subject of thought, as the greatest indeed which can occupy the human mind, yet not as the adequate or direct scope of its institution. Yet I suppose it is not impossible for a literary layman to wince at the idea, and to shrink from the proposal, of taking part in a scheme for the formation of a Catholic Literature, under the apprehension that in some way or another he will be entangling himself in a semi-clerical occupation. It is not uncommon, on expressing an anticipation that the Professors of a Catholic University will promote a Catholic Literature, to have to encounter a vague notion that a lecturer or writer so employed must have something polemical about him, must moralize or preach, must (in Protestant language) *improve the occasion,* though his subject is not at all a religious one; in short, that he must do something else besides fairly and boldly go right on, and be a Catholic speaking as a Catholic spontaneously will speak, on the Classics, or Fine Arts, or Poetry, or whatever he has taken in hand. Men think that he cannot give a lecture on Comparative Anatomy without being bound to digress into the Argument from Final Causes; that he cannot recount the present geological theories without forcing them into an interpretation *seriatim* of the first two chapters of Genesis. Many, indeed, seem to go further still, and actually pronounce that, since our own University has been recommended by the Holy See, and is established by the Hierarchy, it cannot but be engaged in teaching religion and nothing else, and must and will have the discipline of a Seminary; which is about as sensible and logical a view of the matter as it would be to maintain that the Prime Minister *ipso facto* holds an ecclesiastical office, since he is always a Protestant; or that the members of the House of Commons must necessarily have been occupied in clerical duties, as long as they took an oath about Transubstantiation. Catholic Literature is not synonymous with Theology, nor does it supersede or interfere with the work of catechists, divines, preachers, or schoolmen.

§. 2. In its relation to Science.

I.

And next, it must be borne in mind, that when we aim at providing a Catholic Literature for Catholics, in place of an existing literature which is of a marked Protestant character, we do not, strictly speaking, include the pure sciences in our *desideratum.* Not that we should not feel pleased and proud to find Catholics distinguish themselves in publications on abstract or experimental philosophy, on account of the honour it does to our religion in the eyes of the world; – not that we are insensible to the congruity and respectability of depending in these matters on ourselves, and not on others, at least as regards our text-books; – not that we do not confidently anticipate that Catholics of these countries will in time to come be able to point to authorities and discoverers in science of their own, equal to those of Protestant England, Germany, or Sweden; – but because, as regards mathematics, chemistry, astronomy, and similar subjects, one man will not, on the score of his religion, treat of them better than another, and because the works of even an unbeliever or idolator, while he kept within the strict range of such studies, might be safely admitted into Catholic lecture-rooms, and put without scruple into the hands of Catholic youths. There is no crying demand, no imperative necessity, for our acquisition of a Catholic Euclid or a Catholic Newton. The object of all science is truth; – the pure sciences proceed to their enunciations from principles which the intellect discerns by a natural light, and by a process recognized by natural reason; and the experimental sciences investigate facts by methods of analysis or by ingenious expedients, ultimately resolvable into instruments of thought equally native to the human mind. If then we may assume that there is an objective truth, and that the constitution of the human mind is in correspondence with it, and acts truly when it acts according to its own laws; if we may assume that God made us, and that what He made is good, and that no action from and according to nature can in itself be evil; it will follow that, so long as it is man who is the geometrician, or natural philosopher, or mechanic, or critic, no matter what man he be, Hindoo, Mahometan, or infidel, his conclusions within his own science, according to the laws of that science, are unquestionable, and not to be suspected by Catholics, unless Catholics may legitimately be jealous of fact and truth, of divine principles and divine creations.

I have been speaking of the scientific treatises or investigations of those who are not Catholics, to which the subject of Literature leads me; but I might even go on to speak of them in their persons as well as in their books. Were it not for the scandal which they would create; were it not for the example they would set; were it not for the certain tendency of the human mind involuntarily to outleap the strict boundaries of an abstract science, and to teach it upon extraneous principles, to embody it in concrete examples, and to carry it on to practical conclusions; above all, were it not for the indirect influence, and living energetic presence, and collateral duties, which accompany a Professor in a great school of learning, I do not see (abstracting from him, I repeat, in hypothesis, what never could possibly be abstracted from him in fact), why the chair of Astronomy in a Catholic University should not be filled by a La Place, or that of Physics by a Humboldt. Whatever they might wish to say, still, while they kept to their own science, they would be unable, like the heathen Prophet in Scripture, to "go beyond the word of the Lord, to utter any thing of their own head."

2.

So far the arguments hold good of certain celebrated writers in a Northern Review, who, in their hostility to the principle of dogmatic teaching, seem obliged to maintain, because subject-matters are distinct, that living opinions are distinct too, and that men are abstractions as well as their respective sciences. "On the morning of the thirteenth of August, in the year 1704," says a justly celebrated author, in illustration and defence of the anti-dogmatic principle in political and social matters, "two great captains, equal in authority, united by close private and public ties, but of different creeds, prepared for battle, on the event of which were staked the liberties of Europe . . . Marlborough gave orders for public prayers; the English chaplains read the service at the head of the English regiments; the Calvin-istic chaplains of the Dutch army, with heads on which hand of Bishop had never been laid, poured forth their supplications in front of their country-men. In the meantime the Danes might listen to the Lutheran ministers; and Capuchins might encourage the Austrian squadrons, and pray to the Virgin for a blessing on the arms of the holy Roman Empire. The battle com-mences; these men of various religions all act like members of one body: the Catholic and the Protestant generals exert themselves to assist and to surpass each other; before sunset the Empire is saved; France has lost in a day the fruits of eight years of intrigue and of victory; and the allies, after conquering together, return thanks to God separately, each after his own form of worship."[61]

The writer of this lively passage would be doubtless unwilling himself to carry out the principle which it insinuates to those extreme conclusions to which it is often pushed by others, in matters of education. Viewed in itself, viewed in the abstract, that principle is simply, undeniably true; and is only sophistical when it is carried out in practical matters at all. A religious opinion, though not formally recognized, cannot fail of influencing *in fact* the school, or society, or polity in which it is found; though in the abstract that opinion is one thing, and the school, society, or polity, another. Here were Episcopalians, Lutherans, Calvinists, and Catholics found all fighting on one side, it is true, without any prejudice to their respective religious tenets: and, certainly, I never heard that in a battle soldiers did do any thing else but fight. I did not know they had time for going beyond the matter in hand; yet, even as regards this very illustration which he has chosen, if we were bound to decide by it the controversy, it does so happen that that danger of interference and collision between opposite religionists actually does occur upon a campaign, which could not be incurred in a battle: and at this very time some jealousy or disgust has been shown in English popular publications, when they have had to record that our ally, the Emperor of the French, has sent his troops, who are serving with the British against the Russians, to attend High Mass, or has presented his sailors with a picture of the Madonna.

If, then, we could have Professors who were mere abstractions and phantoms, marrowless in their bones, and without speculation in their eyes; or if they could only open their mouths on their own special subject, and in their scientific pedantry were dead to the world; if they resembled the well known character in the Romance, who was so imprisoned or fossilized in his erudition, that, though "he stirred the fire with some address," nevertheless, on attempting to snuff the candles, he "was unsuccessful, and relinquished that ambitious post of courtesy, after having twice reduced the parlour to total darkness," then indeed Voltaire himself might be admitted, not without scandal, but without risk, to lecture on astronomy or galvanism in Catholic, or Protestant, or Presbyterian Colleges, or in all of them at once; and we should have no practical controversy with philosophers who, after the fashion of the author I have been quoting, are so smart in proving that we, who differ from them, must needs be so bigotted and puzzle-headed.

And in strict conformity with these obvious distinctions, it will be found that, so far as we *are* able to reduce scientific men of anti-Catholic opinions to the type of the imaginary bookworm to whom I have been alluding, we do actually use them in our schools. We allow our Catholic student to use them, so far as he can surprise them (if I may use the expression), in their formal treatises, and can keep them close prisoners there.

Vix defessa senem passus componere membra,
Cum clamore ruit magno, manicisque jacentem
Occupat.[62]

The fisherman, in the Arabian tale, took no harm from the genius, till he let him out from the brass bottle in which he was confined. "He examined the vessel and shook it, to see if what was within made any noise, but he heard nothing." All was safe till he had succeeded in opening it, and "then came out a very thick smoke, which, ascending to the clouds and extending itself along the sea shore in a thick mist, astonished him very much. After a time the smoke collected, and was converted into a genius of enormous height. At the sight of this monster, whose head appeared to reach the clouds, the fisherman trembled with fear." Such is the difference between an unbelieving or heretical philosopher in person, and in the mere disquisitions proper to his science. Porson was no edifying companion for young men of eighteen, nor are his letters on the text of the Three Heavenly Witnesses to be recommended; but that does not hinder his being admitted into Catholic schools, while he is confined within the limits of his Preface to the Hecuba. Franklin certainly would have been intolerable in person, if he began to talk freely, and throw out, as I think he did in private, that each solar system had its own god; but such extravagances of so able a man do not interfere with the honour we justly pay his name in the history of experimental science. Nay, the great Newton himself would have been silenced in a Catholic University, when he got upon the Apocalypse; yet is that any reason why we should not study his Principia, or avail ourselves of the wonderful analysis which he, Protestant as he was, originated, and which French infidels have developed? We are glad, for their own sakes, that anti-Catholic writers should, in their posthumous influence, do as much real service to the human race as ever they can, and we have no wish to interfere with it.

3.

Returning, then, to the point from which we set out, I observe that, this being the state of the case as regards abstract science, viz., that we have no quarrel with its anti-Catholic commentators, till they thrust their persons into our Chairs, or their popular writings into our reading-rooms, it follows that, when we contemplate the formation of a Catholic Literature, we do not consider scientific works as among our most prominent *desiderata*. They are to be looked for, not so much for their own sake, as because they are indications that we have able scientific men in our communion; for if we have such, they will be certain to write, and in proportion as they increase in number will there be the chance of really profound, original, and standard books issuing from our Lecture-rooms and Libraries. But, after all, there is no reason why these should be better than those which we have already received from Protestants; though it is at once more becoming and more agreeable to our feelings to use books of our own, instead of being indebted to the books of others.

Literature, then, is not synonymous with Science; nor does Catholic education imply the exclusion of works of abstract reasoning, or of physical experiment, or the like, though written by persons of another or of no communion.

There is another consideration in point here, or rather prior to what I have been saying; and that is, that, considering certain scientific works, those on Criticism, for instance, are so often written in a technical phraseology, and since others, as mathematical, deal so largely in signs, symbols, and figures, which belong to all languages, these abstract studies cannot properly be said to fall under English *Literature* at all; – for by Literature I understand Thought, conveyed under the forms of some particular language. And this brings me to speak of Literature in its highest and most genuine sense, viz., as an historical and national fact; and I fear, in this sense of the word also, it is altogether beside or beyond any object which a Catholic University can reasonably contemplate, at least in any moderate term of years; but so large a subject here opens upon us that I must postpone it to another Section.

§. 3. In its relation to Classical Literature.

I .

I have been directing the reader's attention, first to what we do not, and next to what we need not contemplate, when we turn our thoughts to the formation of an English Catholic Literature. I said that our object was neither a library of theological nor of scientific knowledge, though theology in its literary aspect, and abstract science as an exercise of intellect, have both of course a place in the Catholic encyclopædia. One undertaking, however, there is, which not merely does not, and need not, but unhappily cannot, come into the reasonable contemplation of any set of persons, whether members of a University or not, who are desirous of Catholicizing the English language, as is very evident; and that is simply the creation of an *English Classical Literature,* for that has been done long ago, and would be a work beyond the powers of any body of men, even if it had still to be done. If I insist on this point here, no one must suppose I do not consider it to be self-evident; for I shall not be aiming at proving it, so much as at bringing it home distinctly to the mind, that we may, one and all, have a clearer perception of the state of things with which we have to deal. There is many an undeniable truth which is not practically felt and appreciated; and, unless we master our position in the matter before us, we may be led off into various wild imaginations or impossible schemes, which will, as a matter of course, end in disappointment.

Were the Catholic Church acknowledged from this moment through the length and breadth of these islands, and the English tongue henceforth baptized into the Catholic faith, and sealed and consecrated to Catholic objects, and were the present intellectual activity of the nation to continue, as of course it would continue, we should at once have an abundance of Catholic works, which would be English, and purely English, literature and high literature; but still all these would not constitute "English Literature," as the words are commonly understood, nor even then could we say that the "English Literature" was Catholic. Much less can we ever aspire to affirm it, while we are but a portion of the vast English-speaking world-wide race, and are but striving to create a current in the direction of Catholic truth, when the waters are rapidly flowing the other way. In no case can we, strictly speaking, form an English Literature; for by the Literature of a Nation is meant its Classics, and its Classics have been given to England, and have been recognized as such, long since.

2.

A Literature, when it is formed, is a national and historical fact; it is a matter of the past and the present, and can be as little ignored as the present, as little undone as the past. We can deny, supersede, or change it, then only, when we can do the same towards the race or language which it represents. Every great people has a character of its own, which it manifests and perpetuates in a variety of ways. It developes into a monarchy or republic; – by means of commerce or in war, in agriculture or in manufactures, or in all of these at once; in its cities, its public edifices and works, bridges, canals, and harbours; in its laws, traditions, customs, and manners; in its songs and its proverbs; in its religion; in its line of policy, its bearing, its action towards foreign nations; in its alliances, fortunes, and the whole course of its history. All these are peculiar, and parts of a whole, and betoken the national character, and savour of each other; and the case is the same with the national language and literature. They are what they are, and cannot be any thing else, whether they be good or bad or of a mixed nature; before they are formed, we cannot prescribe them, and afterwards, we cannot reverse them. We may feel great repugnance to Milton or Gibbon as men; we may most seriously protest against the spirit which ever lives, and the tendency which ever operates, in every page of their writings; but there they are, an integral portion of English Literature; we cannot extinguish them; we cannot deny their power; we cannot write a new Milton or a new Gibbon; we cannot expurgate what needs to be exorcised. They are great English authors, each breathing hatred to the Catholic Church in his own way, each a proud and rebellious creature of God, each gifted with incomparable gifts.

We must take things as they are, if we take them at all. We may refuse to say a word to English literature, if we will; we may have recourse to French or to Italian instead, if we think either of these less exceptionable than our own; we may fall back upon the Classics of Greece and Rome; we may have nothing whatever to do with literature, as such, of any kind, and confine ourselves to purely amorphous or monstrous specimens of language; but if we do once profess in our Universities the English language and literature, if we think it allowable to know the state of things we live in, and that national character which we share, if we think it desirable to have a chance of writing what may be read after our day, and praiseworthy to aim at providing for Catholics who speak English a Catholic Literature then – I do not say that we must at once throw open every sort of book to the young, the weak, or the untrained, – I do not say that we may dispense with our ecclesiastical indexes and emendations, but – we must not fancy ourselves creating what is already created in spite of us, and which never could at a moment be created by means of us, and we must recognize that historical literature, which is in occupation of the language, both as a fact, nay, and as a standard for ourselves.

There is surely nothing either "temerarious" or paradoxical in a statement like this. The growth of a nation is like that of an individual; its tone of voice and subjects for speech vary with its age. Each age has its own propriety and charm; as a boy's beauty is not a man's, and the sweetness of a treble differs from the richness of a bass, so it is with a whole people. The same period does not produce its most popular poet, its most effective orator, and its most philosophic historian. Language changes with the progress of thought and the events of history, and style changes with it; and while in successive generations it passes through a series of separate excellences, the respective deficiencies of all are supplied alternately by each. Thus language and literature may be considered as dependent on a process of nature, and admitting of subjection to her laws. Father Hardouin indeed, who maintained that, with the exception of Pliny, Cicero, Virgil's Georgics, and Horace's Satires and Epistles, Latin literature was the work of the medieval monks, had the conception of a literature neither national nor historical; but the rest of the world will be apt to consider time and place as necessary conditions in its formation, and will be unable to conceive of classical authors, except as either the elaboration of centuries, or the rare and fitful accident of genius.

First-rate excellence in literature, as in other matters, is either an accident or the outcome of a process; and in either case demands a course of years to secure. We cannot reckon on a Plato, we cannot force an Aristotle, any more than we can command a fine harvest, or create a coal field. If a literature be, as I have said, the voice of a particular nation, it requires a territory and a period, as large as that nation's extent and history, to mature in. It is broader and deeper than the capacity of any body of men, however gifted, or any system of teaching, however true. It is the exponent, not of truth, but of nature, which is true only in its elements. It is the result of the mutual action of a hundred simultaneous influences and operations, and the issue of a hundred strange accidents in independent places and times; it is the scanty compensating produce of the wild discipline of the world and of life, so fruitful in failures; and it is the concentration of those rare manifestations of intellectual power, which no one can account for. It is made up, in the particular language here under consideration, of human beings as heterogeneous as Burns and Bunyan, De Foe and Johnson, Goldsmith and Cowper, Law and Fielding, Scott and Byron. The remark has been made that the history of an author is the history of his works; it is far more exact to say that, at least in the case of great writers, the history of their works is the history of their fortunes or their times. Each is, in his turn, the man of his age, the type of a generation, or the interpreter of a crisis. He is made for his day, and his day for him. Hooker would not have been, but for the existence of Catholics and Puritans, the defeat of the former and the rise of the latter; Clarendon would not have been without the Great Rebellion; Hobbes is the prophet of the reaction to scoffing infidelity; and Addison is the child of the Revolution and its attendant changes. If there be any of our classical authors, who might at first sight have been pronounced a University man, with the exception of Johnson, Addison is he; yet even Addison, the son and brother of clergymen, the fellow of an Oxford Society, the resident of a College which still points to the walk which he planted, must be something more, in order to take his place among the Classics of the language, and owed the variety of his matter to his experience of life, and to the call made on his resources by the exigencies of his day. The world he lived in made him and used him. While his writings educated his own generation, they have delineated it for all posterity after him.

3.

I have been speaking of the authors of a literature, in their relation to the people and course of events to which they belong; but a prior consideration, at which I have already glanced, is their connection with the language itself, which has been their organ. If they are in great measure the creatures of their times, they are on the other hand in a far higher sense the creators of their language. It is indeed commonly called their mother tongue, but virtually it did not exist till they gave it life and form. All greater matters are carried on and perfected by a succession of individual minds; what is true in the history of thought and of action is true of language also. Certain masters of composition, as Shakespeare, Milton, and Pope, the writers of the Protestant Bible and Prayer Book, Hooker and Addison, Swift, Hume, and Goldsmith, have been the making of the English language; and as that language is a fact, so is the literature a fact, by which it is formed, and in which it lives. Men of great ability have taken it in hand, each in his own day, and have done for it what the master of a gymnasium does for the bodily frame. They have formed its limbs, and developed its strength; they have endowed it with vigour, exercised it in suppleness and dexterity, and taught it grace. They have made it rich, harmonious, various, and precise. They have furnished it with a variety of styles, which from their individuality may almost be called dialects, and are monuments both of the powers of the language and the genius of its cultivators.

How real a creation, how *sui generis,* is the style of Shakespeare, or of the Protestant Bible and Prayer Book, or of Swift, or of Pope, or of Gibbon, or of Johnson! Even were the subject-matter without meaning, though in truth the style cannot really be abstracted from the sense, still the style would, on that supposition, remain as perfect and original a work as Euclid's elements or a symphony of Beethoven. And, like music, it has seized upon the public mind; and the literature of England is no longer a mere letter, printed in books, and shut up in libraries, but it is a living voice, which has gone forth in its expressions and its sentiments into the world of men, which daily thrills upon our ears and syllables our thoughts, which speaks to us through our correspondents, and dictates when we put pen to paper. Whether we will or no, the phraseology and diction of Shakespeare, of the Protestant formularies, of Milton, of Pope, of Johnson's Tabletalk, and of Walter Scott, have become a portion of the vernacular tongue, the household words, of which perhaps we little guess the origin, and the very idioms of our familiar conversation. The man in the comedy spoke prose without knowing it; and we Catholics, without consciousness and without offence, are ever repeating the half sentences of dissolute playwrights and heretical partizans and preachers. So tyrannous is the literature of a nation; it is too much for us. We cannot destroy or reverse it; we may confront and encounter it, but we cannot make it over again. It is a great work of man, when it is no work of God's.

I repeat, then, whatever we be able or unable to effect in the great problem which lies before us, any how we cannot undo the past. English Literature will ever *have been* Protestant. Swift and Addison, the most native and natural of our writers, Hooker and Milton, the most elaborate, never can become our co-religionists; and, though this is but the enunciation of a truism, it is not on that account an unprofitable enunciation.

4.

I trust we are not the men to give up an undertaking because it is perplexed or arduous; and to do nothing because we cannot do everything. Much may be attempted, much attained, even granting English Literature is not Catholic. Something indeed may be said even in alleviation of the misfortune itself, on which I have been insisting; and with two remarks bearing upon this latter point I will bring this Section to an end.

I. First, then, it is to be considered that, whether we look to countries Christian or heathen, we find the state of literature there as little satisfactory as it is in these islands; so that, whatever are our difficulties here, they are not worse than those of Catholics all over the world. I would not indeed say a word to extenuate the calamity, under which we lie, of having a literature formed in Protestantism; still, other literatures have disadvantages of their own; and, though in such matters comparisons are impossible, I doubt whether we should be better pleased if our English Classics were tainted with licentiousness, or defaced by infidelity or scepticism. I conceive we should not much mend matters if we were to exchange literatures with the French, Italians, or Germans. About Germany, however, I will not speak; as to France, it has great and religious authors; its classical drama, even in comedy, compared with that of other literatures, is singularly unexceptionable; but who is there that holds a place among its writers so historical and important, who is so copious, so versatile, so brilliant, as that Voltaire who is an open scoffer at every thing sacred, venerable, or high-minded? Nor can Rousseau, though he has not the pretensions of Voltaire, be excluded from the classical writers of France. Again, the gifted Pascal, in the work on which his literary fame is mainly founded, does not approve himself to a Catholic judgment; and Descartes, the first of French philosophers, was too independent in his inquiries to be always correct in his conclusions. The witty Rabelais is said, by a recent critic,[63] to show covertly in his former publications, and openly in his latter, his "dislike to the Church of Rome." La Fontaine was with difficulty brought, on his death-bed, to make public satisfaction for the scandal which he had done to religion by his immoral *Contes,* though at length he threw into the fire a piece which he had just finished for the stage. Montaigne, whose Essays "make an epoch in literature," by "their influence upon the tastes and opinions of Europe;" whose "school embraces a large proportion of French and English literature;" and of whose "brightness and felicity of genius there can be but one opinion," is disgraced, as the same writer tells us, by "a sceptical bias and great indifference of temperament;" and "has led the way" as an habitual offender, "to the indecency too characteristic of French literature."

Nor does Italy present a more encouraging picture. Ariosto, one of the few names, ancient or modern, who is allowed on all hands to occupy the first rank of Literature, is, I suppose, rightly arraigned by the author I have above quoted, of "coarse sensuality." Pulci, "by his sceptical insinuations, seems clearly to display an intention of exposing religion to contempt." Boccaccio, the first of Italian prose-writers, had in his old age touchingly to lament the corrupting tendency of his popular compositions; and Bellarmine has to vindicate him, Dante, and Petrarch, from the charge of virulent abuse of the Holy See. Dante certainly does not scruple to place in his *Inferno* a Pope, whom the Church has since canonized, and his work on *Monarchia* is on the Index. Another great Florentine, Macchiavel, is on the Index also; and Giannone, as great in political history at Naples as Macchiavel at Florence, is notorious for his disaffection to the interests of the Roman Pontiff.

These are but specimens of the general character of secular literature, whatever be the people to whom it belongs. One literature may be better than another, but bad will be the best, when weighed in the balance of truth and morality. It cannot be otherwise; human nature is in all ages and all countries the same; and its literature, therefore, will ever and everywhere be one and the same also. Man's work will savour of man; in his elements and powers excellent and admirable, but prone to disorder and excess, to error and to sin. Such too will be his literature; it will have the beauty and the fierceness, the sweetness and the rankness, of the natural man, and, with all its richness and greatness, will necessarily offend the senses of those who, in the Apostle's words, are really "exercised to discern between good and evil." "It is said of the holy Sturme," says an Oxford writer, "that, in passing a horde of unconverted Germans, as they were bathing and gambolling in the stream, he was so overpowered by the intolerable scent which arose from them that he nearly fainted away." National Literature is, in a parallel way, the untutored movements of the reason, imagination, passions, and affections of the natural man, the leapings and the friskings, the plungings and the snortings, the sportings and the buffoonings, the clumsy play and the aimless toil, of the noble, lawless savage of God's intellectual creation.

It is well that we should clearly apprehend a truth so simple and elementary as this, and not expect from the nature of man, or the literature of the world, what they never held out to us. Certainly, I did not know that the world was to be regarded as favourable to Christian faith or practice, or that it would be breaking any engagement with us, if it took a line divergent from our own. I have never fancied that we should have reasonable ground for surprise or complaint, though man's intellect *puris naturalibus* did prefer, of the two, liberty to truth, or though his heart cherished a leaning towards licence of thought and speech in comparison with restraint.

5.

2. If we do but resign ourselves to facts, we shall soon be led on to the second reflection which I have promised – viz., that, not only are things not better abroad, but they might be worse at home. We have, it is true, a Protestant literature; but then it is neither atheistical nor immoral; and, in the case of at least half a dozen of its highest and most influential departments, and of the most popular of its authors, it comes to us with very considerable alleviations. For instance, there surely is a call on us for thankfulness that the most illustrious amongst English writers has so little of a Protestant about him that Catholics have been able, without extravagance, to claim him as their own, and that enemies to our creed have allowed that he is only not a Catholic, because, and as far as, his times forbade it. It is an additional satisfaction to be able to boast that he offends in neither of those

two respects, which reflect so seriously upon the reputation of great authors abroad. Whatever passages may be gleaned from his dramas disrespectful to ecclesiastical authority, still these are but passages; on the other hand, there is in Shakespeare neither contempt of religion nor scepticism, and he upholds the broad laws of moral and divine truth with the consistency and severity of an Æschylus, Sophocles, or Pindar. There is no mistaking in his works on which side lies the right; Satan is not made a hero, nor Cain a victim, but pride is pride, and vice is vice, and, whatever indulgence he may allow himself in light thoughts or unseemly words, yet his admiration is reserved for sanctity and truth. From the second chief fault of Literature, as indeed my last words imply, he is not so free; but, often as he may offend against modesty, he is clear of a worse charge, sensuality, and hardly a passage can be instanced in all that he has written to seduce the imagination or to excite the passions.

A rival to Shakespeare, if not in genius, at least in copiousness and variety, is found in Pope; and *he* was actually a Catholic, though personally an unsatisfactory one. His freedom indeed from Protestantism is but a poor compensation for a false theory of religion in one of his poems; but, taking his works as a whole, we may surely acquit them of being dangerous to the reader, whether on the score of morals or of faith.

Again, the special title of moralist in English Literature is accorded by the public voice to Johnson, whose bias towards Catholicity is well known.

If we were to ask for a report of our philosophers, the investigation would not be so agreeable; for we have three of evil, and one of unsatisfactory repute. Locke is scarcely an honour to us in the standard of truth, grave and manly as he is; and Hobbes, Hume, and Bentham, in spite of their abilities, are simply a disgrace. Yet, even in this department, we find some compensation in the names of Clarke, Berkeley, Butler, and Reid, and in a name more famous than them all. Bacon was too intellectually great to hate or to contemn the Catholic faith; and he deserves by his writings to be called the most orthodox of Protestant philosophers.

§. 4. In its relation to the Literature of the Day.

I .

The past cannot be undone. That our English Classical Literature is not Catholic is a plain fact, which we cannot deny, to which we must reconcile ourselves, as best we may, and which, as I have shown above, has after all its compensations. When, then, I speak of the desirableness of forming a

Catholic Literature, I am contemplating no such vain enterprise as that of reversing history; no, nor of redeeming the past by the future. I have no dream of Catholic Classics as still reserved for the English language. In truth, classical authors not only are national, but belong to a particular age of a nation's life; and I should not wonder if, as regards ourselves, that age is passing away. Moreover, they perform a particular office towards its language, which is not likely to be called for beyond a definite time. And further, though analogies or parallels cannot be taken to decide a question of this nature, such is the fact, that the series of our classical writers has already extended through a longer period than was granted to the Classical Literature either of Greece or of Rome; and thus the English language also may have a long course of literature still to come through many centuries, without that Literature being classical.

Latin, for instance, was a living language for many hundred years after the date of the writers who brought it to its perfection; and then it continued for a second long period to be the medium of European correspondence. Greek was a living language to a date not very far short of that of the taking of Constantinople, ten centuries after the date of St. Basil, and seventeen hundred years after the period commonly called classical. And thus, as the year has its spring and summer, so even for those celebrated languages there was but a season of splendour, and, compared with the whole course of their duration, but a brief season. Since, then, English has had its great writers for a term of about three hundred years, – as long, that is, as the period from Sappho to Demosthenes, or from Pisistratus to Arcesilas, or from Æschylus and Pindar to Carneades, or from Ennius to Pliny, – we should have no right to be disappointed if the classical period be close upon its termination.

By the Classics of a national Literature I mean those authors who have the foremost place in exemplifying the powers and conducting the development of its language. The language of a nation is at first rude and clumsy; and it demands a succession of skilful artists to make it malleable and ductile, and to work it up to its proper perfection. It improves by use, but it is not every one who can use it while as yet it is unformed. To do this is an effort of genius; and so men of a peculiar talent arise, one after another, according to the circumstances of the times, and accomplish it. One gives it flexibility, that is, shows how it can be used without difficulty to express adequately a variety of thoughts and feelings in their nicety or intricacy; another makes it perspicuous or forcible; a third adds to its vocabulary; and a fourth gives it grace and harmony. The style of each of such eminent masters becomes henceforth in some sort a property of the language itself;

words, phrases, collocations, and structure, which hitherto did not exist, gradually passing into the conversation and the composition of the educated classes.

2.

Now I will attempt to show how this process of improvement is effected, and what is its limit. I conceive then that these gifted writers act upon the spoken and written language by means of the particular schools which form about them respectively. Their style, using the word in a large sense, forcibly arrests the reader, and draws him on to imitate it, by virtue of what is excellent in it, in spite of such defects as, in common with all human works, it may contain. I suppose all of us will recognize this fascination. For myself when I was fourteen or fifteen, I imitated Addison; when I was seventeen, I wrote in the style of Johnson; about the same time I fell in with the twelfth volume of Gibbon, and my ears rang with the cadence of his sentences, and I dreamed of it for a night or two. Then I began to make an analysis of Thucydides in Gibbon's style. In like manner, most Oxford undergraduates, forty years ago, when they would write poetry, adopted the versification of Pope, Darwin, and the Pleasures of Hope, which had been made popular by Heber and Milman. The literary schools, indeed, which I am speaking of, as resulting from the attractions of some original, or at least novel artist, consist for the most part of mannerists, none of whom rise much above mediocrity; but they are not the less serviceable as channels, by means of which the achievements of genius may be incorporated into the language itself, or become the common property of the nation. Henceforth, the most ordinary composer, the very student in the lecture-room; is able to write with a precision, a grace, or a copiousness, as the case may be, unknown before the date of the authors whom he imitates, and he wonders at, if he does not rather pride himself on, his

novas frondes, et non sua poma.[64]

If there is any one who illustrates this remark, it is Gibbon; I seem to trace his vigorous condensation and peculiar rhythm at every turn in the literature of the present day. Pope, again, is said to have tuned our versification. Since his time, any one, who has an ear and turn for poetry, can with little pains throw off a copy of verses equal or superior to the poet's own, and with far less of study and patient correction than would have been demanded of the poet himself for their production. Compare the choruses of the Samson Agonistes with any stanza taken at random in Thalaba: how

much had the language gained in the interval between them! Without denying the high merits of Southey's beautiful romance, we surely shall not be
wrong in saying, that in its unembarrassed eloquent flow, it is the language
of the nineteenth century that speaks, as much as the author himself.

I will give an instance of what I mean: let us take the beginning of the
first chorus in the Samson: –

> Just are the ways of God,
> And justifiable to men;
> Unless there be who think not God at all;
> If any be, they walk obscure,
> For of such doctrine never was there school,
> But the heart of the fool,
> And no man therein doctor but himself.
> But men there be, who doubt His ways not just,
> As to His own edicts found contradicting,
> Then give the reins to wandering thought,
> Regardless of His glory's diminution;
> Till, by their own perplexities involved,
> They ravel more, still less resolved,
> But never find self-satisfying solution.[65]

And now take the opening stanza of Thalaba: –

> How beautiful is night!
> A dewy freshness fills the silent air;
> No mist obscures, nor cloud, nor speck, nor stain,
> Breaks the serene of heaven.
> In full-orb'd glory yonder Moon divine
> Rolls through the dark blue depths.
> Beneath her steady ray
> The desert circle spreads,
> Like the round ocean girdled with the sky.
> How beautiful is night![66]

Does not Southey show to advantage here? yet the voice of the world
proclaims Milton pre-eminently a poet; and no one can affect a doubt of the
delicacy and exactness of his ear. Yet, much as he did for the language in
verse and in prose, he left much for other artists to do after him, which they
have successfully accomplished. We see the fruit of the literary labours of
Pope, Thomson, Gray, Goldsmith, and other poets of the eighteenth century,
in the musical eloquence of Southey.

3.

So much for the process; now for its termination. I think it is brought about in some such way as the following: –

The influence of a great classic upon the nation which he represents is twofold; on the one hand he advances his native language towards its perfection; but on the other hand he discourages in some measure any advance beyond his own. Thus, in the parallel case of science, it is commonly said on the continent, that the very marvellousness of Newton's powers was the bane of English mathematics: inasmuch as those who succeeded him were content with his discoveries, bigoted to his methods of investigation, and averse to those new instruments which have carried on the French to such brilliant and successful results. In Literature, also, there is something oppressive in the authority of a great writer, and something of tyranny in the use to which his admirers put his name. The school which he forms would fain monopolize the language, draws up canons of criticism from his writings, and is intolerant of innovation. Those who come under its influence are dissuaded or deterred from striking out a path of their own. Thus Virgil's transcendent excellence fixed the character of the hexameter in subsequent poetry, and took away the chances, if not of improvement, at least of variety. Even Juvenal has much of Virgil in the structure of his verse. I have known those who prefer the rhythm of Catullus.

However, so summary a result is not of necessary occurrence. The splendour of an author may excite a generous emulation, or the tyrannous formalism of his followers a re-action; and thus other authors and other schools arise. We read of Thucydides, on hearing Herodotus read his history at Olympia, being incited to attempt a similar work, though of an entirely different and of an original structure. Gibbon, in like manner, writing of Hume and Robertson, says: "The perfect composition, the nervous language, the well-turned periods of Dr. Robertson, inflamed me to the ambitious hope that I might one day tread in his footsteps; the calm philosophy, the careless inimitable beauties of his friend and rival, often forced me to close the volume with a mixed sensation of delight and despair."[67]

As to re-actions, I suppose there has been something of the kind against the supremacy of Pope, since the time that his successors, Campbell especially, have developed his peculiarities and even defects into extravagance. Crabbe, for instance, turned back to a versification having much more of Dryden in it; and Byron, in spite of his high opinion of Pope, threw into his lines the rhythm of blank verse. Still, on the whole, the influence of a

Classic acts in the way of discouraging any thing new, rather than in that of exciting rivalry or provoking re-action.

And another consideration is to be taken into account. When a language has been cultivated in any particular department of thought, and so far as it has been generally perfected, an existing want has been supplied, and there is no need for further workmen. In its earlier times, while it is yet unformed, to write in it at all is almost a work of genius. It is like crossing a country before roads are made communicating between place and place. The authors of that age deserve to be Classics, both because of what they do and because they can do it. It requires the courage or the force of great talent to compose in the language at all; and the composition, when effected, makes a permanent impression on it. In those early times, too, the licence of speech unfettered by precedents, the novelty of the work, the state of society, and the absence of criticism, enable an author to write with spirit and freshness. But, as centuries pass on, this stimulus is taken away; the language by this time has become manageable for its various purposes, and is ready at command. Ideas have found their corresponding expressions; and one word will often convey what once required half a dozen. Roots have been expanded, derivations multiplied, terms invented or adopted. A variety of phrases has been provided, which form a sort of compound words. Separate professions, pursuits, and provinces of literature have gained their conventional terminology. There is an historical, political, social, commercial style. The ear of the nation has become accustomed to useful expressions or combinations of words, which otherwise would sound harsh. Strange metaphors have been naturalized in the ordinary prose, yet cannot be taken as precedents for a similar liberty. Criticism has become an art, and exercises a continual and jealous watch over the free genius of new writers. It is difficult for them to be original in the use of their mother tongue without being singular.

Thus the language has become in a great measure stereotype; as in the case of the human frame, it has expanded to the loss of its elasticity, and can expand no more. Then the general style of educated men, formed by the accumulated improvements of centuries, is far superior perhaps in perfectness to that of any one of those national Classics, who have taught their countrymen to write more clearly, or more elegantly, or more forcibly than themselves. And literary men submit themselves to what they find so well provided for them; or, if impatient of conventionalities, and resolved to shake off a yoke which tames them down to the loss of individuality, they adopt no half measures, but indulge in novelties which offend against the genius of the language, and the true canons of taste. Political causes may co-operate in a revolt of this kind; and, as a nation declines in patriotism, so does its language in purity. It seems to me as if the sententious, epigram-matic style of writing, which set in with Seneca, and is seen at least as late as in the writings of St. Ambrose, is an attempt to escape from the simplicity of Cæsar and the majestic elocution of Cicero; while Tertullian, with more of genius than good sense, relieves himself in the harsh originality of his provincial Latin.

There is another impediment, as time goes on, to the rise of fresh classics in any nation; and that is the effect which foreigners, or foreign literature, will exert upon it. It may happen that a certain language, like Greek, is adopted and used familiarly by educated men in other countries; or again, that educated men, to whom it is native, may abandon it for some other language, as the Romans of the second and third centuries wrote in Greek instead of Latin. The consequence will be, that the language in question will tend to lose its nationality – that is, its distinctive character; it will cease to be idiomatic in the sense in which it once was so; and whatever grace or propriety it may retain, it will be comparatively tame and spiritless; or, on the other hand, it will be corrupted by the admixture of foreign elements.

4.

Such, as I consider, being the fortunes of Classical Literature, viewed gen-erally, I should never be surprised to find that, as regards this hemisphere, for I can prophesy nothing of America, we have well nigh seen the end of English Classics. Certainly, it is in no expectation of Catholics continuing the series here that I speak of the duty and necessity of their cultivating English literature. When I speak of the formation of a Catholic school of writers, I have respect principally to the matter of what is written, and to composition only so far forth as style is necessary to convey and to recom-mend the matter. I mean a literature which resembles the literature of the day. This is not a day for great writers, but for good writing, and a great deal of it. There never was a time when men wrote so much and so well, and that, without being of any great account themselves. While our literature in this day, especially the periodical, is rich and various, its language is elaborated to a perfection far beyond that of our Classics, by the jealous rivalry, the incessant practice, the mutual influence, of its many writers. In point of mere style, I suppose, many an article in the *Times* newspaper, or Edin-burgh Review, is superior to a preface of Dryden's, or a Spectator, or a pamphlet of Swift's, or one of South's sermons.

Our writers write so well that there is little to choose between them. What they lack is that individuality, that earnestness, most personal yet most unconscious of self, which is the greatest charm of an author. The very form of the compositions of the day suggests to us their main deficiency. They are anonymous. So was it not in the literature of those nations which we consider the special standard of classical writing; so is it not with our own Classics. The Epic was sung by the voice of the living, present poet. The drama, in its very idea, is poetry in persons. Historians begin, "Herodotus, of Halicarnassus, publishes his researches;" or, "Thucydides, the Athenian, has composed an account of the war." Pindar is all through his odes a speaker. Plato, Xenophon, and Cicero, throw their philosophical dissertations into the form of a dialogue. Orators and preachers are by their very profession known persons, and the personal is laid down by the Philosopher of antiquity as the source of their greatest persuasiveness. Virgil and Horace are ever bringing into their poetry their own characters and tastes. Dante's poems furnish a series of events for the chronology of his times. Milton is frequent in allusions to his own history and circumstances. Even when Addison writes anonymously, he writes under a professed character, and that in a great measure his own; he writes in the first person. The "I" of the Spectator, and the "we" of the modern Review or Newspaper, are the respective symbols of the two ages in our literature. Catholics must do as their neighbours; they must be content to serve their generation, to promote the interests of religion, to recommend truth, and to edify their brethren to-day, though their names are to have little weight, and their works are not to last much beyond themselves.

5.

And now having shown what it is that a Catholic University does not think of doing, what it need not do, and what it cannot do, I might go on to trace out in detail what it is that it really might and will encourage and create. But, as such an investigation would neither be difficult to pursue, nor easy to terminate, I prefer to leave the subject at the preliminary point to which I have brought it.

III.

CHRISTIANITY AND PHYSICAL SCIENCE.

A LECTURE IN THE SCHOOL OF MEDICINE.

I.

Now that we have just commenced our second Academical Year, it is natural, Gentlemen, that, as in November last, when we were entering upon our great undertaking, I offered to you some remarks suggested by the occasion, so now again I should not suffer the first weeks of the Session to pass away without addressing to you a few words on one of those subjects which are at the moment especially interesting to us. And when I apply myself to think what topic I shall in consequence submit to your consideration, I seem to be directed what to select by the principle of selection which I followed on that former occasion to which I have been referring. Then we were opening the Schools of Philosophy and Letters, as now we are opening those of Medicine; and, as I then attempted some brief investigation of the mutual bearings of Revelation and Literature, so at the present time I shall not, I trust, be unprofitably engaging your attention, if I make one or two parallel reflections on the relations existing between Revelation and Physical Science.

This subject, indeed, viewed in its just dimensions, is far too large for an occasion such as this; still I may be able to select some one point out of the many which it offers for discussion, and, while elucidating it, to throw light even on others which at the moment I do not formally undertake. I propose, then, to discuss the antagonism which is popularly supposed to exist between Physics and Theology; and to show, first, that such antagonism does not really exist, and, next, to account for the circumstance that so groundless an imagination should have got abroad.

I think I am not mistaken in the fact that there exists, both in the educated and half-educated portions of the community, something of a surmise or misgiving, that there really is at bottom a certain contrariety between the declarations of religion and the results of physical inquiry; a suspicion such, that, while it encourages those persons who are not over-religious to anticipate a coming day, when at length the difference will break out into open conflict, to the disadvantage of Revelation, it leads religious minds, on the other hand, who have not had the opportunity of considering accurately the state of the case, to be jealous of the researches, and prejudiced against the discoveries of Science. The consequence is, on the one side, a certain contempt of Theology; on the other, a disposition to undervalue, to deny, to ridicule, to discourage, and almost to denounce, the labours of the physiological, astronomical, or geological investigator.

I do not suppose that any of those gentlemen who are now honouring me with their presence are exposed to the temptation either of the religious or of the scientific prejudice; but that is no reason why some notice of it may not have its use even in this place. It may lead us to consider the subject itself more carefully and exactly; it may assist us in attaining clearer ideas than before how Physics and Theology stand relatively to each other.

2.

Let us begin with a first approximation to the real state of the case, or a broad view, which, though it may require corrections, will serve at once to illustrate and to start the subject. We may divide knowledge, then, into natural and supernatural. Some knowledge, of course, is both at once; for the moment let us put this circumstance aside, and view these two fields of knowledge in themselves, and as distinct from each other in idea. By nature is meant, I suppose, that vast system of things, taken as a whole, of which we are cognizant by means of our natural powers. By the supernatural world is meant that still more marvellous and awful universe, of which the Creator Himself is the fulness, and which becomes known to us, not through our natural faculties, but by superadded and direct communication from Him. These two great circles of knowledge, as I have said, intersect; first, as far as supernatural knowledge includes truths and facts of the natural world, and secondly, as far as truths and facts of the natural world are on the other hand data for inferences about the supernatural. Still, allowing this interference to the full, it will be found, on the whole, that the two worlds and the two kinds of knowledge respectively are separated off from each other; and that, therefore, as being separate, they cannot on the whole contradict each other. That is, in other words, a person who has the fullest knowledge of one of these worlds, may be nevertheless, on the whole, as ignorant as the rest of mankind, as unequal to form a judgment, of the facts and truths of the other. He who knows all that can possibly be known about physics, about politics, about geography, ethnology, and ethics, will have made no approximation whatever to decide the question whether or not there are angels, and how many are their orders; and on the other hand, the most learned of dogmatic and mystical divines, – St.

Augustine, St. Thomas, – will not on that score know more than a peasant about the laws of motion, or the wealth of nations. I do not mean that there may not be speculations and guesses on this side and that, but I speak of any conclusion which merits to be called, I will not say knowledge, but even opinion. If, then, Theology be the philosophy of the supernatural world, and Science the philosophy of the natural, Theology and Science, whether in their respective ideas, or again in their own actual fields, on the whole, are incommunicable, incapable of collision, and needing, at most to be connected, never to be reconciled.

Now this broad general view of our subject is found to be so far true in fact, in spite of such deductions from it that have to be made in detail, that the recent French editors of one of the works of St. Thomas are able to give it as one of their reasons why that great theologian made an alliance, not with Plato, but with Aristotle, because Aristotle (they say), unlike Plato, confined himself to human science, and therefore was secured from coming into collision with divine.

"Not without reason," they say, "did St. Thomas acknowledge Aristotle as if the Master of human philosophy; for, inasmuch as Aristotle was not a Theologian, he had only treated of logical, physical, psychological, and metaphysical theses, to the exclusion of those which are concerned about the supernatural relations of man to God, that is, religion; which, on the other hand, had been the source of the worst errors of other philosophers, and especially of Plato."[68]

3.

But if there be so substantial a truth even in this very broad statement concerning the independence of the fields of Theology and general Science severally, and the consequent impossibility of collision between them, how much more true is that statement, from the very nature of the case, when we contrast Theology, not with Science generally, but definitely with Physics! In Physics is comprised that family of sciences which is concerned with the sensible world, with the phenomena which we see, hear, and handle, or, in other words, with matter. It is the philosophy of matter. Its basis of operations, what it starts from, what it falls back upon, is the phenomena which meet the senses. Those phenomena it ascertains, catalogues, compares, combines, arranges, and then uses for determining something beyond themselves, viz., the order to which they are subservient, or what we commonly call the laws of nature. It never travels beyond the examination of cause and effect. Its object is to resolve the complexity of phenomena into simple elements and principles; but when it has reached those first elements, principles, and laws, its mission is at an end; it keeps within that material system with which it began, and never ventures beyond the "flammantia mœnia mundi." It may, indeed, if it chooses, feel a doubt of the completeness of its analysis hitherto, and for that reason endeavour to arrive at more simple laws and fewer principles. It may be dissatisfied with its own combinations, hypotheses, systems; and leave Ptolemy for Newton, the alchemists for Lavoisier and Davy; – that is, it may decide that it has not yet touched the bottom of its own subject; but still its aim will be to get to the bottom, and nothing more. With matter it began, with matter it will end; it will never trespass into the province of mind. The Hindoo notion is said to be that the earth stands upon a tortoise; but the physicist, as such, will never ask himself by what influence, external to the universe, the universe is sustained; simply because he *is* a physicist.

If indeed he be a religious man, he will of course have a very definite view of the subject; but that view of his is private, not professional, – the view, not of a physicist, but of a religious man; and this, not because physical science says any thing different, but simply because it says nothing at all on the subject, nor can do so by the very undertaking with which it set out. The question is simply *extra artem.* The physical philosopher has nothing whatever to do with final causes, and will get into inextricable confusion, if he introduces them into his investigations. He has to look in one definite direction, not in any other. It is said that in some countries, when a stranger asks his way, he is at once questioned in turn what place he came from: something like this would be the unseasonableness of a physicist, who inquired how the phenomena and laws of the material world primarily came to be, when his simple task is that of ascertaining what they are. Within the limits of those phenomena he may speculate and prove; he may trace the operation of the laws of matter through periods of time; he may penetrate into the past, and anticipate the future; he may recount the changes which they have effected upon matter, and the rise, growth, and decay of phenomena; and so in a certain sense he may write the history of the material world, as far as he can; still he will always advance from phenomena, and conclude upon the internal evidence which they supply. He will not come near the questions, what that ultimate element is, which we call matter, how it came to be, whether it can cease to be, whether it ever was not, whether it will ever come to nought, in what its laws really consist, whether they can cease to be, whether they can be suspended, what causation is, what time is, what the relations of time to cause and effect, and a hundred other questions of a similar character.

Such is Physical Science, and Theology, as is obvious, is just what such Science is not. Theology begins, as its name denotes, not with any sensible facts, phenomena, or results, not with nature at all, but with the Author of nature, – with the one invisible, unapproachable Cause and Source of all things. It begins at the other end of knowledge, and is occupied, not with the finite, but the Infinite. It unfolds and systematizes what He Himself has told us of Himself; of His nature, His attributes, His will, and His acts. As far as it approaches towards Physics, it takes just the counterpart of the questions which occupy the Physical Philosopher. He contemplates facts before him; the Theologian gives the reasons of those facts. The Physicist treats of efficient causes; the Theologian of final. The Physicist tells us of laws; the Theologian of the Author, Maintainer, and Controller of them; of their scope, of their suspension, if so be; of their beginning and their end. This is how the two schools stand related to each other, at that point where they approach the nearest; but for the most part they are absolutely divergent. What Physical Science is engaged in I have already said; as to Theology, it contemplates the world, not of matter, but of mind; the Supreme Intelligence; souls and their destiny; conscience and duty; the past, present, and future dealings of the Creator with the creature.

4.

So far, then, as these remarks have gone, Theology and Physics cannot touch each other, have no intercommunion, have no ground of difference or agreement, of jealousy or of sympathy. As well may musical truths be said to interfere with the doctrines of architectural science; as well may there be a collision between the mechanist and the geologist, the engineer and the grammarian; as well might the British Parliament or the French nation be jealous of some possible belligerent power upon the surface of the moon, as Physics pick a quarrel with Theology. And it may be well, – before I proceed to fill up in detail this outline, and to explain what has to be explained in this statement, – to corroborate it, as it stands, by the remarkable words upon the subject of a writer of the day: – [69]

"We often hear it said," he observes, writing as a Protestant (and here let me assure you, Gentlemen, that though his words have a controversial tone with them, I do not quote them in that aspect, or as wishing here to urge any thing against Protestants, but merely in pursuance of my own point, that Revelation and Physical Science cannot really come into collision), "we often hear it said that the world is constantly becoming more and more

enlightened, and that this enlightenment must be favourable to Protestantism, and unfavourable to Catholicism. We wish that we could think so. But
we see great reason to doubt whether this is a well-founded expectation. We
see that during the last two hundred and fifty years the human mind has
been in the highest degree active; that it has made great advances in every
branch of natural philosophy; that it has produced innumerable inventions
tending to promote the convenience of life; that medicine, surgery, chemistry, engineering, have been very greatly improved, that government, police,
and law have been improved, though not to so great an extent as the physical sciences. Yet we see that, during these two hundred and fifty years, Protestantism has made no conquests worth speaking of. Nay, we believe that,
as far as there has been change, that change has, on the whole, been in
favour of the Church of Rome. We cannot, therefore, feel confident that the
progress of knowledge will necessarily be fatal to a system which has, to
say the least, stood its ground in spite of the immense progress made by the
human race in knowledge since the days of Queen Elizabeth.

"Indeed, the argument which we are considering seems to us to be
founded on an entire mistake. There are branches of knowledge with respect to which the law of the human mind is progress. In mathematics,
when once a proposition has been demonstrated, it is never afterwards
contested. Every fresh story is as solid a basis for a new superstructure as
the original foundation was. Here, therefore, there is a constant addition to
the stock of truth. In the inductive sciences, again, the law is progress . . .

"But with theology the case is very different. As respects natural religion (Revelation being for the present altogether left out of the question), it
is not easy to see that a philosopher of the present day is more favourably
situated than Thales or Simonides. He has before him just the same evidences of design in the structure of the universe which the early Greeks
had . . . As to the other great question, the question what becomes of man
after death, we do not see that a highly educated European, left to his
unassisted reason, is more likely to be in the right than a Blackfoot Indian.
Not a single one of the many sciences, in which we surpass the Blackfoot
Indians, throws the smallest light on the state of the soul after the animal life
is extinct . . .

"Natural Theology, then, is not a progressive science. That knowledge
of our origin and of our destiny which we derive from Revelation is indeed
of very different clearness, and of very different importance. But neither is
Revealed Religion of the nature of a progressive science . . . In divinity
there cannot be a progress analogous to that which is constantly taking

place in pharmacy, geology, and navigation. A Christian of the fifth century with a Bible is neither better nor worse situated than a Christian of the nineteenth century with a Bible, candour and natural acuteness being of course supposed equal. It matters not at all that the compass, printing, gunpowder, steam, gas, vaccination, and a thousand other discoveries and inventions, which were unknown in the fifth century, are familiar to the nineteenth. None of these discoveries and inventions has the smallest bearing on the question whether man is justified by faith alone, or whether the invocation of saints is an orthodox practice . . . We are confident that the world will never go back to the solar system of Ptolemy; nor is our confidence in the least shaken by the circumstance that so great a man as Bacon rejected the theory of Galileo with scorn; for Bacon had not all the means of arriving at a sound conclusion . . . But when we reflect that Sir Thomas More was ready to die for the doctrine of Transubstantiation, we cannot but feel some doubt whether the doctrine of Transubstantiation may not triumph over all opposition. More was a man of eminent talents. He had all the information on the subject that we have, or *that, while the world lasts, any human being will have* . . . *No progress that science has made, or will make,* can add to what seems to us the overwhelming force of the argument against the Real Presence. We are therefore unable to understand why what Sir Thomas More believed respecting Transubstantiation may not be believed to the end of time by men equal in abilities and honesty to Sir Thomas More. But Sir Thomas More is one of the choice specimens of human wisdom and virtue; and the doctrine of Transubstantiation is a kind of proof charge. The faith which stands that test will stand any test . . .

"The history of Catholicism strikingly illustrates these observations. During the last seven centuries the public mind of Europe has made constant progress in every department of secular knowledge; but in religion we can trace no constant progress . . . Four times since the authority of the Church of Rome was established in Western Christendom has the human intellect risen up against her yoke. Twice that Church remained completely victorious. Twice she came forth from the conflict bearing the marks of cruel wounds, but with the principle of life still strong within her. When we reflect on the tremendous assaults she has survived, we find it difficult to conceive in what way she is to perish."

You see, Gentlemen, if you trust the judgment of a sagacious mind, deeply read in history, Catholic Theology has nothing to fear from the progress of Physical Science, even independently of the divinity of its doctrines. It speaks of things supernatural; and these, by the very force of the words, research into nature cannot touch.

5.

It is true that the author in question, while saying all this, and much more to the same purpose, also makes mention of one exception to his general statement, though he mentions it in order to put it aside. I, too, have to notice the same exception here; and you will see at once, Gentlemen, as soon as it is named, how little it interferes really with the broad view which I have been drawing out. It is true, then, that Revelation has in one or two instances advanced beyond its chosen territory, which is the invisible world, in order to throw light upon the history of the material universe. Holy Scripture, it is perfectly true, does declare a few momentous facts, so few that they may be counted, of a physical character. It speaks of a process of formation out of chaos which occupied six days; it speaks of the firmament; of the sun and moon being created for the sake of the earth; of the earth being immovable; of a great deluge; and of several other similar facts and events. It is true; nor is there any reason why we should anticipate any difficulty in accepting these statements as they stand, whenever their meaning and drift are authoritatively determined; for, it must be recollected, their meaning has not yet engaged the formal attention of the Church, or received any interpretation which, as Catholics, we are bound to accept, and in the absence of such definite interpretation, there is perhaps some presumption in saying that it means this, and does not mean that. And this being the case, it is not at all probable that any discoveries ever should be made by physical inquiries incompatible at the same time with one and all of those senses which the letter admits, and which are still open. As to certain popular interpretations of the texts in question, I shall have something to say of them presently; here I am only concerned with the letter of the Holy Scriptures itself, as far as it bears upon the history of the heavens and the earth; and I say that we may wait in peace and tranquillity till there is some real collision between Scripture authoritatively interpreted, and results of science clearly ascertained, before we consider how we are to deal with a difficulty which we have reasonable grounds for thinking will never really occur.

And, after noticing this exception, I really have made the utmost admission that has to be made about the existence of any common ground upon which Theology and Physical Science may fight a battle. On the whole, the two studies do most surely occupy distinct fields, in which each may teach without expecting any interposition from the other. It might indeed have pleased the Almighty to have superseded physical inquiry by revealing the truths which are its object, though He has not done so: but whether it had pleased Him to do so or not, anyhow Theology and Physics would be distinct sciences; and nothing which the one says of the material world ever can contradict what the other says of the immaterial. Here, then, is the end of the question; and here I might come to an end also, were it not incumbent on me to explain how it is that, though Theology and Physics cannot quarrel, nevertheless, Physical Philosophers and Theologians have quarrelled in fact, and quarrel still. To the solution of this difficulty I shall devote the remainder of my Lecture.

6.

I observe, then, that the elementary methods of reasoning and inquiring used in Theology and Physics are contrary the one to the other; each of them has a method of its own; and in this, I think, has lain the point of controversy between the two schools, viz., that neither of them has been quite content to remain on its own homestead, but that, whereas each has its own method, which is the best for its own science, each has considered it the best for all purposes whatever, and has at different times thought to impose it upon the other science, to the disparagement or rejection of that opposite method which legitimately belongs to it.

The argumentative method of Theology is that of a strict science, such as Geometry, or deductive; the method of Physics, at least on starting, is that of an empirical pursuit, or inductive. This peculiarity on either side arises from the nature of the case. In Physics a vast and omnigenous mass of information lies before the inquirer, all in a confused litter, and needing arrangement and analysis. In Theology such varied phenomena are wanting, and Revelation presents itself instead. What is known in Christianity is just that which is revealed, and nothing more; certain truths, communicated directly from above, are committed to the keeping of the faithful, and to the very last nothing can really be added to those truths. From the time of the Apostles to the end of the world no strictly new truth can be added to the theological information which the Apostles were inspired to deliver. It is possible of course to make numberless deductions from the original doctrines; but, as the conclusion is ever in its premises, such deductions are not, strictly speaking, an addition; and, though experience may variously guide and modify those deductions, still, on the whole, Theology retains the severe character of a science, advancing syllogistically from premises to conclusion.

The method of Physics is just the reverse of this: it has hardly any principles or truths to start with, externally delivered and already ascertained. It has to commence with sight and touch; it has to handle, weigh, and measure its own exuberant *sylva* of phenomena, and from these to advance to new truths, – truths, that is, which are beyond and distinct from the phenomena from which they originate. Thus Physical Science is experimental, Theology traditional; Physical Science is the richer, Theology the more exact; Physics the bolder, Theology the surer; Physics progressive, Theology, in comparison, stationary; Theology is loyal to the past, Physics has visions of the future. Such they are, I repeat, and such their respective methods of inquiry, from the nature of the case.

But minds habituated to either of these two methods can hardly help extending it beyond its due limits, unless they are put upon their guard, and have great command of themselves. It cannot be denied that divines have from time to time been much inclined to give a traditional, logical shape to sciences which do not admit of any such treatment. Nor can it be denied, on the other hand, that men of science often show a special irritation at theologians for going by antiquity, precedent, authority, and logic, and for declining to introduce Bacon or Niebuhr into their own school, or to apply some new experimental and critical process for the improvement of that which has been given once for all from above. Hence the mutual jealousy of the two parties; and I shall now attempt to give instances of it.

7.

First, then, let me refer to those interpretations of Scripture, popular and of long standing, though not authoritative, to which I have already had occasion to allude. Scripture, we know, is to be interpreted according to the unanimous consent of the Fathers; but, besides this consent, which is of authority, carrying with it the evidence of its truth, there have ever been in Christendom a number of floating opinions, more or less appended to the divine tradition; opinions which have a certain probability of being more than human, or of having a basis or admixture of truth, but which admit of no test, whence they came, or how far they are true, besides the course of events, and which meanwhile are to be received at least with attention and deference. Sometimes they are comments on Scripture prophecy, sometimes on other obscurities or mysteries. It was once an opinion, for instance, drawn from the sacred text, that the Christian Dispensation was to last a thousand years, and no more; the event disproved it. A still more exact and plausible tradition, derived from Scripture, was that which asserted that, when the Roman Empire should fall to pieces, Antichrist should appear, who should be followed at once by the Second Coming. Various Fathers thus interpret St. Paul, and Bellarmine receives the interpretation as late as the sixteenth century. The event alone can decide if, under any aspect of

Christian history, it is true; but at present we are at least able to say that it is not true in that broad plain sense in which it was once received.

Passing from comments on prophetical passages of Scripture to those on cosmological, it was, I suppose, the common belief of ages, sustained by received interpretations of the sacred text, that the earth was immovable. Hence, I suppose, it was that the Irish Bishop who asserted the existence of the Antipodes alarmed his contemporaries; though it is well to observe that, even in the dark age in which he lived, the Holy See, to which reference was made, did not commit itself to any condemnation of the unusual opinion. The same alarm again occupied the public mind when the Copernican System was first advocated: nor were the received traditions, which were the ground of that alarm, hastily to be rejected; yet rejected they ultimately have been. If in any quarter these human traditions were enforced, and, as it were, enacted, to the prejudice and detriment of scientific investigations (and this was never done by the Church herself), this was a case of undue interference on the part of the Theological schools in the province of Physics.

So much may be said as regards interpretations of Scripture; but it is easy to see that other received opinions, not resting on the sacred volume, might with less claim and greater inconvenience be put forward to harass the physical inquirer, to challenge his submission, and to preclude that process of examination which is proper to his own peculiar pursuit. Such are the dictatorial formulæ against which Bacon inveighs, and the effect of which was to change Physics into a deductive science, and to oblige the student to assume implicitly, as first principles, enunciations and maxims, which were venerable, only because no one could tell whence they came, and authoritative, only because no one could say what arguments there were in their favour. In proportion as these encroachments were made upon his own field of inquiry would be the indignation of the physical philosopher; and he would exercise a scepticism which relieved his feelings, while it approved itself to his reason, if he was called on ever to keep in mind that light bodies went up, and heavy bodies fell down, and other similar maxims, which had no pretensions to a divine origin, or to be considered self-evident principles, or intuitive truths.

And in like manner, if a philosopher with a true genius for physical research found the Physical Schools of his day occupied with the discussion of final causes, and solving difficulties in material nature by means of them; if he found it decided, for instance, that the roots of trees make for the river, *because* they need moisture, or that the axis of the earth lies at a certain angle to the plane of its motion by *reason* of certain advantages thence accruing to its inhabitants, I should not wonder at his exerting himself for a great reform in the process of inquiry, preaching the method of Induction, and, if he fancied that theologians were indirectly or in any respect the occasion of the blunder, getting provoked for a time, however unreasonably, with Theology itself.

I wish the experimental school of Philosophers had gone no further in its opposition to Theology than indulging in some indignation at it for the fault of its disciples; but it must be confessed that it has run into excesses on its own side for which the school of high Deductive Science has afforded no precedent; and that, if it once for a time suffered from the tyranny of the logical method of inquiry, it has encouraged, by way of reprisals, encroachments and usurpations on the province of Theology far more serious than that unintentional and long obsolete interference with its own province, on the part of Theologians, which has been its excuse. And to these unjustifiable and mischievous intrusions made by the Experimentalists into the department of Theology I have now, Gentlemen, to call your attention.

8.

You will let me repeat, then, what I have already said, that, taking things as they are, the very idea of Revelation is that of a direct interference from above, for the introduction of truths otherwise unknown; moreover, as such a communication implies recipients, an authoritative depositary of the things revealed will be found practically to be involved in that idea. Knowledge, then, of these revealed truths, is gained, not by any research into facts, but simply by appealing to the authoritative keepers of them, as every Catholic knows, by learning what is a matter of teaching, and by dwelling upon, and drawing out into detail, the doctrines which are delivered; according to the text, "Faith cometh by hearing." I do not prove what, after all, does not need proof, because I speak to Catholics; I am stating what we Catholics know, and ever will maintain to be the method proper to Theology, as it has ever been recognized. Such, I say, is the theological method, deductive; however, the history of the last three centuries is only one long course of attempts, on the part of the partisans of the Baconian Philosophy, to get rid of the method proper to Theology and to make it an experimental science.

But, I say, for an experimental science, we must have a large collection of phenomena or facts: where, then, are those which are to be adopted as a basis for an inductive theology? Three principal stores have been used, Gentlemen: the first, the text of Holy Scripture; the second, the events and transactions of ecclesiastical history; the third, the phenomena of the visible world. This triple subject-matter, – Scripture, Antiquity, Nature, – has been taken as a foundation, on which the inductive method may be exercised for the investigation and ascertainment of that theological truth, which to a Catholic is a matter of teaching, transmission, and deduction.

Now let us pause for a moment and make a reflection before going into any detail. Truth cannot be contrary to truth; if these three subject-matters were able, under the pressure of the inductive method, to yield respectively theological conclusions in unison and in concord with each other, and also contrary to the doctrines of Theology as a deductive science, then that Theology would not indeed at once be overthrown (for still the question would remain for discussion, which of the two doctrinal systems was the truth, and which the apparent truth), but certainly the received deductive theological science would be in an anxious position, and would be on its trial.

Again, truth cannot be contrary to truth; – if, then, on the other hand, these three subject-matters, – Scripture, Antiquity, and Nature, – worked through three centuries by men of great abilities, with the method or instrument of Bacon in their hands, have respectively issued in conclusions contradictory of each other, nay, have even issued, this or that taken by itself, Scripture or Antiquity, in various systems of doctrine, so that on the whole, instead of all three resulting in one set of conclusions, they have yielded a good score of them; then and in that case – it does not at once follow that no one of this score of conclusions may happen to be the true one, and all the rest false; but at least such a catastrophe will throw a very grave shade of doubt upon them all, and bears out the antecedent declaration, or rather prophecy, of theologians, before these experimentalists started, that it was nothing more than a huge mistake to introduce the method of research and of induction into the study of Theology at all.

Now I think you will allow me to say, Gentlemen, as a matter of historical fact, that the latter supposition has been actually fulfilled, and that the former has not. I mean that, so far from a scientific proof of some one system of doctrine, and that antagonistic to the old Theology, having been constructed by the experimental party, by a triple convergence, from the several bases of Scripture, Antiquity, and Nature, on the contrary, that empirical method, which has done such wonderful things in physics and other human sciences, has sustained a most emphatic and eloquent reverse in its ursurped territory, – has come to no one conclusion, – has illuminated no definite view, – has brought its glasses to no focus, – has shown not even a tendency towards prospective success; nay, further still, has already confessed its own absolute failure, and has closed the inquiry itself, not indeed by giving place to the legitimate method which it dispossessed, but by announcing that nothing can be known on the subject at all, – that religion is not a science, and that in religion scepticism is the only true philosophy; or again, by a still more remarkable avowal, that the decision lies *between* the old Theology and none at all, and that, certain though it be that religious truth is nowhere, yet that, *if* anywhere it is, it undoubtedly is not in the new empirical schools, but in that old teaching, founded on the deductive method, which was in honour and in possession at the time when Experiment and Induction commenced their brilliant career. What a singular break-down of a noble instrument, when used for the arrogant and tyrannical invasion of a sacred territory! What can be more sacred than Theology? What can be more noble than the Baconian method? But the two do not correspond; they are mismatched. The age has mistaken lock and key. It has broken the key in a lock which does not belong to it; it has ruined the wards by a key which never will fit into them. Let us hope that its present disgust and despair at the result are the preliminaries of a generous and great repentance.

I have thought, Gentlemen, that you would allow me to draw this moral in the first place; and now I will say a few words on one specimen of this error in detail.

9.

It seems, then, that instead of having recourse to the tradition and teaching of the Catholic Church, it has been the philosophy of the modern school to attempt to determine the doctrines of Theology by means of Holy Scripture, or of ecclesiastical antiquity, or of physical phenomena. And the question may arise, *why,* after all, should not such informations, scriptural, historical, or physical, be used? and if used, why should they not lead to true results? Various answers may be given to this question: I shall confine myself to one; and again, for the sake of brevity, I shall apply it mainly to one out of the three expedients, to which the opponents to Theology have had recourse. Passing over, then, what might be said respecting what is called Scriptural Religion, and Historical Religion, I propose to direct your attention, in conclusion, to the real character of Physical Religion, or Natural Theology, as being more closely connected with the main subject of this Lecture.

The school of Physics, from its very drift and method of reasoning, has, as I have said, nothing to do with Religion. However, there is a science which avails itself of the phenomena and laws of the material universe, as exhibited by that school, as a means of establishing the existence of Design in their construction, and thereby the fact of a Creator and Preserver. This science has, in these modern times, at least in England, taken the name of Natural Theology;[70] and, though absolutely distinct from Physics, yet Physical Philosophers, having furnished its most curious and interesting data, are apt to claim it as their own, and to pride themselves upon it accordingly.

I have no wish to speak lightly of the merits of this so-called Natural or, more properly, Physical Theology. There are a great many minds so constituted that, when they turn their thoughts to the question of the existence of a Supreme Being, they feel a comfort in resting the proof mainly or solely on the Argument of Design which the Universe furnishes. To them this science of Physical Theology is of high importance. Again, this science exhibits, in great prominence and distinctness, three of the more elementary notions which the human reason attaches to the idea of a Supreme Being, that is, three of His simplest attributes, Power, Wisdom, and Goodness.

These are great services rendered to faith by Physical Theology, and I acknowledge them as such. Whether, however, Faith on that account owes any great deal to Physics or Physicists, is another matter. The Argument from Design is really in no sense due to the philosophy of Bacon. The author I quoted just now has a striking passage on this point, of which I have already read to you a part. "As respects Natural Religion," he says, "it is not easy to see that the philosopher of the present day is more favourably situated than Thales or Simonides. He has before him just the same evidences of design in the structure of the universe which the early Greeks had. We say, just the same; for the discoveries of modern astronomers and anatomists *have really added nothing* to the force of that argument which a reflecting mind finds in every beast, bird, insect, fish, leaf, flower, and shell. The reasoning by which Socrates, in Xenophon's hearing, confuted the little atheist, Aristodemus, is exactly the reasoning of Paley's Natural Theology. Socrates makes precisely the same use of the statues of Polycletus and the pictures of Zeuxis, which Paley makes of the watch."

Physical Theology, then, is pretty much what it was two thousand years ago, and has not received much help from modern science: but now, on the contrary, I think it has received from it a positive disadvantage, – I mean, it has been taken out of its place, has been put too prominently forward, and thereby has almost been used as an instrument against Christianity, – as I will attempt in a few words to explain.

10.

I observe, then, that there are many investigations in every subject-matter which only lead us a certain way towards truth, and not the whole way: either leading us, for instance, to a strong probability, not to a certainty, or again, proving only some things out of the whole number which are true. And it is plain that if such investigations as these are taken as the measure of the whole truth, and are erected into substantive sciences, instead of being understood to be, what they really are, inchoate and subordinate processes, they will, accidentally indeed, but seriously, mislead us.

I. Let us recur for a moment, in illustration, to the instances which I have put aside. Consider what is called Sciptural Religion, or the Religion of the Bible. The fault which the theologian, over and above the question of private judgment, will find with a religion logically drawn from Scripture only, is, not that it is not true, as far as it goes, but that it is not the whole truth; that it consists of only some out of the whole circle of theological doctrines, and that, even in the case of those which it includes, it does not always invest them with certainty, but only with probability. If, indeed, the Religion of the Bible is made subservient to Theology, it is but a specimen of useful induction; but if it is set up, as something complete in itself, against Theology, it is turned into a mischievous paralogism. And if such a paralogism has taken place, and that in consequence of the influence of the Baconian philosophy, it shows us what comes of the intrusion of that philosophy into a province with which it had no concern.

2. And so, again, as to Historical Religion, or what is often called Antiquity. A research into the records of the early Church no Catholic can view with jealousy: truth cannot be contrary to truth; we are confident that what is there found will, when maturely weighed, be nothing else than an illustration and confirmation of our own Theology. But it is another thing altogether whether the results will go to the full lengths of our Theology; they will indeed concur with it, but only as far as they go. There is no reason why the data for investigation supplied by the extant documents of Antiquity should be sufficient for all that was included in the Divine Revelation delivered by the Apostles; and to expect that they will is like expecting that one witness in a trial is to prove the whole case, and that his testimony actually contradicts it, unless it does. While, then, this research into ecclesiastical history and the writings of the Fathers keeps its proper place, as subordinate to the magisterial sovereignty of the Theological Tradition and the voice of the Church, it deserves the acknowledgments of theologians; but when it (so to say) sets up for itself, when it professes to fulfil an office

for which it was never intended, when it claims to issue in a true and full teaching, derived by a scientific process of induction, then it is but another instance of the encroachment of the Baconian empirical method in a department not its own.

3. And now we come to the case of Physical Theology, which is directly before us. I confess, in spite of whatever may be said in its favour, I have ever viewed it with the greatest suspicion. As one class of thinkers has substituted what is called a Scriptural Religion, and another a Patristical or Primitive Religion, for the theological teaching of Catholicism, so a Physical Religion or Theology is the very gospel of many persons of the Physical School, and therefore, true as it may be in itself, still under the circumstances is a false gospel. Half of the truth is a falsehood: – consider, Gentlemen, what this so-called Theology teaches, and then say whether what I have asserted is extravagant.

Any one divine attribute of course virtually includes all; still if a preacher always insisted on the Divine Justice, he would practically be obscuring the Divine Mercy, and if he insisted only on the incommunicableness and distance from the creature of the Uncreated Essence, he would tend to throw into the shade the doctrine of a Particular Providence. Observe, then, Gentlemen, that Physical Theology teaches three Divine Attributes, I may say, exclusively; and of these, most of Power, and least of Goodness.

And in the next place, what, on the contrary, are those special Attributes, which are the immediate correlatives of religious sentiment? Sanctity, omniscience, justice, mercy, faithfulness. What does Physical Theology, what does the Argument from Design, what do fine disquisitions about final causes, teach us, except very indirectly, faintly, enigmatically, of these transcendently important, these essential portions of the idea of Religion? Religion is more than Theology; it is something relative to us; and it includes our relation towards the Object of it. What does Physical Theology tell us of duty and conscience? of a particular providence? and, coming at length to Christianity, what does it teach us even of the four last things, death, judgment, heaven, and hell, the mere elements of Christianity? It cannot tell us anything of Christianity at all.

Gentlemen, let me press this point upon your earnest attention. I say Physical Theology cannot, from the nature of the case, tell us one word about Christianity proper; it cannot be Christian, in any true sense, at all: – and from this plain reason, because it is derived from informations which existed just as they are now, before man was created, and Adam fell. How can that be a real substantive Theology, though it takes the name, which is but an abstraction, a particular aspect of the whole truth, and is dumb almost as regards the moral attributes of the Creator, and utterly so as regards the evangelical?

Nay, more than this; I do not hesitate to say that, taking men as they are, this so-called science tends, if it occupies the mind, to dispose it against Christianity. And for this plain reason, because it speaks only of laws; and cannot contemplate their suspension, that is, miracles, which are of the essence of the idea of a Revelation. Thus, the God of Physical Theology may very easily become a mere idol; for He comes to the inductive mind in the medium of fixed appointments, so excellent, so skilful, so beneficent, that, when it has for a long time gazed upon them, it will think them too beautiful to be broken, and will at length so contract its notion of Him as to conclude that He never could have the heart (if I may dare use such a term) to undo or mar His own work; and this conclusion will be the first step towards its degrading its idea of God a second time, and identifying Him with His works. Indeed, a Being of Power, Wisdom, and Goodness, and nothing else, is not very different from the God of the Pantheist.

In thus speaking of the Theology of the modern Physical School, I have said but a few words on a large subject; yet, though few words, I trust they are clear enough not to hazard the risk of being taken in a sense which I do not intend. Graft the science, if it is so to be called, on Theology proper, and it will be in its right place, and will be a religious science. Then it will illustrate the awful, incomprehensible, adorable Fertility of the Divine Omnipotence; it will serve to prove the real miraculousness of the Revelation in its various parts, by impressing on the mind vividly what are the laws of nature, and how immutable they are in their own order; and it will in other ways subserve theological truth. Separate it from the supernatural teaching, and make it stand on its own base, and (though of course it is better for the individual philosopher himself), yet, as regards his influence on the world and the interests of Religion, I really doubt whether I should not prefer that he should be an Atheist at once than such a naturalistic, pantheistic religionist. His profession of Theology deceives others, perhaps deceives himself.

Do not for an instant suppose, Gentlemen, that I would identify the great mind of Bacon with so serious a delusion: he has expressly warned us against it; but I cannot deny that many of his school have from time to time in this way turned physical research against Christianity.

But I have detained you far longer than I had intended; and now I can only thank you for the patience which has enabled you to sustain a discussion which cannot be complete, upon a subject which, however momentous, cannot be popular.

IV.

CHRISTIANITY AND SCIENTIFIC INVESTIGATION.

A LECTURE WRITTEN FOR THE SCHOOL OF SCIENCE.

I.

This is a time, Gentlemen, when not only the Classics, but much more the Sciences, in the largest sense of the word, are looked upon with anxiety, not altogether ungrounded, by religious men; and, whereas a University such as ours professes to embrace all departments and exercises of the intellect, and since I for my part wish to stand on good terms with all kinds of knowledge, and have no intention of quarrelling with any, and would open my heart, if not my intellect (for that is beyond me), to the whole circle of truth, and would tender at least a recognition and hospitality even to those studies which are strangers to me, and would speed them on their way, – therefore, as I have already been making overtures of reconciliation, first between Polite Literature and Religion, and next between Physics and Theology, so I would now say a word by way of deprecating and protesting against the needless antagonism, which sometimes exists in fact, between divines and the cultivators of the Sciences generally.

2.

Here I am led at once to expatiate on the grandeur of an Institution which is comprehensive enough to admit the discussion of a subject such as this. Among the objects of human enterprise, – I may say it surely without extravagance, Gentlemen, – none higher or nobler can be named than that which is contemplated in the erection of a University. To set on foot and to maintain in life and vigour a real University, is confessedly, as soon as the word "University" is understood, one of those greatest works, great in their difficulty and their importance, on which are deservedly expended the rarest intellects and the most varied endowments. For, first of all, it professes to teach whatever has to be taught in any whatever department of human knowledge, and it embraces in its scope the loftiest subjects of human thought, and the richest fields of human inquiry. Nothing is too vast, nothing too subtle, nothing too distant, nothing too minute, nothing too discursive, nothing too exact, to engage its attention.

This, however, is not the reason why I claim for it so sovereign a position; for, to bring schools of all knowledge under one name, and call them a University, may be fairly said to be a mere generalization; and to proclaim that the prosecution of all kinds of knowledge to their utmost limits demands the fullest reach and range of our intellectual faculties is but a truism. My reason for speaking of a University in the terms on which I have ventured is, not that it occupies the whole territory of knowledge merely, but that it is the very realm; that it professes much more than to take in and to lodge as in a caravanserai all art and science, all history and philosophy. In truth, it professes to assign to each study, which it receives, its own proper place and its just boundaries; to define the rights, to establish the mutual relations, and to effect the intercommunion of one and all; to keep in check the ambitious and encroaching, and to succour and maintain those which from time to time are succumbing under the more popular or the more fortunately circumstanced; to keep the peace between them all, and to convert their mutual differences and contrarieties into the common good. This, Gentlemen, is why I say that to erect a University is at once so arduous and beneficial an undertaking, viz., because it is pledged to admit, without fear, without prejudice, without compromise, all comers, if they come in the name of Truth; to adjust views, and experiences, and habits of mind the most independent and dissimilar; and to give full play to thought and erudition in their most original forms, and their most intense expressions, and in their most ample circuit. Thus to draw many things into one, is its special function; and it learns to do it, not by rules reducible to writing, but by sagacity, wisdom, and forbearance, acting upon a profound insight into the subject-matter of knowledge, and by a vigilant repression of aggression or bigotry in any quarter.

We count it a great thing, and justly so, to plan and carry out a wide political organization. To bring under one yoke, after the manner of old Rome, a hundred discordant peoples; to maintain each of them in its own privileges within its legitimate range of action; to allow them severally the indulgence of national feelings, and the stimulus of rival interests; and yet withal to blend them into one great social establishment, and to pledge them to the perpetuity of the one imperial power; – this is an achievement which carries with it the unequivocal token of genius in the race which effects it.

"Tu regere imperio populos, Romane, memento."[71]

This was the special boast, as the poet considered it, of the Roman; a boast as high in its own line as that other boast, proper to the Greek nation, of literary preeminence, of exuberance of thought, and of skill and refinement in expressing it.

What an empire is in political history, such is a University in the sphere of philosophy and research. It is, as I have said, the high protecting power of all knowledge and science, of fact and principle, of inquiry and discovery, of experiment and speculation; it maps out the territory of the intellect, and speculation; it maps out the territory of the intellect, and sees that the boundaries of each province are religiously respected, and that there is neither encroachment nor surrender on any side. It acts as umpire between truth and truth, and, taking into account the nature and importance of each, assigns to all their due order of precedence. It maintains no one department of thought exclusively, however ample and noble; and it sacrifices none. It is deferential and loyal, according to their respective weight, to the claims of literature, of physical research, of history, of metaphysics, of theological science. It is impartial towards them all, and promotes each in its own place and for its own object. It is ancillary certainly, and of necessity, to the Catholic Church; but in the same way that one of the Queen's judges is an officer of the Queen's, and nevertheless determines certain legal proceedings between the Queen and her subjects. It is ministrative to the Catholic Church, first, because truth of any kind can but minister to truth; and next, still more, because Nature ever will pay homage to Grace, and Reason cannot but illustrate and defend Revelation; and thirdly, because the Church has a sovereign authority, and, when she speaks *ex cathedra,* must be obeyed. But this is the remote end of a University; its immediate end (with which alone we have here to do) is to secure the due disposition, according to one sovereign order, and the cultivation in that order, of all the provinces and methods of thought which the human intellect has created.

In this point of view, its several professors are like the ministers of various political powers at one court or conference. They represent their respective sciences, and attend to the private interests of those sciences respectively; and, should dispute arise between those sciences, they are the persons to talk over and arrange it, without risk of extravagant pretensions on any side, of angry collision, or of popular commotion. A liberal philosophy becomes the habit of minds thus exercised; a breadth and spaciousness of thought, in which lines, seemingly parallel, may converge at leisure, and principles, recognized as incommensurable, may be safely antagonistic.

3.

And here, Gentlemen, we recognize the special character of the Philosophy I am speaking of, if Philosophy it is to be called, in contrast with the method of a strict science or system. Its teaching is not founded on one idea, or reducible to certain formulæ. Newton might discover the great law of motion in the physical world, and the key to ten thousand phenomena; and a similar resolution of complex facts into simple principles may be possible in other departments of nature; but the great Universe itself, moral and material, sensible and supernatural, cannot be gauged and meted by even the greatest of human intellects, and its constituent parts admit indeed of comparison and adjustment, but not of fusion. This is the point which bears directly on the subject which I set before me when I began, and towards which I am moving in all I have said or shall be saying.

I observe, then, and ask you, Gentlemen, to bear in mind, that the philosophy of an imperial intellect, for such I am considering a University to be, is based, not so much on simplification as on discrimination. Its true representative defines, rather than analyzes. He aims at no complete catalogue, or interpretation of the subjects of knowledge, but a following out, as far as man can, what in its fulness is mysterious and unfathomable. Taking into his charge all sciences, methods, collections of facts, principles, doctrines, truths, which are the reflexions of the universe upon the human intellect, he admits them all, he disregards none, and, as disregarding none, he allows none to exceed or encroach. His watchword is, Live and let live. He takes things as they are; he submits to them all, as far as they go; he recognizes the insuperable lines of demarcation which run between subject and subject; he observes how separate truths lie relatively to each other, where they concur, where they part company, and where, being carried too far, they cease to be truths at all. It is his office to determine how much can be known in each province of thought; when we must be contented not to know; in what direction inquiry is hopeless, or on the other hand full of promise; where it gathers into coils insoluble by reason, where it is absorbed in mysteries, or runs into the abyss. It will be his care to be familiar with the signs of real and apparent difficulties, with the methods proper to particular subject-matters, what in each particular case are the limits of a rational scepticism, and what the claims of a peremptory faith. If he has one cardinal maxim in his philosophy, it is, that truth cannot be contrary to truth; if he has a second, it is, that truth often *seems* contrary to truth; and, if a third, it is the practical conclusion, that we must be patient with such appearances, and not be hasty to pronounce them to be really of a more formidable character.

It is the very immensity of the system of things, the human record of which he has in charge, which is the reason of this patience and caution; for that immensity suggests to him that the contrarieties and mysteries, which meet him in the various sciences, may be simply the consequences of our necessarily defective comprehension. There is but one thought greater than that of the universe, and that is the thought of its Maker. If, Gentlemen, for one single instant, leaving my proper train of thought, I allude to our knowledge of the Supreme Being, it is in order to deduce from it an illustration bearing upon my subject. He, though One, is a sort of world of worlds in Himself, giving birth in our minds to an indefinite number of distinct truths, each ineffably more mysterious than any thing that is found in this universe of space and time. Any one of His attributes, considered by itself, is the object of an inexhaustible science: and the attempt to reconcile any two or three of them together, – love, power, justice, sanctity, truth, wisdom, – affords matter for an everlasting controversy. We are able to apprehend and receive each divine attribute in its elementary form, but still we are not able to accept them in their infinity, either in themselves or in union with each other. Yet we do not deny the first because it cannot be perfectly reconciled with the second, nor the second because it is in apparent contrariety with the first and the third. The case is the same in its degree with His creation material and moral. It is the highest wisdom to accept truth of whatever kind, wherever it is clearly ascertained to be such, though there be difficulty in adjusting it with other known truth.

Instances are easily producible of that extreme contrariety of ideas, one with another, which the contemplation of the Universe forces upon our acceptance, making it clear to us that there is nothing irrational in submitting to undeniable incompatibilities, which we call apparent, only because, if they were not apparent but real, they could not co-exist. Such, for instance, is the contemplation of Space; the existence of which we cannot deny, though its idea is capable, in no sort of posture, of seating itself (if I may so speak) in our minds; – for we find it impossible to say that it comes to a limit anywhere; and it is incomprehensible to say that it runs out infinitely; and it seems to be unmeaning if we say that it does not exist till bodies come into it, and thus is enlarged according to an accident.

And so again in the instance of Time. We cannot place a beginning to it without asking ourselves what was before that beginning; yet that there should be no beginning at all, put it as far back as we will, is simply incomprehensible. Here again, as in the case of Space, we never dream of denying the existence of what we have no means of understanding.

And, passing from this high region of thought (which, high as it may be, is the subject even of a child's contemplations), when we come to consider the mutual action of soul and body, we are specially perplexed by incompatibilities which we can neither reject nor explain. How it is that the will can act on the muscles, is a question of which even a child may feel the force, but which no experimentalist can answer.

Further, when we contrast the physical with the social laws under which man finds himself here below, we must grant that Physiology and Social Science are in collision. Man is both a physical and a social being; yet he cannot at once pursue to the full his physical end and his social end, his physical duties (if I may so speak) and his social duties, but is forced to sacrifice in part one or the other. If we were wild enough to fancy that there were two creators, one of whom was the author of our animal frames, the other of society, then indeed we might understand how it comes to pass that labour of mind and body, the useful arts, the duties of a statesman, government, and the like, which are required by the social system, are so destructive of health, enjoyment, and life. That is, in other words, we cannot adequately account for existing and undeniable truths except on the hypothesis of what we feel to be an absurdity.

And so in Mathematical Science, as has been often insisted on, the philosopher has patiently to endure the presence of truths, which are not the less true for being irreconcileable with each other. He is told of the existence of an infinite number of curves, which are able to divide a space, into which no straight line, though it be length without breadth, can even enter. He is told, too, of certain lines, which approach to each other continually, with a finite distance between them, yet never meet; and these apparent contrarieties he must bear as he best can, without attempting to deny the existence of the truths which constitute them in the Science in question.

4.

Now, let me call your attention, Gentlemen, to what I would infer from these familiar facts. It is, to urge you with an argument *à fortiori:* viz., that, as you exercise so much exemplary patience in the case of the inexplicable truths which surround so many departments of knowledge, human and divine, viewed in themselves; as you are not at once indignant, censorious, suspicious, difficult of belief, on finding that in the secular sciences one truth is incompatible (according to our human intellect) with another or inconsistent with itself; so you should not think it very hard to be told that there exists, here and there, not an inextricable difficulty, not an astounding contrariety, not (much less) a contradiction as to clear facts, between

Revelation and Nature; but a hitch, an obscurity, a divergence of tendency, a temporary antagonism, a difference of tone, between the two, – that is, between Catholic opinion on the one hand, and astronomy, or geology, or physiology, or ethnology, or political economy, or history, or antiquities, on the other. I say that, as we admit, because we are Catholics, that the Divine Unity contains in it attributes, which, to our finite minds, appear in partial contrariety with each other; as we admit that, in His revealed Nature are things, which, though not opposed to Reason, are infinitely strange to the Imagination; as in His works we can neither reject nor admit the ideas of space, and of time, and the necessary properties of lines, without intellectual distress, or even torture; really, Gentlemen, I am making no outrageous request, when, in the name of a University, I ask religious writers, jurists, economists, physiologists, chemists, geologists, and historians, to go on quietly, and in a neighbourly way, in their own respective lines of speculation, research, and experiment, with full faith in the consistency of that multiform truth, which they share between them, in a generous confidence that they will be ultimately consistent, one and all, in their combined results, though there may be momentary collisions, awkward appearances, and many forebodings and prophecies of contrariety, and at all times things hard to the Imagination, though not, I repeat, to the Reason. It surely is not asking them a great deal to beg of them, – since they are forced to admit mysteries in the truths of Revelation, taken by themselves, and in the truths of Reason, taken by themselves, – to beg of them, I say, to keep the peace, to live in good will, and to exercise equanimity, if, when Nature and Revelation are compared with each other, there be, as I have said, discrepancies, – not in the issue, but in the reasonings, the circumstances, the associations, the anticipations, the accidents, proper to their respective teachings.

It is most necessary to insist seriously and energetically on this point, for the sake of Protestants, for they have very strange notions about us. In spite of the testimony of history the other way, they think that the Church has no other method of putting down error than the arm of force, or the prohibition of inquiry. They defy us to set up and carry on a School of Science. For their sake, then, I am led to enlarge upon the subject here. I say, then, he who believes Revelation with that absolute faith which is the prerogative of a Catholic, is not the nervous creature who startles at every sudden sound, and is fluttered by every strange or novel appearance which meets his eyes. He has no sort of apprehension, he laughs at the idea, that any thing can be discovered by any other scientific method, which can contradict any one of the dogmas of his religion. He knows full well there is no science whatever, but, in the course of its extension, runs the risk of infringing, without any meaning of offence on its own part, the path of other sciences: and he knows also that, if there be any one science which, from its sovereign and unassailable position can calmly bear such unintentional collisions on the part of the children of earth, it is Theology. He is sure, and nothing shall make him doubt, that, if anything seems to be proved by astronomer, or geologist, or chronologist, or antiquarian, or ethnologist, in contradiction to the dogmas of faith, that point will eventually turn out, first, *not* to be proved, or, secondly, not *contradictory,* or thirdly, not contradictory to any thing *really revealed,* but to something which has been confused with revelation. And if, at the moment, it appears to be contradictory, then he is content to wait, knowing that error is like other delinquents; give it rope enough, and it will be found to have a strong suicidal propensity. I do not mean to say he will not take his part in encouraging, in helping forward the prospective suicide; he will not only give the error rope enough, but show it how to handle and adjust the rope; – he will commit the matter to reason, reflection, sober judgment, common sense; to Time, the great interpreter of so many secrets. Instead of being irritated at the momentary triumph of the foes of Revelation, if such a feeling of triumph there be, and of hurrying on a forcible solution of the difficulty, which may in the event only reduce the inquiry to an inextricable tangle, he will recollect that, in the order of Providence, our seeming dangers are often our greatest gains; that in the words of the Protestant poet,

> The clouds you so much dread
> Are big with mercy, and shall break
> In blessings on your head.[72]

5.

To one notorious instance indeed it is obvious to allude here. When the Copernican system first made progress, what religious man would not have been tempted to uneasiness, or at least fear of scandal, from the seeming contradiction which it involved to some authoritative tradition of the Church and the declaration of Scripture? It was generally received, as if the Apostles had expressly delivered it both orally and in writing, as a truth of Revelation, that the earth was stationary, and that the sun, fixed in a solid firmament, whirled round the earth. After a little time, however, and on full consideration, it was found that the Church had decided next to nothing on questions such as these, and that Physical Science might range in this sphere of thought almost at will, without fear of encountering the decisions of ecclesiastical authority. Now, besides the relief which it afforded to Catholics to find that they were to be spared this addition, on the side of Cosmology, to their many controversies already existing, there is something of an argument in this very circumstance in behalf of the divinity of their Religion. For it surely is a very remarkable fact, considering how widely and how long one certain interpretation of these physical statements in Scripture had been received by Catholics, that the Church should not have formally acknowledged it. Looking at the matter in a human point of view, it was inevitable that she should have made that opinion her own. But now we find, on ascertaining where we stand, in the face of the new sciences of these latter times, that in spite of the bountiful comments which from the first she has ever been making on the sacred text, as it is her duty and her right to do, nevertheless, she has never been led formally to explain the texts in question, or to give them an authoritative sense which modern science may question.

Nor was this escape a mere accident, but rather the result of a providential superintendence; as would appear from a passage of history in the dark age itself. When the glorious St. Boniface, Apostle of Germany, great in sanctity, though not in secular knowledge, complained to the Holy See that St. Virgilius taught the existence of the Antipodes, the Holy See was guided what to do; it did not indeed side with the Irish philosopher, which would have been going out of its place, but it passed over, in a matter not revealed, a philosophical opinion.

Time went on; a new state of things, intellectual and social, came in; the Church was girt with temporal power; the preachers of St. Dominic were in the ascendant: now at length we may ask with curious interest, did the Church alter her ancient rule of action, and proscribe intellectual activity? Just the contrary; this is the very age of Universities; it is the classical period of the schoolmen; it is the splendid and palmary instance of the wise policy and large liberality of the Church, as regards philosophical inquiry. If there ever was a time when the intellect went wild, and had a licentious revel, it was at the date I speak of. When was there ever a more curious, more meddling, bolder, keener, more penetrating, more rationalistic exercise of the reason than at that time? What class of questions did that subtle, metaphysical spirit not scrutinize? What premiss was allowed without examination? What principle was not traced to its first origin, and exhibited in its most naked shape? What whole was not analyzed? What complex idea was not elaborately traced out, and, as it were, finely painted for the contemplation of the mind, till it was spread out in all its minutest portions as perfectly and delicately as a frog's foot shows under the intense scrutiny of the microscope? Well, I repeat, here was something which came somewhat nearer to Theology than physical research comes; Aristotle was a somewhat more serious foe then, beyond all mistake, than Bacon has been since. Did the Church take a high hand with philosophy then? No, not though that philosophy was metaphysical. It was a time when she had temporal power, and could have exterminated the spirit of inquiry with fire and sword; but she determined to put it down by *argument,* she said: "Two can play at that, and my argument is the better." She sent her controversialists into the philosophical arena. It was the Dominican and Franciscan doctors, the greatest of them being St. Thomas, who in those medieval Universities fought the battle of Revelation with the weapons of heathenism. It was no matter whose the weapon was; truth was truth all the world over. With the jawbone of an ass, with the skeleton philosophy of pagan Greece, did the Samson of the schools put to flight his thousand Philistines.

Here, Gentlemen, observe the contrast exhibited between the Church herself, who has the gift of wisdom, and even the ablest, or wisest, or holiest of her children. As St. Boniface had been jealous of physical speculations, so had the early Fathers shown an extreme aversion to the great heathen philosopher whom I just now named, Aristotle. I do not know who of them could endure him; and when there arose those in the middle age who would take his part, especially since their intentions were of a suspicious character, a strenuous effort was made to banish him out of Christendom. The Church the while had kept silence; she had as little denounced heathen philosophy in the mass as she had pronounced upon the meaning of certain texts of Scripture of a cosmological character. From Tertullian and Caius to the two Gregories of Cappadocia, from them to Anastasius Sinaita, from him to the school of Paris, Aristotle was a word of offence; at length St. Thomas made him a hewer of wood and drawer of water to the Church. A strong slave he is; and the Church herself has given her sanction to the use in Theology of the ideas and terms of his philosophy.

6.

Now, while this free discussion is, to say the least, so safe for Religion, or rather so expedient, it is on the other hand simply necessary for progress in Science; and I shall now go on to insist on this side of the subject. I say, then, that it is a matter of primary importance in the cultivation of those sciences, in which truth is discoverable by the human intellect, that the investigator should be free, independent, unshackled in his movements; that he should be allowed and enabled, without impediment, to fix his mind intently, nay, exclusively, on his special object, without the risk of being distracted every other minute in the process and progress of his inquiry, by charges of temerariousness, or by warnings against extravagance or scandal. But in thus speaking, I must premise several explanations, lest I be misunderstood.

First, then, Gentlemen, as to the fundamental principles of religion and morals, and again as to the fundamental principles of Christianity, or what are called the *dogmas* of faith, – as to this double creed, natural and revealed, – we, none of us, should say that it is any shackle at all upon the intellect to maintain these inviolate. Indeed, a Catholic cannot put off his thought of them; and they as little impede the movements of his intellect as the laws of physics impede his bodily movements. The habitual apprehension of them has become a second nature with him, as the laws of optics, hydrostatics, dynamics, are latent conditions which he takes for granted in the use of his corporeal organs. I am not supposing any collision with dogma, I am but speaking of opinions of divines, or of the multitude, parallel to those in former times of the sun going round the earth, or of the last day being close at hand, or of St. Dionysius the Areopagite being the author of the works which bear his name.

Nor, secondly, even as regards such opinions, am I supposing any direct intrusion into the province of religion, or of a teacher of Science actually laying down the law *in a matter of Religion;* but of such unintentional collisions as are incidental to a discussion pursued on some subject of his own. It would be a great mistake in such a one to propose his philosophical or historical conclusions as the formal interpretation of the sacred text, as Galileo is said to have done, instead of being content to hold his doctrine of the motion of the earth as a scientific conclusion, and leaving it to those whom it really concerned to compare it with Scripture. And, it must be confessed, Gentlemen, not a few instances occur of this mistake at the present day, on the part, not indeed of men of science, but of religious men, who, from a nervous impatience lest Scripture should for one moment seem inconsistent with the the results of some speculation of the hour, are ever proposing geological or ethnological comments upon it, which they have to alter or obliterate before the ink is well dry, from changes in the progressive science, which they have so officiously brought to its aid.

And thirdly, I observe that, when I advocate the independence of philosophical thought, I am not speaking of any *formal teaching* at all, but of investigations, speculations, and discussions. I am far indeed from allowing, in any matter which even borders on Religion, what an eminent Protestant divine has advocated on the most sacred subjects, – I mean "the liberty of Prophesying." I have no wish to degrade the professors of Science, who ought to be Prophets of the Truth, into mere advertisers of crude fancies or notorious absurdities. I am not pleading that they should at random shower down upon their hearers ingenuities and novelties; or that they should teach even what has a basis of truth in it, in a brilliant, off-hand way, to a collection of youths, who may not perhaps hear them for six consecutive lectures, and who will carry away with them into the country a misty idea of the half-created theories of some ambitious intellect.

Once more, as the last sentence suggests, there must be great care taken to avoid scandal, or shocking the popular mind, or unsettling the weak; the association between truth and error being so strong in particular minds that it is impossible to weed them of the error without rooting up the wheat with it. If, then, there is the chance of any current religious opinion being in any way compromised in the course of a scientific investigation, this would be a reason for conducting it, not in light ephemeral publications, which come into the hands of the careless or ignorant, but in works of a grave and business-like character, answering to the medieval schools of philosophical disputation, which, removed as they were from the region of popular thought and feeling, have, by their vigorous restlessness of inquiry, in spite of their extravagances, done so much for theological precision.

7.

I am not, then, supposing the scientific investigator (1) to be *coming into collision with dogma;* nor (2) venturing, by means of his investigations, upon any interpretation of *Scripture,* or upon other conclusion *in the matter of religion;* nor (3) of his *teaching,* even in his own science, religious paradoxes, when he should be investigating and proposing; nor (4) of his recklessly *scandalizing the weak;* but, these explanations being made, I still say that a scientific speculator or inquirer is not bound, in conducting his researches, to be every moment adjusting his course by the maxims of the schools or by popular traditions, or by those of any other science distinct from his own, or to be ever narrowly watching what those external sciences have to say to him, or to be determined to be edifying, or to be ever answering heretics and unbelievers; being confident, from the impulse of a generous faith, that, however his line of investigation may swerve now and then, and vary to and fro in its course, or threaten momentary collision or embarrassment with any other department of knowledge, theological or not, yet, if he lets it alone, it will be sure to come home, because truth never can really be contrary to truth, and because often what at first sight is an "exceptio," in the event most emphatically "probat regulam."

This is a point of serious importance to him. Unless he is at liberty to investigate on the basis, and according to the peculiarities, of his science, he cannot investigate at all. It is the very law of the human mind in its inquiry after and acquisition of truth to make its advances by a process which consists of many stages, and is circuitous. There are no short cuts to knowledge; nor does the road to it always lie in the direction in which it terminates, nor are we able to see the end on starting. It may often seem to be diverging from a goal into which it will soon run without effort, if we are but patient and resolute in following it out; and, as we are told in Ethics to gain the mean merely by receding from both extremes, so in scientific researches error may be said, without a paradox, to be in some instances the way to truth, and the only way. Moreover, it is not often the fortune of any one man to live through an investigation; the process is one of not only many stages, but of many minds. What one begins another finishes; and a true conclusion is at length worked out by the co-operation of independent schools and the perseverance of successive generations. This being the case, we are obliged, under circumstances, to bear for a while with what we feel to be error, in consideration of the truth in which it is eventually to issue.

The analogy of locomotion is most pertinent here. No one can go straight up a mountain; no sailing vessel makes for its port without tacking. And so, applying the illustration, we can indeed, if we will, refuse to allow of investigation or research altogether; but, if we invite reason to take its place in our schools, we must let reason have fair and full play. If we reason, we must submit to the conditions of reason. We cannot use it by halves; we must use it as proceeding from Him who has also given us Revelation; and to be ever interrupting its processes, and diverting its attention by objections brought from a higher knowledge, is parallel to a landsman's dismay at the changes in the course of a vessel on which he has deliberately embarked, and argues surely some distrust either in the powers of Reason on the one hand, or the certainty of Revealed Truth on the other. The passenger should not have embarked at all, if he did not reckon on the chance of a rough sea, of currents, of wind and tide, of rocks and shoals; and we should act more wisely in discountenancing altogether the exercise of Reason than in being alarmed and impatient under the suspense, delay, and anxiety which, from the nature of the case, may be found to attach to it. Let us eschew secular history, and science, and philosophy for good and all, if we are not allowed to be sure that Revelation is so true that the altercations and perplexities of human opinion cannot really or eventually injure its authority. That is no intellectual triumph of any truth of Religion, which has not been preceded by a full statement of what can be said against it; it is but the ego vapulando, ille verberando, of the Comedy.

Great minds need elbow-room, not indeed in the domain of faith, but of thought. And so indeed do lesser minds, and all minds. There are many persons in the world who are called, and with a great deal of truth, geniuses. They had been gifted by nature with some particular faculty or capacity; and, while vehemently excited and imperiously ruled by it, they are blind to everything else. They are enthusiasts in their own line, and are simply dead to the beauty of any line *except* their own. Accordingly, they think their own line the only line in the whole world worth pursuing, and they feel a sort of contempt for such studies as move upon any other line. Now, these men may be, and often are, very good Catholics, and have not a dream of any thing but affection and deference towards Catholicity, nay, perhaps are zealous in its interests. Yet, if you insist that in their speculations, researches, or conclusions in their particular science, it is not enough that they should submit to the Church generally, and acknowledge its dogmas, but that they must get up all that divines have said or the multitude believed upon religious matters, you simply crush and stamp out the flame within them, and they can do nothing at all.

This is the case of men of genius: now one word on the contrary in behalf of master minds, gifted with a broad philosophical view of things, and a creative power, and a versatility capable of accommodating itself to various provinces of thought. These persons perhaps, like those I have already spoken of, take up some idea and are intent upon it; – some deep, prolific, eventful idea, which grows upon them, till they develop it into a great system. Now, if any such thinker starts from radically unsound principles, or aims at directly false conclusions, if he be a Hobbes, or a Shaftesbury, or a Hume, or a Bentham, then, of course, there is an end of the whole matter. He is an opponent of Revealed Truth, and he means to be so; – nothing more need be said. But perhaps it is not so; perhaps his errors are those which are inseparable accidents of his system or of his mind, and are spontaneously evolved, not pertinaciously defended. Every human system, every human writer, is open to just criticism. Make him shut up his portfolio; good! and then perhaps you lose what, on the whole and in spite of incidental mistakes, would have been one of the ablest defences of Revealed Truth (directly or indirectly, according to his subject) ever given to the world.

This is how I should account for a circumstance, which has sometimes caused surprise, that so many great Catholic thinkers have in some points or other incurred the criticism or animadversion of theologians or of ecclesiastical authority. It must be so in the nature of things; there is indeed an animadversion which implies a condemnation of the author; but there is another which means not much more than the "piè legendum" written against passages in the Fathers. The author may not be to blame; yet the ecclesiastical authority would be to blame, if it did not give notice of his imperfections. I do not know what Catholic would not hold the name of Malebranche in veneration;[73] but he may have accidentally come into collision with theologians, or made temerarious assertions, notwithstanding. The practical question is, whether he had not much better have written as he has written, than not have written at all. And so fully is the Holy See accustomed to enter into this view of the matter, that it has allowed of its application, not only to philosophical, but even to theological and ecclesiastical authors, who do not come within the range of these remarks. I believe I am right in saying that, in the case of three great names, in various departments of learning, Cardinal Noris, Bossuet, and Muratori, while not concealing its sense of their having propounded each what might have been said better, nevertheless it has considered, that their services to Religion were on the whole far too important to allow of their being molested by critical observation in detail.

8.

And now, Gentlemen, I bring these remarks to a conclusion. What I would urge upon every one, whatever may be his particular line of research, – what I would urge upon men of Science in their thoughts of Theology, – what I would venture to recommend to theologians, when their attention is drawn to the subject of scientific investigations, – is a great and firm belief in the sovereignty of Truth. Error may flourish for a time, but Truth will prevail in the end. The only effect of error ultimately is to promote Truth. Theories, speculations, hypotheses, are started; perhaps they are to die, still not before they have suggested ideas better than themselves. These better ideas are taken up in turn by other men, and, if they do not yet lead to truth, nevertheless they lead to what is still nearer to truth than themselves; and thus knowledge on the whole makes progress. The errors of some minds in scientific investigation are more fruitful than the truths of others. A Science seems making no progress, but to abound in failures, yet imperceptibly all the time it is advancing, and it is of course a gain to truth even to have learned what is not true, if nothing more.

On the other hand, it must be of course remembered, Gentlemen, that I am supposing all along good faith, honest intentions, a loyal Catholic spirit, and a deep sense of responsibility. I am supposing, in the scientific inquirer, a due fear of giving scandal, of seeming to countenance views which he does not really countenance, and of siding with parties from whom he heartily differs. I am supposing that he is fully alive to the existence and the power of the infidelity of the age; that he keeps in mind the moral weakness and the intellectual confusion of the majority of men; and that he has no wish at all that any one soul should get harm from certain speculations to-day, though he may have the satisfaction of being sure that those speculations will, as far as they are erroneous or misunderstood, be corrected in the course of the next half-century.

Notes

Newman's footnoting was both incomplete and unsystematic. These notes reprint some of his, supplement others, and add materials for which he did not provide references. Brackets [ ] indicate direct quotes from Newman's own notes. Other notes cite works for which Newman usually provided rather vague references. Newman either translated classical quotations or quoted from the Greek and Latin. These notes refer to standard translations, which may not be the same as Newman's, but which are used for his untranslated quotes. Biblical references are from the Catholic Bible. The editor has omitted one footnote and subsequent long Latin citation from the work of Ludovico Muratori, which Newman included in "Christianity and Physical Science."

The editor wishes to acknowledge his indebtedness to the critical edition of *The Idea of a University,* edited by Ian Ker and published by Clarendon Press (1976), and to the notes of Martin J. Svaglic, in the University of Notre Dame Press edition of *The Idea of a University* (1982), in composing these notes.

1. Victor Aimé Huber, *The English Universities* (London: W. Pickering, 1843), II, Pt. 1, pp. 331 ff.

2 "For I judged not myself to know anything among you, but Jesus Christ; and him crucified." I Cor. 2:2.

3. Hyacinthe Sigismonde Gerdil, *Opere* (Rome, 1806–21), 3: 353. "One does not find true opposition between the spirit of Academies and that of Universities; there are only differing views. Universities are established to *teach* sciences *to students* who wish to form themselves; the Academies propose to carry out *new research* in the development of the sciences. The Italian Universities provided men who have honored the Academies; and these have given to the Universities Professors who have filled their chairs with the greatest distinction." Literary academies dated from the sixteenth century, and scientific societies from the seventeenth. Both were organized bodies of learned persons some of whom devoted themselves to research, but none of whom taught students as a part of the life of the academies.

4. "To have thoroughly studied the liberal arts softens the manners."

Ovid, *Pontex Epistles,* II, ix, 47–48, in *The Fasti, Tristia, Pontex Epistles, Ibis, and Halieuticon of Ovid,* tr. Henry T. Ritz (London: George Bell, 1890), p. 414.

5. A portion of a line, the full translation of which is
"Grammarian, painter, augur, rhetorician
Geometer, quack, conjurer, and musician,
All arts his own the hungry Greekling counts."
Juvenal, *Satires,* iii, 76–77, in *D. Junius Juvenalis Satirae,* tr. P. Austen Nuttal, new ed. (London: Nichols, 1836), p. 41.

6. "Cords have fallen to me in goodly places; for mine inheritance is goodly unto me." Ps. 16:6.

7. "Every man is to be trusted in his own art, in the business or profession that he follows." See *Ancient and Modern Familiar Quotations* (Philadelphia: Lippincott, 1881), p. 100.

8. J. A. Lalanne, *Influence des Pères de l'Église sur l'éducation publique pendant les cinques premiers siècles de l'ère chrétienne* (Paris, 1850), pp. 52–56.

9. Hugh Paulinus or Serenus Cressy, *The Church History of Brittany from the Beginning of Christianity to the Norman Conquest* (Rouen, 1668), p. 451.

10. [In Roman law it means a Corporation.] Georg Gottfried Keuffel, *Historia Originis ac Progressus Scholarum inter Christianos* (Helmstedt, 1743), p. 319.

11. Johann Lorenz von Mosheim, *Institutes of Ecclesiastical History, Ancient and Modern,* tr. J. Murdock and ed. H. Soames, 4 vols. (London, 1841), 2: 529.

12. Lord Brougham, *Inaugural Discourse on being installed Lord Rector of the University of Glasgow, Wednesday, April 6, 1815* (Glasgow: J. Smith, 1825), pp. 47–48.

13. Mixed Education refers to the practice of educating members of different religious groups in the same institution.

14. David Hume, *An Enquiry Concerning the Human Understanding,* Section X in David Hume, *Enquiries Concerning Human Understanding and Concerning the Principles of Morals,* ed. L. A. Selby-Bigge and P. H. Nidditch, 3d ed. (Oxford: Clarendon Press, 1979), p. 137.

15. Aristotle, *Nichomachean Ethics,* iii, 3, in *The Basic Works of Aristotle,* ed. Richard McKeon (New York: Random House, 1941), p. 969.

16. "Let not the shoemaker go beyond his last." See *Ancient and Modern Familiar Quotations,* p. 287.

17. Newman here distinguishes between *natural theology* understood as

theology based on the use of natural human faculties and *physical theology* understood as theological conclusions based on the empirical examination of nature. At the time Newman wrote, many authors used the two terms interchangeably. Newman did not.

18. Wesleyan was the name frequently applied to the Methodists, after the religion's founder, John Wesley.

19. Francis Bacon, *The Advancement of Learning,* in *Works of Francis Bacon,* ed. J. Spedding, R. L. Ellis, and D. D. Heath (London: Longman, 1858–74), 3: 292–93.

20. Nassau William Senior, *Introductory Lecture on Political Economy, delivered before the University of Oxford, on the 6th of December, 1826* (London: M. Mawman, 1827), pp. 1, 7, 6, 11–12.

21. Bacon, *The Advancement of Learning,* 3: 292.

22. Senior, *Introductory Lecture on Political Economy,* p. 16.

23. [Vid. Abelard, for instance.]

24. [Pursuit of Knowledge under Difficulties, Introd.] George Lillie Craik, *The Pursuit of Knowledge under Difficulties,* a new ed. (London: Charles Knight, 1845), 1: 5.

25. For the various passages Newman is quoting, see Cicero, *On Duties,* ed. M. T. Griffin and E. M. Atkins (Cambridge: Cambridge University Press, 1991), pp. 6–9.

26. Τέχνη τύχην ἔστερξε καὶ τύχη τέχνην.
"Art loves chance and chance loves art."
Aristotle quoting the dramatist Agathon in *Nichomachean Ethics,* vi, 4, ll. 18–19, in *The Basic Works of Aristotle,* p. 1025.

27. Aristotle, *Rhetoric,* i, 5, ll. 15–19, in *The Basic Works of Aristotle,* p. 1341.

28. [It will be seen that on the whole I agree with Lord Macaulay in his Essay on Bacon's Philosophy. I do not know whether he would agree with me.]

29. [De Augment. iv. 2, vid. Macaulay's Essay; vid. also "In principio operis ad Deum Patrem, Deum Verbum, Deum Spiritum, preces fundimus humillimas et ardentissimas, ut humani generis ærumnarum memores, et peregrinationis istius vitæ, in quâ dies paucos et malos terimus, *novis suis eleemosynis, per manus nostras,* familiam humanam dotare dignentur. Atque illud insuper supplices rogamus, ne *humana divinis officiant;* neve *ex reseratione viarum sensûs,* et accensione majore luminis naturalis, *aliquid incredulitatis* et noctis, animis nostris erga divina mysteria oboriatur," etc. *Præf.* Instaur. Magn.] "Wherefore, seeing that these things do not depend upon myself, at the outset of

the work I most humbly and fervently pray to God the Father, God the Son, and God the Holy Ghost, that remembering the sorrows of mankind and the pilgrimage of this our life wherein we wear out days few and evil, they will vouchsafe through my hands to endow the human family with new mercies. This likewise I humbly pray, that things human may not interfere with things divine, and that from the opening of the ways of sense and the increase of natural light there may arise in our minds no incredulity or darkness with regard to the divine mysteries." Francis Bacon, Preface to *The Great Instauration,* in *Works of Francis Bacon,* 4: 20.

30. [Fouqué's Unknown Patient.] A story by Friedrich Heirrich Karl de la Motte Fouqué (1777–1843) published in *Romantic Fiction: Select Tales from the German of De la Motte Fouqué and Others* (London, 1843).

31. [The pages which follow are taken almost *verbatim* from the author's 14th (Oxford) University Sermon, which, at the time of writing this Discourse, he did not expect ever to reprint.] John Henry Newman, *Fifteen Sermons Preached before The University of Oxford between A.D. 1826 and 1843,* new ed. (London: Rivingtons, 1880), pp. 278ff.

32. "Happy, who had the skill to understand
Nature's hid causes, and beneath his feet
All terrors cast, and earth's relentless doom,
And the loud roar of greedy Acheron."
Virgil, *Georgics,* ii, 490–93, in *The Poems of Virgil,* tr. James Rhoades (Chicago: Encyclopaedia Brittanica, 1952), p. 65.

33. Beginning of the line, which when fully translated is, "Money stored up is for each his lord or his slave." Horace, *Epistles,* I, 10, 47, in *Horace: Satires, Epistles and Ars Poeticae,* tr. H. Rushton Fairclough (Cambridge: Harvard University Press, 1970), p. 319.

34. "Strength, joined with folly, falls by its own weight." Horace, *Odes,* III, iv, 65, in *The Odes of Horace,* tr. Edward Marsh (London: Macmillan, 1941), p. 104.

35. Shakespeare, *As You Like It,* I, 2, l. 12.

36. [Crabbe's Tales of the Hall. This Poem, let me say, I read on its first publication, above thirty years ago, with extreme delight, and have never lost my love of it; and on taking it up lately, found I was even more touched by it than heretofore. A work which can please in youth and age, seems to fulfil (in logical language) the *accidental definition* of a Classic. (A further course of twenty years has past, and I bear the same witness in favour of this Poem.)]

37. This famous critique of Oxford University appeared in articles, in the *Edinburgh Review,* by John Playfair, 11 (1808): 249–84; Richard Payne Knight, 14 (1809): 429–41; Sydney Smith, 15 (1809): 40–53; and Knight, Playfair, and Smith, 16 (1810): 158–87. See the essay by Martha Garland in this volume for a discussion of this dispute.

38. [Mr. Keble, Vicar of Hursley, late Fellow of Oriel, and Professor of Poetry in the University of Oxford.]

39. John Locke, "Some Thoughts Concerning Education," in *The Works of John Locke, the twelfth edition* (London: C. and J. Rivington, 1824), 8: 86–87, 167, 152–53.

40. Sydney Smith, *Edinburgh Review,* 15 (1809): 51–52, 48–49.

41. Edward Copleston, *Reply to the Calumnies of the Edinburgh Review against Oxford* (Oxford: Printed for the author, 1810), pp. 107–12. Newman edited these quotations, omitting some material.

42. John Milton, "On Education," in John Milton, *Complete Poems and Major Prose,* ed. Merritt Y. Hughes (New York: Odyssey Press, 1957), p. 632.

43. John Davison, *The Quarterly Review,* 6 (1811): 173–76.

44. William Cowper, *The Task,* II, p. 206.

45. [I do not consider I have said above any thing inconsistent with the following passage from Cardinal Gerdil, though I have enlarged on the favourable side of Julian's character. "Du génie, des connaissances, de l'habilité dans le métier de la guerre, du courage et du désintéressement dans le commandement des armées, des actions plutôt que des qualités estimables, mais le plus souvent gâtées par la vanité qui en était le principe, la superstition jointe à l'hypocrisie; un esprit fécond en ressources éclairé, mais susceptible de petitesse; des fautes essentielles dans le gouvernement; des innocens sacrifiés à la vengeance; une haine envenimée contre le Christianisme, qu'il avait abandonné; un attachement passionné aux folies de la Théurgie; tels étaient les traits sous lesquels on nous preignait Julien." *Opere,* 10: 54.] "I do not consider I have said above any thing inconsistent with the following passage from Cardinal Gerdil, though I have enlarged on the favourable side of Julian's character. 'Of genius, of knowledge, of the capacity for warfare, of courage and disinterestedness in the command of armies, of estimable actions rather than qualities, but the more often tainted by vanity which was its principle, superstition joined to hypocrisy; a spirit rich in enlightened resources, but susceptible to pettiness; of essential faults in government, innocents sacrificed to vengeance; a venomous hatred against Christianity, which it had abandoned; a passionate at-

tachment to Theurgy, such were the traits under which one paints Julien
for us.' "

46. Edward Gibbon, *The Decline and Fall of the Roman Empire* (New
    York: Modern Library, n.d.), 1: 828–29.

47. Newman in the following section quotes extensively from Lord
    Shaftesbury, *Characteristics of Men, Manners, Opinions, Times* (1711),
    in *Works of Lord Shaftesbury* (London: J. Darby, 1732), 1: 97, 2: 55, 1:
    135–36, 138, 142, 336, 338–39, 3: 177, 1: 128, 151, 173–75.

48. "Stick to your own judgment." Persius, *Satires,* I, 7, in *The Satires of
    Persius,* tr. W. S. Merwin (Bloomington: Indiana University Press,
    1961), p. 5.

49. Edmund Burke, *Reflections on the Revolution in France,* in *The Works
    of the Right Honourable Edmund Burke* (London: Bell and Daldy,
    1864), 2: 348.

50. Shakespeare, *Hamlet,* III, iv, ll. 147–49.

51. *Works of Lord Shaftesbury,* 1: 15–16, 19.

52. Bacon, *The Advancement of Learning,* 4: 363.

53. Francis Bacon, "Translation of the 'De Augmentis,' " in *Works of
    Francis Bacon,* 3: 478.

54. "Whatever wild desires have swell'd the breast,
    Whatever passions have the soul possest,
    Joy, Sorrow, Fear, Love, Hatred, Transport, Rage."
    Juvenal, *Satires,* i, 85–86, in *D. Junius Juvenalis Satirae, p. 11.

55. John Henry Newman, *Parochial and Plain Sermons,* new ed. (London:
    Longmans, Green, 1894), 1: 325 ff.

56. P. G. Bacci, *The Life of St. Philip Neri,* tr. F. W. Faber (London, 1847),
    1: 192, 2: 98.

57. Victor Aimé Huber, *The English Universities* (London: W. Pickering,
    1843), 1: 34.

58. Freely translated from *Greek Anthology,* bk. 16, epigram 297, 298
    (London: Heinemann, 1926), 5.

59. "Now stands my tower four-square, outlasting bronze." Horace, *Odes,*
    III, xxx, 1, in *The Odes of Horace,* tr. Marsh, p. 147.

60. The works referred to are Charles Daniel, *Des Études classiques dans
    la société chrétienne* (Paris, 1853), and Jean François Anne Thomas
    Landriot, *Recherches historiques sur les écoles littéraires du Chris-
    tianisme* (Brussels, 1852).

61. T. B. Macaulay, "Gladstone on Church and State," in *Miscellaneous
    Works of Lord Macaulay, Edited by His Sister Lady Trevelyan* (New
    York: Harper and Brothers, n.d.), 2: 566–67.

62. "Scarce suffering him compose his agèd limbs,
    With a great cry leapt on him, and ere he rose
    Forestalled him with the fetters."
    Virgil, *Georgics,* iv, 438–40, in *The Poems of Virgil,* p. 65.

63. Henry Hallam, *Introduction to the Literature of Europe in the Fifteenth, Sixteenth, and Seventeenth Centuries,* 3d ed. (London: John Murray, 1847), 1: 443.

64. "Strange leaves . . . and fruitage not its own." Virgil, *Georgics,* ii, 82, in *The Poems of Virgil,* p. 54.

65. John Milton, *Samson Agonistes,* ll. 293–306.

66. Robert Southey, *Thalaba,* ll. 1–10.

67. [Misc. Works, p. 55.] *The Miscellaneous Works of Edward Gibbon, Esq., with Memoirs of his Life and Writings, composed by himself: Illustrated from his Letters, with Occasional Notes and Narrative, by John, Lord Sheffield* (London: B. Blake, 1837), p. 55.

68. Newman has translated a passage from P. C. Roux-Lavergne, E. D'Yzalguier, and E. Germer-Durand, eds., *De Veritate Catholicae Fidei contra Gentiles seu Summa Philosophica* (Nemausi, 1853), 1: vii.

69. Macaulay, "Ranke's History of the Popes," in *Miscellaneous Works of Lord Macaulay,* 2: 616–21.

70. [I use the word, not in the sense of "Naturalis Theologia," but in the sense in which Paley uses it in the work which he has so entitled.]

71. "Remember Roman, thou, / To rule the nations as their master." Virgil, *Aeneid,* vi, 851, in *The Poems of Virgil,* p. 234.

72. William Cowper, "Light Shining Out of Darkness," ll. 10–12.

73. [Cardinal Gerdil speaks of his "Metaphysique," as "brillante à la verité, mais non moins solide" (p. 9.), and that "la liaison qui enchaine toutes les parties du système philosophique du Père Malebranche, . . . pourra servir d'apologie à la noble assurance, avec laquelle il propose ses sentiments." (*Opere,* 4: 12.)] "Cardinal Gerdil speaks of his 'Metaphysique,' as 'brilliant in truth, but no less solid,' and that 'the connection which holds together all the elements of the philosophical system of Father Malebranche, . . . provides a noble assurance of the justification with which he puts forward his views.' "

Glossary of Names

The purpose of this glossary is simply to identify very briefly the enormous number of religious and secular figures whom Newman cites or mentions in the course of *The Idea of a University*. Many of these names were commonplace at the time, but have since become less well known. Others were no doubt as unfamiliar to many of Newman's Victorian readers as they are to readers today. Names of saints are listed separately.

The editor gratefully acknowledges his indebtedness to the scholarship of Ian Ker and the extensive notes that Ker provided in his critically annotated edition of *The Idea of a University* (Oxford: Clarendon Press, 1976). This glossary would have been impossible without Ker's edition, as well as other standard works of reference.

Abelard, Peter (1079–1142): medieval theologian noted for his logic.

Addison, Joseph (1672–1719): English poet and Whig essayist.

Adrian (seventh century): early Christian missionary to England.

Aeschylus (fifth century B.C.E.): Greek tragedian.

Alcuin (ca. 735–804): Carolingian scholar who founded a palace school for Charlemagne.

Alexander the Great (356–323 B.C.E): king of Macedonia, pupil of Aristotle, and conqueror of much of the Ancient World from Greece to India.

Alfred the Great (849–899): Saxon king.

Anastasius Sinaita (d. ca. 700): abbot of monastery on Mt. Sinai who opposed Monophysite heresy.

Anaxagoras of Ionia (fifth century B.C.E.): Greek natural philosopher.

Animuccia, Giovanni (ca. 1500–1571): choirmaster at St. Peter's and later at St. Philip Neri's oratory.

Antoninus Pius (86–161): Roman emperor, 138–161.

Apollinaris (ca. 310–390): Christian author of biblical commentaries whose ideas came to be regarded as heretical.

Aquila of Pontus (second century): author of literal translation of the Hebrew Bible into Greek.

Arcesilas (316–241 B.C.E.): once head of the ancient Academy founded by Plato.

Ariosto, Ludovico (1474–1533): Italian epic poet best known for *Orlando Furioso.*

Aristotle (fourth century, B.C.E.): Greek philosopher, pupil of Plato, teacher of Alexander the Great, exerted enormous influence over Western philosophy after the twelfth century C.E.

Arouet, François Marie (1694–1778): French poet, historian, playwright, and philosopher strongly critical of Christianity; wrote under the name Voltaire.

Bacon, Francis (1561–1626): British statesman, essayist, and philosopher who argued in favor of inductive philosophy and the pursuit of useful knowledge.

Bacon, Roger (ca. 1214–1292): medieval Oxford natural philosopher associated with early scientific experimentalism.

Balaam: prophet in the Book of Numbers in the Hebrew Bible.

Baronius, Cesare (1538–1607): ecclesiastical historian and Librarian of the Vatican.

Baxter, Richard (1615–1691): Puritan theologian active both before and after the English Civil War.

Beethoven, Ludwig van (1770–1827): the major figure of early-nineteenth-century music.

Benedict XIV (1675–1758): scholar who became pope in 1740.

Bennett: see St. Benedict Biscop.

Bentham, Jeremy (1748–1832): English legal reformer regarded as the founder of English utilitarianism, which emphasized the principle of the greatest happiness for the greatest number.

Bentley, Richard (1662–1742): influential and controversial classical scholar.

Berkeley, George (1685–1753): bishop of the Church of Ireland and major empiricist philosopher.

Beseleel: biblical personality cited in Exodus 31:1–7.

Beveridge, William (1637–1708): Anglican scholar of the church fathers.

Boccaccio, Giovanni (1313–1375): Italian poet known for the *Decameron.*

Bonaparte, Napoleon (1769–1821): French revolutionary war general who became emperor of France and conquered much of Europe; he was defeated in 1815.

Boniface VIII (ca. 1234–1303): became pope in 1294; noted for defending papacy against state authorities.

Borromeo, Federigo (1564–1631): founder of the Ambrosian Library in Milan.

Bossuet, Jacques (1627–1704): French Roman Catholic theologian, preacher, and bishop.

Boswell, James (1740–1795): Scottish author most famous for his *Life of Samuel Johnson.*

Brougham, Henry, Lord (1778–1868): Scottish statesman closely associated with the Society for the Diffusion of Useful Knowledge.

Brutus, Marcus Junius (first century B.C.E.): assassin of Julius Caesar and major participant in subsequent Roman civil wars.

Buffon, Georges Louis (1707–1788): French naturalist.

Bull, George (1634–1710): English bishop and theologian.

Bunyan, John (1628–1688): Puritan author of *Pilgrim's Progress.*

Burke, Edmund (1729–1797): Irish-born British statesman and author of *Reflections on the Revolution in France.*

Burman, Pieter (1668–1741): Dutch classical scholar.

Burnet, Gilbert (1643–1715): Church of England bishop who wrote broadly on political and ecclesiastical matters; he supported the settlement following the Revolution of 1688.

Burnet, Thomas (d. 1750): Church of England theologian.

Burns, Robert (1759–1796): Scottish poet.

Butler, Joseph (1692–1752): eighteenth-century English bishop, theologian, and philosopher of ethics.

Byron, George Gordon, Lord (1788–1824): English Romantic poet.

Caesar, Julius (100–44 B.C.E.): Roman general and statesman whose activities brought an end to the Roman Republic and opened the way for the Roman Empire.

Caius (third century): Christian author.

Campbell, Thomas (1777–1844): Scottish poet.

Carneades (214–129 B.C.E.): Greek philosopher whose writings influenced Cicero.

Cato (the Elder), Marcus Porcius (234–149 B.C.E.): advocate of austere Roman life; opposed introduction of Greek philosophy and foreign luxury into Rome.

Cato (the Younger), Marcus Porcius (95–46 B.C.E.): major political
opponent of Julius Caesar; he was known for austere personal political
morality.

Catullus (first century B.C.E.): Roman poet.

Cervantes, Miguel del (1547–1616): Spanish author of *Don Quixote*.

Charlemagne (742–814): Frankish monarch and crowned first of the Holy
Roman emperors in 800.

Charles II (1630–1685): restored as English monarch in 1660 following
the civil wars.

Churchill, John, first duke of Marlborough (1650–1722): leading English
general in the wars against the France of Louis XIV.

Cicero, Marcus Tullius (106–43 B.C.E.): Roman orator, statesman, and
philosopher.

Clarendon, earl of: see Hyde, Edward.

Clarke, Samuel (1675–1729): author of works of English natural theology
based on Newtonian physics.

Cooper, Anthony Ashley, third earl of Shaftesbury (1671–1713):
influential early-eighteenth-century moral philosopher.

Copleston, Edward (1776–1849): provost of Oriel College, Oxford, who
defended Oxford against its early-nineteenth-century *Edinburgh
Review* critics and later became a bishop in the Church of England.

Cowper, William (1731–1800): English religious poet.

Crabbe, George (1754–1832): English poet.

Craik, George Lillie (1798–1866): a writer associated with the Society for
the Diffusion of Useful Knowledge.

Cudworth, Ralph (1617–1688): philosopher associated with Cambridge
Platonism.

Cuvier, Georges Léopold (1769–1832): French naturalist associated with
the founding of comparative anatomy.

Dante (1265–1321): major medieval Italian poet and author of *The Divine
Comedy*.

Darwin, Erasmus (1731–1802): English poet whose works were
suggestive of evolution; grandfather of Charles Darwin.

David: king of Israel in the Hebrew Bible.

Davison, John (1777–1834): fellow of Oriel College, Oxford, and
religious writer; he defended Oxford against its *Edinburgh Review*
critics.

Davy, Humphrey (1778–1829): English chemist.

Defoe, Daniel (1660–1731): author of *Robinson Crusoe*.

Demosthenes (fourth century B.C.E.): Athenian orator.

Descartes, René (1596–1650): French philosopher of rationalism and originator of analytic geometry.

Dio Cocceianus (ca. 40–112): Greek orator.

Dryden, John (1631–1700): Roman Catholic English poet.

Duns Scotus, John (ca. 1264–1308): medieval philosopher.

Du Pin, Louis Ellies (1657–1719): French Roman Catholic theologian.

Edgeworth, Richard Lovell (1744–1817): inventor; father of novelist Maria Edgeworth.

Edward II (1284–1327): English king.

Elias: another name for the prophet Elijah in the Hebrew Bible.

Elmsley, Peter (1773–1825): Oxford classical scholar.

Ennius, Quintus (239–169 B.C.E.): influential early Latin epic poet.

Euclid (fourth century B.C.E.): founder of geometry.

Eusebius (ca. 260–340): Church historian, for a time associated with the Arian heresy.

Fabricius, Gaius: see Luscinus, Gaius Fabricius.

Fell, John (1625–1686): Anglican scholar of the church fathers.

Fénelon, François (1651–1715): French Roman Catholic bishop.

Fielding, Henry (1707–1754): English novelist.

Francis, Lord Jeffrey (1773–1850): Scottish judge writing for the *Edinburgh Review.*

Franklin, Benjamin (1706–1790): American founder noted for his association with Enlightenment science and commonsense philosophy of life.

Galilei, Galileo (1564–1642): major figure of the Scientific Revolution; he was forced by Roman Catholic authorities to recant his scientific views.

Gerdil, Hyacinthe Sigismonde (1718–1802): Vatican writer on education.

Giannone, Pietro (1676–1748): anticlerical Italian historian.

Gibbon, Edward (1737–1794): author of *The Decline and Fall of the Roman Empire,* which was notably hostile to early Christianity.

Gilbert, William (1540–1603): major figure of the Scientific Revolution; he worked with electricity and magnetism.

Gilbertus: see Gilbert, William.

Goethe, Johann Wolfgang von (1749–1832): foremost German poet and dramatist of his day.

Goldsmith, Oliver (1728–1774): English poet and historian.

Gray, Thomas (1716–1771): English poet, author of "Elegy Written in a Country Churchyard."

Gregory VII (ca. 1020–1085): became pope in 1073 and made the most extensive claims to authority of any medieval pontiff.

Hardouin, Jean (1646–1729): French Jesuit noted for eccentric views of biblical composition.

Heber, Reginald (1783–1826): English bishop of Calcutta and hymn writer.

Herbert of Cherbury, Lord (1583–1648): English philosopher whose thought foreshadowed deism.

Herodotus (fifth century B.C.E.): ancient Greek historian of the Persian Wars.

Hesiod (eighth century B.C.E.): ancient Greek poet.

Hobbes, Thomas (1588–1679): English political philosopher and author of *Leviathan.*

Homer: ancient Greek poet of the *Iliad* and the *Odyssey.*

Hooker, Richard (1554–1600): major Anglican writer and author of *Treatise on the Laws of Ecclesiastical Polity.*

Horace: (first century B.C.E.): Roman poet.

Humboldt, F. H. Alexander, Baron von (1769–1859): Prussian scientist known for his explorations and geographical writings.

Hume, David (1711–1776): major Scottish philosopher and historian.

Huss, John (ca. 1373–1415): Czech church leader influenced by Wycliffe, later condemned for his views and burned at the stake.

Hyde, Edward, earl of Clarendon (1609–1674): royalist leader in and historian of the English Civil War.

Isaac: in the Hebrew Bible, son of Abraham.

Jabal: in the Hebrew Bible, a descendant of Cain.

Jacob: in the Hebrew Bible, one of the sons of Isaac.

Jansen, Cornelius (1585–1638): Dutch Roman Catholic theologian whose strict views of predestination and other topics received papal condemnation after his death; followers known as Jansenists.

John the Deacon (d. ca. 882): medieval scholar.

John XXII (1249–1334): became pope in 1316; defended papacy against state authorities.

John of Salisbury (ca. 1115–1180): scholar of Latin learning and bishop of Chartres.

Johnson, Samuel (1709–1784): renowned English essayist; author of dictionary of the English language.

Joseph II (1741–1790): Hapsburg emperor whose religious policies attempted to impose state direction on much of the life of the Roman Catholic Church in his domains.

Julian (331–363): became Roman emperor in 361 and attempted to return the empire to paganism, hence known as Julian the Apostate.

Justinian (483–565): emperor of the Byzantine Empire; associated with legal code receiving his name.

Juvenal, D. Junius (d. ca. 140): Roman satirist.

Keble, John (1792–1866): English clergyman and poet who was a leader of the Oxford Movement.

Knight, Richard Payne (1750–1824): English classicist who criticized Oxford University in the *Edinburgh Review.*

Laberius (second century B.C.E.): ancient sage.

La Fontaine, Jean de (1621–1695): French author of fables.

Laplace, Pierre Simon de (1749–1827): French scientist known for his nebular hypothesis, which suggested that the universe arose from material accident rather than from divine design.

Lavoisier, Antoine Laurent (1743–1794): French chemist noted for discovery of oxygen.

Law, William (1686–1761): writer of English devotional works.

Lawrence, William (1783–1867): professor of anatomy in the College of Surgeons; in the second decade of the nineteenth century his research led to his being accused of materialism.

Livy, Titus (first century B.C.E.): Roman historian.

Locke, John (1632–1704): major English philosopher of empirical psychology, liberal politics, and religious toleration.

Luscinus, Gaius Fabricius (third century B.C.E.): Roman general known for his absolute patriotism and integrity.

Luther, Martin (1483–1546): progenitor of the German Protestant Reformation.

Lycurgus: legendary reformer and lawgiver in ancient Sparta.

Macaulay, Thomas Babington (1800–1859): English essayist and historian.

Machiavelli, Niccolò (1469–1527): Florentine statesman, political philosopher, and author of *The Prince.*

Mailduf (seventh century): monk who founded school at Malmesbury.

Malebranche, Nicolas de (1638–1715): French philosopher.

Maltby, Edward (1770–1859): bishop of Durham, who offered prayer at the founding of University College, London, and an opponent of Newman while the latter was a member of the Church of England.

Malthus, Thomas (1766–1834): English clergyman and economist whose principle of population argued that the number of human beings increases more rapidly than the food supply.

Marcus Aurelius (121–180): Roman emperor and Stoic philosopher.

Marlborough, duke of: see Churchill, John.

Menander (fourth century B.C.E.): Greek dramatist.

Michelangelo (1475–1564): major Italian painter, sculptor, and architect.

Milman, Henry Hart (1791–1868): liberal English clergyman, wrote histories of the Jews and of early Christianity.

Milton, John (1608–1674): Puritan author of *Paradise Lost* and *Samson Agonistes*.

Montaigne, Michel de (1533–1592): skeptical French essayist.

More, Sir Thomas (1478–1535): lord chancellor of England; later executed for his opposition to the English Reformation; canonized in the twentieth century.

Moses: lawgiver in the Hebrew Bible.

Mosheim, Johann Lorenz von (1694–1755): German ecclesiastical historian.

Muratori, Ludovico (1672–1750): Italian scholar who pursued historical criticism.

Nero (37–68): Roman emperor infamous for his tyranny and persecution of Christians.

Newton, Isaac (1642–1727): foremost figure of the Scientific Revolution and formulator of the theory of universal gravitation.

Niebuhr, Barthold Georg (1776–1831): German historian of Rome who cast doubt on the historical validity of early Roman myths and legends.

Nimrod: in the Hebrew Bible, founder of kingdom of Babel.

Noris, Henry (1631–1704): authority on Augustine whose work was condemned by Spanish Inquisition, but then later approved in 1748 by Pope Benedict XIV.

Occam, William of (ca. 1300–ca. 1349): medieval philosopher of nominalism.

Origen (ca. 185–ca. 254): Christian writer in Alexandria; later accused of heterodox views.

Orpheus: musician in Greek myth.

Ovid (first century): Roman poet.

Palestrina, Giovanni Pierluigi da (ca. 1525–1594): major composer of music according to the decrees of the Council of Trent.

Paley, William (1743–1805): widely read author of natural theology and arguments for the proofs of miracles.

Palladio, Andrea (1518–1580): influential Italian architect.

Parr, Samuel (1747–1825): supporter of Copleston.

Pascal, Blaise (1623–1662): French mathematician and Jansenist.

Pearson, John (1613–1686): Anglican scholar of the church fathers and author of a widely consulted volume on the Creed.

Peel, Sir Robert (1788–1850): as member of Parliament for Oxford supported Catholic Emancipation; later as prime minister led the Conservative Party to accommodate itself to liberal political reform.

Petrarch, Francesco (1304–1374): Italian poet and early admirer of ancient literature.

Pindar (fifth century B.C.E.): Greek poet.

Pisistratus (sixth century B.C.E.): Athenian tyrant.

Pitt the Younger, William (1759–1806): English prime minister.

Pius IV (1499–1565): became pope in 1559 and brought Council of Trent to a conclusion.

Pius IX (1792–1878): became pope in 1846; led a major Roman Catholic resurgence against political and intellectual liberalism.

Plato: (fifth century B.C.E.): Greek philosopher.

Playfair, John (1748–1819): mathematician and geologist critical of Oxford University in the *Edinburgh Review.*

Pliny (the Younger), Gaius (62–113): Roman writer and administrator.

Plutarch (first century): Greek historian who wrote comparative lives of major Greeks and Romans.

Pole, Reginald (1500–1558): English renaissance humanist who defended the Roman Catholic Church during the Reformation.

Polemo of Athens (d. 273 B.C.E.): Greek philosopher converted from life of dissipation to one of temperance.

Pope, Alexander (1688–1744): English Roman Catholic poet and translator of Homer.

Porson, Richard (1759–1808): Cambridge scholar of Greek language and tragedy.

Priestley, Joseph (1733–1804): English chemist and Unitarian theologian.

Ptolemy (second century): Egyptian astronomer.

Pulci, Luigi (1432–1484): Italian Renaissance epic poet.

Pythagoras (sixth century B.C.E.): Greek mathematician and philosopher.

Python: name of the serpent guarding the oracle at Delphi, killed by Apollo; term later applied to the general idea of persons pursuing divination.

Quintilian, Marcus Fabius (first century): Roman author of works on rhetoric.

Rabelais, François (1494–1553): French satirist.

Raffaelle [Raphael] (1483–1520): major Italian painter.

Regulus, Marcus Atilius (d. ca. 250 B.C.E.): Roman general who, after failing to negotiate a settlement between Rome and Carthage, returned to Carthage, where he had been a prisoner, and was executed.

Reid, Thomas (1710–1796): founder of the Scottish philosophy of Common Sense.

Ricci, Flaminio (sixteenth century): follower of St. Philip Neri.

Robertson, William (1721–1793): moderator of the Scottish Kirk and major Enlightenment historian.

Rousseau, Jean-Jacques (1712–1778): author of numerous works radically criticizing the society of his day.

Saladin (1138–1193): Islamic commander who resisted the Crusaders.

Sallust (first century B.C.E.): Roman historian.

Salmasius, Claudius (1588–1653): French classical scholar.

Samuel: prophet in the Hebrew Bible.

Sappho (seventh century B.C.E.): Greek poet.

Savonarola, Girolamo (1452–1498): austere Dominican monk who for a time dominated Florence and was then burned at the stake.

Scipio Africanus, Publius Cornelius (237–183 B.C.E.): Roman general who defeated Hannibal in battle of Zama in 202.

Scott, Walter (1771–1832): enormously popular Scottish historical novelist.

Seneca (first century): Roman dramatist and moral philosopher in the age of Nero.

Senior, Nassau William (1790–1864): first professor of political economy at Oxford.

Shaftesbury, earl of: see Cooper, Anthony Ashley.

Shakespeare, William (1564–1616): foremost dramatist of the English renaissance.

Sibyl: a supposed source of oracles in the Greek world.

Simonides (sixth century B.C.E.): Greek poet.

Smith, Sydney (1771–1845): Scottish clergyman and essayist who criticized Oxford in the *Edinburgh Review*.

Socrates (fifth century B.C.E.): Athenian philosopher whom the city condemned to death.

Solomon: in the Hebrew Bible, the son of King David noted for his wisdom.

Sophocles (fifth century B.C.E.): Greek tragedian.

South, Robert (1634–1716): Church of England clergyman and author of sermons.

Southey, Robert (1774–1843): English poet laureate (1813–1843), also known for his essays and histories.

Statius, Publius (first century B.C.E.): Roman poet.

Swift, Jonathan (1667–1745): Anglo-Irish satirist and author of *Gulliver's Travels*.

Sylvester II (ca. 940–1003): became pope in 999; interested in scientific knowledge.

Symmachus (second century): Christian writer who emphasized law of the
   Hebrew Bible and de-emphasized the divinity of Jesus of Nazareth.

Tacitus (first century): Roman historian.

Tarpeia: daughter of Roman governor who betrayed the city to the
   Sabines; they then killed her.

Taylor, Jeremy (1613–1667): Anglican devotional writer.

Terence (second century B.C.E.): Roman dramatist.

Tertullian (d. ca. 230): church father.

Thales (d. 546 B.C.E.): Greek mathematician and philosopher.

Theocritus (third century B.C.E.): Greek poet.

Theodore (ca. 350–428): Christian bishop associated with the Arian and
   Nestorian heresies.

Theodotion (second century): produced a Greek version of the Hebrew
   Bible.

Thomson, James (1700–1748): Scottish poet.

Thucydides (fifth century B.C.E.): Greek historian of the Peloponnesian
   War.

Ticonius (d. ca. 400): a spokesman for the Donatist heresy, according to
   which the validity of sacraments is dependent upon the quality of life
   and belief of the administering priest.

Tillotson, John (1630–1694): archbishop of Canterbury noted for rational
   theology.

Titus (first century): Roman emperor who conquered Jerusalem.

Tooke, John Horne (1736–1812): English philologist associated with
   radical politics.

Tubalcain: in the Hebrew Bible, a descendant of Cain.

Ussher, James (1581–1656): Anglican scholar of the church fathers and
   author of famous biblical chronology.

Virgil (first century): Roman poet and author of *The Aeneid.*

Voltaire: see Arouet, François Marie.

Watson, Richard (1737–1816): Cambridge regius professor of divinity.

Wellington, Arthur Wellesley, duke of (1769–1852): British statesman and
   victor over Napoleon.

Wesley, John (1703–1791): founder of the Methodist movement, which
   originated in the Church of England and later became a separate
   denomination.

Wiclif, John (ca. 1320–1384): early critic of medieval Church abuses;
   usually regarded as a forerunner of the Protestant Reformation.

Wren, Sir Christopher (1632–1723): English architect of St. Paul's
   Cathedral in London.

Xenophon (fourth century B.C.E.): Greek historian and general.

Zazzara, Francesco (sixteenth century): follower of St. Philip Neri.

SAINTS

St. Aidan (d. 651): missionary monk to the isle of Iona in the Hebrides.

St. Aldhelm (d. 709): abbot of the monastery at Malmesbury.

St. Ambrose (304?–394): bishop of Milan and teacher of St. Augustine.

St. Athanasius (293–373): foremost opponent of the Arian heresy.

St. Augustine (354–430): bishop of Hippo, church father, author of *Confessions* and *City of God*.

St. Augustine of Canterbury (d. ca. 604): missionary to England.

St. Basil the Great (ca. 330–379): defender of orthodoxy at the time of the Arian controversy.

St. Bede (ca. 673–735): monk who is regarded as the first English historian.

St. Robert Bellarmine (1542–1621): major apologist of the Catholic Reformation.

St. Benedict Biscop (ca. 628–690): English Benedictine abbot of Canterbury.

St. Boniface (680–754): English missionary to Germany.

St. Cajetan (1480–1547): founder of congregation of priests whose primary purpose was pastoral care.

St. Charles Borromeo (1538–1584): archbishop of Milan and spokesman for the Catholic Reformation.

St. Cuthbert (d. 687): missionary and bishop of Hexham.

St. Cyprian (d. 258): martyred bishop of Carthage.

St. Dionysius the Areopagite: mentioned in Acts 17:34 as having been converted by St. Paul.

St. Egbert of Northumbria (d. 729): missionary monk to Ireland.

St. Francis de Sales (1567–1622): major figure in the Catholic Reformation.

St. Francis Xavier (1506–1552): Jesuit missionary to Far East.

St. Gregory (540–604): became pope in 590; sent missionaries to Britain.

St. Gregory of Nazianzus (fourth century): opponent of Arianism.

St. Gregory of Nyssa (fourth century): brother of St. Basil and opponent of Arianism.

St. Ignatius Loyola (1491–1556): founder of the Society of Jesus, the Jesuits.

St. Jerome (ca. 342–420): Christian scholar and translator of the Vulgate version of the Bible.

St. John Chrysostom (ca. 347–407): bishop of Constantinople.

St. John of Beverley (d. 721): scholarly bishop of York.

St. Leo (390?–461): major early pope and defender of Catholic unity.

St. Mary the Virgin: term applied by Newman and others in the mid-nineteenth century to the mother of Jesus.

St. Patrick (ca. 389–ca. 461): most famous of missionaries to Ireland.

St. Paul (first century): Jewish persecutor of Christians; converted to Christianity and later wrote numerous epistles of the New Testament.

St. Philip Neri (1515–1595): founder of the Congregation of the Oratory in Rome, a branch of which Newman founded in Birmingham, England.

St. Sturmius (d. 779): missionary to Germany.

St. Theodore of Tarsus (ca. 602–690): archbishop of Canterbury who unified the English church.

St. Thomas Aquinas (1225–1274): medieval philosopher who sought to reconcile the philosophy of Aristotle with Christian thought.

St. Thomas of Canterbury (Thomas Becket) (1118–1170): allowed himself to be appointed archbishop of Canterbury at request of Henry II of England but later clashed with the monarch and was assassinated by the monarch's henchmen.

St. Vincent of Lérins (fifth century): Christian writer who defined the notes or essential features of true Catholic Church doctrine.

St. Virgilius (700–784): Irish monk who became bishop of Salzburg.

St. Wilfrid (634–709): bishop of York and founder of monasteries.

St. Willibrod (658–739): English missionary monk to Ireland.

Rethinking
The Idea of a University

Introduction to

Interpretive Essays

A critical reading of *The Idea of a University* invites the reader to rethink both Newman's rich Victorian text and the situation of universities toward the close of the twentieth century. The issues that Newman raised – the place of religion and moral values in the university setting, the competing claims of liberal and professional education, the character of the academic community, the cultural role of literature, the possibility of different kinds of literature, the relationship of religion and science – continue to be germane, and many are gaining new attention and relevance. Rethinking Newman's major propositions, some of which are explicitly expressed and others implicitly assumed, requires us to rethink our own views of those institutions and of the goals of higher education. Coming to grips with Newman's ideas and arguments demands that we make clear to ourselves our own stated and unstated presuppositions about the life of universities. Whatever our thoughts about education as we enter upon reading *The Idea of a University,* they will be different upon our completing it, if for no other reason than that Newman demands that we defend our own thinking when it contrasts with or goes beyond his.

Newman's mid-nineteenth-century meditations on the university continued a debate over the function of universities that had begun more than forty years earlier. Martha Garland explores the character and organization of the early-nineteenth-century English universities, upon which Newman based much of the vision he set forth in his Dublin lectures and later essays. Her discussion portrays the background of the lively controversy over Oxford University education that had raged during the first quarter of the century and to which Newman makes frequent reference. The participants in those heated exchanges carried out in quarterly reviews and pamphlets expounded the differing virtues of liberal learning and useful knowledge. Those earlier ideas and rhetoric deeply informed Newman's presentation of his argument for a university in which knowledge would be pursued as an end in itself rather than for utilitarian or professional purposes.

Although Newman frequently spoke and wrote in grand generalizations, Garland emphasizes the numerous religious and cultural tensions involved in the setting and the content of his lectures. Nothing about the proposed Catholic university or the Irish environment was so simple or self-evident as Newman's magisterial prose often made it appear. Garland traces the very fine line Newman had to tread between the differing educational ideas and values of the Irish Catholic ecclesiastical authorities and the Irish Catholic laity. In particular, she points to the significant confusion at the time over whom the projected Catholic university was to serve. Newman came to Ireland and delivered his lectures under the mistaken assumption that he was to found a university for Catholics rather than for Irish Catholics, but the hierarchy intended the institution for Ireland alone.

That confusion stimulated Newman's thought and proved important to the later impact of his book. When Newman delivered the lectures that became *The Idea of a University,* he had in mind an audience wider than that which sat before him in Dublin. He ultimately found that wider audience, not during his university administrative labors in Dublin but rather as his book developed a broad readership from the 1860s to the present day. Newman's sense of the issues relevant to university life during the next century were almost prophetic, even if not wholly complete.

The issues that Newman had made his own reappeared in the life of both old and new institutions in the second half of the nineteenth century. The English universities had just undergone important reforms and would during the next several decades find themselves required to accommodate a new democratic politics. New universities were founded in Europe, Great Britain, and the United States, all of which lacked traditions and whose leaders and faculties often looked at least in part to Newman's ideals. As the new universities were founded, there arose a vigorous debate across the Western world over the role of professional education, useful learning, and the sciences versus the more traditional liberal learning that Newman had championed.

Those same decades witnessed intense rivalry among religious groups and demands that secular education replace religious instruction. Newman's work initially appealed to numerous readers who believed that religious faith whether Roman Catholic or Protestant should inform education. Later, his emphasis on liberal education contributing to public life and a polite society gave many university and college teachers, who did not accept his religious views, a sense of vocation. In this regard Newman's emphasizing a historical canon of literature and philosophy appealed to religious and nonreligious educators who often feared that new ideas might prove socially disruptive. Newman provided those same teachers with arguments for confronting the pressures for vocational education. In this latter guise Newman's vision of the liberal arts came to form a secular religion that was supposed to provide moral values and a spiritual ethos in college and university settings, where, contrary to Newman's own views, formal religion had come to play a minimal role.

Newman's *Idea of a University* again provided a rhetoric and a conceptual framework for higher education during its vast expansion after World War II. His emphasis on learning for its own sake became a rallying point for those who thought universities might be overextending themselves and who sought a core value for institutions that had become internally varied in their educational goals. It is the impact of Newman's influence in that past half-century that the editor's essay examines. The editor portrays the counterinstinctive manner in which Newman's argument that liberal learning should be useless became one of its strongest modern defenses. At the same time the editor contends that despite the ongoing presence of Newman's rhetoric in discussions of universities, the reality has changed markedly from his ideal. In particular, he stresses how faculties who teach the traditional liberal arts have themselves become highly professionalized. In the process the experience of student learning and faculty responsibility to students have often been forgotten. He suggests that the countervailing educational pressure may now, paradoxically, arise from professional schools themselves, which demand more liberally educated students.

The editor also observes how Newman's language and values have created presuppositions that are at odds with both the structural and financial realities of contemporary university life. The emphasis on universal learning has led universities to extend their programs beyond their financial resources. Although Newman created important ideals for university life, he provided few ways for institutions to choose among them. The essay suggests that present-day universities are ill-equipped to make such decisions and that Newman's expansive view of the university as a place of universal knowledge has contributed to institutional confusion and difficulty in establishing a strong sense of mission.

For his own part Newman held out one clear mission for his university: to establish Theology as a science of the sciences. Religion – and more specifically, Roman Catholicism – was to provide the ethos and the fundamental framework for education. Since Newman wrote, the role of religion and theology in colleges and universities has sharply diminished, first within secular institutions, not informed by religious values to begin with, and then later in colleges and universities founded by religious denominations.

George Marsden, who in another context described this process in the United States as a movement from Protestant establishment to established unbelief, asks what has been the intellectual cost of this diminishment of religious influence on higher education. He points to the manner in which the absence of religious concerns and content in university curricula has often come about with little formal planning. He argues that ignoring religion and the failure to address the traditional questions raised by religion have created an intellectual vacuum in universities. One result is the restriction of scholarship and other intellectual experiences generated by university teaching and research. Furthermore, the avowedly secular point of view in universities has itself become generally unquestioned and uncriticized. Marsden suggests that this situation be reconsidered and that the questions raised by religion receive the intellectual and academic respect for which Newman argued. Marsden thus also implicitly brings to the fore the issue of how universities, which claim to educate their students in critical thinking, can apply such thinking to their own enterprise and actually become arenas of open thought.

If the diminishment of religion in higher education has provoked relatively little controversy, questions surrounding the teaching of literature and the humanities have in the past decade and a half often led to heated discussions within universities and professional learned societies. These debates, frequently associated in the media with the term "political correctness," have usually taken place under the banners of Western Civilization versus Multiculturalism or Eurocentrism versus Diversity. The terms and the rhetoric, as so often in university controversies, often conceal as much or more than they reveal, and the debates have on more than one occasion generated more heat than light. Yet no single aspect of contemporary higher education (except for athletic programs) has received so much public attention.

Sara Castro-Klarén explores the implications of Newman's views on education and literature for the present debates. Newman's equation of civilization with the culture of the Mediterranean and Europe and his emphasis upon an established literary canon seem at first to make his position relatively simple. Castro-Klarén links his general view of reading literature to an understanding of education in which students simply accumulate or bank information. She observes how this general approach reflects Newman's assumption that writing is active and creative while reading is passive and receptive. Such an outlook ignores how the life experience of the reader helps to determine the reader's response to the written word. In this respect, Castro-Klarén explains how Newman's assumptions about both the production of books and the act of reading, in addition to mid-Victorian prejudice toward non-European culture, made it difficult for him and his contemporaries to appreciate or even creatively to approach those cultures.

At the same time, Castro-Klarén observes the inner tensions of Newman's thought. He rejected subjective emotional and intellectual impulses, which he feared might lead to religious or cultural disorder, yet he admired the literary classics that were the product of the creative subjectivity of those he considered to be the great writers of the English language. This admiration contained the possibility of recognizing the creativity of subjectivities other than those of European writers. In other words, Newman consciously chose among writers, and the same values that led him to admire the English classics could with a leap of his imagination have led him to discern classics in other languages. Even if Newman could not make that leap, modern readers may be capable of doing so.

Castro-Klarén concludes her essay with a consideration of the reciprocity of cultural and intellectual respect within the study of literature, which arises from a mutual recognition of subjectivities of persons from differing cultural backgrounds and experiences. She points to Newman's hesitancy or inability to pursue that reciprocity and mutual need. Castro-Klarén's analysis suggests, however, that while our thinking about literature in university curricula must go beyond Newman, it need not at the same time reject all that he upheld.

Each of the preceding essays assumes that university curricula, religious concerns, and organization may change, but that universities will remain places with campuses where students read books, write papers, and participate in traditional student-life activities and where faculty will teach and pursue research as part of a local community with individual disciplinary ties to a wider profession. Such on the whole were Newman's assumptions about the broad contours of university life and structure. George Landow's essay requires that we consider what the advent of advanced but readily available forms of electronic communication will mean to the teaching, research, and community of universities and to the values that Newman championed. Landow observes that Newman's vision of the university is a historical construct that because of its time and place assumes that faculty and students dwell and work within the world of print culture. The other authors in this volume have made similar assumptions, even though the Open University in Great Britain is now more than two decades old.

Landow by contrast envisions an "electronic university," one no longer operating only within the bounds of print culture. Students and faculty, communicating across vast distances, will share information and research more rapidly than ever before. They will have more access to more information than any university generation in human history. Although the printed book is unlikely to disappear, students will in all likelihood accumulate, manipulate, and assimilate increasing amounts of information electronically. Teachers and students will be able to interact from different locations and different institutions. The present reality of colleges and universities as particular places may be transformed and in large measure eradicated. Consequently both teachers and students will come to think differently about learning and their place and roles in it.

Landow meditates on the meaning of these vast changes for the traditional idea, espoused by Newman and many other writers on education before and after him, that colleges and universities are largely defined by a sense of place and shared community. Landow asks the radical question of what happens to university life when the traditional sense and reality of place disappears and when teachers and students – whose separate roles may themselves become conflated into that of collegial learners – may find themselves part of a far-flung electronic community rather than in traditional classroom settings. Furthermore, he asks what will become of the nature of learning when through hypertext and other forms of computer discourse the very act of reading is transformed into an experience that is inherently open-ended and indeterminate.

Landow's future may prove much nearer than some believe as technology proves a cost-efficient way to deliver educational services to student bodies who increasingly are no longer of the traditional college age and many of whom cannot attend classes held in a traditional manner. Technology already can make available extraordinary lecturers to a wider array of students, provide supplements to traditional instruction, and teach many routine mathematical and linguistic skills that may better be taught through interactive drills. Furthermore, many students who will have grown up using computers and other means of electronic communication may find the electronic university can provide them with a new sense and experience of the learned community, one within which they will participate actively long after graduation. In such an electronic world, education might well become more an ongoing end in itself, such as Newman demanded, than at present when many people take simultaneous leave of intellectual growth and their college setting.

One sign of the genius of Newman's work as a true classic of the Western tradition is that it both allows and demands that we transcend our own time. Through the following essays one finds that rethinking *The Idea of a University* ultimately requires us to think critically about the past in which it was written, the university world in which we now dwell, and a future in which rapidly changing technology may well redefine the university.

Newman in His Own Day

MARTHA McMACKIN GARLAND

For more than a century, in the English-speaking world at least, John Henry Newman's *The Idea of a University* has frequently served as a foundational document in considerations of an ideal framework for higher education. Yet Newman's work contains much that is confusing if not actually confused: several ideas seem paradoxical at best, some assertions apparently contradict each other, and much of the work seems at odds with common sense, the common sense, that is, of twentieth-century America.

That despite these weaknesses the book has become so popular and influential must, I think, be seen as a reflection more of the reputation of the author than of the work itself. During the later years of his life Newman achieved extraordinary public esteem, which has grown to near adulation in more recent times. To nineteenth-century British Roman Catholics, of course, Newman became almost immediately after his 1845 conversion something of a cultural hero. Many Anglicans at first felt exactly the opposite – they saw Newman as having been deceitful and manipulative as he had worked his way through the Oxford Movement, and they viewed his conversion as apostasy and betrayal. But over time, and especially after 1864, when he published *Apologia pro Vita Sua,* his highly popular autobiographical response to an ill-spirited attack on his integrity, even Protestants gradually came to view Newman as a saintly man who had made real personal sacrifices to remain true to his religious beliefs. Interestingly, although Newman had been extremely right-wing – that is, very High Church – as an Anglican, he became something of a "liberal" Catholic. Indeed, his commitment to the Roman faith and to a life of dedicated rationality has transformed him into an embodiment of the ideal of reasoning Catholicism, as the existence of "Newman Centers" on numerous American secular campuses will attest.

No matter what the man has come to symbolize, however, the book remains filled with – in addition to a number of interesting ideas – a series of complicated contradictions. And since these contradictions grew in many cases directly out of the complexity of Newman's background and situation when he wrote the book, it is useful here to remind ourselves of the circumstances he faced.

In the late 1840s Pope Pius IX expressed a strong wish that a Catholic university be established in Ireland. It is not surprising that when the Irish Archbishop Paul Cullen set out to support such a project, he began by asking Newman, a highly visible and well-regarded recent convert to Catholicism, to assume the role of rector (roughly equivalent to president or chancellor in a modern American university). And it should be no surprise to learn that as Newman contemplated the establishment of a new university, he had in mind the Oxford model in which he had grown up.

For whatever else he was, Newman was first and foremost an Oxford man. He had gone up to the University as an undergraduate in 1817 and stayed on as a fellow of Oriel until his break with the Church of England in 1845, holding official posts as a college tutor, a university examiner, and the vicar of St. Mary's, the university church. To be sure, as his religious views had developed, and especially after the 1841 publication of the notorious, inflammatory Tract 90, Newman had increasingly withdrawn from Oxford life. And after his conversion and subsequent ordination into the Catholic priesthood (1847) he had committed himself to the establishment and leadership of a semi-monastic community of "oratorians." But it is fair to say that Newman's adult career up until the 1850s had been essentially within the context of Oxford University.

Unfortunately, the Oxford that Newman had experienced was a most imperfect model for a new Catholic university in Ireland. In several ways, during Newman's tenure Oxford itself had been in a state of development and even turmoil, hardly providing a stable ideal for replication. Throughout the first half of the nineteenth century external critics in Parliament and the popular press had attacked the way business was conducted at both Oxford and Cambridge. One issue particularly frustrating to some people was the religious exclusiveness of the two ancient foundations. By tradition going back more than six hundred years these universities were lavishly endowed and completely untaxed, the theory being that they existed to provide valuable educational services to the nation at large. But because the colleges that made up Oxford and Cambridge had originally been founded as religious seminaries, university membership – both student and faculty – had been limited to men who belonged to the established church. With respect to Roman Catholics there had long been a remarkable irony in this arrangement, since the oldest (and often most prestigious) colleges' property, donated originally to create Catholic seminaries, had been seized and "established" along with many other resources into the Anglican church at the time of Henry VIII. Various other Christian non-conformists (for example, Methodists, Presbyterians, Congregationalists, Baptists, Unitarians) had less of a historically grounded claim to admission to Oxbridge; but as the industrial revolution created newly wealthy families, many of them from dissenting backgrounds, public pressure mounted to remove the exclusionary admissions requirements. The 1830s saw a relatively vigorous but ultimately unsuccessful campaign to "open" the old universities (a campaign, incidentally, in which John Henry Newman and his Oxford Movement friends were among the most vociferous defenders of the status quo). By the early 1850s public pressure could no longer be resisted; in 1852 and 1854 bills passed Parliament requiring various reforms at Oxford and Cambridge, including access for students who were not conforming members of the established church.

Another issue under critical public discussion about the Oxford of Newman's day was the arguably deplorable intellectual quality of the undergraduate experience. University education at both Oxford and Cambridge had sunk to a shockingly low standard during the eighteenth century. Part of the problem came from the narrowness of the curriculum: students were required only to familiarize themselves with classical literature, a limited amount of theological reading, and – only at Cambridge – Euclidean geometry. Despite the fact that all over Europe great strides had been made in the physical sciences, that calculus-based mathematics was advancing rapidly in France and even in Scotland, and that in Germany literary and historical criticism were being done "scientifically," scholars at English universities were still being educated in a pale, watered-down version of the old medieval trivium and quadrivium.

Furthermore the widespread neglect of real teaching by what we would today call the faculty – the "fellows" of the colleges – rendered this inadequate curriculum even less effective. A fellowship (that is, permanent housing in college and a relatively comfortable stipend, tenable so long as the fellow remained unmarried) was granted to a graduate not with the expectation of his teaching or carrying out research but only as a reward for doing well on the undergraduate examinations. It was therefore quite possible for the senior members of the college to commit little energy to intellectual activity, making it necessary for students who had hopes of graduating with honors to hire private tutors. It was widely understood that, except in a few of the largest and richest colleges, useful instruction could *not* be expected to come from the fellows of one's college. And there was virtually no useful *university* instruction at all. That is, although most colleges did little to assure effective teaching, they were fiercely jealous of their rights and their endowments and so refused to contribute resources toward centralized laboratories, libraries, or other expensive facilities for general use.

In fact, at least during the first half of the nineteenth century, *intellectual* improvement was not the essential point of an undergraduate education at Oxbridge. Instead of rigorous scholarship, what was expected of and for students was more of a socialization process. Young men of the wealthier classes were sent there to become acquainted and acquire social skills (aptitude at public debate or talent at recognizing good port ranked high) and to make connections that would prove valuable in later life, when they assumed their roles in the leadership elite of their country. As a German observer of British higher education noted in 1843: "Our universities produce learned men in the several sciences, or men for practical life. . . . The English Universities on the contrary, content themselves with producing the first and most distinctive flower of the national life, *a well educated 'Gentleman.'* . . . [A] glance at the University Calendars [enrollment lists] may convince us that in all the world one cannot be in better company than 'on the books' of the larger Oxford or Cambridge colleges."[1]

As time passed, this social ideal came under increasing attack, in part because of its exclusiveness. Claiming that national resources were being wasted, and on too narrow a range of the citizenry, observers outside the old universities became increasingly strident in their criticism of the low-quality education, and a number of faculty members (called "dons") within Oxford and Cambridge came to agree that something needed to be done. In point of fact, John Henry Newman was one of the university teachers able to see relatively early some faults in the instructional system of his alma mater. In the late 1820s he actually attempted to improve the tutorial system in his college. However, he was completely frustrated, and thereafter cut off from any direct access to undergraduate students, by a provost dedicated to the old customs. Newman then turned his attention entirely to theological issues and joined in the development of the Oxford Movement. In general, instructional reform was very slow, brought about only through the individual efforts of committed teachers and not coming to fruition until the second half of the century; in fact, thorough reform would require parliamentary action.[2]

1. V. A. Huber, *The English Universities* (London, 1843), vol. 2, pt 1, pp. 320, 324.

2. Good treatments of these later developments can be found in Sheldon Rothblatt's *Revolution of the Dons: Cambridge and Society in Victorian England* (Cambridge, 1981) and *Tradition and Change in English Liberal Education* (London, 1976); or see A. J. Engel's *From Clergyman to Don: The Rise of the Academic Profession in Nineteenth-Century Oxford* (Oxford, 1983).

Newman may have been concerned about the quality of Oxford teaching. But he did not criticize another fundamental aspect of his alma mater at mid-century – its utter lack of focus on what we would now call "research." If England's old universities were unsuccessful as centers of teaching, they were even less effective as centers of learning. The same jealous self-protectiveness of the colleges, which prevented centralized university teaching, made centralized university research a complete impossibility. So while German and Scottish universities were becoming research institutes, the French were using the Academy of Science to expand intellectual boundaries, and even American institutions were turning toward research, the old British universities remained essentially expensive clubs designed to change boys into gentlemen.

The Oxford in which Newman had grown up professionally had therefore perhaps not prepared him optimally to found a new university. But in addition he faced other issues – of a more personal nature, both social and ideological – that would influence him as he undertook his new work.

Questions related to social class must loom large in any analysis of early-nineteenth-century England, for in the century after roughly 1750 Britain experienced remarkable and dramatic social transformation. The industrial revolution meant that the country, no longer an essentially agrarian, rural, aristocratic, and hierarchical society, was becoming largely industrial, urban, and democratic, with the rise of a new moneyed (as opposed to propertied) middle class. And as landowning ceased to be the only (or at least main) indicator of social status, other markers – including one's participation in the educational system – assumed increased importance.

John Newman and his family were exactly located in the midst of this broad social change. Newman senior was a banker, at first successful enough to maintain a large middle-class home in London but later forced by financial reverses to exchange banking for brewing and to move his family to Hampshire. John Newman and his brother attended the highly regarded Ealing grammar school and later Oxford, affiliations that served to affirm the family's position in the developing society. Furthermore, Newman's profound commitment not only to the Church of England but especially to its most conservative wing confirmed his position as a true member of the establishment, in all senses of that word.

Ideologically – one might almost say "psychologically" – Newman tended in his early years toward an extremely conservative, even authoritarian stance. This attitude (by no means uncommon among Englishmen of his era) can be seen in his deferential relationships with his parents, in his commitment to traditional views about education, and in his rather abstemious way of life. But his conservatism can best be observed in his religious ideas. Brought up in a strict evangelical home, he was increasingly drawn to ritual, to ancient church tradition, to the teachings of the early church fathers, and to the authority of the church throughout history.

As long as he remained within the Church of England, Newman's social and psychological viewpoints were consistent and supported his secure position in his society and in an intellectual and emotional framework. But going over to Rome stood all this security on its head. Instead of being the highly respectable, if controversial, Oxford and Anglican social insider, he was suddenly cut off from the polite society that he had always known. Forced to leave Oxford, which had been his only home for more than a quarter of a century, and very harshly criticized publicly and privately for his religious views and his conversion, he became instantaneously a member of a discriminated-against minority. Furthermore, although as an Anglican he had put a very high value on the authority of the ancient church and (toward the end) of the papacy, once he became a Catholic Newman found that his education had made him in some sense essentially "liberal" – that is, he had been taught to think for himself, and he valued the freedom (and responsibility) of his individual mind. For centuries British public opinion had equated the acceptance of papal authority with a kind of intellectual slavishness; such ideas were not easy for Newman to shake off, despite his undoubted emotional commitment to his new religion.

Thus, when Newman, a relatively recent convert, tried to work out a manifesto for his new Catholic university in Dublin, he was operating with his social and psychological foundations knocked out from under him. Anyone undertaking such a large project would strive for consistency, for coherence; but Newman's new life – and his new project – were radically inconsistent with his old life, including his personal views and his social position. It is not surprising, therefore, that his proposal seems to lack coherence. Nor is it hard to understand why the actual university failed in several ways to solve the problems that had prompted its foundation. Specifically, as he wrote *The Idea of a University,* Newman seemed ambivalent about three fundamental questions. First, for what social class was this new university being designed? Second, was the university to be mainly for Ireland and the Irish, or was it to serve English-speaking Catholics from all over the world, especially England? And third, what role was the Catholic religion to play in the curriculum and in the university in general?

As I indicated earlier, class considerations shaped education at Oxford, clearly the example Newman had in mind as he began his planning. The old

English universities existed to educate future leaders of society, young men whose financial situation would make it unnecessary for them to get and keep a job or to practice a profession. Many would spend at least part of their lives in government (clearly a task for the wealthy – MP's remained unsalaried until well into the twentieth century). Others would manage family estates or – especially as the nineteenth century wore on – large family businesses. And some would be expected to enter the church. But even this last vocation usually entailed as much management or politics as direct care of souls, for important positions in the church were distributed on the basis of exam results or social connections or both, and involved significant properties that produced admirable incomes. Professions that are today honorable and lucrative – law, medicine, and engineering, for example – were studied not within the old universities but through systems more like apprenticeships.

That Oxford and Cambridge saw themselves as serving an appropriate sector of society, and serving that sector appropriately, was made clear by their spokesmen during the public debates about the quality of the old universities. In the early nineteenth century Sydney Smith in the *Edinburgh Review* (whom Newman refers to as "a Northern Critic") had ridiculed both Oxford's curriculum and its instructional quality, prompting the reply by Edward Copleston that Newman quotes extensively in Discourses V and VII. It was during this debate that Copleston and others spelled out clearly that Oxford had no intention of teaching students anything "useful." Oxford undergraduates were being educated to exercise leadership, guide others, and make public policy, and it would be inappropriate for the curriculum to convey specialized knowledge or practical skills.

Indeed, *usefulness* was a particularly tainted concept because of its association with the political radicalism of the late eighteenth and early nineteenth centuries. The philosophy of "utilitarianism" – widely disseminated by Jeremy Bentham, in the writings of William Paley, and later by John Stuart Mill – had become the dominant articulation of left-wing views, playing in the politico-moral sphere the role of "*laissez-faire* liberalism" in economic discourse. Arguing essentially that "the good" is equivalent to "the useful" and that "general happiness" lies in "the greatest good for the greatest number," utilitarianism had obvious populist, even revolutionary overtones, highly unattractive to Britons badly frightened by late-eighteenth-century events in France. Worse still, because "utility" was to be calculated entirely in human terms, the whole philosophy purported to provide a moral system separate from a divine context. In what seems today a peculiar inversion of common sense – but note, an inversion that Newman embraced – the defenders of Oxford therefore actively rejected any commitment to and even seemed fearful of the concept of usefulness.

The university aimed instead at providing its students with a "liberal education," through which a man's intellectual and logical skills would be strengthened (much as gymnastics would strengthen the body). Through this process he would become "civilized," by acquaintance with the best of human thought and learning – that is, classical literature. There are some interesting unquestioned but perhaps questionable premises in this formulation: that the mind works like a muscle, and that the literatures and histories of ancient Greece and Rome are the best (actually the only appropriate) sources from which to study the human condition. But his discourses make it clear that Newman was not troubled by such issues and that he found the Oxford framework, as defended by Copleston, to be a valuable structure for undergraduate education. After all, this was the educational experience through which he himself had traveled, and it is one he advocated in general and specifically for the Catholic University of Dublin.

Unfortunately, in Ireland it would be difficult to populate a university only with those who were to become members of Parliament, manage large estates and businesses, or provide ecclesiastical leadership (even for the Catholic Church). Ireland's social system was entirely different from that of England, especially if we focus on southern Ireland, where most of the Catholics lived. Functionally and economically nineteenth-century Ireland was one of the colonies of the British Empire. There were wealthy landholders in Ireland, but most of them were of English descent and were members of the Church of Ireland (Anglicanism in Ireland) rather than Roman Catholics. In southern Ireland there were few Catholic landholders of any size; and since industrialization had barely touched the island, there was little commercial or industrial wealth in the hands of either Catholics or Protestants. The majority of the population, instead, were agricultural workers, many of them living in dreadful conditions as tenant farmers. What Ireland needed desperately was a middle class, people with useful educations who would become doctors or attorneys or engineers or accountants. And if some of them became educated in order to go into the church or to become leaders of local government, they would typically not live in comfortable leisure as part of an entitled class but would use church and government more effectively for the well-being of the Irish people.

Newman's goal of using a liberal education to make "gentlemen," therefore, while hardly an evil concept, was in some fundamental ways ill-suited to the needs of the society he was trying to serve. At a strictly logical level perhaps nothing requires that gentlemanliness be a class-based concept. The gentleman's qualities that Newman lists at the end of Discourse V – "a cultivated intellect, a delicate taste, a candid, equitable, dispassionate mind, a noble and courteous bearing in the conduct of life" (89) – could in principle be achieved by a person brought up in poverty and without financial resources. In practice, however, in education as elsewhere, time is money. A person without financial resources may well find that the time spent acquiring knowledge of the classical languages so as to develop "a delicate taste" might have been better spent acquiring a practical understanding of something that would be helpful in earning a living. And when a whole society is as poor, underdeveloped, and economically exploited as was mid-nineteenth-century Ireland, the wholesale production of gentlemen may seem a luxury that a new educational system could ill afford.

At a practical level Newman did recognize the need for a compromise between the old Oxford formulation and what was required for Ireland. While he kept the liberal studies at the heart of his educational program, he did assume that most students, especially in their later years of training, would specialize in something. While rector he established at the Catholic University the beginnings of an engineering program and a medical school, the latter a highly successful institution that in the twentieth century merged with the permanent National University. And he clearly recognized that while a generalist education might be best for the individual, society at large required that many people be educated as specialists so as to provide the technical and professional expertise that would enable a complex society to work.

But Discourse VII, "Knowledge Viewed in Relation to Professional Skill," in which Newman explicitly examines the tension between liberal and professional education, is a rather disappointing collection of competing quotations drawn from the published debates criticizing Oxford. Even when Newman was composing and first delivering his discourses, these earlier squabbles (and the combatants involved) must have been largely forgotten by his listeners; and now at the end of the twentieth century the extended passages borrowed from the *Edinburgh Review* and "Mr. Davison" lack much of either persuasive or historic interest. Newman's own contributions are largely a series of paragraphs in which he jousts somewhat weakly with his own formulation of utilitarianism, followed by a reiteration of his faith in the gentlemanly virtues imparted by general, liberal studies. His book is interesting – and also frustrating – precisely when Newman wrestles with this problem of professional versus liberal education: interesting because finding the right balance between general and specialist education remains an important challenge as we contemplate modern curricula, and frustrating because Newman seems to insist that in his complex, convoluted, and ultimately somewhat sloppy formulation he has found the right balance.

Given his wariness of overspecialization and practical knowledge, what certainly does not emerge in his plan is a university committed to research. In Newman's understanding, Teaching, not Learning, was the point of a university. Specialist professors might be hired to instruct the students in the various disciplines of the liberal arts, but providing the professors themselves with resources in order to advance their scholarship was not part of Newman's plan, either in *The Idea of a University* or in practice when he started setting up his institution. If he had made a commitment to research, it would have been most remarkable, inasmuch as this was such an alien concept within his own experience. But it is interesting to imagine the economic impact, had a "land-grant" institution or two, of the contemporary American type, been established in Ireland.

The second fundamental question complicating Newman's thinking as he began his university project involved nationality: was the Catholic University in Dublin to be mainly "Catholic" or mainly "in Dublin"? That is, were the main targets of Newman's effort to be English-speaking Catholics no matter where they came from, or was this to be a university essentially for Ireland? For reasons that remain obscure, Newman was at first somewhat confused about exactly what his charge was. His understanding was that the pope intended the new university to serve all English-speaking Catholics, a goal that Newman found most appealing. He had earlier actually proposed establishing a Catholic college near the outskirts of Oxford itself, and he would obviously welcome a project that combined his two central lifelong concerns, higher education and religion. That the location of the new institution was to be Dublin was clear from the outset, but Newman did not seem to understand all the implications of that choice. Perhaps his confusion stemmed in part from his own determination, and his belief that the pope and the Irish hierarchy understood and accepted this determination, to maintain his association with the Birmingham Oratory while working with the new university. It was as if he believed that since he himself would be actively involved in institutions in both England and Ireland, his university, too, would become genuinely international. Throughout his tenure as rector he was to spend a great deal of time away from Dublin, a pattern that hardly contributed to his being seen as committed to the *Irish* project.

A final aspect of the English-Irish tension must be mentioned: unquestionably, at a personal, social level Newman would have been gratified by an institution of higher learning designed for English Catholics. Since the Reformation, a small number of elite English Roman Catholic families – members of the gentry and even of the nobility, who had refused to convert with Henry VIII – had been excluded from many formal avenues to power in the English state. But they had retained their wealth and remained a closely knit community, a sort of counter-aristocracy; the families in Evelyn Waugh's *Brideshead Revisited* exemplify this group. Had the old universities not had religious exclusionary clauses, these families would have sent their sons to Oxford and Cambridge. It is not surprising, therefore, that the Oxford Movement and the conversions it spawned had been extremely cheering to these old Catholic families. Newman, Henry Manning, and other converts and the members of this older group of the wealthy faithful had immediately embraced one another warmly, exchanging social for intellectual credibility. To develop an educational system to meet the needs of these English families would have been an ideal project for Newman, and it seems that in some sense he thought that is what he had been asked to do.

Unfortunately, with the possible (but not probable) exception of the pope, Newman was the only person who understood his task in this light. In fact, in Ireland there was very little collective clarity of vision about several issues regarding the new university. To be sure, different parties, with different perspectives, argued that Ireland did need a new institution of higher education, one specifically suited to serve its Catholic citizens. And from the outset it was agreed that the new university would be in Dublin, with even Newman – despite his English longings – understanding that the site made sense. On almost nothing else in connection with the proposed Catholic University, however, was there any general agreement.

Prior to the nineteenth century, university education in Ireland had been provided by the University of Dublin (Trinity College), founded in 1591 and until 1793 open only to members of the Anglican church. In that year Parliament had abolished religious tests for admission, so during the first half of the nineteenth century a small number of middle-class Irish Catholics had attended and received degrees from Trinity College. But control of the curriculum and the general regulation of the institution remained strictly in Anglican hands. The prizes and fellowships continued to be closed to anyone except members of the Church of Ireland, and of course theological training suitable for Catholics was not available in that context. Preparation for the Catholic priesthood had since 1795 been conducted at a government-supported Catholic seminary at Maynooth, but there was no institution analogous to Oxford and Cambridge where Catholic laity could be educated alongside potential members of the clergy.

General political unrest in Ireland, exacerbated by the terrible famine of the mid-1840s, led Robert Peel's government to propose various measures to improve conditions in Ireland, among them a concentrated attack on the problem of higher education. In 1845 the seminary at Maynooth was awarded, along with some capital funds, a significant increase in its annual grant, putting it on a sound financial basis for the foreseeable future. Peel then turned to lay education, establishing three new colleges, two Catholic, one Presbyterian, to be incorporated as the Queen's College. None of these colleges was located in Dublin, to avoid hostile competition with Trinity College. Although each new college was designed especially to appeal to its religious group, each was technically open to students of any denomination and the instructional programs were understood to be nonsectarian. This formulation – open admission, no fixed religious instructional agenda – was referred to as "mixed education," that is, Catholic and Protestant students and curricula in one institution.

This, then, was the situation to which various groups were responding when they began contemplating a "Catholic University in Dublin": on the one hand a long-existing, socially prestigious, basically Anglican institution in Dublin, which Catholics could attend but only as second-class citizens; and on the other, two new colleges, one in Cork, one in Galway, that would welcome Catholics but only into a secular educational structure. This situation had enormous potential for dividing Irish opinion.

Many, perhaps most, Irish Catholics, lay and clerical alike, deeply resented the educational and political liabilities under which their coreligionists labored. A university that could give them complete and open access to the kind of education they needed, both for their careers and within a religious context, would clearly be a boon to Catholics in Ireland, and possibly to Ireland at large. Seeing "mixed" education as inherently dangerous to the faith and morals of Catholic students, the hierarchy, especially Pope Pius IX and Archbishop Cullen of Dublin, forbade their attendance at the new Queen's College, directing instead that a specifically Catholic university be founded where undergraduates' liberal education would "ground them in literature and science in conformity with the Church's teaching."[3] Many Irish laymen, and even some members of the lower

3. J. H. Newman, "Memorandum: Catholic University," in *Autobiographical Writings,* ed. Henry Tristam (London, 1957), p. 323.

clergy, worried about this approach, seeing it as an effort by Rome to exert papal control over the Irish Catholic church and to extend, inappropriately, clerical control in general. Such views were strongly held especially by Irish nationalists, who suspected Rome of being extremely conservative and therefore likely to counter any effort toward Irish independence.[4] In fact, some laymen felt that the mixed-education experiment should be given a fair trial, in that it would bring Irishmen of various religions together, perhaps ultimately to work for Irish national causes.

Thus even after it was agreed that a Catholic university in Dublin should be undertaken, many essentially political arguments still had to be adjudicated: Was control to be papal and hierarchical or local clerical? Must control be clerical at all, as opposed to lay? To what extent was Church doctrine, as defined by an increasingly "infallible" papacy, to determine the content of instruction? Would instructors reflect an Irish nationalist agenda? Or was such an orientation dangerous to the faith and to good education? And with obvious socioeconomic implications was the critical curricular question: was Newman's liberal education ideal appropriate, or was something more practical, something oriented toward careers for middle-class Catholics, what was wanted?

Newman himself further complicated matters by raising the issue of how English the new university was to be, with respect to recruiting either students or faculty. Actually, although it clearly interested Newman, the student part of this question was essentially a red herring, for – as his English Catholic friends indicated, to his disappointment – there was never any likelihood that a significant number of upper-class English families would send their offspring to Dublin to be educated, no matter who the university's rector was. The question of English faculty members was not discussed, certainly not in *The Idea of a University,* but in practice Newman was frequently at odds with Irish public opinion when he tried to employ a scholar from across the Irish Channel. On the other hand, he ran into vigorous ecclesiastical opposition when he engaged two Irish political theorists who were perceived to be unsafely radical.

Unfortunately, as he himself readily admitted, Newman was remarkably naive about Irish matters and hardly the person to wend his way adroitly through the tangles of political opinion. And he was not motivated to try. In a memorandum written in the 1870s Newman said that he would not have undertaken the university project if he had understood that it was aimed

4. This was a reasonable fear; Pius IX had had bad experiences with the radical Young Italy Movement and viewed the much more moderate Young Ireland with considerable suspicion.

only at the Irish. He had no special knowledge of the Irish or of Irish problems and, one gets the sense, not much sympathy either. As he later wrote, "What came home clearly to me was, that I was spending my life in the service of those who had not the claim upon me which my own country-men had: that, in the decline of life, I was throwing myself out of that sphere of action and those connexions which I had been forming for myself so many years. All work is good, but what special claim had a University exclusively Irish upon my time?"[5]

The third cluster of questions Newman needed to address as he wrote *The Idea of a University* and undertook the founding of a new institution had to do with religion. What role would Catholicism play in determining what was to be taught? Were secular books – on science, for example – to be tested against sacred teaching and measured against a papal index, formal or informal? Some of the political questions mentioned above were actually ecclesiastical, if not theological: What role would the Church hierarchy in Rome have in Ireland? Would it determine the structure and curriculum of the university? And how much direct theological teaching would the curric-ulum include?

Here, as with the other issues, Newman's present role and responsibility were to some extent complicated by his past. As previously noted, his position within Anglicanism had been conservative, even authoritarian, and the Roman church might well have expected Newman to remain a staunch protector of all aspects of Church authority, from the papacy to explicit control of curricular matters. But, again as noted above, Newman the Cath-olic was more liberal than Newman the Anglican. Within a year or two of his conversion some of his ultramontane colleagues thought him inade-quately committed to papal authority, and in later years, on such matters as the temporal power of Rome and papal infallibility, he would consistently take a position of "wise and gentle minimism."[6] With respect to the practi-cal issues he faced in the founding of the Catholic University, Newman in almost every case espoused the more liberal solution, preferring local cleri-cal control to direction from the papal hierarchy, encouraging the employ-ment of laity on the instructional staff, and denying theology active censor-ship of the curriculum.

Still, he would not have been interested in founding a Catholic univer-sity if he had not seen a special role for Catholicism in the curriculum; that role saw religion as "the science of the sciences." It would determine the

5. Ibid., p. 330.

6. J. H. Newman, "Autobiographical Sketches: Supplement," ibid., p. 15.

proper interrelationship of all the other disciplines, and it would make all the disparate issues in the various disciplines come together in a kind of coherence. This is somewhat obscure, but Newman seemed to mean that the Catholic faith would form the overarching context for all the academic work of the new university. The teaching of other subjects would not be checked against some sort of Church party line. Rather, students would be expected – with their instructors' conscientious, explicit help, and in all their classes – to remember that they were Catholics; to integrate their understanding of classics, mathematics, and the sciences into their own religious worldview; and to make sense of everything in terms of the understanding they had of their relationship to their church and to their God.

Having noted all these various tensions that Newman faced in founding the Catholic University of Dublin, and having read the book in which he tried to enunciate principles by which to resolve these problems, we are interested in asking how well we think his book succeeded. Were his answers coherent and logical? Or do they seem in some sense self-serving, justifying positions to which he had been brought by his own educational and personal history, not by careful reasoning? Was his "manifesto" a useful document for dealing with higher education in nineteenth-century Ireland? In fact, we know that Newman left his new university and Ireland after only seven years, clearly regarding his efforts as less than successful; and the university he founded led a troubled existence for some fifty years, never recognized by the state and essentially disappearing into the new National University (founded in 1908). But are those practical, historical outcomes relevant as we evaluate *The Idea of a University?* Or at the end of the twentieth century, does the merit – if any – of Newman's book lie elsewhere?

For historians of the Victorian period – student or professional – *The Idea of a University* retains its fascination in part as a primary document that can give us considerable insight into the man and the period that produced it. Newman was by no means "typical" of the Victorian period; indeed, no single individual could be an accurate reflection of the complexities of that rich and varied era. But his life and his writings did illuminate some of the period's most important issues. Newman's economic background and educational experiences exemplified those of the developing upper middle class in England, and the social views produced thereby are mirrored in *The Idea of a University*. Newman's scholarship, especially on theology and church history, was also important in his time, having a profound impact on the English (and American) understanding of Roman Catholicism. It is not too much to say that the wave of conversions-to-Rome, in which he played such an important part, revived the old faith in the British Isles. And his personal life, combining the religious devotion of a nearly monastic Catholic priest and many elements of Victorian respectability, came to serve as a model of decorum and decency as well as devotion.

But *The Idea of a University* continues to interest people who are not particularly concerned about understanding nineteenth-century culture. Certainly the book raises two large questions that remain relevant to the quality of modern higher education. First, whether or not we are satisfied by Newman's notion of "science of the sciences" (or what he elsewhere refers to as the proper operation of an "imperial intellect"), by his claiming this role for religion, he vigorously calls attention to the critical significance of an *integrated* curriculum. Whether we believe that his vision worked itself out in Dublin, Newman challenges us to identify for ourselves some coherent framework within which to undertake our undergraduate educational process. With the exception of a few church-related institutions, American colleges and universities have abandoned efforts to produce such integration in their students' educational experience. Generally speaking today moral or religious values, whereby students may possibly integrate the various elements of the curriculum, come from their experience outside the college or university.

Strictly secular institutions, on the other hand, frequently try to inculcate coherent intellectual values through the development of an integrated "core" of liberal arts courses. This approach, propaganda for which is frequently drawn from *The Idea of a University,* often falters at two important points. First, although many of us read Newman's words about liberal education and long for that ideal, we are not willing to do the hard intellectual work required for us to define that ideal in a way appropriate to the institutions of our day. Faculties face enormous difficulties in agreeing about the basic principles for such a core. Too often, instead of collectively thinking through opinions about how people learn or the information that is crucial to further learning, faculty members in modern American universities do battle to the near-death over academic turf, frantically concerned about enrollment statistics and budget implications for departments and programs. And faculties also fight fierce political battles, dividing into ideological camps that either vehemently oppose or vigorously support traditional parts of the curriculum just because they are traditional.

Even when an institution has developed a framework for liberal education, however imperfect, only infrequently is the school able to articulate that framework to its students and reward those faculty who sustain it. Most academics feel – or used to feel – that teaching at a university is good and noble work, that it has something important to do with molding the young, and that a liberal education is at the heart of that value system. But most academics have now turned resolutely away from any responsibility for helping younger students to recognize the exciting way that ideas fit together. Consequently, academic "advising" and mentoring are among the least-honored and -rewarded activities of faculty members. Institutions whose faculties have devised basic education requirements turn the task of checking the pick-and-choose lists over to part-time employees, often graduate students. Until faculty members spend time with students, discussing the institution's hopes and expectations for them, and sympathetically explaining the value of the math or language requirement, students will not understand what a liberal education is supposed to be, much less receive one.

In addition to the issue of the coherence of the curriculum, Newman also demands that we pay attention to the tension between "liberal" and "useful" education. The balance struck by Newman may seem inappropriate today. It is unlikely that we, any more than nineteenth-century Ireland, can afford to educate our elites only to be elegant generalists, ladies or gentlemen. The problems we do confront, and which our students will confront as they take their place in the world, will surely require that we educate talented specialists familiar with science and technology. Certainly we cannot as a society afford to neglect the remarkable advances in all kinds of knowledge that have grown and will continue to grow naturally out of academic specialization and research. At the same time, it will also be extremely helpful if students and future citizens have studied and understood the lessons of the humanistic disciplines so that they know how responsibly to make use of their specialties. In the present climate, Newman's chief demand may be not that liberal studies win out over useful studies, but rather that all concerned stop to think about what is truly useful in education. Pondering this question should in no small measure lead to a greater appreciation of learning for its own sake. It might also lead universities to a clearer sense of their mission within democracies.

Newman's University and Ours

FRANK M. TURNER

In 1851 the Roman Catholic bishops of Ireland invited John Henry Newman, a recent convert to their faith, to organize and preside over a newly
projected Irish Catholic university in Dublin. Rather than hire a public
relations firm or a vice president for communications to explain the role of
the new university in Irish Catholic life, Archbishop Paul Cullen, the chief
patron of the university, asked Newman himself to deliver a series of lectures on the scope and purpose of the proposed institution. This request
resulted in the series of lectures and later essays that became *The Idea of a
University*. No work in the English language has had more influence on the
public ideals of higher education. No other book on the character and
purposes of universities has received so frequent citation and praise by
other academic commentators. That such became the situation is not without its paradoxes and ironies.

The language of Western political thought originated in the ancient
Greek polis, which had virtually no resemblance to the modern state. Similarly, much of the language with which for more than a century academic
people have discussed their purposes and aspirations originated in Newman's meditations about a no longer existent, provincial, Irish Catholic
institution in almost no way resembling the modern research university.
Like the negotiator who succeeds by being the first person to get his material on the table, Newman against all odds and experience established the
framework within which later generations have considered university academic life. Newman provided the vocabulary, ideas, and ideals with which
to discuss the concerns, character, and purpose of the university and of
higher education generally. He furthermore articulated a vision of the university against which alternative visions despite their relevance, usefulness,
and practicality make the activity of the university seem intellectually and
morally diminished.

At one point in his discussion of English Catholic literature Newman
argued that neither English nor Irish Roman Catholics who spoke the English language would produce a distinctive literature of their own because

non-Roman Catholic cultural forces had already forged the English language and its literature. In that passage Newman contended,

> Certain masters of composition, as Shakespeare, Milton, and Pope, the writers of the Protestant Bible and Prayer Book, Hooker and Addison, Swift, Hume, and Goldsmith, have been the making of the English language. . . . They have made it rich, harmonious, various, and precise. . . . And, like music, it has seized upon the public mind; and the literature of England is no longer a mere letter, printed in books, and shut up in libraries, but it is a living voice, which has gone forth in its expressions and its sentiments into the world of men, which daily thrills upon our ears and syllables our thoughts, which speaks to us through our correspondents, and dictates when we put pen to paper. (188–189)

Newman's own prose about the university has similarly gone forth into later Western culture as such music. His language has established the style and the essential mode of discourse with which to speak and write of the academic life. Virtually everything else written about universities has lacked his harmony and style and the capacity of his ideas to resonate with the desire that the educational process, whatever else it may do, rise above the humdrum of everyday existence and transform the immature into the mature, the unformed into the formed, the unreflective into the reflective, the youth into the adult.

On the face of it, virtually every circumstance surrounding the conception, the character, and the contents of *The Idea of a University* apparently works against its ongoing claims to relevance. Newman's experience in this Irish institution bore little resemblance to that of a modern university administrator. There was no state legislature to which he had to answer. There was no board of trustees to manage, though the Irish bishops were never far from sight. His faculty was not unionized, nor was it overly concerned with academic freedom or issues of governance. He had to spend little or no time on student services. Because his institution was just in the process of being founded, he had no concern with alumni relations. He did not have to deal with government regulation. He was apparently uninterested in the issues of town and gown. Not insignificantly, despite using analogies drawn from athletic training, Newman seems never to have had to think about the ethics and finances of athletic policy, let alone hire or fire a coach.

The distinctly "Victorian" character of Newman's treatise also works against its present-day influence. The book was published in 1852, only two years after the Great Exhibition, during the most prosperous decade of the Victorian era, and exudes the confident conviction that it is possible to establish a university of broad intellectual scope and purview. Such an ebullient climate is today missing from both the university world and the general economy of the West. Like most other leading Victorian writers, Newman assumed the unity of truth and rejected the early inroads of moral and cultural relativism and the pervasive angst and doubt that they would later foster. Newman also displayed a wholehearted, if not fierce, ethno-centricity. "Civilization" for him rarely extended beyond the lands and culture of the Mediterranean world. Along with others of his generation, he unhesitatingly embraced the metaphors of imperialism, proudly portraying the university itself as a vast "imperial intellect" (221) and likening it to an empire. He also presumed that the world of learning and education would pertain to men. His audience, which included women, he always addressed as "Gentlemen," and one goal of his educational enterprise was to produce "the gentleman."

To the inhabitant of a modern university Newman's may seem a voice from an academic time warp. He may have seemed so to many in 1852. Newman championed the values and experiences of early-nineteenth-century unreformed Oxford, where there was little research and virtually no instruction in useful or applied knowledge. Even as he spoke, Newman's vision, based on an Oxford that was itself disappearing, was ill adapted to post-famine Ireland, one of the poorest and most economically under-developed countries in Europe. Newman's backward-looking attitude is all the more peculiar when it is remembered that he first published his book only a few years before the Morrill Act (1862) opened the way for land-grant colleges in the United States, and the founders of Johns Hopkins and Cornell established those institutions as nonreligious research universities.

Newman was out of touch with the major trends in the university world of his own time. Although affirming a larger role for research than is indi-cated in the much quoted preface, Newman did not envision universities as engines for the generation of new knowledge. Indeed, he seemed largely uninterested in new knowledge. He declared the importance of history but also stated that the biblical story of Noah's ark was fundamental to an understanding of the human past. He wrote about science, opened a school of science, and acquired a school of medicine while at the same time strongly criticizing the legacy of Francis Bacon and the ideal of useful knowledge. Newman's was not a voice of the academic future.

If Newman's provincial setting, his quintessential Victorianism, his spurning of useful knowledge and vigorous research do not disqualify him from possessing standing in the world of modern higher education, then surely his previous university experience may raise doubts about his ability to provide direction to university life. For more than fifteen years he had been the chief disruptive academic personality in Oxford. In point of fact, John Henry Newman had been the kind of faculty member whom every university administrator dreads, trustees deplore and fail to understand, and more staid alumni find embarrassing, but whom students and the young among the faculty and alumni cheer toward further extravagances.

During the late 1820s, as a don in Oriel College, Newman had pressed for dramatic changes in the tutorial system. His campaign for pedagogical reform eventually ended with the Provost of Oriel College forbidding him to teach students. Shorn of instructional responsibilities but retaining all the other benefits of his lifetime college fellowship, Newman then became the leading voice in the Tractarian Movement, which denounced the Whig government's policy toward the Church of England and asserted that the Church of England must take a more aggressive stand against all other Christian denominations. By the middle of the 1830s, through his preaching as the vicar of St. Mary's, the university church, Newman made himself the center of an undergraduate personality cult. From that point to the mid-1840s, he or his followers initiated disruptive incidents over the appointment of the Regius Professor of Divinity as well as the elections of the Professor of Poetry and the Vice Chancellor. He and his supporters repeatedly appealed to the alumni of Oxford, who could vote on many university issues, to come back and overturn or challenge policies set forth by the university authorities. During the same period Newman pursued a religious experiment pressing Anglican devotional and theological life toward a position more nearly compatible with Roman Catholicism. As part of that campaign, in 1841 Newman introduced enormous confusion and division into the Church of England by asserting that potential clergymen could receive ordination though interpreting the Thirty-nine Articles in a manner soon condemned by virtually every bishop of that church. Newman eventually resigned his pulpit at St. Mary's and later his Oriel College fellowship, and in 1845 he converted to Roman Catholicism, much to the relief of most of the Oxford University authorities and his local Anglican bishop, who thought Newman would now be someone else's problem. Such was the unlikely figure who by 1852 had been charged to establish a new Roman Catholic university in Ireland.

Indeed, there appears little about Newman's life and outlook or the character of his institution to qualify the book that arose from those experiences as one of the educational and literary masterpieces of the Western world. Yet there *The Idea of a University* stands, a challenge to its own time and a rebuke to much of the character of the late-twentieth-century

university. At their peril those concerned with modern university life –
students, faculty, trustees, alumni, and parents – may ignore Newman's
volume, but if they read it and think seriously about it, whether in agreement or disagreement, they cannot remain indifferent to what he wrote –
unless they are fundamentally indifferent to higher education to begin with.

Two primary themes inform *The Idea of a University*. Both contribute to
the moral ethos of the book, which has attracted many readers and which
has caused considerable difficulty to others. These are, first, Newman's
contention that a university must include theology as part of its curriculum
and, second, his assertion that a university should teach universal knowledge as an end in itself. The former has frequently been left quietly un-
discussed by commentators; the latter has received usually uncritical admiration, which does not seem to comprehend the implications of Newman's
argument in his own day.

For many readers, the religious character of the new Roman Catholic
university in Dublin has raised serious questions about Newman's authority
in regard to present-day secular universities and colleges. John Henry Newman spoke and wrote as a Roman Catholic, and he spoke and wrote with the
zeal of the convert. His firm Roman Catholic orientation caused him some
difficulty even in 1852. Many in his audience, drawn from Dublin's Irish
Catholic middle class and professional groups, disliked the idea of a distinctly Catholic university and would have preferred one of mixed religious
faiths so their sons could associate with the more socially and politically
prominent Protestants of the city.

Later commentators and anthologizers have tended to ignore, downplay,
or excise Newman's uncompromising Roman Catholicism. Yet his religion
cannot be omitted from any rethinking of the book: his commitment to the
Roman Catholic faith provided the moral and conceptual frame for the rest
of the work in which he emphasized the liberal education as an end in itself.
As will be seen, it was in order to justify including Roman Catholic theology in the curriculum that Newman insisted that a university must be a
place of universal knowledge. More to the present point, thinking through
the implications of Newman's religious stance provides considerable illumination on late-twentieth-century university life. Curiously, perhaps, no
other feature of his book has so many unexpected modern resonances.

In Newman's mind, theology is a realm of knowledge, and religious
truth undergirds and informs all other truth. One can dismiss this religious
conviction as a nineteenth-century phenomenon that need no longer be of
concern now that most universities as well as colleges – even including
those founded under religious auspices – are largely secularized. But to do

so would be to ignore important groups in and around the contemporary academy who still accept much of Newman's argument, even if they do not necessarily share all his premises or conclusions.

In addition to modern Roman Catholic universities, there still exist other religiously oriented universities and colleges of numerous faiths, many of which provide rigorous education in liberal arts and learned professions. Within these as well as in nonreligious institutions a lively conversation has begun about the right and even the possible responsibility of faculty members to discuss their personal faith-commitments in relation to the subject matter they teach. There have also arisen spokesmen for more fervent religious positions. For many years, from Oxford and Cambridge in England across the campuses of the United States, religious groups usually associated with Protestant evangelicalism have attacked what they regard as the inadequacy of wholly secular education. Within the past decade the debate over the impact of "secular humanism" on American education resounded through the popular media. That same impulse against secular learning is now touching the universities in Islamic nations.

In many though by no means all respects these religious spokesmen and critics are at one with Newman, but so are others, people in the university who would not see themselves as religious in any sense. From the other end of the political and cultural spectrum ideological positions articulated in the name of so-called political correctness or in the cause of making universities "morally better" places than the surrounding culture – positions that no less than religious fundamentalism may involve limitations on freedom of thought and speech in the academy – clearly represent a secularized version of the religious truth that Newman saw conditioning all other thought and teaching in the life of a university. Both the religious and secular critics seek to find or impose a wider framework of truth or understanding within which the university and its activities should function.

Newman believed in the appropriateness and even the necessity of faith-commitments being related to undergraduate teaching and the university's moral ethos. In contrast, however, to modern religious and secular fundamentalists, Newman himself established considerable space for intellectual freedom. He constructed it in a rather awkward way, but he established it nonetheless. Understanding Newman's position allows us to see how he could combine religion with secular learning to the consternation of religious fundamentalists and how he could also separate secular learning from moral transformation to the consternation of those who would have universities be the agents of cultural and political transformation.

Newman affirmed throughout his many books and articles that there existed two settings for human history. First, there was the *sacred history,* which involved the dealings of God with fallen humankind – the covenant with the Jews; the life, death, and resurrection of Jesus of Nazareth; the history of the Christian church; and judgment at the end of time. It was in this sacred history, rather than through humankind's natural or secular development toward civilization on earth, that God redeemed the human race. Understanding of this redemptive process was the realm of knowledge afforded by theology and the teaching of the Roman Catholic Church. From the era of the apostles, the Church had carried and taught the message of human redemption and knowledge of human virtue understood through the Christian dispensation. This knowledge was supernatural in its origins and had to be so in order to save some human beings from the sinfulness of the world. The points of reference for this sacred order were to be found not on earth but in the wisdom of God in eternity.

Second, for Newman, there existed a *natural or secular history* of human beings, which originated with the creation, involved the fall in the Garden of Eden, and then continued through the civilizing development of the fallen human race as it forged an earthly life and society. The natural history of humankind was co-extensive with civilization, that is, with human secular development. This achievement included the rise of literature, in which Homer stood as "the first Apostle of Civilization" (171); pursuit of the arts; the establishment of civil society; and the generation of scientific knowledge. Knowledge of this natural human development and accomplishment, whether in literature, history, or science, constituted for Newman the basis of the liberal education. Disciplined knowledge of these subjects produced the gentleman.

His separation of human history and human life into secular-natural and sacred-supernatural spheres meant that Newman, unlike many persons in the late-twentieth-century university, labored under no illusion that a liberal education can lead to either moral virtue or religious faith. Paradoxically Newman's faith that human sinfulness requires supernatural redemption limited the moral aspirations of his university. In his view the liberal education addressed only the natural human being in a natural civic setting. The liberal education could not address the issues relating to human redemption. As he remarked,

> Knowledge is one thing, virtue is another; good sense is not conscience, refinement is not humility, nor is largeness and justness of view faith. Philosophy, however enlightened, however profound, gives no command over the passions, no influential motives, no vivifying principles.

Liberal Education makes not the Christian, not the Catholic, but the gentleman. It is well to be a gentleman, it is well to have a cultivated intellect, a delicate taste, a candid, equitable, dispassionate mind, a noble and courteous bearing in the conduct of life; – these are the connatural qualities of a large knowledge; they are the objects of a University; I am advocating, I shall illustrate and insist upon them; but still, I repeat, they are no guarantee for sanctity or even for conscientiousness, they may attach to the man of the world, to the profligate, to the heartless, – pleasant, alas, and attractive as he shows when decked out in them. . . . Quarry the granite rock with razors, or moor the vessel with a thread of silk; then may you hope with such keen and delicate instruments as human knowledge and human reason to contend against those giants, the passion and the pride of man. (89–90)

For Newman, the liberal education led to "intellectual excellence" (90), but that excellence was not to be confused with moral transformation. It was the Roman Catholic *Church* not the Roman Catholic *University* that opened the path to divine truth and human redemption.

Newman was no educational utopian. Only a generation of scholars, having imbibed various secular utopian traditions and having learned to live without the internal or external underpinnings of religious faith, has come to expect universities to do what the church and the great religions have in the past been expected to do. Newman and those scholars who look to liberal education to bring about some kind of human regeneration agree in their perception of the world as evil, unjust, and full of suffering. They differ on the ways to eradicate that evil. Newman thought that redemption or radical transformation of human society could not arise from the evil world or from a university that whatever its religious orientation was part of that world. Newman believed that the larger answers to the evils of the human condition must come from a divine order of truth, which the Roman Catholic Church possessed and taught. Modern scholars and other university-associated people who see university education as fundamentally addressing or eradicating the evils of the world expect that transformation from the world itself. Newman would believe that they misunderstood both the larger scope of human history and the essential moral limitations of a university and the human knowledge that it teaches.

Curiously, Newman's vision, despite its potential for religious interference, possessed a wider sphere for intellectual freedom in the university than the vision of those who conceive education as capable of radically transforming the pride and passion of human beings. Newman was willing to provide instruction in secular literature, philosophy, and history, which showed human beings in all their sinfulness and depravity because such knowledge was a product of natural rather than sacred history. He believed that its teaching would not undermine or replace sacred knowledge, so long as the latter was also taught. Newman was not caught in the intellectual bind of present-day censor-prone scholars who, lacking any transcendental faith, must seek from the finite, secular world the spiritual regeneration that Newman found only in the realm of the sacred. At the same time he also displayed rather more confidence in religious faith and truth than those who would establish institutions to protect students from secular humanism.

Newman's articulation of the university's mission, as providing knowledge that is an end in itself within the ethos of Catholicism, proved transportable and mutable well beyond Dublin. His vision transformed the university into an institution that, whether or not distinctly religious, possessed a character that transcended everyday life, the realm of useful, instrumental knowledge. Newman succeeded in making the university a socially sacred place first for Irish Roman Catholics, then for English and Americans of many religious faiths, and finally for English-speaking peoples throughout the world who may have had little or no religious faith but who sought some institution that possessed an aura of the sacred or of the nonmundane in a secular world. Through at least World War II, even in those public and private universities in the United States that did not embrace a particular confessional outlook, there existed a conviction that education should nourish students in moral values either directly Judeo-Christian or derivatively so. The desire to surround the liberal education even in its contemporary professional form with a larger system of values has persisted among scholars who for the most part may have become religiously nonobservant. The emphasis on teaching universal knowledge as an end in itself became for many scholars a kind of secular religion that raised the goal of their own vocation above others in the bourgeois societies in which universities especially have flourished.

By making the function of the university transcend any narrow utility, Newman associated the university with the ideal of organic wholeness, as opposed to mechanistic division, that has proved so powerful in modern thought from Rousseau and Burke to Marx and Wagner. This outlook linked Newman's work to an intellectual tradition broader than that of Roman Catholicism and allowed his work to speak to audiences who might spurn religious faith but who no less fervently spurned the values of middle-class society associated with useful knowledge. Drawing upon ancient classical writers long championed by his own Oxford teachers whom he quotes at such length, Newman urged that university knowledge is "not merely a means to something beyond it, or the preliminary of certain arts into which it naturally resolves, but an end sufficient to rest in and to pursue for its own sake" (78). He continued, "[T]hat alone is liberal knowledge, which stands on its own pretensions, which is independent of sequel, expects no complement, refuses to be *informed* (as it is called) by any end, or absorbed into any art, in order duly to present itself to our contemplation" (81).

Newman thus set himself and the institution whose idea he articulated against the ideals of utility and useful knowledge and consequently made the distinguishing value of the university its apparent *uselessness*. The usefulness, indeed the higher calling, of the university was its very lack of direct social and economic utility. That transcendent uselessness, even more than the various protections of law, contract, and custom, has preserved much of the freedom of university life. It has allowed universities to be havens where students may pursue studies and activities not directly or practically applicable to later life while they mature toward adulthood. It has provided faculties with the possibility of pursuing teaching and research that need not necessarily be directly useful. It has provided the possibility of contained eccentric creativity.

Newman's rhetoric of knowledge as an end in itself has also, however, introduced into university life a vocabulary that is distinctly anti-utilitarian, anti-commercial, and even potentially anti-intellectual. Newman's thought has fostered internal discord, as those who pursue useless learning in the traditional liberal arts often criticize or look down upon those who pursue useful or applied knowledge, whether teaching foreign languages, English composition, engineering, journalism, education, management, or agriculture. Part of this tension arises from professional envy rooted in salary differentials between, for example, persons who do similar work in economics departments and management schools or in biology departments and medical schools. But another part of that tension arises from the failure of universities to work through a sense of mission that embraces the pursuit of both liberal and useful knowledge, which is the function of virtually all modern universities.

The word *University* has remained the same from Newman's day to ours while the reality it describes has not. Many university presidents, provosts, and deans continue to speak of universities as places where knowledge is pursued for its own sake, but the reality they seek to administer has become something quite different. Universities now constitute one of the chief venues in Western society for the pursuit of useful and profitable knowledge. In the United States, for example, after World War II the federal government turned to the universities as the settings for most of the sponsored research in science and medicine. In this regard the earlier role of the land-grant universities in the development of American agriculture was transferred to other areas of scientific research. Again since World War II, more and more businesses have turned to faculties from economics departments and business schools for their expertise. Television stations and even movie producers look to university scholars across the academic spectrum for advice, as do museums. Social scientists advise politicians on taking both polls and policy positions while federal, state, and municipal agencies look to them for counsel on topics from child care to environmental standards to fish hatcheries. Many university administrators believe today that their science and medical faculties must interact with private enterprise. These and many other new relationships have emerged in recent decades without much thought or clearly articulated structure. The language, rhetoric, and ideas of Newman cannot contain or direct these initiatives.

By drawing the research function into the university setting, governments, private foundations, businesses, and faculties have radically transformed the character of the university as understood and articulated by Newman. He could declare, "[W]hether or no a Catholic University should put before it, as its great object, to make its students 'gentlemen,' still to make them something or other *is* its great object, and not simply to protect the interests and advance the dominion of Science" (6). Today, many university people, certainly privately if not publicly, contend that university life has the reverse function. Faculties not infrequently find their responsibilities to students and especially undergraduates an obstacle to research and to reputation and financial gain beyond the walls of the university.

It is the university appointment that provides the accreditation for work on the outside. University scholars seek to perpetuate that situation by making the Ph.D. or other advanced professional degrees the indication of expertise and the union ticket for consulting. University scholars normally scorn scholars who work independently outside the academy, no matter how important their work. In that regard university people now seek to have it both ways – they defend their distinctiveness on the argument of liberal learning as an end in itself and defend their access to extramural income on the basis of their monopoly on usefulness.

No matter how much Newman's description and prescription of university life differ from the contemporary reality, no alternative rhetoric has succeeded in substituting itself for Newman's in the sphere of public discourse on higher education. Consequently, his concepts and ideals, which some even at the time thought aimed too high, stand like Banquo's ghost at the feast of the modern university community. As administrators and faculties continue to turn to Newman's language about the value of the liberal education and the priority of teaching to describe the functions of their institutions, their words and the values embodied therein repeatedly condemn much of the reality to which they apply that language. Particular irony surrounds the public boasts by universities about pursuing and valuing knowledge for its own sake when the financing of all higher education, public as well as private, arises from moneys earned either in the past or present through the application of useful knowledge.

Newman's argument that university study should eschew usefulness has produced another unexpected, harmful result for the life of modern universities – the absence of a clear understanding and articulation of mission. The otherworldly or perhaps more correctly nonworldly stance elaborated by Newman has led to a situation in which universities and colleges are often not expected to be financially well administered. Trustees, alumni, and the general public too often assume that faculties and administrators are by nature or disposition unconcerned about the so-called real world. Indeed, trustees often tolerate financial and administrative practices in universities that they would under no circumstances tolerate in their own for-profit or "useful" organizations or even in other not-for-profit institutions such as hospitals. Faculties for their part criticize the operational side of the university, including the management of janitors, repair personnel, and secretaries, but rarely their own educational activities. University faculties all too rarely seek high standards of efficiency or responsibility or accountability because they expect the non-university world and outside donors to pay for educational inefficiency. Newman's argument for uselessness has become a rationalization for academic inefficiency and the consequent rise in costs to students.

Some of Newman's most influential and oft-quoted passages in *The Idea of a University* have also directly contributed to paralysis in university decision making. In the first sentence of his preface, beyond which numerous academic commentators in campus addresses seem not to have ventured, Newman stated that a university is "a place of *teaching* universal *knowledge*" (3). Newman knowingly used a false etymology for the word *university* to emphasize throughout his book an argument that assumes infinite financial resources for universities. The ideal of academic universality refers not to quality or excellence but only to the teaching of universal knowledge of some kind, whether of high quality or not. It works directly against preserving quality. As universities both public and private confront financial limitations, this ideal provides absolutely no guidance in setting priorities. Indeed, it works directly against selecting what programs universities should offer.

This situation was no accident or oversight on Newman's part. He personally argued for teaching universal knowledge so that his university would have to include theology. Many of the Roman Catholic laity in his audience were willing to send their sons to a mixed university or other academic institutions that did not provide Roman Catholic instruction. University College London, founded by the English Utilitarians, had specifically excluded theology. Newman from conviction as well as from the instructions of Archbishop Cullen and Pope Pius IX undertook to demonstrate that a real university must include theology. His deductive strategy was to contend that an institution could only truly be a university if it taught universally and that such universality must include theology. Consequently the argument for the university as a place of teaching universal knowledge, which is employed today to inhibit reshaping the universities ("I cannot imagine a university that does not include . . ."), had its own roots in special pleading and faulty scholarship. The argument has rarely been able to overcome the morally and intellectually expedient character of its origins.

Despite his rhetoric Newman did make choices. As he later planned for the Catholic University in Ireland, he thought it would include the traditional liberal arts, medicine, law, and engineering. At the same time he clearly excluded many activities that, as will be seen, took place in contemporary learned institutions not associated with universities. Within universities Newman seems to have expected some form of substantial but not well-articulated sorting of priorities. In a justly famous passage, he declared,

> What an empire is in political history, such is a University in the sphere of philosophy of research. It is . . . the high protecting power of all knowledge and science, of fact and principle, of inquiry and discovery, of experiment and speculation; it maps out the territory of the intellect, and sees that the boundaries of each province are religiously respected, and that there is neither encroachment nor surrender on any side. It acts as umpire between truth and truth, and, taking into account the nature and importance of each, assigns to all their due order of precedence. It maintains no one department of thought exclusively, however ample and noble; and it sacrifices none. It is deferential and loyal, according to their respective weight, to the claims of literature, of physical research, of history, of metaphysics, of theological science. It is impartial towards them all, and promotes each in its own place and for its own object. (220)

Newman may have thought that universities would simply grow as the areas of knowledge grew, but he does not explain how to decide what will or will not be included. In the phrase "taking into account the nature and importance of each" there is, however, the suggestion that current social values will in part aid in making that decision, but Newman gives little guidance as to who will delineate "the importance of each" or how they should carry out their task. Later university people have not done much better in setting limits or learning how to constrain or contract activity.

Newman believed that students would benefit from the presence of many disciplines, but he also seems to suppose that the faculty would achieve some meaningful sense of shared purpose. Assuming such unity and shared goals in universities, Newman wrote,

> It is a great point then to enlarge the range of studies which a University professes, even for the sake of the students; and, though they cannot pursue every subject which is open to them, they will be the gainers by living among those and under those who represent the whole circle. This I conceive to be the advantage of a seat of universal learning, considered as a place of education. An assemblage of learned men, zealous for their own sciences, and rivals of each other, are brought, by familiar inter-course and for the sake of intellectual peace, to adjust together the claims and relations of their respective subjects of investigation. They learn to respect, to consult, to aid each other. Thus is created a pure and clear atmosphere of thought, which the student also breathes, though in his own case he only pursues a few sciences out of the multitude. (77)

Yet in his day and in the present a shared unifying vision has eluded most universities, which have become holding companies. The real life of a university takes place in its departments, schools, libraries, museums, cen-ters, and institutes, which function in relative autonomy. Many of those units retain their own independent sources of income, making them largely immune from external supervision. The general absence of interaction and institutional bonds among the various parts of the university accounts for the absence of shared vision and in turn for the internal confusion that many universities confront in establishing priorities and clarifying their mission. Indeed, most universities simply will not even attempt to formulate a mis-sion statement, which might provide some guidance.

As a result, universities frequently display the inability to make serious, long-range decisions about themselves. There is virtually no broadly ac-cepted mechanism in higher education to make Newman's envisioned "im-perial intellect" function the way any intellect must function – by making choices. Faculties confront enormous difficulties in making transdepartmental decisions about quality. Even appointment committees drawn from across departments or across schools rarely choose to challenge the decisions of the initiating faculty. It is often noted that universities are very good at creating new programs and very poor at closing old ones or those of relatively low quality, even though the guarantees of tenure would protect the livelihoods of the affected faculty. Rather than close, reduce, or restructure low-quality units, faculties and university administrations, including trustees, tolerate lesser academic quality or mediocrity, squandering institutional resources that could be more usefully applied elsewhere. Indeed, the refusal of academic people to make choices within their own institutions represents nothing less than a form of academic anti-intellectualism.

When Newman wrote, there existed circumstances that mitigated some of the institutional dangers inherent in his advocacy of universal learning and his emphasis on teaching rather than research. At that time the major research or creation of new knowledge in the sciences, economics, history, literary criticism, and the classics took place outside the university setting. Newman could assume, and quite properly so, that universities would live off the intellectual research and growing capital of knowledge being produced among academies, learned societies, museums, and private scholars. That situation permitted him to contemplate a wide range of courses that would not necessarily be expensive because teachers would not be involved with generating new knowledge. He also assumed that scholars pursuing research outside the university might be retained to teach from time to time.

Within Newman's ideal of educating the young in knowledge as an end in itself, there also lurked more worldliness than may at first appear. Later teachers, using Newman's language, have often urged their students not to be concerned with social mobility or with relating their education to future employment. They are well intentioned and properly seek to produce students who will have moral lives and imaginations beyond the world in which they work. Yet Newman's view was more complicated and subtle. Newman had no doubt that university education was a path to social advancement, and he understood that many of the Irish Catholic youth who would attend his university lacked social skills. He did not doubt that the education he advocated would allow them to function within genteel society, which the lack of education and the prejudice of the day had closed to their forebears. He knew from his Oxford days that non-utilitarian university learning opened the higher echelons of British society more rapidly than professional or useful knowledge. There was thus no little social utility to a vocationally useless education.[1]

A liberal education conceived as an end in itself may not have embraced professional knowledge in the middle of the nineteenth century, but it was nonetheless the mode of learning that led to social mobility throughout the British Isles and across Europe. And social mobility for their sons was one of the promises that Newman implicitly made to the Irish Catholic laypersons he addressed:

> Robbed, oppressed, and thrust aside, Catholics in these islands have not been in a condition for centuries to attempt the sort of education which is necessary for the man of the world, the statesman, the landholder, or the opulent gentleman. Their legitimate stations, duties, employments, have been taken from them, and the qualifications withal, social and intellectual, which are necessary both for reversing the forfeiture and for availing themselves of the reversal. The time is come when this moral disability must be removed. Our desideratum is, not the manners and habits of gentlemen . . . but the force, the steadiness, the comprehensiveness and the versatility of intellect, the command over our own powers, the instinctive just estimate of things as they pass before us, which sometimes indeed is a natural gift, but commonly is not gained without much effort and the exercise of years.
>
> This is the real cultivation of mind; and I do not deny that the characteristic excellences of a gentleman are included in it. (7)

Newman expected the Roman Catholic University to train young men to assume positions of leadership that anti-Catholic discrimination had prevented them from achieving. His ideal of the gentleman would allow Irish Roman Catholic youth to mix on the same intellectual and social plane with their English and Anglo-Irish rivals.

It is important to recall that Newman spoke in the provincial setting of a city far removed from the mainstream of Victorian life. He could have appealed to provincial bias, but he did not. Given his and Archbishop

---

1. During the second half of the century, under the guidance of Benjamin Jowett, professor of Greek at Oxford and master of Balliol College, the civil service examinations for Britain and for India were designed so persons skilled in Greek and Latin had a very considerable advantage over persons trained in modern languages including those of the non-Western world. This device made classical training an extremely useful education in late Victorian Britain.

Cullen's desire for a distinctly Roman Catholic institution, Newman could have urged a more clearly Catholic-oriented program of study, but he did not. He could also have played to the nationalistic sympathies of his audience by associating the university curriculum with things Irish, but he did not. Newman's call to liberal learning was a call to Irish Catholics to abandon their religious and nationalistic provincialism and to look to a wider world in which to realize their talents and ambitions.

That outlook holds special relevance today and gives the experience of the liberal education ever-renewed vitality. Within contemporary universities various groups advocate retreat into provincialisms of ethnicity, gender, sexual orientation, or some other form of commutarian identity. These exclusionist tendencies stand in direct opposition to liberal learning. They constitute the xenophobic mentality of the small town located far from the major metropolis, where wider learning, excitement, and opportunity abound. They champion the world of village athletes smug in their neighborhoods, never testing themselves against big-league teams. To the extent that university people resist or disparage the liberalizing possibilities of higher education – the possibility of drawing oneself outside the community of one's birth and the experiences of one's rearing – they confine students and themselves in new provincialisms. These, whether political, religious, racial, or gender-related, will in the not long run prove as dreary, boring, and limiting to personal imagination and achievement as have all provincial towns through the ages.

But there is also another, less-discussed new academic provincialism. Across the nation, within undergraduate institutions that claim to provide a liberal education, academically professionalized training in the arts and sciences is replacing liberal education. Professors of the liberal arts who criticize undergraduate programs in business administration or other applied fields are themselves often instructing their students in a similarly preprofessional manner. Much of the undergraduate experience is increasingly academically "professional" while the professional schools, which are supposed to be narrow, have often become self-espoused advocates of liberal learning, in part as a response to the defective undergraduate education their incoming students have received.

In the past three decades there has occurred a vast though largely unheralded redirection among those in the United States and in many European nations who instruct undergraduates in the liberal arts. With their own professional advancement linked to specialized research, both older and younger instructors tend to conceive of undergraduate education in academically professional terms rather than in terms of liberal learning. Their goals – rather than the needs of undergraduates for a broadening intellectual experience, preparation for participation in civic life, or even preparation for future graduate and professional schools – now in no small measure set the agenda for undergraduate education.

Although undergraduate institutions have broad requirements in various areas of study, the courses that students now encounter have frequently become excessively specialized in a professional scholarly manner. Indeed, the "core curriculum" of one leading university actually spurns the broad survey course. Another leading university does not offer a survey course in American history. The public justification is usually that high schools now provide adequate broad education through advanced placement courses, that requiring such courses undercuts the independence of undergraduates, or that broad courses are intellectually shallow. Quite often, however, these public arguments conceal the refusal or, more disturbingly, the inability of specialized professional scholars to provide general education. Young instructors emerge from the very best graduate schools in the United States unprepared and unconcerned to offer such instruction and fearing that it will prove professionally damaging. Too often such young faculty only reflect the attitude of their older colleagues who may feel no responsibility for providing the foundations of general education in their fields. Their own graduate courses are narrowly specialized and provide little or no background either for future teaching or for research after the dissertation.

Through this academic professionalism faculties of arts and sciences have themselves turned against liberal education and liberal learning. Their action or inaction constitutes academic professionalism and careerism run amok. Across the nation faculties of arts and sciences in their various disciplines seem to have concluded that the education of undergraduates in the precise knowledge of a few things of dubious significance, except for the instructor's own research and possible career advancement, is better than even attempting to discuss large questions about the human situation or about particular fields of study for which there may exist only uncertain answers. The faculties of arts and sciences, rather than the faculties of professionals schools, have come to equate knowledge with professionalized knowledge and vocation with life. Here is the treason of the clerks at the close of the twentieth century, and it is led not by the weakest educational institutions but by the allegedly most outstanding.

Paradoxically, in contrast to Newman's day, the contemporary academy may require professional schools to defend liberal learning and to demand that the students whom they admit possess such learning because in the present day it may be primarily within the realm of professional training that the value of the liberal education most readily manifests itself. The desirability, usefulness, and wisdom of liberal learning is not new to the professions. In a memorable passage describing the skills required of a jurist and by implication of all persons involved with the legal system, Judge Learned Hand once commented,

> I dare hope that it may now begin to be clearer why I am arguing that an education which includes the "humanities" is essential to political wisdom. By "humanities" I especially mean history; but close beside history and of almost, if not quite, equal importance are letters, poetry, philosophy, the plastic arts, and music. Most of the issues that mankind sets out to settle, it never does settle. They are not solved because . . . they are incapable of solution properly speaking, being concerned with incommensurables. At any rate, even if that be not always true, the opposing parties seldom do agree upon a solution; and the dispute fades into the past unsolved, though perhaps it may be renewed as history, and fought over again. It disappears because it is replaced by some compromise that, although not wholly acceptable to either side, offers a tolerable substitute for victory; and he who would find the substitute needs an endowment as rich as possible in experience, an experience which makes the heart generous and provides the mind with an understanding of the hearts of others.[2]

One would be hard pressed today to find a graduate student in the arts and sciences receiving such advice from a mentor.

In a very real manner inherently recognized by Newman, professional education serves the arts and sciences by nurturing a university environment in which academic pursuits are directly related to life experiences. Indeed, professional education stands as a voice of one of the great traditions in Western culture. From ancient times, disagreement has existed between advocates of the active life and of the contemplative life – the life of action versus the life of thought. As in most sharply drawn dichotomies, the choice is less certain than it appears. Nonetheless, within the university setting, the professional schools symbolize that part of human life devoted to action and to the intense interface of higher education and the larger society.

Professional schools, like Aristotle in Raphael's painting *The School of Athens,* remind the modern university that the great questions cannot remain "academic" and that the academy must reach the larger world. In that

2. Irving Dillard, ed., *The Spirit of Learned Hand* (New York, 1959), p. 214.

painting of Plato and Aristotle conversing, Plato holds the *Timaeus,* which speculates on natural philosophy and a mystical cosmology, and Aristotle holds his *Ethics,* which explores the role of morality in the good society. Plato's hand points toward the heavens and perhaps also to the realm of his beloved ideal forms. By contrast, Aristotle strides forth pointing directly to the earth. Within the life of a university the professional schools play that Aristotelian role, attending to the concerns of the earth and to the pursuit of the ideal in the concrete. When thinking of this relation of the professional schools and liberal learning, we should recall that Aristotle advocated a vast role for the arts while Plato banished the poets from his republic.

Newman's vision of the university contained a clear appreciation of the active life. In addition to the pursuit of knowledge for its own sake, Newman asserted a direct social purpose for universities – "that of training good members of society" (125). The art of the university, he declared, "is the art of social life, and its end is fitness for the world." In the same passage he explained,

> [A] University training is the great ordinary means to a great but ordinary end; it aims at raising the intellectual tone of society, at cultivating the public mind, at purifying the national taste, at supplying true principles to popular enthusiasm and fixed aims to popular aspiration, at giving enlargement and sobriety to the ideas of the age, at facilitating the exercise of political power, and refining the intercourse of private life. (125–126)

These remain worthy ends for universities. If universities do not achieve them, their own position in the larger society will no longer be secure. In the future one can only hope that university people – faculties, administrators, and trustees – will rediscover those goals and retreat from the mindless professionalism that now drives so much of university life.

But that recovery must occur within the areas of the university where liberal learning has traditionally resided – the faculties of arts and sciences. There scholar-teachers must learn to rediscover and appreciate the personal consolation and wider social value, and even usefulness, of the pursuit of knowledge as an end in itself. They must learn once again to value the ordinarily extraordinary achievement of teaching students to think critically, to speak articulately, and to write clearly. In the process they should recall that these skills, when joined to those of mathematics, have stood at the core of intellectual, social, and moral amelioration for the past three centuries.

Theology and the University: Newman's Idea and Current Realities

GEORGE M. MARSDEN

Suppose John Henry Newman were somehow able to return to survey the state of modern universities a century and a half after his famous lectures. Let us say, for instance, that he had an opportunity to tour the universities of the United States, which today may lay claim to providing the prototypical university being exported around the world. What would he think?

The most striking first impression would be the way higher education had become a mass enterprise. Newman presumably would not be appalled simply by the huge numbers, but he would be alarmed by the degree to which the demands of mass education had created universities in which technical and narrowly vocational studies had overwhelmed everything else. Modern universities, he would soon realize, were not shaped by any unifying "idea." They were products of the market.

Closer examination might brighten the picture, however. A resourceful guide, say a university president, might point out to Newman that even in the United States, where among Western countries technical emphases and mass education are the most rampant, a considerable elite among university and college students still seek a substantial liberal arts education. Some even read *The Idea of a University*. This humane elite who raise questions about the grand purposes of education is probably larger, relative to the whole population, than that of the fortunate few white males who attended the tiny universities and colleges of Newman's time. For all the laments about higher education today, proportionately more people, it might be argued, now receive a first-rate humane education than ever before.

Newman, however, would be far from satisfied with this line of reassurance. He would have to point out that his idea of a university was not simply about maintaining the humane educational ideals of the West. His educational ideal must be viewed as a unified whole. In fact, the survival of his secondary ideals would be worse than useless in a system that so systematically excluded the essential component of his educational design.

What would alarm Newman most (although it would surprise him least) about current higher education is the absence of theology. In the major universities in the United States that set the standards for others, theological study is rarely even an option in undergraduate curricula. Catholic universities are exceptions, but are in that respect usually regarded as behind the times. Some major American universities with Protestant backgrounds still have divinity schools, which others often regard as vestiges of a more religious past that have no relation to the rest of higher education. In fact, most academics today take for granted that invoking a normative theological concern would contaminate one's scholarship. Even some of Newman's most ardent admirers part with him on this crucial point. A striking example is Jaroslav Pelikan in *The Idea of the University: A Reexamination* (1992). Pelikan, a distinguished historian of theology, presents his book as a dialogue with Newman. Yet when Pelikan describes his supposedly Newmanian ideal for the contemporary university, he leaves theology on the periphery.

For Newman, by contrast, theology is pivotal to the idea of a university. After Discourse I, theology is his first topic. "A University," he argues, "by its very name professes to teach universal knowledge: Theology is surely a branch of knowledge: how then is it possible for it to profess all branches of knowledge, and yet to exclude from the subjects of its teaching one which, to say the least, is as important and as large as any of them?" (25)

Newman is not arguing for merely including theology among the sciences studied in the university; he intends something more basic. Theology's presence provides a necessary context for the proper conduct of the other disciplines. Essential to Newman's outlook is that all knowledge is connected. Truths about any part of the universe are qualified by their relation to truths about other parts of the universe. This interrelatedness of all truth is essential to his ideal of an educated person. "[T]rue enlargement of mind," he writes, "is the power of viewing many things at once as one whole, of referring them severally to their true place in the universal system, of understanding their respective values, and determining their mutual dependence." (99) If a university fosters such integrated learning, each of the arts and the sciences needs to reckon with the insights of all others. Since relationships to God are the most important of human relationships, no university can fulfill its task of pursuing universal knowledge if knowledge about God is not part of the context for all other knowledge.

Newman correctly identified one of the major afflictions of academic thought since his time. Each discipline tends to aggrandize its way of looking at reality and to ignore other ways. Economists, for example, see economics as basic for understanding human experience. Psychologists see psychological factors as basic. Sociologists may reduce everything to social forces and class. Biologists may see it as all in the genes. Literary students see human problems as reducible to linguistic constructions. And so forth. Communications among disciplines becomes almost impossible. Today specialists in closely related subdisciplines sometimes cannot understand each other. Or, even if they can communicate, they cannot keep up with other fields. Thus, although we have accumulated incredibly more information and expertise in the past century and a half, we have far less sense than our ancestors did of how one part of our experience relates to the rest.

Even apart from the question of theology's place, this fragmentation of knowledge undermines the possibility of a coherent ideal for a university. "The idea of a multiversity" seems a contradiction in terms. Universities today have no central point of reference, no overarching philosophy. Rather, they are clearinghouses for numerous special interests in the production of information and opinion. Students become educated in parcels of specialized knowledge, but they are poorly equipped to evaluate the interrelationships of these parcels or to weigh their relative importance.

Newman, seeing the beginnings of modern academic specialization and the tendency of each discipline to regard itself as primary, argued that for a university to survive as a coherent entity, philosophy would have to play a central role as the "science of sciences." Philosophers, who should look at human knowledge as a whole, could balance the claims of the various disciplines, including, of course, theology. In today's multiversity, philosophy is a marginal, specialized discipline. Theology is altogether absent from the mainstream intellectual enterprise.

Newman saw this trend for theology developing already at the Anglican universities of Oxford and Cambridge. It would, he recognized, accelerate as modern universities emerged. Speaking for his opponents, Newman declared in one of the University Subjects lectures not included in this volume:

> The proper procedure, then, is not to oppose Theology, but to rival it. Leave its teachers to themselves; merely aim at the introduction of other studies, which, while they have the accidental charm of novelty, possess a surpassing interest, richness, and practical value of their own. Get possession of these studies, and appropriate them, and monopolize the use of them to the exclusion of the votaries of religion. Take it for granted, and protest, for the future, that Religion has nothing to do with the studies to which I am alluding, nor those studies with Religion.[1]

1. John Henry Newman, *The Idea of a University,* ed. I. T. Ker, (Oxford, 1976), pp. 321–22.

Newman's emphasis on theology as essential to a true university was, as he makes clear, not to turn a university into a theological seminary. Rather it was based on the larger ideal that universal knowledge must involve the interrelations of what humans know. So theology must be included as a most important dimension of human inquiry. If other sciences hope to understand the most significant truths about human experience, they must take the truths of theology into account. Otherwise, they are engaged in a futile attempt to understand essential questions about the universe without considering it as a whole. They are attempting to understand the creation without any knowledge of the creator.

Newman's Ideal and Higher Education Today

Today Newman's ideal that theology must play a crucial role if we are to have true universities seems to many people like something from the Dark Ages. Not only is theology not a point of reference for other disciplines, it is not even a discipline at most universities. Moreover, if a young sociologist or psychologist, let us say, announced that theological insight would guide his or her setting a research agenda, the chances for a successful academic career would probably be greatly diminished. Even though relating one's faith to the rest of one's thought has a distinguished intellectual heritage, most academics today regard it as unprofessional and entirely out of place. Reporting on the suggestion that faith and scholarship might mix, the *Chronicle of Higher Education* summarized one prominent historian's response: "The notion that scholars' personal beliefs are compatible with their academic interests is 'loony' and reflects a 'self-indulgent professoriate.' "[2] According to this view, religious beliefs are purely "personal," and hence it would be "self-indulgent" to introduce them into one's professional thought.

Given such prejudices, most religious academics, especially younger ones, learn to keep quiet about their faith. In the United States the anomaly this creates is particularly striking. Most of the population professes rather traditional Christian beliefs about fundamental dimensions of reality, and many such believers study in universities. Yet within the universities themselves, there is almost no effort to relate these dimensions of human experience. For instance, most disciplines do not have schools of Christian

---

2. Carolyn J. Mooney, "Devout Professors on the Offensive," *Chronicle of Higher Education,* May 4, 1994, p. A 18, quoting Bruce Kuklick.

thought, in which scholars might wrestle with the relation of their faith to their learning. There is nothing comparable to feminist studies, which explore the implications of gender for other fields of study. Or contrast the role of Christians in academia to that of Marxists, who seem threatened with extinction in the rest of the nation's population, but have prominent representatives in many academic fields.

One common remark about the near absence of theological reference in modern mainstream university education is nonetheless to insist that this is just the way it should be. Particularly if Newman is being invoked to make this point, it is easy to understand such negative reactions. Newman's ideal in its pure form would be out of place in the multiversities of today. He was speaking as the rector of a small Catholic institution in which everyone could be expected to subscribe to the same theological tradition. In the diverse universities of today such expectations would seem wildly inappropriate.

Yet Newman's broader points should not be so easily dismissed, even in the setting of today's universities. Questions remain for such institutions. If contemporary universities are to be truly diverse and inclusive, should there not be room for scholars who explicitly relate the theological implications of their faith to the rest of their learning? Each of the major religious traditions, after all, includes some intellectually rigorous traditions informed by the insights of that faith. Should those traditions exist only as objects of study in contemporary universities?

The suggestion that today's universities be open to efforts to integrate religious traditions with learning needs to be qualified by a number of ground rules. Many people in every religion use faith as a substitute for learning, professing to rely for all their answers on religious authority. They are accordingly dogmatic and see the academic arena as another place to proselytize – attitudes that are not appropriate to the diverse modern academy. Most of modern education is funded by governments and is committed to serving a broad constituency of people of all traditional faiths or of none. In order for such people to get along and to have any fruitful intellectual interchange, they must agree to some common rules. These are the rules of modern scholarly discourse, which make it possible for people to weigh and evaluate another's evidence and arguments. They are analogous to the procedures in a court of law, where more or less disinterested third parties adjudicate disputes as objectively as possible. For an academic community to function effectively, it must allow some room for relatively dispassionate analysis in which all parties are open to some correction of their views. Preempting all discussion by appealing to religious authority or to evidence not accessible to others, or by one-sided preaching or proselytizing, undercuts the possibility of worthwhile exchanges in diverse academic settings.

In the late nineteenth and early twentieth centuries, as modern higher education was being defined, the logic of these considerations led to a much stronger rule regarding the place of religion in the academy. Many academics came to believe that any religion that appealed to an authority higher than the human mind should be banished.[3] This sentiment did not arise solely from intellectual considerations. It was also a strong reaction against Christianity's long dominance of higher education. As late as the time of Newman's university lectures in the mid-nineteenth century, it was still standard practice for universities and colleges to be governed by one Christian denomination or tradition, which controlled the selection of administrators and faculties. The Anglican universities of Oxford and Cambridge had gave religious tests for prospective students. University reformers in the following generation understandably wished to end this clerical control, and some progressive thinkers developed strong antagonisms to traditional Christianity. In the United States such sentiments were compounded by concerns that the government not promote one religion over another. De facto establishment of Protestant teaching at state-sponsored universities understandably seemed unfair to people of other faiths. As twentieth-century universities increasingly tried to serve more diverse communities, the virtual exclusion of religious concerns from scholarship seemed a good way to preserve equity and to help keep the peace.

All these considerations converged toward promoting what has become a very strong rule about religion in mainstream intellectual life – any religious expression is widely thought to be unscientific, unprofessional, and inappropriate.[4]

Religious Perspectives in Today's Universities?

The question remains, however, whether this strong rule, though its origins are understandable, is a good one. Is it not perhaps an overcorrection for what were real problems? Is there not a way to reopen a university's intel-

3. The exception often was theological study itself, which was usually isolated from the rest of the university, as in divinity schools.

4. I have explored this history in *The Soul of the American University: From Protestant Establishment to Established Nonbelief* (New York, 1994).

lectual life to explicit religious concerns while continuing to guard against religious excesses? Is there not, in other words, a middle way?

In answering these questions, we should recognize that religion has never been entirely absent from contemporary intellectual life, despite what some proponents of a strict separation might imagine. All scholarship takes place in the context of the social location, assumptions, prior commitments, and religious beliefs of the scholars. Religious commitments and assumptions are therefore inevitably present for scholars who are seriously religious. These commitments may be kept in the background and be undeveloped, but they are present nonetheless.

Especially in fields that have to do with human behavior, such prior assumptions and commitments, whatever the source, can have a major impact on scholarship. First, they often determine the subject one chooses to study. Second, they influence what one is likely to see as significant about the subject and to highlight in one's presentation. Third, they incline scholars toward some interpretive theories and against others. Fourth, in any moral judgments or evaluation, whether implicit or explicit, prior commitments are bound to have a significant impact.

Religiously based commitments are not unique in any of these influences. Feminist scholars recently have effectively emphasized the degree to which social location is likely to shape scholarly agendas and evaluation. A feminist scholar is more likely than a nonfeminist male to be concerned with women's activities, to accept theories that emphasize gender construction and roles, and to see the subordination of women as a primary moral concern. Marxist scholars likewise have typical interpretive emphases and moral judgments. So do neo-conservatives and old-style liberals. Whatever social or ideological locations are central to one's identity are likely to be refracted throughout one's scholarship as well.

This observation does not, however, license partisan scholarship that ignores standards of evidence and argument. As some representatives of each of the positions mentioned above have demonstrated, one can be bound by strong social or ideological commitments and still adhere to the highest scholarly standards. In the more technical parts of one's scholarship, or in fields that are largely technical or scientific, one's prior commitments are likely to have little appreciable impact, although they may still determine what is important. As scholarship moves into interpretation, especially in matters that involve human relationships, epistemology, and metaphysics, prior commitments come more into play. The best scholars, however, will still defend their viewpoints with evidence and arguments that are accessible to people of other outlooks. They will also treat their opponents and counterevidence fairly and with respect. Scholars who base their interpretations largely on appeals to the prejudices of their own social or ideological groups may have an impact on those groups, but will likely fail to communicate with, let alone persuade, scholars with widely varied interests and orientations in the modern academy.

Nor is it true that religious commitments and outlooks are unique among the prior commitments of scholars in that religious beliefs are not ultimately based on scientific empirical evidence, while other prior commitments are empirically based. It is true that religious beliefs typically rest on claims that, while they may be supported by considerable evidence, are not susceptible to scientific proof.[5] Many other beliefs that are essential to scholarship, however, have the same difficulty. Few of the cherished moral beliefs of contemporary scholars rest on scientific proof. The belief, for instance, that persons should be treated equally, regardless of race or gender, is not susceptible to scientific demonstration. It rests, rather, on the authority of communities that have accepted a tradition of valuing equality and also on the intuitions of people who have been shaped by those communities. Yet this belief serves as the moral premise for much of modern thought and as the point of departure for much scholarly interpretation. It is not true, then, that religious beliefs can be clearly separated from other beliefs on the basis that religious beliefs rest on appeals to authority and tradition, while acceptable academic beliefs must rest on scientific evidence alone. All scholars bring to their work many background assumptions that do not ultimately rest on any solid evidence. Although these beliefs do not themselves serve as evidence in mainstream scholarship, they shape its parameters. Religious beliefs can influence scholarship in just the same way.

Most philosophers and philosophers of science today have rejected philosophical "foundationalism," or the belief, often associated with the Enlightenment of the early modern era, that the pursuit of truth began with the determination of self-evident and unquestionable philosophical foundations, and then scientific method built up a body of beliefs on which all enlightened people must agree.[6] The idea of such foundations having

5. For a sophisticated philosophical defense of the intellectual justifications for believing in God, see William P. Alston, *Perceiving God: The Epistemology of Religious Experience* (Ithaca, 1991).

6. For reflections on the implications for Christian faith of the critiques of foundationalism, see Nicholas Wolterstorff, *Reason within the Bounds of Religion* (Grand Rapids, Mich., 1976); and Alvin Plantinga and Nicholas Wolterstorff, eds., *Faith and Rationality: Reason and Belief in God* (Notre Dame, 1983).

largely eroded, few scholars today are prepared to defend the thesis that a supposedly neutral scientific method is the highest standard for assessing what considerations are legitimate for scholarship that deals with the human condition. Rather, scholars by and large accept the assumptions on which scholarly subcommunities can agree. On more technical questions, of course, there is wide agreement. But the most important dimensions of the human experience have proven to be not susceptible to technical analysis. The more scholarship deals with high-level interpretive issues, particularly in the humanities and the social sciences, the more it will be divided among parties shaped by various prior commitments, which no scientific method can adjudicate.

It is particularly striking that even some of the most outspoken opponents of the old foundationalism persist in defending its achievement of restricting religious discourse in public life. The anti-foundationalist philosopher, Richard Rorty, for instance, insists that the public sphere ought to be kept thoroughly secular. His argument is that an appeal to a religious revelation is no argument in a public setting where not everyone accepts that revelation. "If," he goes on, "you can give some reasons that don't have to do with revelation, then the question of whether or not your belief is held because of your religion is irrelevant."[7] That is surely not the case, however, unless one is thinking about arguments in a technical philosophical sense. A Mennonite scholar may offer some good arguments against warfare, and a Catholic scholar may offer good arguments against abortion, but in neither case is the religious faith irrelevant to the scholarship. The religious commitments, rather, are important factors that both religious and nonreligious people ought to know about and to reflect upon. It is simply not true that the only relevant way religion can enter into public discourse is as a bald appeal to specially revealed authority.

A Bad Rule

The question is, then, in the contemporary academic setting, should religiously shaped commitments be treated differently from those arising from other sources? During the century following Newman's lectures, the opinion came to prevail that religious perspectives should be in a special category. Aside from the political motivations for such a rule, the intellec-

7. Richard Rorty as quoted in "Towards a Liberal Utopia: An Interview with Richard Rorty," *Times Literary Supplement,* June 24, 1994, p. 14.

tual rationale was based largely on the Enlightenment view that the highest form of truth was supported by scientific evidence and empirical data. This outlook preserved the old foundationalist dream that modern scholarship would produce an ever-expanding body of truth that all right-thinking people should agree on. As an organizing principle for modern higher education, it also had the practical advantage of supplying standards for truth on which people of many persuasions could agree. If they all would suspend or subordinate their sectarian religious beliefs, they could then work together and treat reality as the product of natural forces susceptible to empirical investigation. So the rule gradually emerged that invoking explicit religious belief would be wholly out of place when one was working as a professional member of this modern academic community. Once the rule was established, few mainstream scholars were inclined to re-examine it, even after the intellectual climate changed.

This rule suffers from a number of defects. First, limiting academic inquiry to that which could be studied on a purely naturalistic empirical basis never fulfilled the dream that higher education would eventually unify people on the important questions regarding society and the universe. As academia currently demonstrates, nonreligious schools of interpretation can be just as sectarian and dogmatic as religious thought. Although that does not justify religious dogmatism as a substitute for serious intellectual interchange, it does point out that sectarianism is not unique to religiously based views.

Second, religious commitments, as well as other prior commitments not scientifically based, could not be entirely eliminated from either scholarship or teaching. The academy did put strong pressures on religious people, however, to revise their religious beliefs in light of considerations susceptible to empirical analysis. If some scholars nonetheless persisted in more traditional religious beliefs, they were pressured to keep quiet about those beliefs, view them as personal, and subordinate them to the standards and interests of the dominant scholarly community as much as possible. Thus, although religious perspectives still operate in the academy, they have been put into marginal and often denigrated positions, even though there is no clear intellectual warrant for doing so.

Third, the rule arbitrarily privileges certain types of empirically based knowledge. It rests not on conclusions drawn from science itself, but is rather a premise or working assumption: that the more purely naturalistically one regards reality, the closer one gets to universal truths. That assumption has been immensely compelling to many modern people, because it works extremely well in technical matters. One can settle to the satisfaction of any reasonable person innumerable issues – how certain natural processes work or the most efficient way to get a job done or to save lives. The value of these accomplishments is immense. Moreover, scholars can also collect data and discover patterns of human behavior. And they must always be willing to test their claims against the available empirical evidence. It does not follow, however, that a purely naturalistic empirically based method produces the highest form of truth, by which everything else ought to be tested.

A worldview, or even a set of working principles, in which truth is *limited* to the empirically verified turns out to be constricted. It distorts reality, highlighting only one of its dimensions as worthy of serious consideration. It credits only one way of human knowing as worthy of full trust. If many forces in reality are not entirely susceptible to naturalistic inquiry, then the scientific outlook may, for all its accomplishments, limit human perceptions of reality. The question of spiritual realities aside, many of the most interesting and important subjects dealt with in academia, those involving creativity, the unique aspects of human biography and history, or questions of justice and morality, are not known best through scientific procedures alone.

In the current academic climate, then, there seems little intellectual justification for perpetuating the rule that explicit religious expression should be discouraged in respectable scholarship. Furthermore, many philosophers of science argue that scientific orthodoxies are determined by dominant communities of scientists who are, in turn, shaped in part by their social contexts. In the humanities, postmodern modes of thought, for all their excesses, point out the hopelessness of establishing an intellectual consensus, except on technical matters.

In such a setting, it seems only fair that religiously based viewpoints should not be discriminated against as a class. Rather, those that are intellectually responsible, and follow the various rules of evidence, argument, and civility necessary to scholarly interchange, should be encouraged as legitimate parts of a pluralistic intellectual enterprise. If universities are to be consistent in their pluralism, they cannot single out religious subcommunities as those who must keep silent about or even disregard their most cherished beliefs.

It is sometimes objected, however, that if religious perspectives already implicitly shape some respected scholarship, why is there any need for change? The answer is that the pressures against explicit religious expression in modern universities have inhibited and constricted the explorations of the relation of faith to learning. Even though religiously based commitments and assumptions may have a real impact on scholarship, even most religiously committed scholars are only dimly aware of what that impact might be. John Henry Newman saw as essential to a true university the exploration of the interrelationships of all types of human knowledge, including the theological. In the modern university the relation of the theological to other dimensions has remained a vastly underdeveloped field of inquiry. Scholars whose religion may play a primary role in shaping their viewpoints seldom identify themselves as religious, so people of similar faiths can hardly develop communities of discourse. Outside of theology itself, and recently in the field of philosophy, it has been difficult to identify any body of scholarship marked by religious perspectives.

What Difference Does it Make?

Another frequent question is what difference might theological perspectives make in scholarship in other fields? One example from the major theological traditions will illustrate. A fruitful academic inquiry would be the question of what are the scholarly implications of the belief of Christianity, Judaism, and Islam that God is "the Creator of the heavens and the earth." The affirmation does not settle the question of how God may have created, whether by immediate fiat or by means of natural evolutionary processes. Even with that question left open, the belief that the universe is ultimately the product of an intelligence should make a real difference in many issues. Particularly when natural science, pushed to its limits, moves into metaphysical speculation about the structures of reality (such as, what had to precede the big bang, or is the universe a self-contained entity), this theological affirmation might legitimately affect one's theorizing. Belief in the divine should not limit inquiry into the natural order, but it may caution against regarding the best current natural explanation as ultimately the best one.

It is outside of natural science, however, that the belief in a creator may have the strongest impact. If religious scholars reflect the implications of that belief, it can have an important bearing on what sorts of theories they accept or reject. They might, for instance, be disinclined to view the development of human moral ideals as simply constructions necessary to meet the evolutionary needs of particular cultures. Rather, while recognizing that functional dimension, they might also be inclined to view humans, as creations of God, as embodying, however imperfectly, some moral sense that deals with a right and wrong created into the scheme of things.

Morality, then, would be a social construction, but more as well. The study of human history or of anthropology might thus be part of the often flawed human quest for the good. Such a viewpoint differs in tone from that of much current scholarship, which assumes that "the good" is what works best for one's social group in a particular cultural setting.

Or in approaching the epistemological questions raised by postmodernism, the scholar who was committed to a belief that God created our minds and the reality we encounter might be less inclined to see human knowing as purely relative to one's community or as controlled by those who hold cultural power. We cannot immediately determine what differences would result from including a belief in divine creation in one's thoughts on this point, but it should be clear that the theological issue would provide an intriguing agenda for scholarly reflection.

Religious people take widely differing positions regarding the implications of their beliefs for the rest of their scholarship. So saying that their theological beliefs will bear on their scholarship is not at all to say that they will introduce pat answers drawn from authority. They will, like other scholars, bring some important assumptions into their scholarship. But in most fields they will challenge some of the reigning unproven assumptions in contemporary scholarship. They thus introduce new inquiries and the critical perspectives that can lead to creativity. For example, they might launch effective critiques of the cult of the self, which is so pervasive in popular culture and in academic culture as well.[8] Since religious people often differ among themselves on such questions, such cultural critiques might lead to appraisals of their own religious traditions as well. During the cold war, for instance, Christian scholars sometimes spoke out strongly against their own churches' easy identifications of Christianity with American patriotism.

The varieties of religious people today also help guarantee that consideration of theologically based concerns would not cut off debate or burden campuses with a new religiously based orthodoxy. A Mennonite scholar who teaches about the Vietnam War will probably have an approach different from that of a neo-conservative Catholic, even though each adheres to the best conventions of historical scholarship in presenting evidence and arguments. Each will speak from a point of view shaped by theological concerns, and each may want to reflect on that factor. Similarly, a Jewish scholar writing about the founding of the state of Israel will in all likelihood

8. For example, see Paul Vitz, *Psychology as Religion: The Cult of Self-Worship*, 2d ed. (Grand Rapids, Mich., 1994).

have a perspective very different from that of an Islamic scholar. It would be misleading for such scholars to hide the religious backgrounds that shape their opinions.

The same considerations apply to effective teaching, which involves sensitivity to the beliefs and outlooks of one's audience. But there is no easy formula for determining when identifying one's own religiously based concerns would be appropriate. Some deeply religious teachers will, for pedagogical reasons or because they are addressing diverse audiences, keep their commitments in the background, at least for a time. On the other hand, there is a case for being open about one's religious commitments, simply in the name of truth in advertising. If teachers reveal the major sources of their own perspectives, students are in a better position to weigh and evaluate them. In pluralistic settings, of course, it is always important to make clear that students are not expected to share a teacher's prejudices and that students' own beliefs will be treated with respect.

Even in mainstream universities, then, there should be some room for academic reflection on the implications of theological commitments, so long as that is done in a civil and academically responsible manner.

The Alternative of Religiously Defined Schools

In diverse multiversities, there are serious practical and political limits to how extensively such theological reflection is likely to be pursued, so we should be asking whether contemporary higher education ought not to encourage more institutions that are shaped predominantly by one religious tradition. These would be much closer to what Newman originally had in mind as his prototype for a university, although they would not necessarily be as homogeneous as was his Catholic University in Dublin.

Such institutions have always existed, but the trend today is to discourage them or to treat them as second class. Many people assume that if a college or a university defines itself by its faculty's religious commitments, it is to that extent inferior. Intellectual inquiry and creativity, it is often said, are best fostered in diversity. Governments and accrediting agencies often put subtle, or not so subtle, pressures on such schools to become more open and more like other schools.

Such concerns can easily obscure some major advantages of encouraging the option of schools with religiously defined faculties. In an era when so many faculties seem to present a cacophony of opinions, there ought to be room for more unified alternatives. Much of contemporary higher education is constricted by the demands of diversity, which can actually lower the level of discussion. With little agreement on fundamental issues, discussions often do not proceed much beyond debates about methodologies. At the same time, diverse institutions have their own orthodoxies on certain issues. Lacking intellectual principles that can command general assent, they tend to be controlled by the politics of not giving offense. Some subjects are not discussed or explored. The neglect of theological perspectives in such institutions is only one case in point.

At religiously defined institutions, on the other hand, not every discussion has to go back to square one. Long traditions of debate on fundamental questions allow current discussion to proceed at levels not easily attainable in more diverse settings. Such traditions need by no means be intellectually stagnant or lacking in creativity. Unlike most other discourse in universities today, they involve the wisdom of many past eras and the intellectual fashions of today. Such encounters may generate intense intellectual excitement and creativity. They deal with existentially alive and momentous questions faced by people who have commitments to the wisdom of other eras but who are trying to live responsibly in today's intellectual and moral climate. John Henry Newman himself is an example of the intellectual stature possible among those who identify with a religious tradition and are dedicated to resolving the tensions among the insights of the past and the present. The contemporary world loses much when it reduces the communities of scholars wrestling with the meaning of a tradition. While modern universities pride themselves on their intellectual diversity, few have room for serious engagement with the diversity of the ages.

Of course exciting intellectual environments do not always obtain at religiously defined schools, where strict orthodoxies and close-mindedness can cut off discussion. Especially in this era when the more conservative religious heritages feel culturally beleaguered and when constituencies are looking for easy answers, religious institutions can be narrow and restrictive. Nonetheless, there is a viable point of creative tension between maintaining essential loyalty to a religious heritage and allowing vigorous and creative debate within that heritage.

So with respect to religion in higher education, we should be promoting a broader sort of pluralism than has prevailed in the past generation – that is, pluralism *among* as well as *within* institutions. Today the overwhelming tendency is to allow varieties of ethnic, racial, and gender-based voices equal place within institutions. These legitimate concerns should be expanded to include diverse religious perspectives as well. The downside, however, is that the current pluralist ideals, with their homogenizing formulas for inclusiveness, tend to make every institution of higher education essentially the same. In such a setting, no tradition is wholly free to be itself, there is little engagement of past and present, and often the level of discourse must remain low in order to accommodate all the potential disagreements. A healthier concept of pluralism would recognize that distinct communities need strong educational institutions if they are to survive, flourish, and pass their ideals from one generation to the next.

John Henry Newman's idea for a university took for granted that churches need vigorous educational institutions and that society needs the church. In the intervening century and a half the intellectual lives of churches have been inhibited by struggles simply to survive as recognized voices in modern academic settings. The resulting defensive battles limited the development of some of Newman's fundamental ideas – in particular, that of exploring all academic disciplines within contexts that explicitly include theological perspectives.

Today many of the intellectual forces associated with attacks on established Christianity and with the rise of materialistic worldviews based on natural scientific definitions of intellectual life have weakened. Visions of twentieth-century progress and unity brought about by the spread of a universal science have proven illusory. Perhaps the time has come, then, to take up once again Newman's academic agenda, which includes theological as well as other perspectives. Not everything that Newman proposed seems viable as we approach the twenty-first century, and Newman himself might not be happy with the rather modest proposals presented here to save something of his essential program. Newman worked in an era when established churches were taken for granted, and he had a high regard for the theological authority of the Roman Catholic Church. Nonetheless, the essence of his theologically oriented agenda should challenge people of the twenty-first century seriously to reconsider some of their assumptions about education and theology.

The Paradox of Self in
The Idea of a University

SARA CASTRO-KLARÉN

Whereas the contemporary university has become the site for what one author has termed "culture wars" and another the "battleground of the curriculum," the content of the curriculum assumes a smaller place in Newman's *Idea of a University* than one might expect. Except for the key issue of the inclusion of theology, Newman seems not to believe that the curricular character of his university is especially problematical.

Yet Newman's lectures represent an important point of departure for the current controversy partly because of his assertions, partly because of silences, and partly because of the remarkable intellectual tensions inherent in his prose. Newman calls for the teaching of "universal knowledge," (3) which implies a boundless world of instruction and learning, but he then establishes numerous boundaries. Newman presents himself to his Irish Catholic audience (and later readers) as the voice of a universal church and of English literary culture. Though a convert from the dominant religion in England to a minority religion, he does not defend the interests of cultural or religious minorities. While speaking to a nationalistically minded audience, he does not urge that recognition or development of national identity have a place in university education. Nonetheless, Newman's own language and arguments are complex and display inner doubts hidden within his frequently sweeping assertions. Indeed, if we take Newman literally, he becomes an informed and relevant voice for our contemporary debates on multiculturalism, the ethics of advocacy, the literary canon, and "free inquiry" itself.

I

From the opening of *The Idea of a University,* Newman *struggles* to clarify what he means by a university education. He struggles because he admires the education he received at Anglican Oxford, and at the same time he wants to please both the Roman Catholic Church authorities and the Irish

laity who themselves disagreed about the character of the new Irish Catholic University. He wants to uphold many traditional English and European
intellectual authorities, yet he knows that his own quest from Anglicanism
to Catholicism had involved challenging traditional religious views, and
that his ideal of a liberal education pursued for its own sake involved
directly criticizing a society committed to useful knowledge.

Newman's opening argument for the necessary inclusion of Roman
Catholic theology in the university challenges the presuppositions of his
audience and the tradition of university education in Britain. Such instruction existed in no other British university at the time. Newman's repeated
efforts to equate theological and scientific truth, and thus to justify a university chair for Roman Catholic theology, also jars many present-day readers
who no longer regard theology as the science of sciences. Newman's assertion, however, was a radical claim for a new subject – indeed, a minority
subject – and for legitimating religious ideas, which British society generally spurned. Newman's argument for including Roman Catholic theology
because the university is a place of "universal knowledge" is in part, and
paradoxically, the same argument by which later subjects, such as those
related to multiculturalism, have often been introduced into the conservative world of university education. Newman's radicalism needs to be recognized because he cloaked it in very conservative rhetoric and almost immediately retreated from the radical implications of his argument.

Although urging the presence of theology because of its special status as
part of "universal knowledge," Newman himself quickly circumscribes
that universality. He does not take *universal* to stand for the full geographical expanse of the globe, nor does he mean it to include all (other) knowledge. At the core, "universal knowledge" is the eternal knowledge the
Roman Catholic Church claims on matters human and divine. Education as
a process of critical inquiry into reality or into such questions as how did the
world get to be the way it is said to be? or into the constitution of knowledge
is *not* what Newman understands when he speaks of "universal knowledge." Newman in this regard truncates the full implications of his own
argument. Just such intellectual and cultural truncation, whether advocated
by Newman or others, is being questioned and often rejected in the present-
day university.

Yet, there exists a real tension in Newman's language and argument. He
does see his university as an institution endowed with an "intellectual, not
moral" objective (3). Newman's effort to disentangle the moral charge of
his teaching, his rhetoric of "universal knowledge," and his implicit recognition of modes of knowledge different from those of the Church become

the knotted core for his disquisition on the curriculum. Newman wants to protect Catholicism, but he also wants many subjects not related to it to be included in the university.

As is true for many today, Newman's problem stems from his unwilling-ness or incapacity to confront how inextricably curriculum and cultural politics are bound, especially as related to his claims for theology. He argues, "Revealed Religion [channeled through the teaching of the Roman Catholic Church] furnishes facts to the other sciences, which those sciences, left to themselves, would never reach." He continues, "It is not then that Catholics are afraid of human knowledge, but that they are proud of divine knowledge" (59). Newman would thus privilege Roman Catholic teaching over other religious and philosophical outlooks, but he is reluctant to say that exactly. On some occasions he seems to say that ideas from literature and science may have their own presence, even when contrary to theological ideas, so long as they do not undermine the moral ethos of Catholicism. Newman desires an expansive world of learning, but one in which there are limits to speculation and to the social and political implications of new ideas. Our own university visions are also often blurred by a similar reluctance to admit the uncomfortable and foreboding mix of "freely" pursued knowledge and the power struggles of competing cultural interest groups.

Newman articulates his sense of proper limitation of inquiry and private criticism by frequently contrasting Roman Catholicism and Protestantism. His concept of Protestantism is more cultural than theological. Newman contends that for Protestants, faith is, "not an acceptance of revealed doctrine, not an act of the intellect, but a feeling, an emotion, an affection, an appetency; and, as this view of Faith obtained, so was the connexion of Faith with Truth and Knowledge more and more either forgotten or denied" (30–31). Newman boldly counters this Protestant outlook, which has come to inform many parts of Western culture that have no direct relationship to Protestant churches. He reasserts that Catholic belief is not a matter individuals can decide for themselves, nor is it a matter of habit, custom, loyalty, or law. For Newman and others of his tradition, Catholicism constitutes a body of knowledge into which an individual must be carefully initiated by learned teachers. It is not to be pursued by open, private inquiry.

Newman wishes to educate his students in the use of reason, but he wants to limit the scope of their criticism. Consequently Newman sees a liberal education that holds religion to be a branch of literature or aesthetics as an inimical force that erodes the hegemonic truth claims of the Catholic faith. Further, Newman sees an implicit analogy between what he regards as the anarchical state of Protestant culture, which had spurned Catholic truth, and the intellectual life of the modern world with few, if any, cultural authorities. The university, by teaching both religious faith and a cultural tradition, could prevent cultural disorder.[1]

University teaching, understood as a kind of apostolic and cultural mission, is thus a grave business. Its work, inasmuch as it transmits secular knowledge informed and made uniform by a rigorous system of belief, reaches beyond the academy linking Church and Society. It reinforces the ground for a common culture and for all truth claims about the world. In Newman's plan for a Roman Catholic university we can see all the conditions necessary for the production of Gramsci's "traditional intellectual," the social group that mediates and reproduces the political and cultural power relations between the dominant and subaltern classes. As Gramsci has pointed out, "The education system is the instrument through which intellectuals of various levels are elaborated."[2] These intellectuals set the rules by which knowledge is authorized or excluded from the educational curriculum or the public sphere. Newman implicitly recognizes the political character of his argument, but he averts his eyes from the political implications, pretending to deal with a purely "intellectual" problem. In the present-day university, by contrast, many would argue that "purely intellectual problems" are almost invariably political or filled with political implications.

Within Newman's world of reference, present-day American universities are culturally, if not denominationally, "Protestant." In today's academic and wider public sphere, Luther's idea of faith as a personal, private confidence in the saving power of grace, which originally gained ascendancy in a religious form, has now manifested itself in a secular form. People in the United States generally take it for granted that faith or religious belief is an individual and private matter or choice, which in and of itself cannot constitute the basis for public policy. But it has not always been that way. Only well into this century (1941) did the Supreme Court ruling

1. Perceiving similar challenges to the principles that authorize a "common" culture – the ideal of "doing as one likes" – Matthew Arnold, who had listened to Newman's sermons at Oxford, argued in *Culture and Anarchy* (1869) for the need to contain "spiritual anarchy" with the inculcation of values and sensibilities of the *belles lettres*. In that sense Arnold sought from culture what Newman thought possible only through religion.

2. David Forgacs, ed., *An Antonio Gramsci Reader: Selected Writings, 1916–1935* (New York, 1988), p. 305.

on conscientious objectors put secular and religious beliefs on the same footing by defining religion as any system of beliefs sincerely held by individuals.[3] The ruling not only acknowledged the authority of the individual's conscience and consciousness, a tenet fundamental to Protestant faiths, it also undergirds present assertions of the integrity and particular economy of different cultures and cultural practices. Therefore, for most Americans neither individuals nor separate cultures can be held subject to any self-proclaimed universalizing reason. Today *all* individuals and *all* cultures are theoretically local. Newman for his part regarded with fear and contempt the constant and pervasive production of local or schismatic groups. To such proliferation of difference he opposes the Catholic concept of the special relation of faith and reason.

Newman was afraid of a multiplicity of religious or philosophical or cultural outlooks competing on the basis of equality and on the subjective choices of students. He was fearful of religious schism. This view stands far removed from the contemporary secular modern university. Throughout its history, the United States has been the site of ongoing schisms in religion because of the deep Protestant roots of its culture. Americans retained habits of mind learned in Protestant churches long after regular church attendance declined. Consequently, it is not surprising that as higher education during this century often became a kind of secular religion, education itself should display a similarly schismatic character.

The truth of the matter is, as J. D. Hunter argues in *Culture Wars* (1991), that the struggles over curriculum, the role of intellectuals, and the specific historical circumstances implied in the production of knowledge are profoundly political matters. They are pieces in games of personal and community self-definition and endurance. Hunter observed that in previous cultural debates in the United States, "underlying the disagreements [between Catholics, Protestants, and Jews], there were basic agreements about the order of life in community and nation – agreements forged by biblical symbols and imagery."[4] Today, for many, the Bible is just another document, and binding moral authority resides in personal experience or scientific rationality, not even the rationality of *other* cultures. This intense cultural subjectivity is the source of the current culture wars. It was just such subjectivity in all its forms that Newman perceived and so distrusted in his own day. He found it inherent in Protestant culture and in the drive toward

3. See James Davidson Hunter, *Culture Wars: The Struggle to Define America* (New York, 1991), pp. 258–59.

4. Ibid., p. 42.

useful scientific knowledge. It was to overcome that disunity that he raised the banner of a Catholic universality and praised the manners and literature of an imagined genteel English culture.

There is a close relationship between Newman's restriction on universal learning and his anxiety over cultural Protestantism and the distinction he draws between teaching and research. For Newman the university is an instrument for the diffusion and extension of knowledge, not for pursuing knowledge that might challenge the wisdom of the ages, because he fears the "usurpation" by the sciences of religious truth (74). The teaching function in his university consolidates and disseminates truth, which research, with its emphasis on open inquiry and private criticism, may eventually undermine. Newman would not halt research, but neither would he give it a significant place in his institution. Newman feared that the ever-growing purview of new critical knowledge, especially in the physical sciences and the humanities, would displace religion and religious faith. By restricting the university largely to teaching, Newman was establishing a climate in which knowledge would appear to be more nearly a settled affair rather than an expanding world. Thus Newman urges that the university be a place of universal knowledge so as to include theology, but restricts its mission primarily to teaching so as to offer a modest protection to theology within its walls.

Newman's limitation on the impulse toward new knowledge and new ways of thinking constricts the experience of both the teacher and the student. It leads to what Paulo Freire has criticized as the "banking concept of education," whereby with the teacher as narrator, "education becomes an act of 'depositing.' " The teacher is the expositor of hardened knowledge. The student, by contrast, passively receives the teacher's elaboration, inclusion, exclusion, interpretation, and disposition of knowledge. This concept of education reinforces the hierarchy of authority in which the student is the neophyte and the teacher the fully initiated believer or master. This approach projects onto the student a state of ignorance prior to the encounter with the teacher. It in effect negates education and knowledge as processes of inquiry in which the student recognizes his or her own individual experience and critical self-consciousness. The teacher in turn cannot learn and refashion knowledge from the student's experience and discovery, because knowledge is assumed as largely fixed and thus open inquiry by either teacher or student is discouraged. Many would agree with Freire, in contrast to Newman, that "apart from inquiry, individuals cannot be truly human."[5]

5. Paulo Freire, *Pedagogy of the Oppressed* (New York, 1993), p. 53.

II

Even though Newman avoids direct discussion of the political relations of knowledge to power and to culture, his arguments about the curriculum revolve around this silent but vibrant concern. In the preface, Newman speaks with his most authentic voice when he protests the conditions under which Irish Catholics have been educated – or, rather, denied an education that affirms their history and culture. Here he comes as close as he ever will to calling for a *national* Catholic university or, rather, for the recognition of differing cultural needs on the part of students when he states,

> Robbed, oppressed, and thrust aside, Catholics in these islands have not been in a condition for centuries to attempt the sort of education which is necessary for the man of the world, the statesman, the landholder, or the opulent gentleman. Their legitimate stations, duties, employments, have been taken from them, and the qualifications withal, social and intellectual, which are necessary for . . . [their] reversal. The time is come when this moral disability must be removed. Our desideratum is . . . command over our own powers. (7)

Newman's call for reversing the intellectual and thus political handicap imposed on Irish and English Catholics by an Anglican university system recognizes the cultural and political interests of a subaltern class. Repositioning the English and Irish Catholics' claims to an equal and yet different status in the political hierarchy not only brings Newman's claims to universal knowledge full circle – acknowledgment of the different knowledge needs of the oppressed Catholics – but also connects the actual concerns of his argument – a liberal education capable of connecting, without hostility, with the needs of a Catholic minority – to our own contemporary culture wars. Those who today think about education in America and in much of the rest of the world cannot, like Newman, quietly avoid or simply mention in passing the question of what are the educational needs of those social groups who until the past few decades were largely left out of the educational process or whose cultures were ignored or even disparaged in the education they received.

For that brief moment in the preface, Newman directly confronts the needs of his Irish audience for social and political equality and cultural authenticity. But he quickly retreats from that recognition in order to serve the Church hierarchy that oversees his university and to reassert the dominance of his own familiar English culture. Newman cannot extend his empathy to cultures beyond Europe. In this regard his views replicate those of previous generations of Europeans and foreshadow those of some in the academy today who find it difficult to appreciate unfamiliar human civilizations. Newman disparaged the ways non-European peoples have built complex and durable societies. Even though he realizes that each civilization is *local* and *discrete,* this recognition does not even remotely suggest to him parity between self – European Christianity – and others. Instead, he assumes and accepts the difference, so he can dismiss the Chinese or the Aztecs as irrelevant to any of his concerns with "universal knowledge," art, or literature. For him only one civilization is worthy of the name, and that is European Christianity with its peerless intellectual accomplishments, alphabetic writing, the book. Newman's assumptions may seem uninformed or imperialist or racist. Even if we remove religion from his hierarchy of values, we can still recognize the uncompromising Victorian belief in the superiority of Western culture.

Here it is important to quote Newman in full, because his characterization of other civilizations, let alone "ethnic peoples," fuels the culture and curricular wars in academia today:

> I am not denying of course the civilization of the Chinese, for instance, though it be not our civilization; but it is a huge, stationary, unattractive, morose civilization. Nor do I deny a civilization to the Hindoos, nor to the ancient Mexicans. . . . [B]ut each of these races has its own civilization, as *separate* from one another as from ours. I do not see how they can be all brought under *one* idea. Each stands by itself, as if the other were not; each is local; many of them are temporary; none of them will bear a comparison with the Society and the Civilization which I have described as alone having a claim to those names. (167–168); emphasis added)

Newman had no difficulty recognizing otherness, and he was sensible enough not to lump *them* all together. But he saw nothing held in common with them either. Each is separate in its own alienated strangeness. He is so profoundly taken with the differences, that he readily concedes and accepts the limitations of the universal claims of Christianity. Each segment of humanity stands alone, impermeable by the other's version of humanity, but only Christianity can claim the universal prize for itself. Radicalized, this recognition of cultural impermeability can and has led to the logic of imperialism, segregation, and apartheid.

Though today we readily associate racism with nineteenth-century European colonialism in Africa, India, and Asia and with the treatment of the Amerindians of North America, similar notions of "racial" and cultural impermeability characterized the earlier Spanish conquest and colonialization of the Amerindian civilizations. Newman's attitudes in that regard long predate him. Those attitudes may replicate themselves in contemporary society. The terms of the famous debate between the humanist Juan Ginés de Sepúlveda (1490?–1574) and the Dominican Bartolomé de Las Casas (1474–1566) provide a good example of the ideology of alterity that has accompanied European expansion since its earliest days. This debate was held in 1550 before and between the highest exponents of Spanish theology and in no less a place than the court of Charles V. Its purpose was to settle the question of the day: Were the inhabitants of this hemisphere, the "Indians," human beings or not?

Las Casas used a good part of the European arsenal of knowledge to disprove the "truth" Sepúlveda constructed out of the European archive of alterity. Sepúlveda contended that the Indians, despite their civilizations, were infrahuman. Las Casas had not only visited this hemisphere, but had actually spent a considerable part of his life in the Caribbean and in Meso-America; Sepúlveda could not claim a similar eyewitness authority. However, within Christianity's exclusive claim to reason and civilization, Sepúlveda's view was to prove the more long-lasting and influential. The humanist saw the fundamental difference in the very institutions of everyday life and culture that were supposed to demonstrate the similarities between Europe and the Aztecs. Sepúlveda explained:

> For in the same institutions I see proof on the contrary of the rudeness, the barbarism, and the inherently slavish nature of these people. For the possession of inhabitations, of a fairly rational mode of life, and of a kind of commerce is something that natural necessity itself induces, and only serves to prove that they are not bears and monkeys and are not completely devoid of reason. But on the other hand, they have no private property in their state, and they cannot dispose of or bequeath to their heirs their houses or fields. . . . Such in sum, are the dispositions and customs of these little men – barbarous, uncivilized, inhumane.

Thus, Newman's sense of European superiority and uniqueness is but one link in a long chain that included not only Roman Catholic observers. In 1748 the Scottish philosopher and historian David Hume generalized Sepúlveda's dictum even further when he wrote that he believed that "all other species of men to be naturally inferior to the whites." Hume founded his belief on the "fact" that there "have been no ingenious manufactures amongst them, no arts, no science."[6]

In this respect the intellectual basis of Newman and those who earlier championed European superiority was white Europeans' *possession* of the very kind of useful knowledge that Newman so vehemently spurned in his university lectures. Newman urged that his university resist including useful knowledge, but his evaluations of who were and were not civilized peoples outside of Europe were based on the *possession* of such knowledge. This outlook is all the more pernicious here, because the English often disparaged the Irish for having not embraced the spirit of improvement based on useful knowledge.

As elaborated by both Sepúlveda and Hume, the value assigned to a particular people or culture depended on the presence or absence of alphabetic writing and the production of books. Once again Sepúlveda anticipates Newman and Hume when in the same passage on the Aztecs he "compares" or rather disqualifies pictographs as writing: "These little men, who not only are devoid of learning but do not even have a written language; who preserve no monuments of their history, aside from some vague and obscure reminiscence of past events, represented by means of certain paintings . . . have no written laws but only barbaric customs and institutions."[7] Such reiterated blindness regarding any other system for "writing" the past and the law can be explained only by the indissoluble link forged in Christendom between culture and the book, the sacred-secular order believed to emanate from the writing of the past. In view of this powerful link, all other knowledge must be proven to lack in authority, despite ample evidence for the efficacy of other knowledges and writing systems. Just as Sepúlveda spoke derisively of Aztec pictographs, another of his famous contemporaries, Bishop Diego de Landa (1524–1579), learned to read glyphs from a Maya priest, only to proceed to the zealous burning of more than 40,000 Maya "books." He not only assumed the separation of knowledges (authorized/forbidden or nonexistent), but his actions confirmed all

6. Juan Ginés de Sepúlveda, *Tratado sobre las justas causas de la querra contra las Indias* (Mexico City, 1941), as quoted in Benjamin F. Keen, ed., *Latin American Civilization* (Boulder, 1986), p. 68; David Hume, "Of National Characters," in *The Philosophical Works of David Hume,* ed. Thomas Higg Green and Thomas Hodgte Grose, 4 vols. (Darmstadt, 1964), 3: 252 n. 1.

7. Sepúlveda, quoted in Keen, ed., *Latin American Civilization,* p. 68.

canonical distinctions later drawn by the high priests of literature, taste, or cultural identity politics.

Newman's troubled disquisition on the place of books in the English academy, his ambivalence about the English literary canon and a yet-to-be, maybe impossible, Irish Catholic literature in English, echo those attitudes and situate him in the middle of the current battle about books and the debates over electronic representations and other knowledges. For Newman the book is the locus of learning and communication, but only those books of which he culturally or religiously approves. He cannot imagine or appreciate learning from another culture. In that respect his mode of universal knowledge is curiously limited. Yet his emphasis on *the idea of the universal* lingers with all its other extensive meanings, so modern teachers and students may follow his urging to universality and go far beyond him to appreciate cultures and civilizations he disparaged. He would not have wished to make that journey, but he nonetheless pointed the way.

With unusual keenness Newman considers briefly the relation between literature and national identity. In a few sentences he states with forceful clarity the political content and the function of literature in the life, growth, and health of a national project. Newman realizes, as we do not, that literature represents all of life, not just aesthetic feeling, not just great oratory, and not just "a way with" language. Literature, he writes, is to mankind as "autobiography is to the individual" (157). Because of the ample scope of literature and precisely because it is a form of knowledge, "Literature stands related to Man as Science stands to Nature; it is his history" (157). Yet Newman has great misgivings about its location and allocation in the university curriculum. His reservations again harbor the seeds for our own culture wars. If literature were only a question of *belles lettres* and a canon established to suit the taste of an elite, in a democratic society members of other groups could similarly dismiss or ignore the "classics" and read what their (inferior, strange, exotic) taste craves. For Newman, however, literature contains powerful, beguiling, pleasure-filled, all-inclusive cultural representations, which themselves produce our understanding of life. The master narratives – novels, plays, poems, films – do indeed stand for the meaning of history.

Newman does not sustain the logic of his own powerful finding. As on previous occasions, he removes his gaze from the difficulty of his own insight. Having chosen the unthreatening position of advocate of a mistreated yet faithful "minority," he cannot press his argument with full force. He seems unable to show or even to understand how a canon of Protestant "classics" inherently diminishes the Irish Catholics, who have been cast in the role of the other (Aztec?) in order to draw the difference. What Newman faces when he longs for, but abandons, the project of a Catholic literature in English is the possibility of a critical and subversive literature that would not only rewrite the English language (as American Black literature does) but would also challenge it and his own "universal" claims for it. Consequently, Newman settles for advocating a university education that will allow the Irish to compete socially with the English elite but that will not clear any space for cultural competition or self-agency. The Irish Catholic, as a liberally educated person, must become the very model of an English gentleman. Newman cannot bring himself to imagine that there might be a distinctly Irish Catholic gentleman with his own religious and cultural characteristics. The Irish may ape or emulate their English betters, but they may not embody their own breed of gentility, qualities the English might do well to imitate.

Here is the problem of the multicultural challenge. Can higher education teach students about a multiplicity of cultural awarenesses? Can this be achieved without mere relativity? Can that multiplicity of cultural awarenesses and emphathies result not in cultural schism but in a new, always already multiple sense of being human? Newman cannot carry us to those questions, but it is clear that because he feared this kind of world, he was wholly aware of its possibility.

III

Newman fears moral, cultural, religious relativism as do many academic commentators today who resist the impact of the various modes of diversity on university campuses and in university curricula. To oppose such relativism Newman appeals to the authority of a Roman Catholic universalism. But he also does something else. He creates fearful images or caricatures of the world in which religion and education are separated.

In his resistance to that separation, Newman compares Protestant England and the Roman world in the centuries after the birth of Christ. This comparison of the English gentleman and the apostate emperor concludes Newman's attack on a liberal education disassociated from religious teaching. In the end such an education is a rudderless or "Godless" pursuit of knowledge for its own sake, a good finally defined negatively. At best it is a meaningless pleasure of the intellect, and at worst it amounts to the abdication of moral authority. In his analogy Newman likens the intellect and ethics of the English gentleman, the product of a liberal education that lacks

Roman Catholic teaching, to the philosophy of a pagan citizen of Rome. He can find no better example than Julian, the fourth-century emperor who rejected Constantine's conversion of the empire to Christianity. The apostate Roman emperor and the Victorian English gentleman share an attitude of tolerance, a personal exercise of intellectual freedom, and a reduction of ethics to a sort of hedonism and a refraining from inflicting pain needlessly. Both look at all religious faiths with a leveling and impartial eye. Religion is thus for both the embodiment of the sublime and the beautiful.

Newman's general critique of a "Godless" liberal education has three major points: the endless branching out of knowledge into new sciences, all of which deny theology equal epistemological status; the usurpation by the sciences – biology, geology, archeology, philology – of religious truth; the repositioning, within the scheme of the free pursuit of knowledge, of religion as a subcategory of aesthetics or, worse yet, of psychology. These intellectual tendencies or developments make human beings think that secular knowledge or science includes all the relevant and great questions of life. These transform the physical universe and the present social world into ends in themselves. The danger of the liberal education unhallowed and unguided by the Catholic faith is that partial knowledge seems to be complete knowledge.

Newman's strategy of conveying his condemnation of such a liberal education through an analogy with a hedonistic, effeminate, tolerant Roman emperor creates a figure upon which every contemporary cultural or moral fear could be projected. Julian was not an English Protestant gentleman, and English Protestant gentlemen were not apostates even if they were not adherents of the Roman Catholic faith. Newman used that comparison to foster a fearful, imaginary opposition between his mode of education and culture and that of others. Although the Catholic church built on the foundations of Greek thought, a dissenting Protestant tradition made use of the same foundation, only to produce a different reading at a different time – namely, the split and disciplined subjective self of modernity. Furthermore, Protestant universities on the Continent, in Scotland, and in the American republic had achieved a liberal education no less hallowed by religious faith and a sense of common culture than that which Newman proposed for Ireland.

Indeed, if Protestantism has not actually been the disruptive cultural force that Newman portrayed, it is just possible that those in present-day higher education calling for more individual choice will no more foment cultural anarchy than did the great Protestant universities and colleges. Similarly, those who fear that diversity and multiculturalism will lead to cultural decline may be projecting their own apprehensions, as is equally the case of those who condemn American humanities curricula as the preserves of dead white European males.

The purpose of Newman's critique of the exploding world of liberal, secular learning, which may lead to modern Julians or cultural Protestants, is as vast as it is daunting. Through a university curriculum founded in the belief that knowledge is a closed circle, Newman attempts to stem the challenge of science and of time – that is, of change itself. In his idea of a university the Roman Catholic Church's perennial claim to hegemonic knowledge stands in open confrontation with the modern European self and its claims to moral autonomy. Newman was attempting to oppose and to roll back the whole thrust of human subjectivity that had been championed in the religious realm by the eighteenth-century Protestant pietistic revivals from Germany to Great Britain and New England and in the secular realm by the poets of the Sturm und Drang and high Romanticism. In that regard Newman appealed to universality against the strongest forces in modern culture – the useful knowledge of the sciences and the subjective sensitivity of new explorations of the inner self. Today what we see in most universities are radical manifestations of the forces Newman tried to stem: science and subjectivism and cultural difference.

Newman, like many of his latter-day followers, attempted to articulate a single unified Western cultural tradition. In point of fact, that tradition has included the Catholic faith as Newman presented it, as well as Greece, Rome, Judaism, Protestantism, science, individualism, democratic aspirations, and a strong penchant for self-criticism. And during the past half-millennium it has defined itself in relation to its constructed others: Amerindians, "Orientals," Africans. Newman may have seen those many elements in the Western experience as antinomian impulses, as three centuries earlier the Puritans of Massachusetts had viewed the demands for liberty by Anne Hutchinson and Roger Williams. Both tendencies – toward authority and toward individualism – pertain to the Western tradition. Today critics of diversity and multiculturalism see those movements as antinomian and as challenges to a unitary culture. They may well be, but they also belong to the Western tradition. People who encounter those forces may thereby better understand their own intellectual and cultural heritage. Those who would oppose diverse modes of thinking as undermining Western culture might well be reminded of the heady debates over the rediscovery of Aristotle through Arabic thought in the twelfth and thirteen centuries in Paris.

The possibility of choosing or embracing differing moral and cultural horizons – despite the universal claims of Christianity, including its self-proclaimed monopoly on civilization – results from the sustained inward march of Western thought from Descartes through Rousseau and Kant to the Romantic ideal of a unique self forever in need of self-expression. Thus the siege that Newman tries to repel involves not only geology's dismissal of the story of Noah's ark and the claim of science to cultural hegemony, but also the more aggravating and more local puritan belief in the autonomous and therefore responsible individual. There follows from these positions a moral obligation *not to believe* what is not supported by enough or good enough evidence. It is this obligation to pursue free and exhaustive inquiry which I recognize as the root of our contemporary culture wars and which Newman wishes to resist with all that is within him.

Yet Newman's position is a complicated one. He seems to inhibit critical freedom of thought, yet he eventually appeals to it. As with so many of the issues he raises, Newman tries to have it both ways on the question of freedom of inquiry. The advance of such freedom has been at the root of much of the struggle since the seventeenth century between science and theology. The place and value assigned to such freedom in Western culture has over the years limited the authority of the Church to teach its "universal" truths as opposed to individuals' prerogative to question them. Pursuit of concrete, inner freedom has traditionally defined liberal education. This self-determining freedom of criticism and inquiry fosters disbelief in any external, preordained arrangement of power or authority. The inner self cultivated by the liberal education is called to originality and thus to authenticity. It cannot be subsumed, therefore, under any systematic set of beliefs, lest it betray its obligation to the voices that emanate from the innermost recesses of its being.[8]

Ironically, a version of this critical subjective self informs Newman's idea of literature as well as his belief in the impossibility of a Catholic literature in English. As with so many of his arguments, he starts from an established hierarchical point. After circumscribing civilization to Christian Europe (167–168), Newman lays down the "standards of education, which the Civilized World . . . has enjoined and requires" (169). This education takes place by means of books the production of which, as noted earlier, he regards as one indication of civilization. Reading them enlarges the mind, cultivates the intellect, and refines the feelings.

Newman contends that, in a manner similar to the establishment of sacred theological texts in the early centuries of the Church, literary texts in

8. Charles Taylor, *Sources of the Self: The Making of Modern Identity* (Cambridge, Mass., 1989), p. 404.

Europe have now been stabilized and have achieved a maturity of two kinds. First, these writings are unalterable in kind and number; and second, they cannot be superseded. In other words, there is a canon of secular classics, which includes both ancients and moderns. Newman's reading list would largely reiterate what was then in use at Oxford. Such views on a canon of literature, and their shortcomings, are familiar enough from current academic debates. They would deserve no further comment were it not that Newman's understanding of several categories of literary analysis – language, voice, genres, author, books – directly contradicts his notion of a stable and fixed canon and highlights some of the most disturbing aspects of his thought in relation to today's realities of cultural difference.

For instance, if literature is, as he argues, more than just fine writing, more than eloquence, and if it does correspond to a permanent record of an essentially personal voice, how can we have *a closed canon,* from which so many voices – across time and space – would have to be, by definition, excluded? Or, if literature is of a "personal character" and "consists in the enunciations and teachings of those who have a right to speak as representatives of their kind, and in whose words their brethren find an interpretation of their sentiments, a record of their own experience, and a suggestion of their own judgments," does it not follow that some readers may find their selves profoundly missed or underrepresented in the Greek or English "classics"?[9] Such a group would need to discover and produce, by either rewriting or writing stories and poems, a literature of their own, stories that represent their sentiments so that self-recognition marks the acts of reading and writing. Here Newman's idea of literature dovetails with the many claims made by multiculturalists who argue for broadening and "enriching" the notion of what it is to be human across a space and time that exceed the experience of the ancient Greeks and the English Protestants.

Indeed, many who would appeal to Newman to support an inherently conservative university education might with discomfort recall his *Essay on the Development of Christian Doctrine,* published seven years before *The Idea of a University.* There Newman rejected the argument that the canon of Scripture alone taught Christian doctrine, contending that many voices in the tradition of the Church over the centuries had to articulate the full meaning of the Bible and the original teachings of the Apostles. He used that argument to justify and defend the various innovations by the Roman Catholic Church. If Newman could defend innovation and change in sacred teaching, how could he consistently deny the same to the canon of secular literature?

9. John Henry Newman, *The Idea of a University,* ed. I. T. Ker, (Oxford, 1976), p. 243.

IV

One contemporary ideal of the individual in a democratic society is to be true to oneself. This quest includes the notion of challenging each other's beliefs at the personal and the institutional level. One is responsible for one's own beliefs, and that responsibility cannot be delegated. Thus, as the individual searches for authentic identity, a liberal education and the encounter with the writings of other subjectivities seem the designated place for reflexivity. Historically Kant's finding the moral imperative in an inner voice was crucial to the modern search for authenticity and freedom.[10] This development is part of what Charles Taylor termed a "massive subjective turn of modern culture, a new form of inwardness in which we come to think of ourselves as beings with inner depth."[11] Authenticity received further emphasis in the Romantic idea that each individual has an original and particular way of being human. The conclusion therefore followed that a person is morally called to live and shape his or her own life, that is, like an "author," he or she has a unique personal style.

This is the image of the self that Newman and later Matthew Arnold in their critique of English *culture* seek to contain. Paradoxically, this is the same subjective self that they embrace in the celebrated writings of the great and unique authors of the canon (Newman) or in readings for an English upper-class *culture* (Arnold).[12] For both Newman and Arnold, an educated elite acquires the wisdom and habits of mind of the "best authors," whose originality has produced a literary legacy for their descendants.

As Newman and Arnold see it, writing is a glorious, creative act by certain especially gifted subjective selves. Reading, in contrast, is a passive act by the less gifted. Writing books is an exercise in authenticity. The silent reader, in contrast, absorbs, observes, receives, accumulates, at best "banks" the classics' masterly expressions of thoughts and feelings. Writing and reading, in Newman's sense of an education – the process by which civilization remains integrated – designate two classes of intellectual activity and two classes of people: writers who plumb the depths of their inner

10. Charles Taylor, *The Ethics of Authenticity* (Cambridge, Mass., 1991), p. 26.

11. Ibid.

12. In "Culture in Genesis: Arnold, Tylor and Culture Theory in Mid-Victorian Britain," David Van Keuren spells out the distinctions between Arnold's idea of culture – an educated elite steeped in the "best ideas" of the past – and E. B. Tylor's sense of culture as a complex whole "produced by natural laws acting ineluctably upon society as a whole" (MS, p. 44, quoted with the gracious permission of the author).

world and readers who enlarge their minds with the gift offered by the writer. Literature is, Newman tells us, essentially a personal work. It proceeds from a given individual, who uses the language in a distinctive way. He contends, "It is the fire within the author's breast which overflows the torrent of his burning, irresistible eloquence. It is the poetry of his inner soul." Even slang is acceptable here – it "breathes of the personal."[13] Reading is part of the banking education, an accumulation of wisdom, beauty, and eloquence bequeathed to us by the *author*-ity.

Newman's romantic concept of the writer exercising subjectivity confers an exceptional status on authors and on literature. But then he has to face the local conditions under which literature formulates correspondingly local worldviews, which have made – in specific historical situations – suitable and convincing universal truth claims. That is, how can Newman distinguish between or allow hierarchies to be established between manifestations of subjectivity in one culture from those in another culture. Both subjectivities could and often do claim to express universal truth.

Newman's design for a university, with its closed circle of knowledge, unravels for a second time, given the students who will study there. The case in point for Newman is Shakespeare, the epitome of English literature. How does a student possessing an authentic English or Irish Catholic consciousness read the greatest writer of the English Protestant tradition? With disbelief? Aren't anti-Catholic sentiments and arguments of Milton or Gibbon ingrained in the English language itself as to produce an experience of misrecognition in an Irish Catholic? Don't these writings violate a Catholic's conscience? Should they not be omitted from a new listing of the canon? Is authenticity of experience not the foundational ground for the experience of reading or rather interpretation as well as for writing? Is not reading, like writing, an active rather than a passive experience?

Newman, however, does not squarely face the problem of the canon as a historical construction for a well-defined, and not at all universal, group of readers. He could not confront the possibility that the canon was itself a cultural problem to those whose voices and experiences were outside it. His contemporary Ralph Waldo Emerson had indirectly addressed that issue a few years earlier when he told an American audience, "Books are the best things well used; abused, among the worst. . . . The one thing in the world, of value, is the active soul. This every man contains within him."[14] Working

13. Newman, *The Idea of a University,* ed. I. T. Ker, pp. 234, 231.

14. Ralph Waldo Emerson, "The American Scholar" (1837), in *Essays and English Traits,* ed. Charles W. Eliot, The Harvard Classics (New York, 1909), pp. 9–10.

out the tensions between Newman's Catholic hierarchy of authors and Emerson's Protestant egalitarianism is the controversial task left to contemporary readers of literature at a time when the hegemony of English and European culture is either losing strength or redefining itself.

Newman as an Englishman addressing an Irish audience could not overcome his own cultural identity and suggest that the Irish might define themselves over and against English literature or produce a literature of their own. Newman as a Roman Catholic addressing Roman Catholics was unwilling to suggest that they challenge the social dominance of Protestant culture. Today, those who think about the humanities in universities where the faculties and the students come from numerous cultural backgrounds cannot escape or finesse such issues, nor can the reader who wishes to rethink *The Idea of a University*.

Newman's preoccupation with the fact that Protestant authors made English "a rich, harmonious, various and precise" language (188) differs little from the task faced by Afro-American writers, Brazilian intellectuals, or Spanish American writers when they attempt to escape the tyranny of established practices that shut out their sense of their own experience and feeling for the language. Neither Newman's system of classics nor the Catholic education of Ibero-American colonials allowed for the possibility that the English, Spanish, and Portuguese languages would be analyzed, broken down, and put together again so as to serve as appropriate vehicles for the representations of other cultures and new sensitivities. Such literary developments would show, among other things, that language and nationality are not a natural couple made in heaven. Rather, they are the product of complex and specific historical, social, and discursive forces. Language and culture can become companions in a variety of cultural processes, of which identity building is only one.

If Newman had been familiar with the cultural history of Latin America, he would, of course, have rejected the anticlerical and Francophile character of the nineteenth-century intellectuals who wrote in consonance with their American identity – an identity they were eager to assume. Yet seen in the longer tradition of Latin American literature, Newman's desire for an English Catholic literature is not unlike the exigency and struggle of local, subaltern intellectuals and artists in colonial situations. From its very outset, with the *Comentarios reales* (1609) by Garcilaso de la Vega, el Inca (1539–1616), what we now call Latin American literature faced the same paradox: how to make the authorized system of representation, by definition inimical, inscribe the subaltern's experience and point of view.[15] The question for Garcilaso, the first New World–born author to write a classic about America, as well as for ensuing generations of Latin American writers, was how to make the Spanish language, already loaded with a hegemonic Catholic, colonialist, and racist ideology, speak authentically for peoples who were the very objects of colonialism.

Newman, who used the language of imperialism and who as an Englishman never doubted English superiority, would have rejected a specific *colonial* solution to the subalterity that defines his own English Catholic identity. He would also have rejected the Latin American "model" because it only too readily acknowledges two problems that Newman preferred to leave in silence. First, reading as well as writing require authenticity inasmuch as the reader must be able to recognize himself or herself in literature's representations of the world. Second, writing, reading, and teaching are not parts of a private impermeable realm; rather, they directly engage the public sphere and therefore questions of power. Instead of placing his confidence in the present English or Irish Catholic reader and a possible writer expressing the inner depth of the (Catholic) individual, a move that would have enabled him to anticipate James Joyce, Newman once again climbs to higher ground and hands down requirements for English Catholic literature, prescriptions that run counter to the demands of an autonomous, authentic self, necessary to writers and to citizens or readers.

The contradiction at the heart of Newman's design for an Irish Catholic university that would recognize the non-Catholic classics as its models and legacy is that the ideal of authenticity implied in his notion of the author already means the decline of hierarchical society. That is, a human agent (author) capable of self-understanding can define his or her identity through human systems of representation alone. This individual no longer needs doctrine to mediate between him and his understanding of self or the world. If the highest value is the writer's originality, one of the crowning glories of Christian civilization, and if the writer is no longer an exceptional case, it follows that the recognition of difference is the only way to acknowledge self-authenticity.

As Charles Taylor has pointed out, this contradiction is part of a poorly articulated debate. While the modern authentic individual must and can seek truth for himself – truth conceived as a process of discovery – he

15. For a modern translation of this work, see Garcilaso de la Vega, *Royal Commentaries of the Incas and General History of Peru,* tr. Harold Livermore, 2 vols. (Austin, Tex., 1966).

nevertheless is not alone. In his quest for re-cognition he seeks the opinion of others. Regardless of his position in the master and slave power game, the individual, like language, is always situated dialogically, so the re-cognition of the good in himself requires an engagement with others. As Taylor has commented, "A perfectly balanced reciprocity takes the sting out of our dependence on opinion, and makes it compatible with liberty."[16] The remedy is not rejecting the importance of the other's gaze; it is to enter into a different contract in which others' freedom and equality can be honored. The dialogue between Protestants and Catholics, averted by Newman's hegemonic response to the Anglican establishment, requires not sovereignty but reciprocity. His assertion of sovereignty, however, justifies his avoidance of dialogue and pluralism.

This sense of equality and mutual need is of course absent from Newman's pages, for his mind was imbued with the sovereignty and self-sufficiency characteristic of the Victorian age and with "universal knowledge." In his idea of a university there is no need for reciprocity. The student comes, like the catechumen of the early Christian church, to read and learn from the best of those who have gone before him. The student walks the well-traveled path, not deviating from it or cutting a new one. In this sense "the idea of a university" denies the central principle of a liberating education for human beings endowed with equal rights and autonomous subjectivities. The engagement of knowledge, as Aristotle said and Newman reiterates, is one of the primary orientations of the mind. It is indeed integral to the idea of being human. But Aristotle's legacy is predicated on a single vast reason, or logos, which after Descartes's proposition of a disengaged subject began to fade and has in a way led to our present subjectivism. Knowledge in our time has become the very ground for a search for freedom. Thus we think of knowledge as an individual and communal process of ongoing discovery, invention, and reinvention, in which truth is always in the making. Newman, for all his personal religious searching, would not embark upon such a journey.

16. Charles Taylor, *Multiculturalism and "The Politics of Recognition"* (Princeton, 1992), p. 48.

Newman and the Idea of an Electronic University

GEORGE P. LANDOW

Except for his years in Dublin, John Henry Newman's entire experience with the life of a university occurred in Oxford. He left that university, resigning his Oriel College fellowship in 1845, when he became a member of the Roman Catholic Church. I shall commence this discussion of the electronic university – the university as an institution in the age of digital information – by allowing Newman to describe his last hours in Oxford. In his *Apologia pro Vita Sua* (1864), Newman carefully relates his parting from university friends, including the man who had been his undergraduate tutor, or faculty advisor and chief instructor in the Oxford system.

> In him I took leave of my first college, Trinity, which was so dear to me, and which held on its foundation so many who had been kind to me both when I was a boy, and all through my Oxford life. Trinity had never been unkind to me. There used to be much snap-dragon growing on the walls opposite my freshman's rooms there, and I had for years taken it as an emblem of my own perpetual residence even unto death in my University.
>
> On the morning of the 22nd [February 1846] I left the Observatory. I have never seen Oxford since, excepting its spires, as they are seen from the railway.[1]

Although a note immediately qualifies this poignant image of Newman's exile – he had visited the university thirty-two years after his departure and fourteen years after he wrote this passage – the image of Newman as a heroic exile-of-conscience remains to emphasize how much his adherence to intellectual and spiritual truth cost him personally.

To anyone concerned with Newman's idea of a university and its relation to late-twentieth-century developments in information technology,

---

1. John Henry Newman, *Apologia pro Vita Sua, Being a History of His Religious Opinions,* ed. Martin J. Svaglic (Oxford, 1967), p. 213.

educational practice, and institutional change, this scene of departure conveys an essential fact about his conception of a university – namely, that it is first of all *a place*. This assumption or premise recurs throughout *The Idea of a University*. Indeed, the notion of spatial location begins his fundamental description of a university, which according to him "is a place of *teaching* universal *knowledge*. This implies that its object is, on the one hand, intellectual, not moral; and, on the other, that it is the diffusion and extension of knowledge rather than the advancement" (3). Further, in his moving eulogy for Oriel College in Discourse VII, he describes "a small plot of ground, hemmed in by public thoroughfares, which has been the possession and the home of one Society for above five hundred years" located "in the heart of Oxford" (111).

Educational institutions have been and remain, in the popular mind, largely defined by place and location. But no less significantly since the Academy in Plato's Athens, educational institutions have also been *places defined by the nature of contemporary information technologies*. The word has undergone major changes as one form replaced another earlier one in the technology of education and cultural memory. First came the spoken word, then the written, and with Gutenberg the printed version, and now the digital word. Thus far, each new information technology partially displaced and replaced earlier versions for certain functions, but did not do away with them. Public speaking continues to have great social and political importance millennia after the invention of writing, and writing retains its importance long after printing had formed and informed Western culture.

One can point out several other crucial facts about the changing ways people have encountered the word, perhaps the most important of which for this examination of future universities is that each information technology, each form of the word, has created its own characteristic educational institution and educational practice. Each of these technologies of cultural memory, furthermore, becomes naturalized. Each, in other words, becomes so expected and obvious a part of its culture that it appears inevitable, natural, *what one expects,* and therefore all but invisible, particularly to those who rely upon it most and whose thoughts and attitudes have been most shaped by it – that is, students, teachers, researchers, and theorists of education.

As it turns out, perhaps ironically, one of the great values of the cultural paradigm shift from printed to digital word is that it enables us – no, better, it forces us – to recognize that certain of our most fundamental cultural assumptions about authorship, intellectual property, creativity, and education depend upon particular information technologies.[2] For example, although Newman clearly envisages both the university he has left and the one he wishes to create as places of wise speech, he assumes that the preaching, lecturing, instruction, and conversation will largely concern books. Take the following two representative facts. First, he delivered a series of lectures and then published them as a book, *The Idea of a University,* and it is the printed form that has had such influence. Second, his controversial career derives in large part from the characteristic qualities of print. Consider, would Newman have written Tract 90 had not the printing press made widely accessible the writings of the church fathers and the documents of church history? As scholars of the Gutenberg revolution have pointed out, the widely distributed fixed text produced by the printing press promoted religious controversy and violent conflict by putting down divisive positions in black and white and making them available to large numbers of people. The coming of the digital word makes it much easier for us to note how the printed book founds Newman's ideas of education and educational institutions.

At the same time that this age of transition grants us the opportunity, the freedom, and the responsibility of recognizing that some of our fundamental assumptions thus relate crucially to particular material conditions, it also reminds us that in every change, in every potential advance, something is gained but something is also lost. Plato, Socrates relates, feared (correctly, it turns out) that writing, which functions as a prosthetic memory, would encourage certain kinds of forgetfulness. People were willing to risk that sacrifice in exchange for a radical new means of preserving exact arguments. Indeed, as Marshall McLuhan and other students of the relation of information paradigms to culture have pointed out, before the achievement of writing many forms of Western thought would have been virtually impossible to conceive and to record and hand on to others.

Some apparently minor changes in the material conditions within which we encounter language have had fundamental cultural effects. For example, until a thousand years ago, materials on which to write were so expensive or so difficult to obtain that scribes were obliged to pack as many words as possible on each page, and in order to do so they omitted spaces between the end of one word and the beginning of the next. Thus, economic reasons directly produced a form of writing that made reading a matter of decipher-

2. For a detailed discussion of these issues, see the works by Bolter, Eisenstein, Kernan, Landow, and McLuhan, in Suggested Reading.

ing streams of alphabetic characters, a process that was best done aloud. In contrast, the availability of less costly surfaces on which to write led directly to silent reading, and with it came new conceptions of private, interior space. Late-twentieth-century college and secondary school teachers who fear the effects of new information paradigms and practices have a long and honorable pedigree: in the fourteenth century, historians of reading remind us, the faculty at the University of Paris repeatedly made rules forbidding undergraduates to read silently, for they feared that without proper guidance students might get into trouble, might get things wrong. This example further reminds us that all new developments in information technology have eventually fostered democratization, though some, like writing itself, took millennia to evolve from the property of the few to the empowerment of the many.

Similarly, the combination of the printing press and movable type had radical and often destabilizing effects on European culture. Gutenberg's invention made multiple copies of individual works widely available, and like the invention of interword spacing hundreds of years before, it had a dramatic cultural impact apparently out of keeping with these few simple facts. As Marshall McLuhan, Elizabeth Eisenstein, and other students of the Gutenberg revolution have shown, the economic need to secure enough readers to pay for the multiple copies led to the predominance of vernacular languages, their official forms, and standardized spelling and grammar. These changes in turn fostered nationalism.

According to Alvin Kernan, print culture also swept away "an older system of polite or courtly letters – primarily oral, aristocratic, authoritarian, court-centered . . . and gradually replaced [it] by a new print-based, market-centered, democratic literary system" that had major effects on individual social life. For example, print technology changed the audience for literature from a few "manuscript readers or listeners . . . to a group of readers . . . who bought books to read in the privacy of their homes. Print also made literature objectively real for the first time, and therefore subjectively conceivable as a universal fact, in great libraries of printed books containing large collections of the world's writing." Print, Kernan demonstrates, also freed authors from the patronage of the wealthy few because it led to "copyright law that made the author the owner of his own writing."[3]

Equally important, scholarship, teaching, and indeed educational institutions as we know them, and as Newman envisioned his, are also largely

3. Alvin Kernan, *Printing Technology, Letters and Samuel Johnson* (Princeton, 1987), pp. 4–5.

the product of the Gutenberg revolution. Printing technology adds fixity and multiplicity to written language. Many copies of the same work permit readers separated in time and space to consult and comment upon it. The printed book costs so much less than the manuscript book, or codex, that it is available in vastly larger numbers; faculty, students, and individuals outside institutions can afford their own personal libraries. With the development of high-speed printing in the early nineteenth century – the age of steam's gift to the reading public – books, periodicals, and other printed information, including college catalogs and, more recently, student evaluations of faculty teaching, become possible.

How will things on campus change with the arrival there of the digital word? Describing a few of the more obvious effects turns out to be fairly easy, since they are already upon us. Most scholarly books, student editions, textbooks, college catalogs – in fact, virtually all the newly produced reading materials one encounters in the modern university – have been computer typeset. This fact reminds us that at present most applications of electronic textuality still lead to printed books and articles. Not only computer typesetting and desk-top publishing but also text-analysis, full-text searching, and similar computer applications work with texts translated into electronic form.

Nonetheless, fully electronic text – text intended to be read on a computer – increasingly shapes the modern college and university. I do not mean the near-universal use of computers for institutional purchasing, payrolls, student records, and the like, but on-line library catalogs, information available on campus-wide networks, and the use, thus far largely for courses in the physical and social sciences, of statistical software. At my own institution, Brown University, as at so many others, students and faculty commonly use the university library's electronic – or so-called on-line – catalog at terminals in various library buildings. This catalog is also accessible from BRUNET, the campus-wide network. Faculty and students who connect to the institution's computing services by telephone can also obtain these services off-campus. In addition, readers consult the *MLA Bibliography* and *Oxford English Dictionary* on CD-ROMs at workstations in the library, and in the near future these resources will be available to readers with access to BRUNET.

These examples of the electronification of our colleges and universities suggest that they are well on the way to becoming cyborg institutions, mixtures of electronic and other media. There is more. Students at my and many other institutions employ simple, easy-to-use so-called point-and-click Macintosh interfaces to obtain the course catalog, university rules and regulations, national news, weather, and the like. Since the digital word so easily crosses the physical boundaries of buildings, departments, and entire institutions, its readers discover that they expend little more time or effort to connect to sources of information located at other institutions, including on-line catalogs, computer conferences, and sources of electronic texts, than to use those at Brown. Indeed, I have a colleague who, given the inadequacy of Brown's library in his field, regularly crosses the continent electronically and consults the on-line catalogs of California institutions.

Restricting ourselves just to computing resources within the electronic bounds of the campus, we can observe other signs of the times. Students can read through electronically linked documents – what are, in essence, combinations of miniature electronic libraries and collaborative work environments – on such subjects as the nuclear weapons and disarmament treaties, the history of religion, nineteenth-century public health, postcolonial literature, literary and cultural theory, Pre-Raphaelite painting, and experiments in electronic fiction and poetry. Many of these hypertext documents (or webs) are unique to Brown, but other materials, such as the justly famous Perseus Project, are now found at hundreds of institutions.

Using Perseus, the Harvard-developed corpus of texts and images of ancient Greek literature, art, and thought, the student who possesses only a rudimentary knowledge of classical Greek, or, for that matter, none at all, can read in ways that until now were possible only to the trained classicist. For example, coming upon the image of the hunt or the net in a play by Aeschylus, a student can open up the text in the original language, use a dictionary to discover the Greek words or phrases, and then follow them throughout a particular play or author, using electronic links to move back and forth between the original Greek and the English translation. At the same time, Perseus, which also has a large database of maps, images, and reference works, permits the student and the scholar to carry out many different kinds of work.

If such electronic materials are already available, how, then, will the future electronic university differ? First of all, such electronic resources will become far more common and increasingly move from being used on a single workstation to being used on or across networks that knit together sources of information widely separated geographically. The most obvious and most exciting example of such geographically dispersed or wide-area-network hypertext is the Internet's World Wide Web using the Mosaic interface, which currently runs on machines with the Macintosh, Unix, or Windows operating systems. Working on a computer connected to the Internet, one enters the World Wide Web simply by starting up Mosaic, after

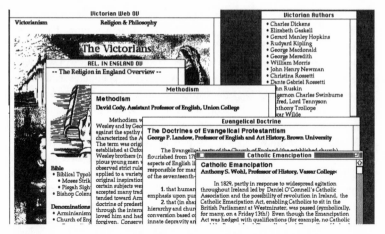

Figure I. Collaboration and interdisciplinarity in hypertext. This snapshot records a session with the Victorian Web, a hypertext document comprising approximately six hundred essays and two thousand links created at Brown University. This hypertext document (or web), which was produced using Eastgate Systems' program Storyspace, includes materials on Victorian literature, art, religion, science, technology, and social and political history. When the web opens, the reader encounters a graphic overview ("Victorian Web OV"), which appears at upper left. After using this overview to open a list of Victorian authors, which appears at the upper right, the reader has begun to explore Victorian religion, beginning with the "Religion in England Overview," using it to obtain, in turn, David Cody's essay on Methodism, George P. Landow's on the defining beliefs of evangelical Protestantism, and Anthony S. Wohl's on the restoration of full civil rights to Britain's Roman Catholics in 1829. Cody designed and wrote this body of linked materials about religion in the U.K., and they are interwoven with a wide variety of subjects, including individual authors, public health, Victorian attitudes toward race and class, and political history. In both principle and practice, electronic linking produces an open-ended, unfinished form of textuality, since later readers can always add new documents and links. In this example, the essay by Wohl, which he created as part of a set of documents on Victorian English attitudes toward the Irish, was added several years after the creation of the "Religion in England" node.

which one uses menus and search tools to read on one's own monitor materials that may be stored on other continents. The first time I encountered World Wide Web, a friend showed me materials about my own university's physics department, and, using a computer mouse, I opened a series of documents, including bibliographies and the actual works cited. Only when my friend pointed out the fact did I realize that part of the "document" I read resided in Providence, Rhode Island, but others, which I experienced as being "in the same place," had in fact come from Switzerland and New Mexico. Next, using Mosaic's search feature, I inquired where on the Internet materials were available on Charles Dickens. Within a minute, the search mechanism produced a list of sites, several of which offered the full text of some of the novels. Within several minutes, I had transferred the text of one of Dickens's stories from Australia to Providence.

If this report of a first encounter with World Wide Web sounds like something out of a science-fiction novel (or a telephone commercial), consider that sites on the World Wide Web, which already exist from Antarctica and Papua, New Guinea to Finland and France, spring up every day, and undergraduates in many institutions have begun to create and maintain them. While many institutions debate the value of wiring their campus with computer networks, or providing access to the Internet for faculty in the humanities, an entire gigantic information infrastructure is being used daily by hundreds of thousands of people.

As such changes might suggest, far more student work will be submitted in electronic, rather than paper, formats, and one result might be that different criteria for judging student exercises will emerge. Access to the Internet will continue to permit those with specific educational and scholarly interests, such as Anglo-Saxon literature, textual editing, poststructuralism, and Vietnam-era literature (the subjects of several active, ongoing computer conference or discussion groups), to communicate with others outside their own institutions. This communication also suggests that anyone can share some of the resources now found largely within individual universities or professional organizations.

All the cultural effects of electronic textuality, including those that have the most impact upon future conceptions of higher education, derive from the fact that the digital word is an electronic code and not a physical mark on a physical surface. Whereas all previous forms of writing have been founded on the ways marks are made on paper or on some other visible, physical surface, the electronic text, image, or number are codes and not things and, moreover, not only exist on a far different scale from words but also cannot be read without the intervention of a machine. From the digital form come three crucial qualities, each of which has potentially far-reaching cultural effects. First, because text and images in digital form are essentially codes, they can be easily manipulated, duplicated, shared, and transported. As anyone who has used even the most primitive word processor knows, the digital word therefore possesses near-instant fluidity and manipulability. This capacity for easily reconfiguring a piece of writing – quickly making corrections and editorial changes – has enabled computers to displace typewriters in fairly short order in many parts of the business and academic worlds.

Second, electronic digital coding produces what we may term *address-ability,* which in turn produces the open text. In so-called analog media in electronic form, such as video, the user or researcher wishing to locate a particular bit of information, be it sound, image, or text, must move through the film, tape, or document in linear order, and that takes significant time and energy. In contrast, someone wishing to locate the same information stored in digital form can locate it almost instantly because computers provide each bit of information with an easily locatable "address." This feature of the digital world, as we shall see shortly, produces hypertext, which emphasizes reader control and possesses great educational potential.

Hypertext adds to the digital word the electronic link connecting words, phrases, images, sounds, and other forms of information. It is composed of blocks of text – what, following Roland Barthes, I term *lexias,* or reading units – and the electronic links that join them. Together they produce an open-ended, perpetually unfinished textuality described by *link, node, network, web,* and *path.* Whereas the digital word leads to the electronic book, hypertext, which combines the digital word with the digital link, leads to something much closer to an electronic library.

Were you reading this essay in a completely realized hypertext, clicking on "Roland Barthes" would have brought you to bibliographical information of the sort usually contained in a foot- or endnote. However, then you could have left this essay and this volume and moved directly to the cited texts or to other discussions of Barthes and hypertext. You could read the works by Barthes, or you might return here. That is, like the scholarly reader wandering through an open-stack library, you might well be productively distracted from one task, or you might make a note about that discovery and return to the so-called main text. Of course, if you were reading this chapter in a complete hypertext form, in which every text participates in what Theodor H. Nelson, who coined the term *hypertext* in the 1960s, calls a "docuverse," you could also have opened the full text of Newman's *Apologia* or *The Idea of a University* at any time in order to check the context of my quotations or just to follow some of Newman's arguments.

In one sense, such reading practice does not seem particularly novel, since it is, after all, pretty much what skilled readers in the sciences, social sciences, and humanities do regularly: they read an annotated text in a professional publication, encounter a foot- or endnote, and either return to the main text or decide to consult a cited article or other work before doing so. Obviously, hypertext makes such reading far easier, quicker, and therefore more likely to occur in more complex forms. At this time, when we will continue to read in both print and electronic environments, hypertext also offers an efficient means for beginning students to develop the higher-order cognitive skills involved in multilinear reading.

Hypertext produces a drastically different experience of reading and of text that has major implications for intellectual property, authorship, and creativity. Print technology emphasizes the discrete, separate work and thereby markedly exaggerates conceptions, precious to our print-based intellectual culture, of isolated creativity. In contrast, reading hypertext emphasizes how much works relate to each other and how much they have in common. Hypertext, which obviously encourages and even demands particularly active readers, transfers to them some of the power – and function – of the author, but it reminds us how every author participates in a work-in-progress to which countless others have already contributed. As readers move through a web or network of texts, they shift the center – and hence the focus or organizing principle – of their investigation and experience. Hypertext, in other words, provides an infinitely re-centerable system whose provisional point of focus depends upon the reader, who becomes truly active in yet another sense.

Other important qualities of hypertext as an educational medium derive from the last two aspects of the digital word to be discussed – its creation of virtuality and its capacity to reside on and travel through electronic networks like the Internet. Even in isolated, so-called stand-alone computers, hypertext draws upon various forms of *virtuality*.

As I have explained elsewhere, since electronic text-processing is a matter of manipulating computer-manipulated codes, all texts that the writer encounters on the screen are virtual texts. Using an analogy to optics, computer scientists speak of "virtual machines" created by an operating system that provides individual users with the experience of working on their own machine when they in fact share a system with as many as several hundred others. Similarly, all texts the reader and the writer encounter on a computer screen exist as a version created specifically for them while an electronic primary version resides in the computer's memory. One therefore works on an electronic copy until such time as both versions converge when the writer commands the computer to "save" his or her version of the text. At this point the text on the screen and in the computer's memory briefly coincide, but the reader always encounters a virtual image of the stored text, not the original version; in fact, when one describes electronic word-processing, such terms and such distinctions no longer make much sense.

Virtuality has a central role when combined with another fundamental feature of digital technology – its ability to join in large, even worldwide networks. The existence of the digital word as a code, which permits an indefinite number of readers on a network to share the same text, also produces several other effects, one of which is a kind of placelessness. I began this essay by pointing out that Newman's assumption that the university had to be a *place* served as an important, if unexamined, premise in his conception of higher education. Such an assumption is entirely appropriate, given the role that traditional conceptions of education granted the idea of presence, to the assumption that student and teacher communicated, however one-sided that relationship might be, in the presence of each other. Until the invention in the past century of physical and then electronic recording of human speech and the invention of the telephone, speech obviously required that speaker and listener, lecturer and audience, teacher and student share a spatial location.

From the Renaissance onward, however, learners have used information technologies to educate themselves outside the presence of individual instructors. Printed books, newspaper and periodical literature, phonograph records, tapes, videodisks, and CD-ROMs form an unbroken continuum that begins with Renaissance self-help manuals, by which people of comparatively low social status acquired knowledge and skills that formerly required a private tutor or educational institution. Like the manuscript or the printed book, digital information technology creates what we may term the *virtual presence* of an absent teacher that students consult at their need and convenience, not those of the instructor. Some means of storing digital information, such as floppy disks and CD-ROMs, share with books and manuscripts a dependence upon specific physical locations; that is, producers or distributors of such materials must deliver them physically to readers, and readers who want to consult them have to be in physical proximity to them. Computer networks promise to redefine the place of learning as radically as did the inventions of writing and printing – in part because networks like World Wide Web enable hundreds and even thousands of people to consult the same texts at the same time, and in part because networks disperse the instructor's virtual presence even farther from the location of the stored text. Placing digital information on giant networks completely changes the learner's experience, conception, and assumptions about the *place* of learning

Newman, we recall, eloquently portrayed his sense of exile from his beloved Oxford, and when I began to think about his ideas of university education in the context of late-twentieth-century developments in educational and other technologies, I first asked myself, Would Newman have felt exiled from a new electronic university in which, as one of my students phrased it, "There's no *there* there"? To the extent that Oxford meant a particular circle of friends, the college setting, and the like, he would obviously still feel the same loss. But to the degree to which the future electronic university exists in cyberspace – in its interchanges on wide-area computer networks – he would not.

In addition to producing cyberspace, networked digital textuality also creates another kind of virtuality that has important educational effects.[4] This form, which we may term *virtual presence,* concerns the way the hypertext reader and writer experience other contributors. Virtual presence is of course a characteristic of all technology of cultural memory based on writing and symbol systems: since we all manipulate cultural codes, particularly language but also mathematics and other symbols, in slightly different ways, each record of it conveys a sense of the one who makes that utterance. Hypertext differs from print technology, however, in several crucial ways that amplify this notion of virtual presence. Because the essential connectivity of hypermedia removes the physical isolation of individual texts in print technology, the presence of individual authors becomes both more available and more important. The characteristic flexibility of this reader-centered information technology means, quite simply, that writers have a much greater presence in the system, not only as potential contributors and collaborative participants but also as readers who choose their own paths through the materials.

The fundamental connectivity of hypertext, which makes it have such potentially powerful educational uses, promises to reconceive many institutions and practices of education as we know it. For example, the electronic linking that so readily crosses the boundaries of individual texts also permits students to move easily from one level of difficulty to another and from one discipline to another. This characteristic of hypermedia obviously demands active students, new forms of evaluating their work, and greater emphasis, even in the humanities, upon the kind of collaboration characteristic of much scientific research. Another effect of linking draws faculty research and student learning closer together than is possible in book-based educational systems – an effect of which Newman, who thought that universities were places for disseminating knowledge and not contributing to its creation, might have approved.

4. I have drawn in this paragraph upon my *Hypertext: The Convergence of Contemporary Critical Theory and Technology* (Baltimore, 1992).

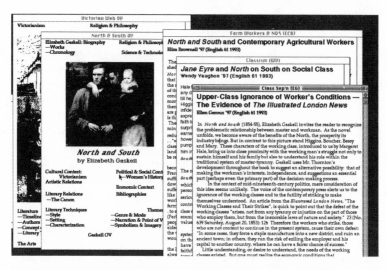

Figure 2. Hypertext as a collaborative writing environment for students. In this second example from the Victorian Web, a reader has used its chief overview, which appears at screen left, to obtain another for Elizabeth Gaskell's industrial novel, *North and South,* and has then begun to explore student-created materials available under the heading "Political & Social Context." Of the nine essays linked to this heading, three appear open here. Although Wendy Vaughon's comparison of the way *Jane Eyre* and *North and South* treat social class takes the form of literary analysis, the essays by Eliza Brownell and Ellen Geroux (which they created for a different assignment) present the results of historical research in the university's Special Collections. There are several important points about this example, the first of which is that, when used as a writing environment, hypertext permits student authors both to make individual contributions and yet inevitably collaborate with one another. Second, hypertext produces a group-created document in which students work collaboratively with faculty authors as well as with other students. Third, hypertext linking, which encourages cross-disciplinary lines, also encourages students to integrate subjects being studied in different courses and different disciplines. Fourth, as the materials on the political and social context of this novel reveal, multi-author hypertext encourages and almost demands that readers encounter differing approaches to whatever issue or topic is under consideration; in this case, the student researchers – all in the first term of their undergraduate education – reproduce much of the contemporary Victorian debate about the causes and solutions of unrest among factory workers by quoting at length from the periodical press, which Newman so disliked. A final fact about hypertext that is not obvious in this example involves the way it produces a course or community memory. Long after they have completed this course, these student authors remain part of it as later classes continue to read and debate their contributions.

He might also have approved of hypertext's creating habits of relational thinking. My own initial work with hypertext suggests how this technology, so apparently alien to Newman, who had little good to say about technology, provides a useful introduction to the way hypertext supports his general educational principles. Most of the earliest attempts to employ computers in education drew upon their abilities to perform simple, repetitive tasks as means of helping students memorize large amounts of factual information. Such computer-assisted learning, often encountered in language acquisition, risks using a rat-maze approach to education, in which students begin at one point and find themselves driven relentlessly through a narrow range of sequences that are often difficult to quit.

In contrast, hypertext, which emphasizes perceiving and making connections as well the reader's choosing his or her path through large fields of information, effectively provides easy access to information and, more important, develops the skills needed to do something with it. Thus, the new educational technology conforms to Newman's insistence that education must consist of more than the simple accumulation of facts. For example, in "Knowledge Viewed in Relation to Learning," Newman explains that he does not mean to disparage

> a well-stored mind, though it be nothing besides, provided it be sober, any more than I would despise a bookseller's shop: – it is of great value to others, even when not so to the owner. Nor am I banishing, far from it, the possessors of deep and multifarious learning from my ideal University; they adorn it in the eyes of men; I do but say that they constitute no type of the results at which it aims; that it is no great gain to the intellect to have enlarged the memory at the expense of faculties which are indisputably higher. (103)

I do not wish to exaggerate or unduly emphasize Newman's possible approval of the aims and effects of such new information technologies, particularly since he had the greatest skepticism about the beneficent educational effects of technology. Newman, after all, expressed hostility to steam-driven, high-speed printing, which made periodicals and books cheap and thus available to a large number of people. It was also responsible for disseminating knowledge in many subjects, including the natural sciences and political economics, down the social and economic scale.

To us who live in an age in which educators and pundits continually elevate reading books as an educational ideal and continually attack television as a medium that victimizes a passive audience, it comes as a shock to encounter Newman claiming that cheap, easily available reading materials similarly victimized the public:

> What the steam engine does with matter, the printing press is to do with mind; it is to act mechanically, and the population is to be passively, almost unconsciously enlightened, by the mere multiplication and dissemination of volumes. Whether it be the school boy, or the school girl, or the youth at college, or the mechanic in the town, or the politician in the senate, all have been the victims in one way or other of this most preposterous and pernicious of delusions. (103)

Part of Newman's rationale for this denunciation lies in the belief that inexpensive periodicals and books supposedly advance the dangerous fallacy that "Learning is to be without exertion, without attention, without toil; without grounding, without advance, without finishing." (103) Like many a conservative elitist in our own day, however, he fears the people unsupervised, and he cannot believe that reading without proper guidance – guidance, that is, from those who know, from those in institutions like Oxford – can produce any sort of valid education. Had Newman encountered self-taught millworkers and artisans who made discoveries in chemistry, astronomy, and geology after reading newly available books, he would likely not have changed his mind.

Like Socrates, who feared the effects of writing, which he took to be an anonymous, impersonal denaturing of living speech, Newman also fears an "impersonal" information technology that people can use without supervision. And also like Socrates, he desires institutions of higher learning – which for the ancient is face-to-face conversation in the form of dialectic – to be sensitive to the needs of specific individuals. Newman therefore argues that "a University is, according to the usual designation, an Alma Mater, knowing her children one by one, not a foundry, or a mint, or a treadmill." (104–105)

Newman's criticism of the flood of printed matter produced by the new technology superficially echoes Thomas Carlyle, whose "Signs of the Times" (1829) had lambasted his age, whose "true Deity is Mechanism." In fact, claims this first of Victorian sages,

> Not the external and physical alone is managed by machinery, but the internal and spiritual also. Here too nothing follows its spontaneous course, nothing is left to be accomplished by old, natural methods. . . . Instruction, that mysterious communing of Wisdom with Ignorance, is

no longer an indefinable tentative process, requiring a study of individual aptitudes, and a perpetual variation of means and methods, to attain the same end; but a secure, universal, straightforward business, to be conducted in the gross, by proper mechanism, with such intellect as comes to hand.[5]

This passage parallels and might have provided a major inspiration for Newman's conceptions of education. In addition, Carlyle attacks those like Newman who propose educational systems and design institutions.

In sentences I omitted from the quoted passage, Carlyle explained that everything, for his contemporaries, "has its cunningly devised implements, its preëstablished apparatus; it is not done by hand but by machinery. Thus we have machines for education: Lancasterian machines; Hamiltonian machines; monitors, maps, and emblems."[6] Or, as Carlyle might say today, we have peer tutoring, core curricula, distribution requirements, work-study programs, and junior years abroad.

What is not at issue here is the practicality of Carlyle's criticisms of the mechanization of education and other human activities – after all, it seems that on the same grounds he would attack any organizational change. No, what is crucial here is that Carlyle, who apparently denies all possibilities for reform of existing institutions, recognizes something about them that Newman, the often admirable theorist of education, does not: that all institutions and forms of social organization are properly to be considered technologies. Carlyle, who pointed out elsewhere that gunpowder and the printing press destroyed feudalism, saw that writing, printing, pedagogical systems, and universities are all technologies of cultural memory. Newman, like most academics of the past few hundred years, considers them, more naively, as natural and inevitable. Consequently, he notices the effects of only those institutions new to him or that he does not like.

The great value of this recognition here is that it reminds us that the idea of an electronic university does not technologize the university or add technology in some way alien to its essential spirit. Digital information technology, in other words, is only the latest one to shape an institution that, as Carlyle reminds us, is itself a form of technology, a mechanism, and has long been influenced by those technologies on which it relies.

Newman would almost certainly be suspicious of educational technol-

5. Thomas Carlyle, "Signs of the Times" (1829), in *A Carlyle Reader,* ed. G. B. Tennyson (Cambridge, 1969), pp. 46, 35.

6. Ibid., p. 35.

ogy. He would also fear the true democratization inherent in such apparent educational anarchy, and he would take the changing intellectual skills as a matter for major concern – even, possibly, as a reason for its ultimate rejection. Nonetheless, there are several points in the new university of which Newman might fully approve.

First of all, educational hypertext's defining emphasis upon making connections – between text and other texts, text and context, and among various approaches – certainly supports Newman's conviction that education consists fundamentally in making connections, something apparent when he describes an intellect "properly trained and formed to have a connected view or grasp of things" (8).

He would also approve of the characteristic multivocality and inter-disciplinarity of hypertext technology, which blurs the borders between individual texts and separate disciplines. Discussing theology, Newman argues that "all knowledge forms one whole, because its subject-matter is one; for the universe in its length and breadth is so intimately knit together, that we cannot separate off portion from portion, operation from operation, except by a mental abstraction" (45). Newman claims that true knowledge, wisdom, and learning are more-than-disciplinary; therefore, anything like hypertext that promises to cross boundaries has the potential to create the education that Newman proposes as an ideal. "These various partial views or abstractions, by means of which the mind looks out upon its object, are called sciences, and embrace respectively larger or smaller portions of the field of knowledge" (42). Newman here virtually defines a chief characteristic of any document once it appears electronically linked to others within a hypertext web. In fact, readers tend to experience documents in a fully linked hypertext corpus, and the entire web itself, as open-ended, perpetually unfinished, and partial to the degree that their current interests guide the axes of their investigations.

Electronically linking various disciplines and approaches to issues within a single field of discourse, or virtual place, creates hypertext's characteristic multivocality, a quality Newman desires in institutions of higher learning. As he explains, "[T]he advantage of a seat of universal learning, considered as a place of education" lies in the way an "assemblage of learned men, zealous for their own sciences, and rivals of each other, are brought, by familiar intercourse and for the sake of intellectual peace, to adjust together the claims and relations of their respective subjects of investigation. They learn to respect, to consult, to aid each other." (77) Anyone who has experienced a modern university, read much about Newman's Oxford, or studied in scholarly literature may well be excused for taking a skeptical glance at his claim, "Thus is created a pure and clear atmosphere of thought, which the student also breathes," but one has to agree that, as Newman asserts, the student "profits by an intellectual tradition, which is independent of particular teachers, which guides him in his choice of subjects, and duly interprets for him those which he chooses. He apprehends the great outlines of knowledge, the principles on which it rests, the scale of its parts, its lights and its shades, its great points and its little, as he otherwise cannot apprehend them" (109). By allowing beginning and advanced students (among whom I include members of the faculty) to immerse themselves in the cultures of various disciplines, hypertext corpora and other forms of electronic textuality permit them more efficiently than ever before to encounter both the conflict and the contributions of separate disciplines, each of which forms part of some greater whole.

The reason we do not recognize the wholeness of knowledge, says Newman, derives from our fallen state. As he explains, the "cultivation" of the human mind "lies in fitting it to apprehend and contemplate truth," but

> the intellect in its present state . . . does not discern truth intuitively, or as a whole. We know, not by a direct and simple vision, not at a glance, but, as it were, by piecemeal and accumulation, by a mental process, by going round an object, by the comparison, the combination, the mutual correction, the continual adaptation, of many partial notions, by the employment, concentration, and joint action of many faculties and exercises of mind. Such a union and concert of the intellectual powers, such an enlargement and development, such a comprehensiveness, is necessarily a matter of training. (109)

Although the experience of teaching and learning with digital media is recent, one thing seems clear: they do enable students to develop their intellects "by going round an object, by the comparison, the combination, the mutual correction, the continual adaptation, of many partial notions."

One implication of Newman's emphasis on the inevitable interdisciplinarity of true knowledge appears in his description of the result of education as the recognition that every subject, every science, every discipline, exists as part of a network of interrelations. "That only is true enlargement of mind," he explains in "Knowledge Viewed in Relation to Learning," "which is the power of viewing many things at once as one whole, of referring them severally to their true place in the universal system, of understanding their respective values, and determining their mutual dependence." (99) This general approach to thought, Newman urges, constitutes the "perfection" of intellect:

Possessed of this real illumination, the mind never views any part of the extended subject-matter of Knowledge without recollecting that it is but a part, or without the associations which spring from this recollection. It makes every thing in some sort lead to every thing else; it would communicate the image of the whole to every separate portion, till that whole becomes in imagination like a spirit, every where pervading and penetrating its component parts, and giving them one definite meaning. (100)

Hypertext, which continually presents all information and all beliefs as part of a greater whole, also inevitably "makes every thing in some sort lead to every thing else," thereby encouraging the particular fundamental approach Newman emphasizes as necessary to the truly educated person.

The idea – or perhaps ideal – of the fast-approaching electronic university has many attractions, not the least of which is the economical, almost inevitable, sharing of resources among institutions of widely varying size, endowment, focus, and stature. Similarly, the economical development, maintenance, and use of materials for interdisciplinary approaches, like the way networked hypertext resources create course and institutional memories, have enormous appeal for many. Then there is the promise of students more involved in their own education and more able to obtain self-paced instruction, particularly for the advanced or interested student.

Such gains, however, have implicit in them certain losses, such as have always accompanied shifts in technological and informational paradigms. Plato rightly feared the devaluing of memory by those who read and write, and those who earlier feared the democratizing effects of technological changes introduced by books, copy machines, and calculators were, from their point of view, absolutely correct.

There are other possible losses to which the wonders of the electronic university may lead. One is decreased institutional loyalty – why, for example, feel sentimental about Alma Mater when the most interesting materials one encountered came from another institution on another continent and when the most important discussions in which one participated took place in electronic space and may not have originated within any particular institution at all?

Another interesting – and potentially troubling – change in the nature of higher education involves cyberspace and the possibilities of computer simulation, which already have proven in certain circumstances to have great educational value. Airlines and air forces have long known that complex computer-based simulations prove economical in human and material terms, and recent projects have shown the clear benefits of such simulation for students of chemistry, trauma surgery, and other fields, including training the handicapped, in which it is better to experience simulated, rather than actual, dangers. In addition, comparatively simple text-based simulations for students of history and culture have suggested that such methods have value in the humanities and social sciences, too.

Given the obvious gains implicit in such educational uses of simulation, where might the losses appear? Cyberspace – or virtual reality, as it is also known – involves more or less fully immersing users in a virtual world. That is, users experience themselves within the data and not facing it or in opposition to it as they do a printed page and a computer screen. This information technology, which has potentially enormous power, offers three possible dangers. First, since any description or representation of reality is a selection that embodies certain assumptions, all instantiations of virtual reality come with built-in, often unexamined ideologies. Of course, one might reply, so do all books and all libraries – just try to carry out research on materials once or now considered unfashionable or beneath academic interest, such as certain areas of nineteenth-century popular culture or religious thought.

Second, both hypertext and virtual reality to differing degrees threaten to devalue intellectual skills traditionally considered the most important. All current information technologies necessarily demand various forms of abstraction. Language and writing to a certain degree compensate for that which is not present. But what happens to skill at abstraction, selection, quotation, or emphasis in an information technology that permits one to offer an apparently realistic simulacrum of an object? Similarly, what will happen in literary studies when one does not have to quote a brief passage but can simply link to it? Hypertext might well do much to prevent authors from quoting material outrageously out of context, but will it also encourage the loss of skills related to selecting, quoting, and discussing extracted passages? Will the ability to make connections, or to proffer particular kinds of examples, become more important than arguments based, essentially, on the absence of the material discussed? I do not know the answer to such questions, but given the way education changed, many would say for the better, with the coming of print, I can only point to the likelihood of new rhetorics, new stylistics, and new modes of reading and writing appropriate to the utopian – or nowhere – space of the electronic university.

What else does this loss of place implied by electronic technology mean to the university, to its students and faculty? A colleague has pointed out to me that Newman thought that the university would nurture virtues by means of a kind of ethos, and most colleges for a long time echoed that goal at least in the opening sentences of their catalogs. Will that sense of the university as a place of values survive a university that is not in a single place? Furthermore, the sense of the university as a place has often nurtured students' personal development. Will the digital university destroy that nurturing?

Again playing devil's advocate, my colleague wonders about the effect of computers upon the social life of universities, particularly upon faculty collegiality and intellectual interchange. He reports that a friend collected a good deal of evidence to suggest that collegiality is dissolving throughout both our colleges and universities, supposedly because faculty, especially in the humanities and the social sciences, spend less time on campus, preferring to work at home on personal computers, which give them access to libraries, databases, and other colleagues all over the world. In that sense the university as a place is disappearing because the people who really constitute the place interact less and less in the traditional university space.

These crucial questions demand three responses, the first of which involves examining the degree to which colleges and universities now provide such nurturing and collegiality. Facing the possibility of electronic universities, we tend, I would argue, to sentimentalize present universities much as those who oppose electronic text sentimentalize books. Many book-lovers both in and out of the academic world who feel threatened by the digital word contrast the present limited version of reading on a computer screen with the pleasures of reading a beautifully designed, printed, and bound leather volume. Many of us pretend that we and our students generally read volumes bound by Sutcliffe, when in fact the materials are unwieldy anthologies, paperbound reprints of classics that dissolve during the week they are used, and, increasingly, packets of photocopied texts. Similarly, although we like to think – *imagine* or *fantasize* would be a more accurate term – that our educational institutions are characterized by Oxbridge tutorials, small seminars, and lots of contact between student and faculty, the great majority of American and European students (many of whom, incidentally, are nonresident or attend institutions without campuses or adequate student facilities) have for half a century or more received their education in lectures with hundreds of others.

Of course, one might well respond that even if a good bit of contemporary university education falls far short of the ideals that the college catalogs proffer to applicants and their parents, those comparatively few schools that maintain small seminars and close contact between student and teacher do not have to abandon their ways in an onrushing electronic world.

Here the answer is, of course not, since the experience of using such electronic materials – electronic text, hypertext, computer conferencing, and other forms of the digital word – supports and supplements these activities, rather than doing away with them.

Much the same can be said about collegiality among faculty members – it is often an ideal more honored in the breach than in the observance. Electronic networks, like telephone lines, connect people, supplementing and strengthening rather than destroying the community based on physical presence. Certainly, the isolated scholar reading, writing, or keystroking away on a personal computer does not thereby participate in collegial activities, but, then, neither does the scholar reading a manuscript, writing notes, or typing up an article on an old-fashioned typewriter. Any destruction of collegiality caused by faculty use of word-processors derives from not enough of a good thing rather than from too much of it. Any destruction of collegiality by electronic technology arises when it is inadequate or incomplete; its essential quality and effect tend to emphasize connection and relation. In other words, personal computers by themselves do not the digital revolution or the electronic university make. In fact, *digital computing joined by networks* make the new information technology and the new university.

The shape of the new intellectual space formed by this networked computing can already be guessed from its earliest forms – electronic mail, electronic conferencing, computer-mediated conferencing, and the World Wide Web. As far as I know, everyone who has studied or experienced computer-mediated communication has pointed out that these contacts produce a new kind of collegiality. My own experiences of computer conferences, in which people from five continents participated, suggest that a defining characteristic is a sense of collegiality, the nurturing experience of conversing with those who have similar interests. Anyone with a scholarly specialty knows the pleasure of leaving one's own institution, where no one else shares or perhaps even understands those interests, and attending a conference of those who do. One feels – at last – understood and even occasionally appreciated for those serious interests. Precisely these kinds of experiences characterize computer conferences: the intellectual community resembles that in a traditional professional conference, but one can participate in it at almost any time and with little expense or inconvenience. Thus a fully digital university will allow those within the institution and without to participate in common interest groups. Some of these participations may well, as they have in my case, eventually lead to private electronic communications and good old-fashioned face-to-face conversations.

Let me close by explaining that I remark on the way we fall short of our ideals of collegiality and close and continuous interaction with students chiefly not to point to the absence of the emperor's new clothes. I do so to remind us that the digital university is coming into being to remedy the shortcomings of the present non-digital one. In the jargon of the technologists, this change is not technology- but need-driven, which is to say that those instructors and scholars who eagerly grasp the new potential of the digital word and digital university do so because they as teachers and scholars need to, though like all solutions to major problems, the electronic university will confront us with a range of new questions and issues.

Suggested Reading

On John Henry Newman and Victorian Universities

Culler, A. Dwight. *The Imperial Intellect: A Study of Newman's Educational Ideal* (New Haven, 1955). Remains the most important and thorough study of the background of Newman's educational thought.

Engel, A. J. *From Clergyman to Don: The Rise of the Academic Profession in Nineteenth-Century Oxford* (Oxford, 1983). A broad treatment of the changes in Oxford during the half-century after Newman's departure in 1845.

Garland, Martha. *Cambridge before Darwin: The Ideal of a Liberal Education, 1800–1860* (Cambridge, 1980). Provides the most thorough available account of the Victorian debate over the liberal education.

Honey, J. R. De S. *Tom Brown's Universe: The Development of the English Public School in the Nineteenth Century* (New York, 1977). A lively account of the public schools from which Victorian boys were then sent to the universities.

Ker, Ian. *John Henry Newman: A Biography* (Oxford, 1988). Provides good coverage of the years of Newman's university administration in Ireland.

McGrath, Fergal. *Newman's University: Idea and Reality* (London and New York, 1951). Coverage of Newman's trials as a day-to-day administrator of his university.

Morrell, Jack, and Arnold Thackray. *Gentlemen of Science: The Early Years of the British Association for the Advancement of Science* (Oxford, 1981). The history of the scientific association whose leaders generally espoused the useful knowledge whose adequacy Newman criticized.

Rothblatt, Sheldon. *The Revolution of the Dons: Cambridge and Society in Victorian England* (London, 1968). Excellent coverage of Cambridge.

Smelser, Neil J. *Social Paralysis and Social Change: British Working-Class Education in the Nineteenth Century* (Berkeley, 1991). The best recent treatment of Victorian education outside the elite universities and public schools.

Ward, W. R. *Victorian Oxford* (Oxford, 1965). Provides background on Oxford politics and education throughout the nineteenth century.

Ward, Wilfrid. *The Life of John Henry Cardinal Newman* (London, 1912). Remains an important biography, but it concentrates on the period after Newman's conversion to Roman Catholicism.

The University Today

Bernstein, Richard. *Dictatorship of Virtue: Multiculturalism and the Battle for America's Future* (New York, 1994). An extremely critical account of the efforts to establish multicultural curricula.

Bloom, Alan. *The Closing of the American Mind: How Higher Education Has Failed Democracy and Impoverished the Souls of Today's Students* (New York, 1987). A now classic attack on the character of American higher education.

Boyer, Ernest L. *College: The Undergraduate Experience in America* (New York, 1987). Remains a significant account of structural changes occurring in American higher education.

——. *Scholarship Reconsidered: Priorities of the Professorate* (New York, 1990). Urges that various forms of academic activity be accounted as scholarship and rewarded as such.

Bromwich, David. *Politics by Other Means: Higher Education and Group Thinking* (New Haven, 1992). A demand that critical independent thinking replace concerns for cultural agendas in higher education.

Carnochan, W. B. *The Battleground of the Curriculum: Liberal Education and American Experience* (Stanford, 1993). One of the more influential discussions.

D'Souza, Dinesh. *Illiberal Education: The Politics of Race and Sex on Campus* (New York, 1991). A critique of recent trends in American universities.

Fuller, Timothy, ed. *The Voice of Liberal Learning: Michael Oakeshott on Education* (New Haven, 1989). Essays on education by a distinguished mid-twentieth-century philosopher who explores many of Newman's themes.

Graff, Gerald. *Professing Literature: An Institutional History* (Chicago, 1989). A discussion of the forces that have brought controversy to the teaching of literature.

Hunter, James Davison. *Culture Wars: The Struggle to Define America* (New York, 1991). An attempt at a synthetic treatment of the conflicts over curriculum and other cultural tensions in the United States.

Jacoby, Russell. *Dogmatic Wisdom: How the Culture Wars Divert Education and Distract America* (New York, 1994). Argues that the debate over the curriculum clouds appreciation for other problems in American education.

Lambropoulos, Vassilis. *The Rise of Eurocentrism: Anatomy of Interpretation* (Princeton, 1993). An important and controversial work on the emergence of those outlooks that are today termed "Eurocentric."

Marsden, George. *The Soul of the American University: From Protestant Establishment to Established Unbelief* (New York, 1994). An important discussion of the historical role of religion in American higher education and the necessity for reopening the question today.

Oakley, Francis. *Community of Learning: The American College and the Liberal Arts Tradition* (New York, 1992). A survey of the contemporary scene by a distinguished historian and former president of Williams College.

Pelikan, Jaroslav. *The Idea of the University: A Reexamination* (New Haven, 1992). An exploration of the modern university in light of Newman's ideal.

Proctor, Robert E. *Education's Great Amnesia: Reconsidering the Humanities from Petrarch to Freud* (Bloomington, 1988). A major reassertion of the humanities' central role in American higher education.

Rosovsky, Henry. *The University: An Owner's Manual* (New York, 1990). Describes the life of a Harvard academic administrator and the forces at work in a major research university.

Sykes, Charles T. *ProfScam: Professors and the Demise of Higher Education* (New York, 1990). A highly critical account of the contemporary American professorate.

Taylor, Charles. *Multiculturalism and "The Politics of Recognition": An Essay* (Princeton, 1992). A leading contemporary philosopher offers a major commentary on this question.

Universities, Print Culture, and the Electronic Future

Benedikt, Michael. *Cyberspace: First Steps* (Cambridge, 1991). An introduction.

Bolter, J. David. *Writing Space: The Computer Hypertext, and the History of Writing* (Hillsdale, N.J., 1990). A discussion of the way the introduction of the computer has transformed the act of writing.

Chartier, Roger. *The Cultural Uses of Print in Early Modern France,* tr. Lydia G. Cochrane (Princeton, 1987). Explores the manner in which print transformed cultural relationships.

Eisenstein, Elizabeth L. *The Printing Press as an Agent of Change:*

Communications and Cultural Transformations in Early-Modern Europe (Cambridge, 1980). The classic work on the subject.

Heim, Michael. *Electric Language: A Philosophical Study of Word Processing* (New Haven, 1987). Speculates on the larger dimensions of the coming of electronic modes of writing.

Kernan, Alvin. *Printing Technology, Letters, and Samuel Johnson* (Princeton, 1987). Explores how the organization of printing affected eighteenth- and early-nineteenth-century literature.

Landow, George P. *Hypertext: The Convergence of Contemporary Critical Theory and Technology* (Baltimore, 1992). The major work on the manner in which the new technology meshes with contemporary critical theory.

Landow, George P., and Paul Delany. *The Digital Word: Text-Based Computing in the Humanities* (Cambridge, Mass., 1993). A major introduction.

McLuhan, Marshall. *The Gutenberg Galaxy: The Making of Typographic Man* (Toronto, 1962). A pioneering study of the subject.

Ong, Walter J. *Orality and Literacy: The Technologizing of the Word* (London, 1982). An influential work on the cultural implications of the movements toward literacy and then to print culture.

Steinberg, S. H. *Five Hundred Years of Printing,* 2d ed. (Baltimore, 1961). A standard history.

Contributors

Martha McMackin Garland is associate professor of history and associate dean of the College of Humanities at Ohio State University. In the latter capacity she oversees curriculum and instruction and in 1994–95 chaired a campuswide committee on the quality of the undergraduate experience. She is the author of *Cambridge before Darwin: The Ideal of a Liberal Education, 1800–1860* (1980).

Sara Castro-Klarén is professor of Latin American Literature and Culture at Johns Hopkins University. She is the author of *Escritura, transgresión y sujeto en la literatura latinoamericana* (1989), *Understanding Mario Vargas Llosa* (1990), "Dancing and the Sacred in the Andes: From the Taqui-Oncoy to Rasu Ñiti," Stephen Greenblatt, ed., *New World Encounters* (1993), and editor along with Sylvia Malloy and Beatriz Sarlos of *Women's Writing in Latin America* (1991).

George P. Landow is professor of English and art history at Brown University. He is the author of *Hypertext: The Convergence of Contemporary Critical Theory and Technology* (1992) and numerous works in Victorian literature and art including *The Aesthetic and Critical Theories of John Ruskin* (1971), *William Holman Hunt and Typological Symbolism* (1979), *Victorian Types, Victorian Shadows: Biblical Typology and Victorian Literature* (1980), and *Elegant Jeremiahs: The Sage from Carlyle to Mailer* (1986).

George M. Marsden is the Francis A. McAnaney Professor of History at the University of Notre Dame. He is the author of *Fundamentalism and American Culture* (1980) and *The Soul of the American University: From Protestant Establishment to Established Nonbelief* (1994). During 1992 he served as president of the American Society of Church History.

Frank M. Turner is the John Hay Whitney Professor of History at Yale University, where he served as provost between 1988 and 1992. He is the author of *Between Science and Religion: The Reaction to Scientific Naturalism in Late Victorian Britain* (1974), *The Greek Heritage in Victorian Britain* (1981), and *Contesting Cultural Authority: Essays in Victorian Intellectual Life* (1993).

Rethinking the Western Tradition

The Idea of a University
JOHN HENRY NEWMAN
Edited by Frank M. Turner,
with essays by Martha McMackin Garland,
Sara Castro-Klarén, George P. Landow,
George M. Marsden, and Frank M. Turner

Since its publication almost 150 years ago, *The Idea of a University* has had an extraordinary influence on the shaping and goals of higher education. The issues that John Henry Newman raised — the place of religion and moral values in the university setting, the competing claims of liberal and professional education, the character of the academic community, the cultural role of literature, and relation of religion and science — have provoked discussion from Newman's time to our own. This edition of *The Idea of a University* includes the full text of "University Teaching" and four selections from "University Subjects" together with five essays by leading scholars that explore the background and the present-day relevance of Newman's themes.

In the essays Martha Garland discusses the character and organization of the early nineteenth-century English universities upon which Newman based much of his vision; Frank M. Turner traces the impact of Newman's influence during the vast expansion of higher education since World War II; George Marsden investigates how the decreasing emphasis on religion has affected higher education; Sara Castro-Klarén examines the implications of Newman's views on education and literature for current debates between proponents of a curriculum based on Western civilization and one based on multiculturalism; and George Landow considers what the advent of electronic communication will mean to university teaching, research, and community.

To aid accessibility the edition also includes a chronology and biographical sketch of Newman's life, an analytical table of contents, questions for discussion, reference notes, and a glossary of names, all of which will help make this volume the standard teaching text for Newman's work.

RETHINKING THE WESTERN TRADITION